ASPEN PUBLISHERS

MW01223116

IT Project Manage

2008 Edition

by Larry Webber and Frederick Webber

IT Project Management Essentials is a hands-on resource book to guide project managers through the process of designing, developing, and implementing an IT goal. This book covers the basic steps in IT project management: scope planning and defining, activity defining and sequencing, resource planning, time estimating, schedule developing, cost estimating, and budget developing. Quality control is discussed as an essential element of every step throughout the process. Advanced IT project management techniques and tools are also covered.

Highlights of the 2008 Edition

The 2008 edition brings you information on the following:

- How to manage virtual project teams. Virtual teams can include people down the street or around the world. Building a virtual team is often cross cultural (and cross time zone).

- Tips on establishing your own virtual project manager office.

- How to build a virtual team when employees in different time zones are working on the same project.

- The tools for the success for a virtual team.

- Managing projects following the Rational Unify Process (RUP).

- What is an iterative project and what makes it agile?

- Using a Project Maturity Model to improve your PMO's performance.

- Comparison of maturity models—which is right for your company?

- How a maturity model can identify training for your project managers.

- Using a maturity model to ensure continuous improvement and lower costs.

11/07

For questions concerning this shipment, billing, or other customer service matters, call our Customer Service Department at 1-800-234-1660.

For toll-free ordering, please call 1-800-638-8437.

IT Project Management Essentials
2008 Edition

ASPEN PUBLISHERS

IT Project Management Essentials
2008 Edition

Larry Webber
Frederick Webber

Wolters Kluwer
Law & Business

AUSTIN   BOSTON   CHICAGO   NEW YORK   THE NETHERLANDS

This publication is designed to provide accurate and authorative information in regard to the subject matter covered. It is sold with the understanding that the publisher is not engaged in rendering legal, accounting, or other professional services. If legal advice or other professional assistance is required, the services of a competent professional person should be sought.

—From a *Declaration of Principles* jointly adopted
by a Committee of the American Bar Association
and a Committee of Publishers and Associations

Printed in the United States of America

1 2 3 4 5 6 7 8 9 0

ISBN 978-0-7355-6633-0

About Wolters Kluwer Law & Business

Wolters Kluwer Law & Business is a leading provider of research information and workflow solutions in key specialty areas. The strengths of the individual brands of Aspen Publishers, CCH, Kluwer Law International and Loislaw are aligned within Wolters Kluwer Law & Business to provide comprehensive, in-depth solutions and expert-authored content for the legal, professional and education markets.

CCH was founded in 1913 and has served more than four generations of business professionals and their clients. The CCH products in the Wolters Kluwer Law & Business group are highly regarded electronic and print resources for legal, securities, antitrust and trade regulation, government contracting, banking, pension, payroll, employment and labor, and healthcare reimbursement and compliance professionals.

Aspen Publishers is a leading information provider for attorneys, business professionals and law students. Written by preeminent authorities, Aspen products offer analytical and practical information in a range of specialty practice areas from securities law and intellectual property to mergers and acquisitions and pension/benefits. Aspen's trusted legal education resources provide professors and students with high-quality, up-to-date and effective resources for successful instruction and study in all areas of the law.

Kluwer Law International supplies the global business community with comprehensive English-language international legal information. Legal practitioners, corporate counsel and business executives around the world rely on the Kluwer Law International journals, loose-leafs, books and electronic products for authoritative information in many areas of international legal practice.

Loislaw is a premier provider of digitized legal content to small law firm practitioners of various specializations. Loislaw provides attorneys with the ability to quickly and efficiently find the necessary legal information they need, when and where they need it, by facilitating access to primary law as well as state-specific law, records, forms and treatises.

Wolters Kluwer Law & Business, a unit of Wolters Kluwer, is headquartered in New York and Riverwoods, Illinois. Wolters Kluwer is a leading multinational publisher and information services company.

ASPEN PUBLISHERS SUBSCRIPTION NOTICE

This Aspen Publishers product is updated on a periodic basis with supplements to reflect important changes in the subject matter. If you purchased this product directly from Aspen Publishers, we have already recorded your subscription for the update service.

If, however, you purchased this product from a bookstore and wish to receive future updates and revised or related volumes billed separately with a 30-day examination review, please contact our Customer Service Department at 1-800-234-1660 or send your name, company name (if applicable), address, and the title of the product to:

ASPEN PUBLISHERS
7201 McKinney Circle
Frederick, MD 21704

Important Aspen Publishers Contact Information

- To order any Aspen Publishers title, go to *www.aspenpublishers.com* or call 1-800-638-8437.
- To reinstate your manual update service, call 1-800-638-8437.
- To contact Customer Care, e-mail *customer.care@aspenpublishers. com,* call 1-800-234-1660, fax 1-800-901-9075, or mail correspondence to Order Department, Aspen Publishers, PO Box 990, Frederick, MD 21705.
- To review your account history or pay an invoice online, visit *www .aspenpublishers.com/payinvoices.*

Wolters Kluwer
Law & Business

About the Authors

Lawrence Webber has more than 30 years' experience in the information services field. He began his career in the U.S. Marine Corps as a digital network repairman and then moved to a position as a COBOL programmer supporting the Marine's Logistics traffic management systems.

After his release from active service, he worked in Kansas City as a COBOL programmer, systems analyst, and IT manager at Waddell & Reed, Temperature Industries, United Telecommunications, and the law offices of Shook, Hardy & Bacon.

For the next 12 years, Mr. Webber held various systems engineering and data processing management positions with International Truck and Bus in Springfield, Ohio, where, among other achievements, he authored an extensive Disaster Recovery plan for the 2-million-square-foot manufacturing facility. He worked as a Disaster Recovery program manager and Six Sigma Black Belt consultant for Computer Science Corporation in Dayton, Ohio. He is currently a Business Continuity Coordinator at R+L Carriers in Wilmington, Ohio.

Mr. Webber has an Associate in Science degree from Darton College in Albany, Georgia, in Data Processing; a Bachelor of Science degree in Business Administration and an MBA both from Rockhurst College in Kansas City, Missouri; and an Associate in Science degree in Industrial Engineering from Sinclair Community College in Dayton, Ohio. He also completed a Master of Project Management degree from West Carolina University.

Mr. Webber is retired from the U.S. Army Reserve as a First Sergeant in the Infantry. He is a certified Project Management Professional by the Project Management Institute, Certified in Production and Inventory Management by APICS, and is a Microsoft Certified Professional. He is an adjunct faculty member at DeVry University Keller Graduate School of Management and has published several articles on disaster recovery topics.

Mr. Webber can be reached by email at *ljwljw88@hotmail.com*. Your comments and suggestions for improving this book are welcome.

Frederick Webber is a graduate of Rose-Hulman Institute of Technology with a double major in Mechanical Engineering and Computer Science. He is currently attending the Air Force Institute of Technology working on a master's degree in Engineering. Mr. Webber has worked on a team that developed the entire technological arm of Elastic Image, a company specializing in pre-decorated thermoformed plastics. Mr. Webber intends to pursue an entrepreneurial career in robotics, artificial intelligence, and mechatronics.

Contents

A complete table of contents for each chapter is included at the beginning of the chapter.

Preface

IT Project Management Essentials is a hands-on resource book that guides anyone assigned as a project manager through the project management process of designing, developing, and implementing an IT goal. This process includes scheduling and management techniques along with the essential tools, such as stakeholder analysis and reports, for handling these techniques.

This book covers the basic steps in IT project management: scope planning and defining, activity defining and sequencing, resource planning, time estimating, schedule developing, cost estimating, and budget developing. Quality control is discussed as an essential element of every step throughout the process. Advanced IT project management techniques and tools are also covered: Six Sigma, Balanced Scorecard, PRINCE2, and Troubled Projects. The book suggests ways to:

- revitalize and optimize an existing project;
- create a corporate team that supports IT needs and goals;
- develop opportunities; and
- improve customer service through portfolio management.

Written in a practical how-to style and organized for fast access to specific information, this book not only explains the project management process but also takes you step-by-step through the implementation of any IT goal. It includes checklists and templates for the project management documents needed in managing the process.

AUDIENCE

This book is directed at IT managers and business analysts who need information about the IT project management process and how to apply it within their organizations to obtain a competitive advantage in the marketplace. CIOs, IT directors, and managers who are engaged in designing, developing, or upgrading an information system environment will find this book to be an invaluable hands-on aid in cost-justifying and implementing an IT solution in a defined, repeatable, and measurable fashion.

There is a dynamic technological environment for enhancing any information system. There is also a need for a set of project management standards, tools, and techniques to help IT professionals to complete very small to very large projects. These projects encompass the addition of hardware, to the addition of a new application, to a major redesign of a network from a client/server paradigm to an object-oriented paradigm.

Most of the new IT technologies require a team effort rather than an individual one. In addition, the introduction of Internet technologies usually requires customer involvement and vendor assistance. Many IT administrators are becoming aware of a need for new management skills. The system administrator or IT technical manager usually does not have the time or the desire to read a number of books on specialized project management techniques. This book addresses the critical need for a practical, comprehensive guide on how to plan, design, develop, implement, and control any IT project.

Learning how to use support tools and techniques is critical to the knowledge of the project management process. This book discusses not only specialized project management tools but also some commonly available tools such as Microsoft Excel and PowerPoint.

Finally, the bottom-line issue for the audience is money. These chapters show how a project can be managed to fit within a given budget. In addition, the importance of cost estimates for a reliable budget is discussed.

The contents of the book can also be found on the accompanying CD-ROM. This permits rapid searching of the entire text to quickly locate ideas, terms, or procedures as needed.

Lawrence Webber
August 2007

Acknowledgments

I would like to thank Gail Williamson for her patient editing of some of the chapters, significantly improving their clarity. I would also like to thank Lou Iannitti for his contributions on virtual teams. Also, a big thanks to Joanne Cursinella and Rosalie L. Donlon at Aspen Publishers, who were a pleasure to work with.

Lawrence Webber
August 2007

Chapter 1

What Is IT Project Management?

§ 1.01   INTRODUCTION

> "Time is a great teacher, but unfortunately, it kills all its pupils."
>
> —Hector Berlioz

Project management is a process for translating a stated requirement into action to create the desired product. It decomposes each dimension of the unknown into its components to separate what is known from what is not. What is known can be easily estimated, while the unknown is an educated guess. Project management is a journey into the unknown. The exact amount of time required, exactly what the finished product looks like, exactly how much it will cost—all of this is only a guess. The larger the undertaking, the longer it requires and the greater the uncertainty of the outcome. This may sound complex, but it is simply a lot of analysis using common sense.

Projects exist because companies have problems. A project creates a product or service that a company needs in order to solve a problem. Project managers must understand that the primary goal of the project is to complete the work product and end the project. Some projects seem to live on and on until the customer finally cuts funding. No one considers such a project to be a success since it did not deliver the solution to the customer's problem.

§ 1.02   SIX PROJECT MANAGEMENT ELEMENTS

There are six distinct project management elements to an IT project and each one is critical to the project's success.

[A]   Element One: Managing Customer Expectations

Many executives avoid involvement in a project. Once it has been assigned, they wash their hands of the issue and only want to be called to inspect the final result. However, project managers must work closely with the project sponsor to clearly identify the project's requirements and ensure design changes made during development are consistent with the sponsor's vision for the final product.

During project definition, the project manager carefully shapes the sponsor's expectations of how the project will be executed and what the final product will look like. How long the project will take to complete, anticipated risks, and assumptions used to facilitate planning must all be discussed and agreed upon in advance. Ensure that the sponsor understands that the project will only deliver what is in the definition and nothing else. It may be necessary to create a mock-up to resolve design tradeoffs.

[B]   Element Two: Project Phases

There are five project phases. It is important to recognize that quality monitoring is an integral function of each phase, although most people associate it only with the testing phase. Each phase results in a set of documents that prepare the project for the next phase or closure. The phases are:

- **Initiating**—Identify the customer need and verify that it is feasible and affordable. Stakeholders must be identified to ensure they are consulted during project definition. The result is a clear project definition of what the final product will look like. Document acceptance criteria in objectively measurable terms.

- **Planning**—Break down the project definition and scope into individual tasks. Estimate the time, cost, and technical support required to complete each task. Sequence the tasks into a project plan. Create a list of planning assumptions and a full risk assessment for the project.

- **Executing**—The project team works according to the plan to create the target product or service.

- **Controlling**—Monitor the project plan and budget progress to ensure plan execution. Risk assessment, issues, and assumptions lists are periodically updated. Address staffing issues as they arise. Ensure all changes are approved through a scope management plan. Obtain customer approval for the finished product.

- **Closing**—Wrap up the project budget, release the people, and collect documents for use in later projects.

[C]   Element Three: Project Activities

Besides managing sponsors and phases, there are activities that include all the managing levels and affect all of the phases of the project. These activities include:

- **Scheduling**—Identify the tasks, their sequencing, and resources required.
- **Budgeting**—Obtain company funding and approval for using internal labor.

- **Managing resources**—Ensure the resources are properly applied to the assigned tasks.

- **Managing risk/opportunity**—Try to anticipate problems or opportunities that may arise, and address them as early as possible.

- **Controlling quality**—Ensure the product under development adheres to the project definition and company standards.

"The expectations of life depend upon diligence; the mechanic that would perfect his work must first sharpen his tools."

—Confucius

[D]   Element Four: Tools

The fourth element is tools. A tool can be as simple as a pencil or as complex as project management software. Tools of project management include:

- Processing historical data or using experience to improve estimates, better the risks gauge, and to evaluate previous resource (labor) performance.

- A scope management plan to ensure there are no changes to the project definition without proper approval, and no unapproved adjustments to the timeline or budget.

- A risk assessment matrix to examine the risks to the project, present and future, and to add mitigation steps into the project plan to reduce the likelihood and impact of their occurrence or to increase the warning that they are about to occur.

- An issues log to track small things that must be done to complete a project task.

- Tasks lists and their corresponding Gantt charts to track the project schedule, illustrate task contingencies, and monitor progress.

- A project budget to project costs and to track actual to projected expenditures.

- A resource management plan to ensure that the necessary resources, time, equipment, technical skills, and money are available at the right time to work on a task.

[E]   Element Five: Analytical Process

The fifth element is the analytical process, which is ingrained in all components of the project management process. Certain areas or functions have come to be set apart for specific analysis processes. These include:

- **Profitability**—This means that the project team is always watching its expenses while adding value to the customer.

- **Learning curve**—This is the time it takes for team members to learn about project management as well as new technologies.

- **Scalability**—This is the degree to which a system can be enhanced without a major change in design.

- **Interoperability**—This refers to the degree to which the various network components work with each other successfully.

- **Portability**—This refers to the degree to which the software can be transferred from one environment to another.

- **Risk**—This is constantly analyzed to head off (or contain) problems before they occur.

- **Legacy**—This refers to both software and hardware that must be included in planning—it is rare that a project is handed a clean slate without a need to interface with legacy technology.

[F]   Element Six: People

The sixth element is people. Although listed last, it is the most important element. People are referred to variously in this book as "the team" and "the customer." People are a project manager's primary tool. It takes both the project team and the customer to achieve project success. On occasion, managing the relationship between the project team and the customer is referred to as conflict management; but perhaps it should be referred to as opportunity management.

"Plans are nothing; planning is everything."

—Dwight D. Eisenhower

---

§ 1.03   PROJECT MANAGEMENT BASIC ACTIVITIES

There are eleven basic types of project management activities. Some of the activities are more dominant in some phases than others; however, any project of any size is dynamic. While scope defining is obviously a part of the planning phase, one may have to return to it more than once during the project.

Some of these eleven basic types of project management activities can be merged together, such as scope planning and scope defining. In a large project, there should be as much of a detailed breakdown of activities as is feasible. The activities that make up the project administrative process discussed in this section of the book are as follows:

1. Scope Planning
2. Scope Defining
3. Activity Planning
4. Activity Sequencing
5. Resource Planning
6. Time Estimating
7. Schedule Developing
8. Cost Estimating
9. Budget Development
10. Quality Controlling
11. Managing Risks and Opportunities

[A]   Scope Planning

One of the first actions of a project manager is to define the goals and performance expectations of the project, and to get the sponsor to agree on them. Then, determine how individual technologies components (protocols, firewalls, servers, e-mail, software, browsers, etc.) fit into the overall objectives. The scope plan is the strategic view of the constraints and assumptions of the project as developed by the project team. It contains:

1. Basic team list
   - People with technical skills (programmers, DBAs, network, intranet, Internet)

- People with project management skills
- Representatives of the product users
- Administrative support (accounting, human resources, facilities, etc.)

2. Criteria for communications (training, documentation, status reporting)—frequency and content of status reports, reports to other stakeholders, issues escalations, etc.

3. Criteria for establishing timelines—guidelines for estimating tasks, such as 90 percent sure dates, 50/50 estimation (the average amount of time required)

4. Criteria for identifying skill requirements—what is an expert, novice, etc. for a specific technology?

5. Criteria for selecting resources—select internal first, external, hire new people, etc.

6. General budgetary requirements—is there a cap, special forms, or format for requesting project funds?

7. General costing requirements—how to estimate the cost for a task, usually associated with hardware, cabling, etc.

8. Performance benchmarks—required performance standards for the final product. These are some of the required test points.

9. Start and end dates of the project—Sometimes this is legally mandated.

10. User or customer expectations—may be vague or specific. The best solution is to include a representative group of users on the team.

11. Validation system benchmarks—success requirements for various milestones and the end of the project. This may be tied to performance bonuses.

In some cases, project funding is "contributed" from a variety of sources. The IT department budget may pay for the hardware; the marketing department may pay for product training, etc. In this case, it is important that the project manager ensure that contributors receive what they paid for and that the expense to validate their support does not exceed their contribution.

[B] Scope Defining

It is amazing how many projects start without a clear idea of what is wanted. Project sponsors are hot to begin the journey of creating the solution even though they lack a clear idea of where they are going or how they are going to get there. Clearly defining the project's scope provides a sound basis for its success. Without a clear idea of what is wanted, when it is wanted, and the constraints on the project, a project plan cannot be written nor can a budget with any semblance of reality be created.

Refer to the benchmarks and criteria discussed above and solidify the ideas in the project request. Get a "firm" first commitment from all the parties involved. Notice it is a *firm*, not *final* commitment. Project goals evolve; scope definition is not final until the end of the project. Scope definition includes the following:

1. Basic definitions of responsibilities
2. An organization chart that shows links among people and their defined responsibilities
3. Clear definition of the project manager's responsibilities
4. Communication policy that includes:
   - Who sends information
   - What kind of information is sent
   - When information is sent
   - Who receives what types of information
   - What type of communication is used
   - Why that type of communication is used
5. Descriptions of the quality control and verification systems used in the planning, design, development, and implementation phases of the project goals
6. Firm project start and end dates
7. Essential milestone dates
8. List of realistic, manageable project goals
9. List of resource estimates: human and material
10. Lists of cost estimates: human, materials, and time
11. Risk benchmarks include from a simple "nothing will be done with a minimal risk" to a complex statement on how to handle very dangerous risks
12. Threat (security) policy that illustrates how types of threats are handled

The framework of scope planning determines how detailed the scope definition will be.

> "Let our advance worrying become advance thinking and planning."
>
> —Winston Churchill

[C] Activity Planning

With the details, definitions, and descriptions of the actions for the project in hand, plan the activities required to complete the plan based on expected goals. Activities cover the following as a minimum:

1. Design, development, control, and implementation functions

2. Expected actions of support team members

3. Firm start and end actions

4. Flowchart of activities (think critical path)

5. How the quality control and assurance systems are to be implemented in all project phases

6. How to handle the established communications policy

7. How to implement a realistic security policy

8. The project manager's administrative activities for this project

9. List of cost estimates associated with each function, application, or service

10. List of key milestones with their importance to the project's expected goals

11. List of realistic manageable activities

12. List of resource and skill estimates associated with each function, application, or service

[D] Activity Sequencing

When sequencing activities to implement project goals, a clear statement about activities and their relationships to each other, including time, people, equipment, materials, and cost is ready. The usual presentation is a flowchart. Items needed at this point are listed below.

1. A flowchart or some other visual presentation that shows the activity sequence

2. Communication points sequenced so that all appropriate parties involved know the project status

3. Criteria for communicating the status of quality control

4. Criteria for being able to change the activity sequence if necessary

5. Critical path of activities (optional)

6. Procurement activities, identified within the sequence

7. Quality control and verification activities scheduled throughout

8. Resource input activities sequenced

Activity sequence as used here means the complete list of activity sequences, including one for each operational area, quality, training, documentation, and project administration. Link each to its project goals.

[E] Resource Planning

Resources come in different forms—people, equipment, and materials. The important human resource is not headcount, but skills. Equipment categories that have to be considered are permanent or temporary, available or unavailable, and legacy or new. Software versions and compatibility of hardware must also be considered.

There are other resource considerations, but they are outside the scope of this book. For example, should resources train the network user to function at an expected defined level of expertise? (Select an e-mail application that is not user friendly and see what happens.) The resource definition should include the following as a minimum:

- Chart on how resources are linked to functions or services
- Firm resource requirements and consequences of not having them
- Policy on who determines resource requirements
- Procedure for turning an unavailable resource into an opportunity
- Resource change policy
- Resource utilization policy
- Resource requirements policy

[F] Time Estimating

Use time management experts or software tools to develop time estimates. This activity can use historical data for establishing benchmarks. Pessimism is better than optimism in doing time estimates. Know either the criteria used by the experts or the tools for establishing the estimates. The primary cause of failure of projects is unrealistic time estimates.

Some types of information needed to complete time estimates are as follows.

1. Criteria for associating cost and time estimates and potential changes

2. Criteria for establishing time measures

3. Criteria for formulating time estimates

4. Methodology for validating time estimates based on the defined project goals

5. Procedure for associating time estimates with tasks and acquisitions

6. Quality control and validation time estimates (20 percent of the project is suggested)

7. Time estimates based on skill types and levels rather than on headcount involved

[G]   Schedule Developing

Use time management software to develop schedules. Scheduling is where ordered activities and fixed times are combined. A schedule can be a simple calendar with activities inserted on milestone days, or an elaborate flowchart with dates placed on directional arrows. Two potential tools for establishing schedules are Gantt charts and PERT/CPM techniques. The schedule should include:

1. Scheduled communications points

2. Consistent and coherent timelines

3. Allocated time for risk management

4. Criteria for changing the schedule

5. Notification schedule for status on project changes

6. Quality control and verification schedule

7. Schedule based on the project scope definition

8. Timeline (calendar, flowchart)

9. Timeline for acquiring skills, equipment, and materials

The schedule should be readable to all involved. An issue with project management software is developing a schedule too complex to understand.

[H] Cost Estimating

Use cost management software tools to develop cost estimates. This activity can use historical data for establishing benchmarks. As with time estimating, it is better to be on the pessimistic side than the optimistic side in doing cost estimates. Points to consider include:

1. Cost estimates based on skill types and levels rather than headcount
2. Criteria for associating cost to time estimates and potential changes
3. Criteria for establishing cost benchmarks
4. Criteria for formulating cost estimates
5. Methodology for validating cost estimates based on the expected project definition
6. Procedure for associating cost estimates with people, equipment, and materials
7. Quality control and validation cost estimates (10 to 20 percent of project costs is suggested)

[I] Budget Development

Budgeting is organizing cost estimates into a formal financial structure. A budget is to cost as a schedule is to time. Each budget item should be associated with a task in the plan. Budget development creates:

1. A budget (or budgets) that is consistent with the project's scope definition
2. A separate budget line for risk management or an identified component of another manager's budget
3. Links between this project's budget and any supporting budgets
4. Procedure for handling outside resources payments
5. Procedure for making changes and updates to the budget reporting system as relevant to agreed-upon project changes
6. Separate budget lines for quality control and verification (optional)

> There should be one project budget, whether it is a part of the formal budget system or not.

[J] Quality Controlling

Following are questions to answer so the unexpected events do not assault expected project goals.

- Are there consistent quality standards?
- Is there an established quality control system for the project?
- Are there formulated verification activities?

Establish benchmarks for the project's quality and performance at the earliest planning sessions. This sets a level of expectation in the project team's mind.

Document the customer's expectations for the project. Be as specific as possible about expectations. Always use objectively measurable quality characteristics.

> "Men often oppose a thing merely because they have had no agency in planning it, or because it may have been planned by those whom they dislike."
>
> —Alexander Hamilton

[K] Managing Risks and Opportunities

Risk is the chance that something will disrupt the project schedule or budget. It is also referred to as "uncertainty." To establish a risk management process:

1. Create a list of assumptions and guidelines for handling potential threats and opportunities.
2. Identify points in the project for re-assessing risks.

Think of a risk as a threat to the project. Sometimes a project manager can turn a risk into an opportunity. Imagine a project six months into development, and then someone invents a utility program that can cut that time in half or less. Can this affect the project? Of course it can! A risk is not necessarily a problem; but it can have an adverse or disastrous consequence on the project's outcome.

When defining the project scope, establish how to handle threats and opportunities. Unfortunately, in risk management most people think only of the threats to the project. What if someone comes up with an idea that a component of a hardware product or a software application can be omitted and still achieve the customer's expectations? This is an opportunity!

Document activities for handling threats. There should also be activities that handle opportunities if they arise. A simple activity rule would be, "Until a threat (an opportunity!) reaches a certain risk level, no action shall be taken."

Risk assessment is important to planning resources. Determine the minimum skill level requirements. Headcount requirement is not the correct way to think. A novice can successfully complete some activities, while others need an expert. If the schedule allows, turn the lack of a skill into a training opportunity.

Sequence tasks in the project to monitor potential threats and opportunities. A minimum recommendation is at least one risk review during each phase of the implementation of the project. At every meeting, the quality assurance and control team should comment on the potential of performance risks.

Set aside time and expense to support the risk management task for each project phase. If there are no threats in that project phase, an opportunity is created for either moving funds to another phase or reducing the budget.

The schedule (activities plus time) should have at each key milestone an activity that assesses the project's status and determines if there are potential threats and opportunities. Include contingency funds in the project budget for risk mitigation. The most logical line is the one to allocate money for contractors. Another line to consider is for quality control and verification. Additional funds may be needed if the product needs more testing than estimated.

§ 1.04   THREE MANAGEMENT LEVELS

As mentioned earlier, there are three distinct management levels at which a project is controlled. These levels are:

- Strategic
- Tactical
- Operational

[A]   Strategic

Many upper-level managers think they do not have a part to play in any project, except perhaps to be critical, which is untrue. These managers establish the strategic position of the project. A strategic manager needs to say more than "I want this enhancement to the information system." The project must include measurable strategic goals from upper-level management. It is based on these goals that a tactical or operational manager is ultimately evaluated. The clearer these goals are, the more secure the managers will be in achieving successful project results.

What does it mean to be a strategic manager? A strategic manager sets strategic goals. Such a goal may be as simple as "Enhance the network to do a specific function within a specific timeframe and within a specific budgetary amount." This statement, with appropriate values, is measurable. The tactical manager's first task is to negotiate the statement so it is realistic and manageable.

> The word *strategy* comes from the Greek word *stratégos*. This word means "general-of-the-army," thus the military connotation of the words *tactical* and *operational*.

A strategic manager should be thought of as an active Greek general, not a twenty-first-century general who is more a bureaucrat than an active participant in the battle. A strategic manager heads an area of the organization that includes the IT project as a part of the manager's performance goals. This manager should have the budget authority and should be assisting the IT project tactical manager with providing resources, equipment, and materials.

[B] Tactical

The tactical manager is the one responsible for the overall flow of the project process so that the strategic goals are met. This manager can be the IT administrator, a business manager, or the project manager.

A military definition of tactics is the handling of field troops, while strategy involves positioning on the battlefield. The word *tactics* comes from the Greek word *taxis*. Tactics is the act of arranging or disposing of the troops for battle. Operations are the place where the work occurs.

> Many new project managers mistakenly believe that merely because they are managers they can automatically rally the support of all those assigned to them. However, respect is earned and not bestowed by title (so hard to gain—so easy to lose). All too often, the respect of the followers is forfeited because of the lack of basic interpersonal or management skills.

[C]   Operational

The operational managers are the people who handle the day-to-day operations or activities that have been defined in the project plan. Notice this is plural because in a large project there may be many operational managers reporting to the tactical manager. These people are often referred to as project leads. The functions are the same no matter the label.

So how does one move from the military management ideas to the present-day corporate environment? The first global companies of the late nineteenth and early twentieth centuries used the military model in their expansions. Of course, many of the ideas, concepts, techniques, and tools that make up what may be defined as IT project management have their origins in projects of the United States military. The foremost example is the development of the first nuclear-powered submarine, *USS Nautilus*, under the management of Admiral Hyman G. Rickover in the mid-1950s.

"Think ahead. Don't let day-to-day operations drive out planning."

—Donald Rumsfeld

---

§ 1.05   EVALUATING PROJECT VIABILITY

One of the fundamental aspects of a project in the pre-proposal stage is the need for adequate research. Evaluating a project with a checklist and *metaquestions* helps to answer many of the issues that the successful project manager will integrate into the bigger picture with the help of upper management. However, if management fails to evaluate the market and scope of the project, success may well be out of reach.

[A]   Using a Project Viability Evaluation

Using a project viability evaluation is like a risk virus vaccine. Create an evaluation form to clarify the customer's objective (see Exhibit 1-1, Sample Project Viability Checklist). If the project's concerns cannot be resolved, review and revise the premises. Such an evaluation also helps the customer clarify the problem. A positive result can be used to gain upper management's buy-in.

Exhibit 1-1: Sample Project Viability Checklist

Project Name:		Comments
1. Are potential materials and equipment available to achieve project results?		
2. Are potential resources available to achieve the project results?		
3. Are potential costs too high to achieve project results?		
4. Are there appropriate project justifications to ensure continuing executive support?		
5. Are there appropriate skills available to achieve project results?		
6. Is there an adequate project budget to achieve the results?		
7. Are there project tools available to control the project?		
8. Do the project results align with the company's strategic goals?		
9. Do the project results reflect efficiency and innovation?		
10. How may project results affect any product pricing?		
11. How may project results meet customer needs?		
12. How stable is the IT organization for achieving the project results?		
13. How stable is the technology required to achieve project results?		
14. How will the results affect the return on investments (ROI)?		
15. Is the deadline realistic to achieve project results?		
16. What are the events that can cause the project to fail?		
17. What are the events that can make the project successful?		
18. What are the possible impacts of the results on the information system?		
19. What are the possible resistant concerns to project results?		
20. What is the project manager's level of authority to achieve the project results?		

The leading questions should look something like this:

- What funding exists for this project?
- What are the project's measurable objectives?

If the answer to the first question is negative or unknown, conduct a conversation with the customer, but not a negotiation. If the customer does have a potential figure in mind, then that becomes the point of negotiation for the response to the second question.

This kind of project manager/customer dialogue can provide a realistic scenario for making intelligent estimates. In addition, the project team can use the responses as a foundation for essential project documents such as the scope plan, activity plan, project schedule, and project budget.

§ 1.06 ASKING THE CORRECT QUESTIONS

The broadest areas for developing any set of project evaluation questions are of course:

- How?
- Why?
- When?
- Where?
- Who?
- What?

These are *metaquestions*, which means first-ordered questions. They are the broadest and simplest questions you can ask; of themselves, they are also the most effective. They are the first categorical steps toward clarification or refinement. How-type questions involve methodology, skill prerequisites, and financial concerns. Why-type questions involve justifications such as cost-benefit analysis, customer expectations, benchmarks, standards, and especially measurable project goals. Questions on benchmarks and standards are important to the quality control assurance process and the risk management program.

When-type questions involve time estimates and a schedule. Where-type questions consider location definitions and resource prerequisites. Who-type questions involve primarily skill types and level prerequisites, and the responsible agents. What-type questions involve resources (skills, equipment, materials, and project duration); that is, production time plus wait time.

The first step in using *metaquestions* is to narrow them down using categorical statements that include the characteristics, functions, and goals of a project, such as a specific customer definition rather than a global one. The second step is classifying a potential project in terms of what is and what is not—the foundation of the forms for a project scope plan. Turn these statements into questions based on the "big six." This process helps ensure as risk-free an environment as possible.

> "To raise new questions, new possibilities, to regard old problems from a new angle, requires creative imagination and marks real advance in science."
>
> —Albert Einstein

§ 1.07 DEVELOPING THE TWENTY QUESTIONS

Do not expect to have questions ready to determine a project's viability at the start of the planning stage. Instead, formulate the inquiry based on the old game that begins with the question, "Is it living or nonliving?" The format establishes two contrasting points and requires a "yes" or "no" answer. Perhaps, the first question to ask is, "Are there measurable goals?" If the answer is "yes," then the second question is, "Are sufficient funds available to complete the customer's measurable goals?"

The game is immediately over if the answer to the first question is "no." Never go to upper management to discuss a project without measurable project goals; instead, discuss an opportunity with upper management if there are no measurable goals.

Before discussing a project's viability with upper management, brainstorm with some of the project staff as well as with those who would be involved in the project. Brainstorming is an excellent technique for generating ideas or suggestions to order into a rational sequence. Do not get hung up on the sequence of the goals, unless one or more is critical to all of the others.

> Always keep a copy of the project's viability study in the project documentation library. It can provide valuable technical and business process information for future projects.

Some questions to stimulate the team during a brainstorming session:

- How complete is the list of measurable goals?
- Why should this project be done?
- How much funding is required to complete the critical goals and any other goals?
- What types of tasks and skills are required?
- When are the goals to be completed?
- When are management tools required?
- What are the required benchmarks and standards?
- Who has tactical responsibility for the project?
- What are the potential impacts on the system's infrastructure?
- How can potential risks be determined?

Some yes-no questions for the project viability process:

- Are there measurable project goals?
- Is there sufficient justification (cost-benefit analysis, customer relationship, or general market environment) to begin this project?
- Is there sufficient funding?
- Does the present staff have the skills to achieve the defined potential tasks?
- Can the goals be achieved within the expected duration (time)?
- Are the necessary management tools available, and are there appropriate skilled personnel available?
- Have the implications for possible benchmarks and standards been considered?
- Is there a written statement of tactical responsibility?
- Are there any critical impacts on the system's infrastructure?
- Have criteria of potential risks been established?

Some project questions in the pre-proposal phase can be used to create a checklist that reflects a set of yes-no responses and to develop a local template. This process is a requirement for any discussion of project viability with upper management. Exhibit 1-2 is a checklist with instructions for creating and using project viability questions.

1. What are the measurable project goals?
   If the project lacks measurable goals, it will be difficult to know how much of something is enough. The customer may make ever increasing demands since the approval criteria was not objectively measurable from the beginning.

Exhibit 1-2: Checklist for Project Visbility Questions

Measurable goals	❑
Acceptable assumptions	❑
Acceptable constraints	❑
Identified deliverables	❑
Identified risks	❑
Identified opportunities	❑
Identified project impacts	❑
Identified stakeholders	❑
Established project process	❑
Adequate duration	❑
Criteria for time estimates	❑
Schedule requirements	❑
Acceptable deadlines	❑
Cost-benefit analysis	❑
ROI impacts	❑
Adequate available funding	❑
Budget requirements	❑
Criteria cost estimates	❑
Project authority adequate	❑
System infrastructure effects	❑
Compatibility	❑
Interoperability	❑
Portability	❑
Scalability	❑
Technology stability	❑
Quality control	❑
Identified process	❑
External standards	❑
Internal standards	❑
External benchmarks	❑
Internal benchmarks	❑
Quality assurance	❑
Identified process	❑

Exhibit 1-2: (*Continued*)

External standards	❑
Internal standards	❑
External benchmarks	❑
Internal benchmarks	❑
Resources	❑
Equipment	❑
Internal	❑
External	❑
Materials	❑
Internal	❑
External	❑
Skills	❑
Internal	❑
External	❑
Contacts	❑
Internal	❑
External	❑
Project management tools	❑
Internal	❑
External	❑
Development tools	❑
Internal	❑
External	❑
Facilities	❑
Internal	❑
External	❑
Logistics requirements	❑
Training requirements	❑
Internal	❑
External	❑
Documentation requirements	❑
Internal	❑
External	❑
Communications requirements	❑
Internal	❑
External	❑

Exhibit 1-2: (*Continued*)

Instructions for Using a Viability Checklist

General Instructions

- This checklist is only a framework for you to create your own 20 questions.
- There are two required questions in any situation:
    1. Is there funding available for a potential project?
    2. Are there measurable goals for a potential project?
- Each of these items will require its own set of questions based on the metaquestions (How?, Why?, When?, Where?, Who?, and What?) that lead to a "yes," "no," or "not applicable." From these questions, the list should be narrowed to 20 for the meeting with the project initiator.
- Do not expect to have an acceptable set of questions on the first try.
- When presenting your questions it might effective to have a slide for each. The potential customer should focus on each question rather than on the 20 as a whole. It is more important to have a visual presentation rather than you just asking each question.
- You might include very brief talking points on each slide such as "Criteria for adequate funding."

Specific Instructions

Measurable goals: "Win the game" appears to be a measurable goal; however, does it mean the game must be won by more than one point? In the same manner, the goal of completing the project on time and on budget is not measurable. What must specifically be completed?

Acceptable assumptions: An assumption is a prediction that an action or an event will be fulfilled. An example is "There will be potential risks, but they will all be overcome."

Acceptable constraints: A constraint is a limitation or parameter such as the duration or funds available for the project.

Identified deliverables: A deliverable is a measurable result, product, or service of the project.

Identified risks: A risk is an event that will bring failure to the project.

Identified opportunities: An opportunity is a situation that can shorten the project's duration or lessen funding requirements.

Identified project impacts: An impact can be either short term or long term. When a long-term risk is forgotten, such as when the maintenance time required for a piece of hardware in the field is ignored in the design of the project, the cost can reduce any profits from the project.

Identified stakeholders: A stakeholder is potentially anyone in the organization, members of an external funding group, users, and interested government regulators.

Established project process: When there is no established project process, there is no management. There is firefighting. Would you want to do business with someone who cannot tell you how they are going to achieve your measurable goals?

Adequate duration: Duration should be defined as to the amount of working days available for the project. An absolute duration includes such things as weekends. One might speak of a six-month duration; however, what is the actual production time?

Criteria for time estimates: If you do not have measurable and object criteria for time estimates, the project will fail.

Schedule requirements: A schedule needs to consider in a project's duration its production time and its wait time. It is an allocation of activities with deadlines or milestones.

Acceptable deadlines: Acceptable deadlines are realistic. They can also be defined within either a pessimistic or an optimistic scenario.

Exhibit 1-2: (*Continued*)

Cost-benefit analysis: An IT cost-benefit analysis is required before determining the viability of the project. Any questions should be formulated within in the context of the results of the cost-benefit analysis.

ROI impacts: A return on investment is more than a financial saving. An ROI could also be an adequate security system that protects data and its loss to a cracker (thief), which could be difficult to quantify.

Adequate available funding: If there is no available funding, the project is only speculation.

Budget requirements: A project budget is a formal structure that is based on changing cost estimates. A project budget is not a corporate annual budget that is based on headcount and activities.

Criteria for cost estimates: If you do not have measurable and object criteria for cost estimates, the project will fail.

Project authority adequate: A written document that establishes the parameters of authority for the project manager must be completed prior to the start of the project.

System infrastructure effects: The infrastructure is more that the visual components (hardware, software, and people). It includes the intangibles: compatibility, interoperability, portability, and scalability.

Technology stability: Do you know of any potential technology that could impact the measurable goals of the project?

Quality control: Quality control is the definition component of a quality program. You need to know the potential impacts of internal and external objective and measurable standards (procedures) and benchmarks (performance level) on completing the project's goals.

Quality assurance: Quality control is the performance (the data gathering) component of a quality program. You need to know the potential uses of internal and external objectives and measurable standards (procedures) and benchmarks (performance level) on completing the project's goals.

Resources: You need to have knowledge as to resource requirement types potentially required before determining the viability of the project. The knowledge should include internal and external equipment requirements, materials, skills, contacts, system and development tools, facility requirements, and finally training and documentation needs. Why do you need all this data up front? You need to be able to judge as adequately as possible your capabilities to do the customer's stated measurable goals.

Training requirements: Training requirements need to consider the availability of internal and external classes. Will the training include hands-on situations? What is the learning curve scenario? What are the potential funding requirements? When is the training requirement to determine the critical path?

Documentation requirements: Documentation requirements have to consider if all or some of the documents are written. What kind of funding is needed? What type of documentation is required (technical, customer, or training)?

Communications requirements: Communications requirements have to consider the methods for getting information to a person in an appropriate manner? Who gets what information must be defined. Do you give weekly reports to the customer using e-mail or do you give monthly presentations of project status? What are the benefits and consequences of using email? Consider that e-mails can be forwarded to people outside of the project's environment and sometimes be interpreted on an emotional level.

Example Questions

Below are 10 questions in the "yes-no" response format for the project viability process

1. Are there measurable project goals?
2. Is there sufficient justification (cost-benefit analysis, customer relationship, or general market environment) to do this project?
3. Is there sufficient funding?
4. Does the present staff have the skills to achieve the defined activities or tasks?
5. Can the goals be achieved in the expected duration (time)?
6. Are the necessary management tools available and are there appropriate skilled personnel available?
7. Have the implications for possible benchmarks and standards been considered?
8. Is there a written statement of tactical responsibility?
9. Are there critical impacts on the system's infrastructure?
10. Have criteria for potential risks been established?

While some of the above questions might not be answered absolutely at a meeting on project viability, they should be answered with a high degree of certainty. A "maybe" answer should be turned into a "yes" or "no" prior to a definite start of a project.

2. What potential materials and equipment are available?
    At this point it should be apparent what types of materials and equipment are to be used for each goal.

3. What and where are available resources?
    A project manager must be a master at obtaining resources—know what the resources are and how to get them. They might be found outside of the IT department or even outside the corporation. Resource availability is one criterion for approving the start of a project.

4. How do project costs compare to expected benefits?
    The project approval should include a basic cost-benefit analysis so that upper management can judge the project's viability.

5. Why should this project be done?
    Without specific justification, why should the project proceed? Customers sometimes are impatient to throw money at a problem without careful consideration or planning.

6. What and when are appropriate skills available?
    Create measurable and specific skill-level descriptions that include technical requirements.

7. How will the project's budget items be funded?
   Unfortunately, budget items for a given project may be scattered over a number of different budgets. Create a project budget, even if it is outside of the formal financial structure to manage the entire process.

8. What and where are the required project management tools for achieving project results?
   Project management tools can be as simple as a set of index cards or as complex as a utility that can manage a project based on performance evaluation and review technique (PERT). Remember, the more complex a tool, the greater the learning curve. The problem is that the more complex the tool, the harder it is to identify the bad data.

9. What benchmarks and standards have been identified in the quality control and assurance program for the deliverables?
   It is critical to identify standards and benchmarks to ensure the success of any project that includes quality management. Remember that a quality deliverable means customer satisfaction.

10. How do the project goals reflect efficiency and innovation?
    Because something may be a buzzword on the customer's tongue does not mean it is tasty. Consider how the project's goals affect the IT infrastructure and its efficiency and how any innovation or enhancement will ripple through the system.

11. What are the critical assumptions and constraints for managing the project's goals?
    The project manager roots them out and records them on a detailed list. Feed these into the risk management plan.

12. Who has responsibility for the project's management?
    The project manager must have *written* authority from executive management to do what is necessary to complete a project on schedule and on budget. This authorization is in the project charter. Do not begin a project without this legitimization.

13. How do deliverables relate to the project goals?
    Maintain a list of deliverables associated with each goal; these could include training or special documentation. Consider the types of presentations to be delivered as each goal is developed and completed.

14. How stable is the technology required to achieve project results?
    Include in the list of assumptions and constraints any technology to be used in the development of deliverables. Introducing a new technology during the project duration could create a devastating ripple effect.

15. How will the results impact the return on investments (ROI)?
    ROI is more that a simple cost-benefit analysis. Its impact might mean a significant improvement in system scalability in a given area, so that the customer would be very satisfied.

16. How realistic are the deadlines to achieve project results?
    There is only one rule at this point: the project *must* have realistic deadlines. Never expect to start a project the day after it is approved. Complex issues need to be resolved first.

17. What are the events that could cause the project to fail?
    Manage risks by considering them before they happen. This activity is a part of defining assumptions and constraints.

18. What are the events that can make the project successful?
    Do not ignore the positive. The project may be happening at the correct time and in the correct place.

19. What are the possible impacts of the results on the company's data systems?
    The IT manager filters all data through the defined goals of the project team.

20. What are the criteria for the various types of estimates?
    Remember, estimates come in three flavors—pessimistic, realistic, and optimistic—so determine the basic project cost and time estimates in each of these three types. Describe potential skill requirements in the same manner.

"Judge a man by his questions rather than by his answers."

—Voltaire

At the pre-proposal survey step, establish clear parameters. As in football, first establish the playing area, the goal posts, the end field, and the yardage lines. If managing the creation of an XML-based application for defining a financial database for corporate budget items, the following data are needed.

- What are the budget items?
- What kind of database is it?
- When is the database to be accessed?
- Where is the database located?

- Why does the application for the database need to be XML-based?
- Who is to access the database?
- How is the database to be accessed?

Just by using the metaquestions, the project manager can quickly establish the types of data needed in this critical area. Other critical areas include:

- Sources of funding
- Basic assumptions and constraints
- Potential impact, especially on the system's infrastructure
- Potential possibilities for risks and opportunities
- Technological requirements

The development of any checklist or form should begin by asking questions about the project. In such a case, consider the potential rather than the actual.

The checklist and instructions in this chapter are examples only. Based on the individual situation, create a project-specific set of questions.

---

§ 1.08 ABCs OF PROJECT MANAGEMENT ISSUES

Below is a list of sources that can generate project management issues. The essential purpose of the scope plan, and ultimately the responsibility of the project manager, is to control the parameters or negative limits of these sources. Each letter is limited to a maximum of five sources because of the defined constraint of the page length for this book. Use this list to determine if the project plans and scope have considered every angle of the project.

- A—acceptance criteria, activity definitions, aims, analysis, assumptions
- B—bargaining, benchmarks, benefits, best practices, budget
- C—champion, communications, constraints, control, cost
- D—data, decisionmaking, deliverables, design, documentation
- E—effectiveness, efficiencies, environment, expectations, expediencies

- F—failure, feedback, financing, functionality, funding
- G—gates, geopolitics, goals, government, groupings
- H—hardware, hiring, historical data, human relations, human resources
- I—idealism, implementation, information, infrastructure, IT strategy
- J—job assessment, job description, job satisfaction, job rotation, just-in-time
- K—kicker, kickoff meeting, KISS principle, knowledge management, kow-towing
- L—lag-lead times, leadership, learning curve, legal concerns, life cycle
- M—marketing, media, methodology, milestones, mission
- N—needs assessment, negotiations, networking, noise, normal
- O—objectives, operational management, organization, obsolescence, ownership
- P—partnering, performing, phasing, planning, prototyping
- Q—qualification, quality, quantification, quantity, quota
- R—reengineering, resistance, rewards, risk management, roles
- S—schedule, skills, stakeholders, standards, strategy
- T—team building, technology, time management, total quality, training
- U—understaffing, unions, upgrading, user friendly, user involvement
- V—validation, value management, variance, verification, version
- W—what if, work authorization, win-win agreement, work environment, workload
- X—X factors (the improbable technical factors)
- Y—you
- Z—Z factors (the improbable emotional factors)

> "One of the greatest and simplest tools for learning more and growing is doing more."
>
> —Washington Irving

§ 1.09   SOME PROJECT MANAGEMENT ADVANTAGES AND LIMITATIONS

Using project management techniques allows the IT project manager to guide and control a process with a clear focus in order to achieve a set of measurable goals with a successful conclusion. As with any technique, project management has both its advantages and its limitations. Some advantages are:

- Clear picture of the task and the participants' responsibilities
- Early identification of performance errors
- Means of accountability
- Product integrity
- Team participation

According to some people, there may be more limitations than advantages; however, here are only two limitations:

- Keep project plans simple to limit misinterpretations.
- Changes in the project may make administrative paperwork intolerable.

§ 1.10   USING ESSENTIAL TERMS

The following 50 terms are essential to a full discussion of any project and form the supports for the framework of this book. Beyond these terms, consider local technical applications of software, hardware, and infrastructure.

> Intangible infrastructure concepts include interoperability, portability, and scalability.

An **assumption** is a prediction that something will be true; either an action or an event that ensures project success.

Authority is the investment in managing and controlling a series of tasks such as a project. For example, the critical statement the project sponsor has to make is, "The project manager has the authority to make all decisions required to achieve a successful project."

A **benchmark** is a specific technical level of excellence.

A **checklist** is an organized list, possibly a standard of action, followed in sequence, to accomplish a specified goal.

A **consultant** is a person from outside the normal resource pool with experience in solving a specific project issue.

Control is the monitoring of progress and the checking for variances in the plan.

A **cost-benefit analysis** is the development of a ratio to determine if a project is financially viable.

A **critical activity** or task if not completed means project failure.

A project **critical chain** is the schedule's critical path after leveling resources requirements (to avoid overcommitments).

A **deliverable** is a clearly defined project result, product, or service.

An **estimate** is a guess based on opinion, or a forecast based on experience. Cost, time, and resource estimates are the foundations for project planning.

Expectation is a stated project goal that can become a perceived undocumented result.

Goal characteristics have to be measurable, specific, and potentially possible.

Interoperability is to what degree the various network components work with each other successfully.

Management is the process of working with people, resources, equipment, and materials to achieve organizational goals.

Management team is a supervisory team that coordinates broad issues that affect the corporation.

The **market analysis report** documents and verifies market opportunities and justifies the features, services, and applications for the project goals.

A **model** is a theoretical environment with as much data as possible to reflect reality adequately for decisionmaking.

An **objective** is a set of measurable goals to achieve a defined target; if not achieved, it has critical results.

An **opportunity** is a situation that will positively affect the project in time, money, resources, or all three in a significant manner.

An **organization** is an entity created to achieve what the separate individuals could not accomplish.

Portability is the degree to which the software can be transferred from one environment to another.

Portfolio management is the management of all of an organization's projects (pending and active) to obtain the greatest benefit.

Process is a systematic and sequential set of activities (tasks) to achieve a set of measurable goals.

A **program** is collection of projects working in the same functional area; for example, the collection of projects to implement a new enterprise resource management system.

A **project** is an organized set of tasks to reach a measurable outcome within a specified duration.

Project management is the managing, controlling, and integrating of tasks, resources, time, and costs to achieve defined measurable outcomes within a specified duration.

A **project management office** (PMO) is an organization that provides services to both project managers and project sponsors to more efficiently manage projects.

A **project manager** is the person with overall responsibility for managing and controlling the project tasks (defined and undefined) to achieve a measurable outcome within a specified schedule and budget.

A **project team** is a temporary organization assembled to achieve measurable goals within a specific time and with limited resources, equipment, and materials.

Quality assurance is the establishment of standards, practices, and measurements to ensure that good things go into a project to get good things out of it. It is all the things done prior to project tasks to prepare them to create good results. It is the complement of quality control.

Quality control is the component of quality management that considers the results of project tasks. It compares the task results to the project definition, standards of performance, etc., to determine the degree of compliance. It is closely associated with testing.

A **resource** is anything that supports the project. This includes money, skills, materials, time, facilities, and equipment.

Resource planning is establishing support requirements for a project as to costs, availability, start date and end date (length of time for use plus duration), and technical specifications.

A **risk** is a potential issue that can have a significant impact on the success of a project or major activity.

Scalability is the degree a system can be enhanced without a major change in design.

The **schedule** is the project plan for the allocation of tasks with estimated durations.

Scope is the boundary of the project. Do everything within it, and nothing outside of it.

Skill level is a factor used by a project manager in planning the project's budget (based on technical staffing), rather than using a headcount.

Specific goals are measurable, unambiguous project goals that match exactly the customer's stated expectations.

The **sponsor** (or primary customer) is the person providing the resources and the working environment to make possible the achievement of project goals.

A **stakeholder** is any person or organization interested in the project's existence or outcome. This includes the customer, the PMO manager, the general public, shareholders, the project team, and interested government regulators.

A **standard** is usually an external, industry-accepted document for achieving quality for one or more of the project-defined expected goals.

A **statement of work** (SOW) is an integrated set of descriptions as to project tasks, goals, risks, and resources to complete a measurable outcome.

A **system** is an interactive set of tasks or groups that form a whole with dynamics that affect all the components.

The **third-party market agreement** provides the plans whereby the project or a part of the project is to be the responsibility of a third-party developer.

Exhibit 1-3: Project Proposal Checklist

Technical Section:	Yes	No	Comments
Executive summary			
Requirements analysis			
Solutions			
Alternate solution			
Scope of work			
Parameters			
Methodology			
Technical solution			
Prototype/Demo			
Beta test			
Installations			
Standards			
Benchmarks			
Maintenance			
Training			
Documentation			
Risk analysis			
Appendix/Glossary			
Index			
Administrative Section:			
Executive summary			
Commitment statement			
Solution			
Statement of work (SOW)			
Activities			
Deliverables			
Organization			
Task responsibilities			
Project management process			
Tracking system			
Reporting system			
Quality control			
Contractors/Consultants			
Personnel qualifications			
Appendix			
Index			

Exhibit 1-3: (*Continued*)

Financial Section:	Yes	No	Comments
Executive summary			
Cost model			
Contract			
Cost summary			
Cost estimate basis			
Payment structure			
Overhead rates			
Facilities rates			
Cost schedule			
Additional cost criteria			
Appendix			
Index			

Exhibit 1-4: Project Planning Checklist

Project:		Date:		
Prepared by:		Yes	No	NA
Acceptable variances from performance have been identified				
Activities are comprehended by the team				
Activity responsibilities have been clearly defined				
Adequate tools to complete activities				
Approval process is satisfactory				
Approved work by responsible managers				
Consultant parameters have been clearly stated				
Contingency policy rather than padding				
Cost estimates are realistic				
Critical path has been identified				
Customer has given measured objectives				
Customers are adequately involved in the project process				
Deliverables have been clearly identified				
Documentation program is adequate				
Exit process exists				
Facilities are adequate				
Flexibility is possible in the project				
Gantt chart available as a working tool				
Historical IT data were used when appropriate				
Identified appropriate standards and benchmarks				
Overtime is minimized				
Performance objectives are clearly defined				
Plan is comprehensive and no unknown omissions				
Political issues have been identified and handled				
Potential consequences analyzed and accepted				
Potential risks identified with contingency solutions				
Procedures to handle resources availability				
Procedures to objectively handle cost estimates				
Procedures to objectively handle time estimates				
Program for recognition is excellent				
Project communication program is adequate				
Project goals enhance the corporate goals				
Project manager has adequate authority to make decisions				
Project mission communicated to the full project team				
Quality control and assurance program in place				
Review process is satisfactory				

Exhibit 1-4: (*Continued*)

Project:		Date:		
Prepared by:		Yes	No	NA
Satisfactory reporting system in place				
Schedule is realistic				
Team members are qualified				
Team members' roles have been clearly described				
There are no activities with lengthy durations				
There is an adequate testing process				
Time estimates are realistic				
Training for project success is adequate				
Written measured project objectives or goals				

Chapter 2

Defining a Project

§ 2.01   INTRODUCTION

> "Project Scope Management includes the processes required to ensure that the project includes all of the work required and only the work required to complete the project successfully."
>
> —PMBOK 2000 edition

A project's definition is an explanation of what the project is trying to accomplish. It might be to construct a building, replace an accounting system, or audit a company for legal compliance. A clear definition allows for accurate timelines and budget estimates. A vague definition introduces more unknowns into the project estimates. These unknown factors waste resources and time.

A project's definition has many components. The limits of a project are its "scope." Scope identifies what is included and excluded from the project. Sometimes the scope is general, such as to replace all of the personal computers within the headquarters building, or specific by identifying the departments or even the individual units involved in the plan. What is "in scope" must be clearly identified and the list must be specific. Everything in scope is in the project plan.

Things excluded from the project are "out of scope." Out of scope items can be described generally, as in "all else is excluded," or specifically, such as "the Materials department is excluded from this project." The description of what is out of scope is often general. A critical responsibility of the project manager is to provide a clear definition of the project's goals and limits to keep the project moving toward completion, with a minimal waste of resources. This chapter discusses:

- Project definition
- Scope defining
- Developing a project charter
- Key components of a project notebook
- Maintaining a project's scope
- Evaluating proposed scope changes

§ 2.02 PROJECT INITIATION—TAKING THE FIRST STEP

Projects fail at the beginning, not in the execution. Too many projects are assigned in the course of casual conversation. The simple one-liner, "Build a new payroll system" is too vague to attempt. Whom will the payroll system support? Is it only intended to support the local office? Will it include the factory in Canada (with different legal requirements)? What sort of payroll is it to support? Does it include hourly workers with time sheets turned in weekly, salaried staff where there are few data entries, or must it determine sales commissions?

When people speak, their words are based in some context. This context must be shared with the listener if the speaker is to convey the intended information. For example, an IT manager who was scolded by an executive about an inaccurate field on an inventory report might shout to the programmer to "Fix the Materials system!" Although the IT manager knew what was meant, the actual requirement passed to the programmer was very broad. It is important that the project manager assigned to a task spend as much time as necessary in the early days of the project clarifying exactly what is needed.

For example, imagine that in an executive meeting, the CEO turns to the IT Director and says, "We need a better handle on all of these computer things. I want an asset inventory. Make it happen!" and the meeting continues its discussion on ways to cut the employee benefits for the nonexecutive personnel.

- The IT Director thinks, "This inventory can be used to build a database for the Help Desk so they will know what each person has on their desk when they call for assistance. I'll need PC technicians, a database consultant, and part of a server."

- The Accounting Manager thinks, "We can use the inventory to tie the unit's serial number to the purchase price and more accurately allocate depreciation expense to each department. I must have these numbers before the next quarter's reports."

- The Materials Manager thinks, "We can add a bar coded tag to each PC and use this asset count to justify our move to RF scan guns. I'll call that salesperson back in and schedule a formal presentation for the staff."

- The Sales Manager thinks, "I can use this to show how computers are unfairly distributed among the departments. I need the results before the next capital budget cycle."

- The CEO thinks that he will finally know how many PCs are in the building. He views this as a one-time physical count of units and anticipates the result in a few days.

It is apparent that the project sponsor (CEO) has a clear idea of what he wants. He sees this project as a brief, one-time count while others are envisioning technology purchases, database programming, and a wide range of data entry. If the IT Director begins work on the project without clarifying the project's mission and characteristics, a lot of time and money will be spent and the project will likely be terminated before anyone on the staff is satisfied.

Project initiation is the official order to begin the project, and in most companies, it is a formal process. The dedication of company resources toward a goal should be a carefully considered action. In other companies or for smaller projects, project initiation can be quite informal. Even the informal companies will use many of the tools discussed in this chapter.

As early in the planning process as possible, appoint a project manager. By participating in the planning, the project manager will have a deeper understanding of the project's motivations, politics, and constraints. Companies initiate projects for a number of business reasons:

- Changes in regulatory requirements—new laws, such as HIPAA or Sarbanes-Oxley compliance

- Perceived business opportunity—Web-based catalogs and e-commerce

- To meet a business threat—"we must do this because our competition did"

- Customer request—provide visibility into our inventory

- To update or replace an existing technology—move company reports to the Web

"A battle is won or lost before the enemy is met, based on the general's preparations."

—Sun Tzu (6th century B.C.), *The Art of War*

§ 2.03 ASSEMBLING A PROJECT NOTEBOOK

Immediately after appointment to the project, the project manager assembles a notebook to hold the project's planning documents. This notebook provides the project's administrative framework and includes auxiliary plans for things such as managing stakeholders, managing risks, etc. Tabs in a typical project notebook might include:

- Mission statement
- Project goals
- Planning assumptions
- Project charter
- Stakeholder analysis
- Stakeholder communications plan
- Risk analysis
- Risk management plan
- Scope validation plan
- Scope management plan
- Project quality plan
- Open issues tracking plan

Some of these tabs pertain to project initiation, and some are for both initiation and execution. Small projects manage nicely with fewer tabs. For example, a small project may have so few stakeholders who regularly work together so that a formal communications plan is not necessary. The larger and more complex a project is, the more critical that methodical planning becomes.

§ 2.04 ASSEMBLING A PROJECT CHARTER

A project charter is similar to a project's birth certificate. It declares the purpose (or desired result) for the project and formally assigns a project manager to carry out the project. If the project is created as the result of a feasibility study, then a draft charter can be pulled together from the study documents. If the project is a fresh start, then the charter must be created from scratch. A project charter:

- Formally establishes the project manager's authority to execute the project
- Validates the project manager's understanding of the project's goals to be sure they are in sync with the sponsor's goals

- Documents the link between the project's purpose and business requirements or strategic plan initiatives
- May identify the time boundaries for the project's start and finish
- May identify a maximum budget amount
- Is signed by the sponsor or senior executive.

See Exhibit 2-1 for a sample project charter.

Exhibit 2-1: Project Charter

Project Name: _____

Project Sponsor: _____ Project Manager: _____

Project Mission Statement:

_____

_____

_____

Start Date: _____ Anticipated End Date: _____

Budget Estimate: _____

Critical Objectives:

Responsibility and authority of the project manager:

• Is the principal point of contact for this project.
• Is responsible for project planning, execution, and performance. The project manager will employ the company's project process tool suite for planning, managing, tracking, and controlling the project.
• Will assemble, train, and direct the project team and evaluate and rate project team member performance
• Assign and reassign work to project team members regardless of their functional assignment within the company
• Will report project status to company management and stakeholders every 30 days from project inception to conclusion
• Control the scope baseline of this project

_____   _____

Approved   Date

Additional examples can be found by searching the Internet for "Project Charter Form."

The project charter is drafted by the project manager and is approved by the project's sponsor or a senior executive. An executive's signature is important since projects are cross-functional and often step out of the normal company management hierarchy. A signed charter informs the department managers of the project manager's authority and that their assistance is required. The charter also announces to the company the existence of the project and authorizes use of company resources for these objectives. It confers authority on the project manager to issue directives toward its completion. A signed contract is a project charter for a contractor.

Each company has its own format for the charter. It may be a single page or include an overview of every tab in the project notebook. At a minimum, it should include the mission statement, identify the project manager by name, and authorize the project manager to use company resources to begin the project. Additional project charter items might include:

- Background information on the problem or project, such as the problem it is to solve or new function it will provide

- Specific goals to be included in the project, such as mandatory, onsite end-user training, no disruption of normal service during installation, etc.

- Specific objectives to be included in the project and how they will be measured, such as software response time

- Specific deliverable items, such as end-user manuals, a transaction audit trail, etc.

- A recap of the organizational scope of the project—which areas of the company are to be involved in the project or benefit

- Specific time constraints, such as legal compliance dates

- Key risks acknowledged for the project—usually for projects where the technology is new or the goal is research

- Key assumptions that must be true for the project to succeed

- Project staffing assignments to quickly align specific people to the project

- Identify the members of the project steering committee and their responsibilities

- Identify milestones when the project manager must formally report on the project's progress

- Any areas specifically outside of the scope for the project.

The secondary purpose of a project charter is for new team members to gain a picture of the project's overall goals. Remember, a project plan is all about communications and the charter is a basic document for the plan. As the project progresses, team members may come and go based on the requirements of the project plan. When all of the team members are busy working on their tasks, the new team members can gain a better understanding of the project's mission by reading the fundamental project documents.

§ 2.05 PROJECT DEFINITION AND SCOPE

Project definition develops the project charter into a project's mission statement and its scope. A project's scope is all that it encompasses, much like the walls of a room. Whatever is within the scope of the project (or within the walls) is in the project.

Anything outside of the scope of the project is for another project on another day. For a task to gain entry to the room, the project manager must open the door. Otherwise, the task cannot become part of the project. Project scope communicates to the team members what to focus on and what to ignore. It sets the expectations of the stakeholders as to what the project's final product should encompass.

Scope planning is an iterative process. It begins at the project's inception, based on what is known at that moment. The deeper the details are dug into, the more likely the project is to succeed.

Scope planning assumes that the requested resources will be available when needed and in the quantity required. This assumption allows planning to proceed until the actual schedule is built and actual resource requirements are identified.

A key project manager responsibility is "scope management," which ensures that all changes to the project scope are made in a controlled manner and that unofficial "side agreements" between team members and end users are never permitted. As the project progresses, some of the assumptions made during the planning process will prove to be false and new obstacles will arise. This requires modifying the scope to reflect new situations. The earlier an obstacle or opportunity is identified in the project, the cheaper the changes are to make in the scope plans.

[A] Creating a Project Mission Statement

> "Would you tell me, please, which way I ought to walk from here?" asked Alice.
> "That depends a good deal on where you want to get to," said the Cat.
> "I don't much care where," said Alice.
> "Then it doesn't matter which way you walk," said the Cat.
>
> —Lewis Carroll, *Alice in Wonderland*

Begin scope planning by identifying what the successful outcome of the project would be. The project manager's vision of the project's successful outcome must be the same as the sponsor's vision. A tool for accomplishing this is a project mission statement. The mission statement is the cornerstone on which the project's planning rests. A mission statement is a high-level, succinct group of sentences that describes the overall intent of the project.

Projects exist to create or to achieve something. This something might be to build a new computer room, to migrate data to a new software version, or just about anything. The cornerstone of a project is its overall goal. The goal consists of "what" is wanted and "why" it is needed. (The "how" is the project plan.) If the project manager does not completely understand what the successful outcome of the project would look like, then how can the project team understand it? If the project manager does not understand the driving forces behind the project, then decisions may be at variance with the business intent.

Some sponsors act as if their role is complete once the project manager has been appointed. This is never the case. As seen in the previous example, the sponsor must effectively communicate his "vision" of the project's results to the project manager and ensure that the project does not deviate from it. The sponsor is also a key player in developing most of the initial project planning documents.

It is the project manager's responsibility to ensure the project's purpose is clearly defined. Sometimes there is a rush to start early. Although some of the administrative details can begin, the project manager must push back on the project sponsor to clarify the project's goals before committing resources.

The persons requesting the project may be intentionally vague. They know generally what they want but cannot describe it specifically. They become increasingly frustrated talking to the project manager since their goal is not clear to them either. Rather than argue with the project sponsor that something cannot be built that is not even fully understood at the concept level, the project manager should propose a feasibility study, which will examine the business need and draft specifications for the final product.

The information elements found in a project mission statement vary from company to company. Often the project mission statement ties the project's goals to a business need or strategic goal. In its final form, the mission statement is an agreement between the project manager and the project's sponsor as to the project's objectives and deliverables. This statement provides a shared vision for all of the team. Sometimes the mission statement includes a recap of the problem the project addresses.

Classic mission statements from history that present a clear vision:

"I believe that this nation should commit itself to achieving the goal, before this decade is out, of landing a man on the moon and returning him safely to the Earth."

—President John F. Kennedy, May 25, 1961

"I will return."

—General Douglas MacArthur, 1942, upon leaving the Philippines.

A well-written mission statement identifies the project's justification and ties it to the business requirement. Sometimes it includes a separate product statement that clearly describes the item or service the project is to create. A project that begins without a clear link to a business object or strategy will be constantly in danger of cancellation. If the sponsor cannot identify such a link, then maybe the project should not exist!

Following is an example of a project mission statement found on the Internet:

http://natureali.org/parrot_project/Mission.htm

"The Purpose of the California Parrot Project" is to:

- Determine the geographical distribution of parrots in California.
- Determine the ecological parameters associated with successful colonization.
- Identify species present and determine their population sizes.
- Establish the extent of interbreeding between closely related congeners.
- Educate the public about naturalized parrots.
- Encourage public participation in the process of the scientific study of urban parrots.

1. The first line of the statement identifies the scope of the project as "California." Therefore any other state or nation is (by inference) out of scope.
2. Clear project goals are described in the other bullet points.

Some sponsors are intentionally vague in their project description hoping to keep their options open for changing the project later. They expect an accurate estimate of the cost and time required for a project when they are not even sure what the final product will look like. They hope in this way to avoid requests for additional time or money!

There are times when vague project goals are appropriate. An example is a research project where the goal is something that has never been done before. The project's mission may be something like building an unmanned ore-mining machine. Since this has never been done before, it is hard to use the experience from previous projects to build the plan. The project manager is unsure of the specific action steps and the budget needed to achieve the goal. This type of project plans only one or two stages ahead and, based on the results, plans the next step. Even though the project plan is murky, the team's efforts are anchored by the project's mission statement.

Information systems projects sometimes start with vague objectives and are expected to clarify themselves as the project progresses. This is often because the project's sponsor lacks a clear vision of what is involved but feels that prompt action is called for. Most business managers do not think as analytically as an IT manager does when considering a problem. By helping them to clarify their vision during the early stages of project planning, the project manager saves everyone considerable frustration later in the project.

An unspoken secondary goal of every project is to complete the project with an optimal utilization of resources. No matter how well run the project is, someone (usually in Accounting) will want to know why some item or other was purchased, nine months after the fact. Good documentation will minimize the time required to address these questions.

Projects have many goals. The mission statement is a general goal that can be broken down into smaller goals. For example, if the mission (goal) is to build an inter-company Web page, the secondary goals would be to build separate Web pages for each department. Objectives are measurable items under these second-level goals, such as building a human resources page that published job openings, benefits, etc.

[B]   Defining Objectives

With a sponsor-approved mission statement in hand, the project manager breaks the mission statement into its functional characteristics. Each functional characteristic becomes a project goal (such as training documentation, number of simultaneous users, etc.). These functional characteristics are known as "criteria of success." Goals are general statements of direction where objectives are specific. Describe objectives in terms of their deliverable items. Include metrics that describe some aspects of the deliverables. Describe each objective according to the acronym SMART.

Specific—A precisely described task

Measurable—Quantified results

Achievable—Don't reach too far

Realistic—Resources must be available

Timed—When the objective must be achieved

Measurements can be specific (such as the object must be 25 feet long), they can be relative (do not exceed $500,000), or they can be comparative when they are compared to a baseline, such as system response time. Whatever measurements are used, keep them easy to understand and unambiguous to measure. Measurements tell the team member when they are done. Metrics provide a "how much" standard that both the customer and the team member can work to.

> "When you measure what you are speaking about and express it in numbers, you know something about it, but when you cannot express it in numbers, your knowledge about it is of a meager and unsatisfying kind."
>
> —Lord Kelvin

If the sponsor announces a mission to build a new payroll system, the project manager breaks this into smaller goals, and then objectives. To create these goals, many questions must be answered by the sponsor. "Who will use or benefit from it?" "How many people will be using the system and where are they located?" "What is the required system availability time, equipment available to support the new system, etc.?" Each of these questions will lead to other questions. Every project characteristic agreed upon is recorded on a project objectives list.

Every project objective becomes a system requirement that must be addressed in the project plan. A single objective can add considerable work to a project. However, a clear definition can also preclude a lot of work. It is very difficult to describe all aspects of an objective. At some point, assumptions must be made. The clearer that an objective is, the easier it will be to plan for and to achieve. Vague objectives are opportunities for scope creep. Programmers can interpret vague objectives to make their own assumptions that will shrink the end product or expand it.

Thoroughness in extracting project objectives out of the stakeholders will result in fewer overlooked tasks on the task plan. Often an objective thought essential may have been just a passing whim by the customer. What are the customer's measurable expectations, the deliverables? There cannot be such a thing as an unspoken priority of the customer.

If the customer cannot settle on specific project objective characteristics, then make assumptions about measurable characteristics and add them to the objective description. Note assumptions and point them out to the customer to approve or modify. Either way, there is a clearer criteria from which to plan.

To aid in the description of the project's objectives, refer to existing information sources. Documents from previous projects are useful in identifying potential obstacles, for estimating task durations, and for strategies to manage specific stakeholders. The project manager can use these documents to assist in developing the plan. Other sources of scope planning information include:

- Published company strategic direction
- Company's management style
- Projected business needs
- Stakeholder interviews
- Organizational policies
- Formal and informal company organization
- Government regulations

§ 2.06   DEFINING ASSUMPTIONS

Assumptions are the "unknowns" of the project. Projects swim in a sea of uncertainty since they involve estimating actions and results of these actions in the future. Each task is an estimation of how much time an activity will require to achieve completion assuming no more than the usual delays (short-duration illness, a lack of technical expertise of the team member, a delay in receiving an important piece of equipment). Planning is guesswork based on experience, suggestions from the project team, and assumptions. Guesswork is necessary to reduce uncertainty.

Assumptions add stability to process planning by assuming all things are stable and unchanging. They allow the planning process to proceed. The key is to capture the assumptions so they can be controlled. Each assumption is related to a project objective. Several months from now, the details of why a course of action was selected based on an assumption will be lost to memory. Write each assumption down now and include it in the project documentation.

Since assumptions are guesses disguised as facts, they have a degree of risk that they might be false (with a corresponding negative impact on the project). Every assumption must be evaluated in the risk assessment as to the negative impact to the project if they prove to be false.

[A]   Standard Assumptions

Some assumptions are taken for granted and are not listed, such as the project manager maintaining good health throughout the life of the project. Another assumption might be that the company's business climate and ability to fund the project will remain constant.

Two key assumptions expedite the planning process. First, assume that the project's mission will not change materially over the life of the project. This provides a constancy of purpose. In reality, it might change but at that point, the plan can be modified to address it. Second, that resources will be available when they are needed and in the quantity they are needed.

[B]   Guiding Assumptions

Assumptions are not open-ended. They exist inside of boundaries. The primary boundary is company policies and procedures. Assume these policies will not materially change over the life of the project. Any assumption that expects to be exempted from company policies must be confirmed immediately and on the surface; it is unlikely to happen. When planning, assume the project budget will not be increased or decreased during the project. Budget changes and time line changes are adjusted through negotiations with the project sponsor based on circumstances at the time.

Any "hard" due dates must be identified and when planning in the beginning, always adjust the plan to meet them. Do not depend on being excused from them. An extension is possible but it is an unlikely assumption unless it is locked in during the project planning process. Firm due dates often are legally mandated and the company will not have the ability to alter them.

[C]   Constraints

A constraint is a specific requirement or measurement that guides plan development. Constraints limit the project manager's freedom of action for planning. They form project boundaries. If they interfere with the project, the project manager should appeal them to the sponsor and the steering committee.

Sometimes to guide the project manager and team members, specific constraints may be added to the project, such as:

- Use existing hardware resources
- Use existing staff (no contract programmers)
- Use a specific programming language
- Migrate historical data to the new database

[D]   Sharpening a Vague Goal

One tool for breaking down a concept into its various components is known as a cause and effect diagram. This is useful since most customers do not understand the basic building blocks of information systems. Each aspect of a system involves tradeoffs such

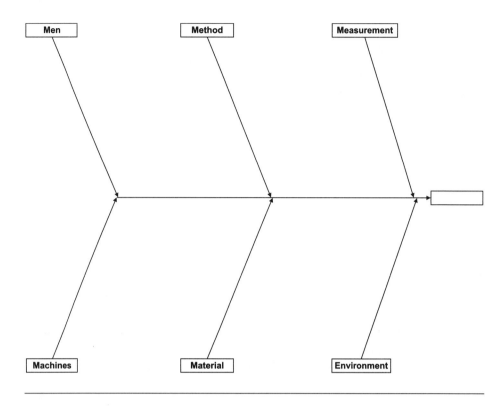

Chart 2-1: Fishbone Five Ms and an E

as "lower cost or faster network" or "fancier Web pages or faster speed." A cause and effect diagram helps to draw out characteristics of the project's mission to speed the identification of characteristics.

A cause and effect diagram uses the analogy of a fish to illustrate a problem. The "head" is the problem or objective. Place a terse statement here, such as "Develop new payroll system." Each of the "fishbones" represents one major aspect of this issue. The name for the "bones" should be the major drivers of the mission. Sometimes this is known as the Five Ms and an E:

- Men—Who are the key people involved with this issue? Add these names to the stakeholder list. This might be the network expert, the critical business manager, the skilled programmer, etc.

- Machines—What equipment is needed for this issue? New workstations? Scanners? CD writers?

- Money—What aspects of this issue will drive its cost? Are there timing issues? Is there a looming price drop for hardware? Is there a financial benefit to the company?

- Method—Existing processes and new processes

- Measurement—How to gauge the quality improvement, and the completeness of the objectives.
- Environment—In the payroll example, this is primarily the legal and tax environments.

§2.07 RISK MANAGEMENT PLAN

Every project has risks (the sea of uncertainty). There are risks of a critical task running longer than planned, throwing off the timetable for the rest of the project. There is a risk of a funding cut. Risks seem to be everywhere. A project manager's job is to manage these risks rather than let them manage the project. To do this, risks must be identified, documented, and tracked.

What risks should be managed? Begin with the list of assumptions. Remember that an assumption is a guess disguised as a fact. By its very nature, an assumption is at risk of being wrong. A project notebook will have a separate section dedicated to risk management. Rate each assumption as to what phase of the project it involves and what the likelihood is that it is wrong—based on what is known at that point in time.

There should be activities in the scope plans that evaluate potential risks and opportunities. Revisit risk assessments periodically and completely review them at every milestone or monthly. As the work evolves, what was once an assumption may become a fact or a fallacy. This change will alter the project plans.

[A] Assessing Project Definition Risks

Risk assessment is an important part of an executing project. However, at this point, the risk analysis is focused on the project definition. It asks the questions:

- Is the final project goal clear?
- Are there any constraints that guide the scope or definition?
- Are the specifications clear and complete?
- If his project depends on other organizations for its success, have they committed to the project's success?
- Is the sponsor committed to the project?
- Are there secondary project sponsors?
- Is the project's completion due date acceptable?
- Is the budget adequate?
- Are any of the key stakeholders opposed to the project?

- Is critical equipment available?
- Are critical labor resources available?
- Is the technology new to the company?
- Does the sponsor have executive backing?

[B] Mitigating Planning Risks

Once a risk is identified, the next step is to determine the likelihood that the risk will occur. If it does occur, how much damage is inflicted to the project and, finally, how much warning will there be before the risk becomes a danger? The study of risk and its mitigation will be addressed at length in a later chapter. At this point, the issue is how to mitigate, or reduce, the damage, should a risk become a damaging reality. Add these mitigation steps into the project plan as a safety measure.

For example, mitigate the possibility (risk) that the project manager does not understand what the project sponsor is asking by requiring that a specifications acceptance document be signed. To identify and overcome stakeholder objections to the project's specifications, the project manager meets with each of them and obtains their viewpoints on the project's goals and objectives.

Some risks may exist but their likelihood is low or their impact is low. Set these risks aside. Focus on the significant ones. For each significant risk identified during the project definition and scope phase, identify a mitigation action as a countermeasure against it.

§ 2.08 SCOPE DEFINITION—DEVELOPING A WORK BREAKDOWN SCHEDULE

Depending on the project and the company's approach to project management, consider using a work breakdown schedule (WBS) to organize the project. This is an important tool for organizing large projects and may not be required for small ones. A work breakdown schedule uses a hierarchical structure to break down the mission statement into "what" must be done, and not "how" to do it. A work breakdown schedule is not a substitute for a project schedule. Rather it is a way to identify and organize the tasks prior to writing the plan.

A work breakdown schedule organizes the project's mission and objectives into logical groupings. The schedule identifies deliverable-oriented groupings of project components that help to define the scope. Possible groupings are:

- Project phases—A software project can be broken down into its five phases of design, code, test, implement, and close.

- Identify components of deliverables—A turnkey system can be broken down into hardware, software, documentation, training, purchasing, disaster recovery planning, and project follow-up.

- Technical discipline—A project can be broken down into the various technical areas that will support it, such as programming, networking, operations, training, and contracting.

Normally, the top level of the hierarchy is the name of the project. The second level details the deliverable items. Below each deliverable is a breakdown of the functional requirements to deliver it. No attempt is made to sequence any of the actions. The goal is to identify all of the tasks that must be included within the project plan. A WBS also brings to light hidden tasks that may significantly impact the timeline and budget.

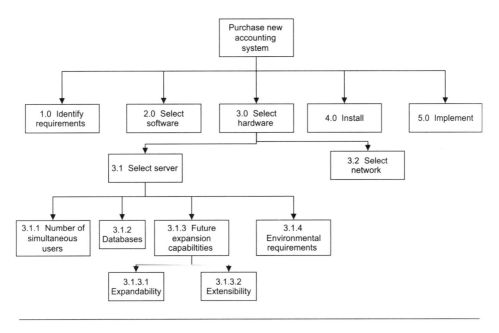

Chart 2-2: WBS Hierarchy

Each of these general groupings is further broken down into ever finer detail until the lowest-level items can be reasonably estimated for resource requirements and duration. These low-level tasks are called "work packages." There is no set number of WBS levels to decompose a mission statement but most experts believe that six levels deep is sufficient. An ideal work package is small enough that the time and cost to create it can be estimated with reasonable certainty.

Assign each item in the work breakdown schedule a unique number for later control and reference. After inserting a task into a work schedule, its number can link it back to its spot in the WBS. Project management software may be able to generate these numbers on request. An advantage to the number approach is the ease of updating a project plan when an objective has been expanded, reduced, or eliminated.

Another example of a WBS is a text version using indentation instead of boxes like an organization chart:

Purchase new accounting system

    1.0   Identify requirements

    2.0   Select software

    3.0   Select hardware

        3.1   Select server

            3.1.1   Determine number of simultaneous users

            3.1.2   Databases

            3.1.3   Future expansion

                3.1.3.1   Expandability

                3.1.3.2   Extensibility

            3.1.4   Environmental requirements

        3.2   Select network

The best way to see how a work breakdown schedule fits with a project is to pull one from a previous company project and use it as a template. The WBS will illustrate local requirements or format expectations.

§ 2.09 SCOPE DEFINITION—DEVELOPING A RESPONSIBILITY MATRIX

Another work breakdown schedule focuses on the people side of the project. On medium to large projects, it is useful to know who to consult for a task and who has final authority to approve something. This is illustrated by a "responsibility matrix." This matrix identifies who should write something, who can approve it, and who is the final approving authority, etc.

Purchase new accounting system

	CEO	Vice President of IT	Sponsor	Project Manager	Applications Support Manager	Network Manager	Help Desk Manager	Vice President of Finance	Accounting Team Representative
Project mission statement	5	3	2	1				3	
Project charter		5	2	1					
Work breakdown schedule			2	1					
Identify accounting's functional requirements					3			5	1
Identify end-user functional requirements					3		3	5	
Identify accounting work flow changes					3			5	1
Establish hardware specifications		5		1	3	3			
Establish software specifications		5		2	1				
Define user documentation requirements			2		3		3	5	1
Define user training requirements			2		3		3	5	1
Define network requirements		5			3	1			
Define computer room specifications		5		1		3			

Writes	1
Approves	2
Must be consulted	3
Must be notified	4
Final approval	5

Chart 2-3: Responsibility Matrix

For example, Chart 2-3 shows that the project manager authors the project mission statement in consultation with the vice-presidents of IT and finance, with a final approval by the CEO.

§ 2.10   PROJECT SCOPE VERIFICATION

Scope verification is part of the ongoing quality assurance for the project. Quality assurance is the process of verifying the quality of a project *before* completing a task. Verifying the work *after* completion is the province of quality control. Project scope validation begins by developing a project mission statement with the sponsor. The validation is a shared vision with the sponsor of what the completed project should look like. As the project progresses, the project plans are compared to the vision to ensure the plan includes the necessary steps to fulfill its mission. As steps are executed, the quality control team verifies that everything completed to that point is contained in the plan.

After validating the mission statement with the project's sponsor, the next step is to review the characteristics to be included in the project's finished product. This is an area where vague ideas are converted into measurable objectives. The scope verification process ensures that there are no major omissions in the plan. Again, confirm that these details are what the sponsor is looking for in the final product.

> For example, a requirement to build data entry screens implies a need to edit the data as entered (close to the source for quickest correction). Scope verification would bring this to the attention of the sponsor since work to accomplish this may extend the project. Or, an accounting system may place a premium value on data integrity. An implied task might be to flag all files downloaded to workstations with a date/time stamp to prevent them from reloading into the main databases.

Scope validation also occurs when the project team meets with the end users to discuss the project details. The outcome of the meeting will probably again result in a meeting with the sponsor to resolve questions and move more items from the assumption list to the task list. This is where the true user details come out; be prepared for them to ask for the moon!

These conversations have the useful result of extracting from all interested parties the expected key features on their minds. Let there be "no unstated expectations." A list of the project's goals and objectives adds flesh to the bones of the mission statement. During these conversations, discuss each of the project assumptions to see if they can be confirmed or converted to project requirements. This reduces uncertainty by reducing the number of assumptions and makes the sponsor more aware of the complexity of the project.

> "Simplicity is the ultimate sophistication."
>
> —Leonardo DaVinci

After assembling the exhaustive "wish list" of project objectives, prioritize the entries. View each item on the list as a cost in time and money. The fewer "wishes" on the list, the simpler the project is and the more likely it is to succeed. Work together with the sponsor and the end user to label each objective: "criticals," "wants," or "nice to have."

Objectives labeled as "nice to have" should be shuttled aside to a list of enhancements to be included in later versions. The more straightforward the project is, the more likely it is to succeed. When moving items off the project plan's scope and onto the system enhancement list, capture the reason why they could be deferred until later.

This discussion will probably arise again and these notes will prove useful. Often a project's sponsor has no idea how easy or difficult a specific feature is to implement. These discussions are an opportunity to educate the sponsor.

Name	Description	Cost		Benefit	Reason Delayed	Date	Requested By
		Time	Materials				

Chart 2-4: Future Enhancements

The final step in scope validation in the planning phase is for the sponsor to provide written approval on the charter document, assumptions list, the WBS, and the list of project objectives.

§ 2.11   SCOPE MANAGEMENT PLAN

Throughout its "life," the project will be pelted with attempts to change its scope to accommodate one issue or another. Many of these change requests are based on sound business principles. The project manager must evaluate each request and then seek approval for those deemed most worthy. Changes to the scope that require additional work must be approved along with the time and funds to support the extra effort. Taking on additional work without additional resources delays a project no matter what the sponsor says to the contrary. As veteran project managers will say, "You can cut the budget, you can crash the schedule, you can add features, but threaten as you might, a project takes as long as it takes."

A project manager maintains a delicate balance between the scope, the budget, and the project completion date. A change made to one of the three unbalances the other two. If the project's budget is decreased and the due date held steady then you must decrease the scope to maintain balance. Increasing the scope means increasing the timeline and/or budget. Like the laws of physics, change one and the other two adjust by themselves.

> To be effective in pushing the project to completion, the project manager must have control over at least two of the three: scope, budget, or completion date.

Scope changes come about for many reasons. Sometimes there is an omission in the project plan when drafted. Now time and financial resources must be added to the

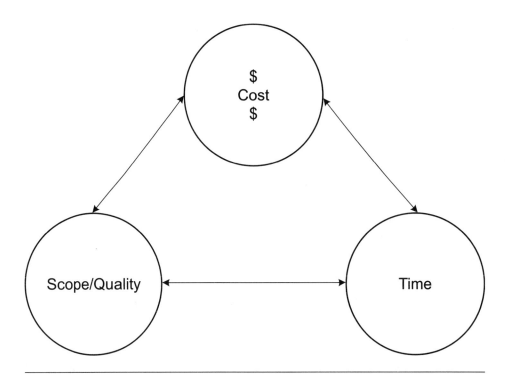

Chart 2-5: Scope—Budget—Timeline

budget and completion date to address this overlooked task. Sometimes an external event causes a change, such as when a business opportunity appears. It could be an opportunity to save work for a later time. Any number of reasons can drive a change request.

Changes to the plan's scope can be intentional or unintentional. An intentional change could be due to a technological breakthrough that causes a goal to be changed, or a feature is dropped from the final product that reduces the scope plan. An unintentional change could be the team looks at the data being loaded to the new system and finds it to be invalid and inconsistent. Another example of an unintentional change is the passing of new legal requirements that the final product must accommodate.

The project team works side by side with the end users to build the product. Sooner or later, as a favor to a friend, a programmer adds "something" to the project. The project manager must prevent side agreements between programmers and users that are outside the scope of the project. Every additional function slipped into the plan adds further maintenance and may disrupt planned work farther along in the schedule. Unofficial scope change will become a deluge if the first instance is not firmly squashed.

These changes test the mettle of the project manager. Unauthorized changes are never benign unless they reduce cost and shorten time estimates. Here are a few more examples of unauthorized changes that the project manager must look for. They can come at any time and from any direction:

- The customer asks for a change and believes it is not really a change. For example, the customer wants the security level to be elevated from minimum to medium.
- The customer asks for a monthly status report on the security server or requests a "small" functional change.
- The team wants to be helpful to the customer and do a little extra, like creating a customized interface to the firewall so the accounting manager can do "something" around the firewall.

Frequently the phrase "scope creep" is used to express a problem of project management. Creep implies a very slow movement. Actually, the term might be better phrased as "scope earthquake." When the scope plan is undermined with unauthorized changes, its carefully crafted list of assumptions, risks, and performance measures have all been shattered.

[A] Changing the Scope

> "No plan survives the first contact with the enemy."
>
> —Helmuth von Moltke the Elder, Chief of Staff, Prussian Army

A project cannot resist changes to its scope for very long. Some changes have very compelling reasons. The key is to manage these changes so that the necessary resources are approved at the same time that the scope is expanded. Without a well-defined scope plan and its supporting documents, such as the business justification, there is not an objective baseline for negotiations on customer expectations, valid cost and time estimates, and workable schedule and budget.

Establish a scope management plan early in the project definition process since it provides a conduit for requests to change the project scope. It involves:

- a simple tracking system to ensure that requests are promptly reviewed and granted or rejected, but never held in limbo,
- a form to collect all of the pertinent information for the request, and
- a simple approval process to accept or reject a request based on its merits.

The scope change process is straightforward:

1. The requestor fills in the scope change request form and forwards it to the project manager. The form explains what changes are proposed to the scope and why they are a good idea.

2. The project manager assigns a request number and logs the request into the scope change request log.

3. The project manager reviews the form to estimate its cost and time impact on the project.

4. The form, along with the estimates, is forwarded to the project steering committee for discussion at the next meeting.

5. The committee votes to accept or reject the change. This places the decision of scope (and the time and money) squarely where it belongs—with the executives. It also removes the project manager from the hot seat.

6. The project manager updates the log with the committee's decision.

7. The project manager informs the requestor as to the committee's decision.

8. The project manager files the request, along with any notes made during the discussion of its merits. The issue may come up again and the notes will be useful.

The form shown in Exhibit 2-2 captures the essential information necessary to evaluate a suggested scope modification.

At the top is some information as to what this involves (project name), who is asking for the change, and when they asked for it.

The second section is a description of what is requested. The description should succinctly indicate what is wanted and why.

The middle section is an analysis of the request's impact on the project according to the project manager. Costs and schedule impact is separately examined and a projected impact on the completion date is provided. (This is where the project management software really saves time by quickly calculating the time added to the schedule based on the additional tasks.)

The bottom section is for approvals. As stated before, the project manager is the gatekeeper to the project and minimizes changes to the project. By signing the document approving the change, the project sponsor agrees to provide the additional resources and adds time to the end of the plan.

The scope change tracking log (see Chart 2-6) tracks scope change requests to ensure prompt handling and resolution. To demonstrate the prompt handling of requests, key dates are recorded as to when the request was received, analyzed by the project manager and passed to the committee for a decision.

Exhibit 2-2: Scope Change Request

Project: _____
Requested by: _____
Date: _____

Requested change:

Cost Impact:

Engineering	
Programming	
Materials	
Indirect Cost	_____
Total Cost:	_____

Schedule Impact:

Tasks Affected:

| Old Completion Date | _____ |
| New Completion Date | _____ |

New Project Completion Date: _____

Request Number: _____

Approval:

_____   _____
(Date)   (Project Manager)

Cost to Implement: _____
Delay in Project Completion: _____

Approval:

_____   _____
(Date)   (Project Sponsor)

Request number: Create a simple numbering system to track the request. If more than one project is being tracked at a time, use a prefix to identify each project.

Task change title: Assign a descriptive name as to what this change is about for clarity.

Submitted by: Provide the name of a specific person for whom to contact with further questions.

Received: This is the date the project manager received the request. Promptly addressing requests helps to set a project tempo of action.

Analysis complete: This is the date the project manager's analysis of the change's impact was complete.

To committee: This is the date the request was submitted to the project steering committee for approval.

Disposition: This is the decision by the committee whether to add the requested change to the scope, to decline the request, or to reconsider it at a future time.

Comments: These are any comments as to why the request was declined or delayed for another time.

What can be done to limit the number of scope change requests? Cut them off at the pass!

An experienced project manager can proactively address this by:

- Asking all stakeholders to sign off on the scope plan and definitions at the kickoff meeting.

- Reviewing the scope change process whenever meeting with stakeholders in order to keep it in the front of their minds

- Discussing the status of the scope plan at each weekly review

- Ensuring that all requested technical changes do not change the scope plan intentionally or unintentionally

- Ensuring that the quality assurance team looks for scope omissions during its audits of the project plans

§ 2.12   PROJECT STEERING COMMITTEE

The chair of a project manager is definitely a hot seat. Many people suggest, demand, plead, threaten, and do practically anything to have their pet idea included in a project. Accommodating all of these requests would throw the project into chaos. Not all ideas are good ones. Not all pet projects are bad ideas. Since everyone cannot be pleased, long-term animosity can build against the project manager. Project managers must "tread lightly" to avoid alienating key company managers. To provide some political cover, most projects use a steering committee.

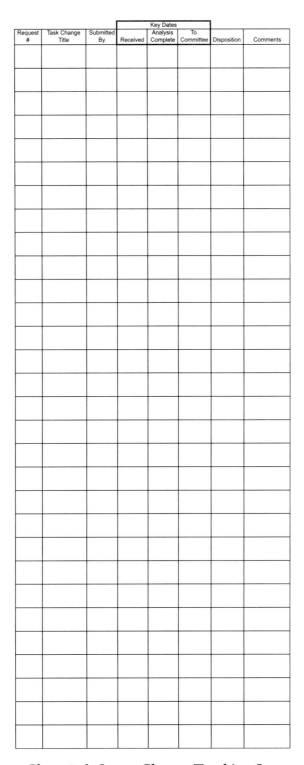

Request #	Task Change Title	Submitted By	Key Dates			Disposition	Comments
			Received	Analysis Complete	To Committee		

Chart 2-6: Scope Change Tracking Log

When a project steering committee is used, they assume the responsibility of being the gatekeeper of the project's scope from the project manager. The committee provides oversight and general direction to the project to keep it aligned with the company's goals.

A project steering committee should include high-level executives to reduce the potential of political bullying intruding on the scope of the project. A typical committee might include:

- Project manager
- Customer
- Accounting budget representative
- Sponsor
- Other interested executives

The committee would meet at least twice per month to review change requests and ensure the project is tracking with changes in the business environment. The project manager keeps minutes on the meeting and issues a report of the decisions made. This provides a record of the events around the approval or denial of scope changes.

§ 2.13 SUMMARY

A project's definition is an explanation of what it is trying to accomplish. It might be to construct a building, replace an accounting system, or audit a company for legal compliance. A clear definition allows for accurate timelines and budget estimates. A vague definition introduces more unknowns into the project estimates. These unknown factors waste resources and time.

A project's definition has many components. The limits of a project are known as its scope. Scope identifies what is included and excluded from the project. The project manager must clearly identify these boundaries and then protect them against changes.

To ensure that the project's definition is correct and includes all essential goals and objectives, the project manager conducts a risk assessment. The result of this assessment is a series of mitigation actions that increase the likelihood of a complete and accurate project definition.

To break down the project mission statement into its component parts, several different tools can be used. The "fishbone" diagram identifies the various factors that the project must consider. An alternative is the work breakdown structure (WBS) which organizes the project's mission and objectives.

All projects are changed at some point during their execution. Business environments change, company priorities change, and budget cycles ebb and flow. To manage changes to the project definition, the project manager establishes a scope management plan to ensure that only approved changes are in the project plan and in tasks executed by the team. Unauthorized changes are never permitted.

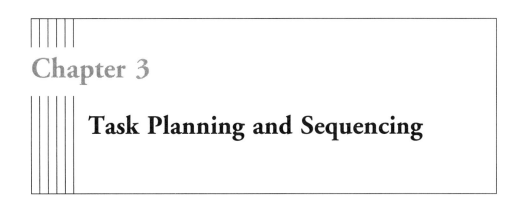

Chapter 3

Task Planning and Sequencing

§ 3.01   INTRODUCTION

Once the project's definition is clear and approved, the next task is to identify the steps required to create a project plan. A sheet of paper and some simple figuring may be adequate for a small project. Complex projects are another matter. The task planning and sequencing phase breaks down the project into smaller pieces to see what it takes to accomplish the assigned mission.

New projects face a risk that the amount of effort or cost may be more than the sponsor/customer is willing to pay. Looking at a project as a whole, it is difficult to do more than guess what it may cost in time or materials to complete it. Until this analysis is completed, the project's cost and time required are a vague estimate with no clear idea of what is required to complete it.

Projects are better understood by breaking them progressively into smaller pieces until they are a series of "work packets." A work packet is small enough to estimate the labor and materials necessary to complete it. This collection of work packets is known as a work breakdown schedule (WBS). The total time and cost estimates for this collection of packets form the project's initial budget.

A WBS groups and sequences packets to make better sense of the project but in itself is not an executable plan. Creating a plan is left for later. The WBS considers resource requirements when creating work packets but detailed estimates are left for later in the plan development.

§ 3.02   CREATING A WORK BREAKDOWN STRUCTURE

People have a limited capacity to comprehend. If more than nine items must be learned, monitored, or coordinated at a time, then people become overwhelmed. To assemble a project plan from a project definition, create a work breakdown schedule. If it is too large to effectively break down, then segment it into subprojects that each have their own WBS.

A WBS is also a tool to verify the scope of a project. If upon examination, the project's hidden but required tasks are too expensive, the project may be cancelled. Many would consider it better to be cancelled than to struggle underfunded for months simply to fail in the long run. The project manager and a team of technical and business experts create a WBS. In addition to being thorough, they look for the hidden pitfalls so they can be addressed early.

Companies bidding for contracts use the WBS technique to break down a project definition into a statement of work (SOW). This ensures that the bidders do not agree to charge for a simple job, but have hidden tasks that require considerably more effort. An SOW is essentially the same as a WBS.

> Hidden tasks can be anything. Imagine a software development project. The goal is to build an interface into the company's database to receive orders directly from the Internet. Money is tight and this project is essential for the company to survive. Unknown to the project manager, the Web software purchased for building the interface requires an upgrade to the operating system. This change causes the old database software to stop working. It requires a multiple-version upgrade. In both cases, the

upgrading expense and the special expertise required to install the new operating system were not foreseen. These added tasks will likely increase the project's duration.

[A] WBS Basics

Task planning is the creation of a "road map" of actions necessary to fulfill the project definition. It is the first step is translating words into deeds. It establishes the base for the project manager to estimate the duration of the project, determine the required resources, and schedule the work. The work breakdown structure is a hierarchical description of all the work that must be done to meet the needs of the customer. Key points to consider in WBS development are:

- An *event* is a point in time, such as the start or end of a task.
- A *task* is a work unit meaningful for tracking a set of activities. Writing a module that handles a specific function is a task.
- *Task sequencing* determines the logical order of activities used in developing a realistic and achievable schedule.

Two important concepts come into play at this point:

- *Decomposition* is the action of breaking broad statements into their individual actions. A project definition is "decomposed" into smaller units until its financial, time, labor, and other resource requirements can be reasonably estimated. If you make the tasks too small, it is micromanaging. Make tasks too large, and the estimates will be too unreliable. Resources are assigned in the schedule development phase of the plan.
- *Sequencing* is the action of placing these tasks in the proper order. An operating system cannot be installed on a new server until it has been ordered, received, unpacked, and set into place. Sequence activities logically and note the ones that may proceed in parallel. Often this reveals possible missing activities from the WBS.

Task planning assumes that a company's dynamic business environment is static. This assumption allows planning to proceed. The project actually exists in an environment that is constantly changing politically, economically, technologically, and socially. Without assuming a steady environment, it would be too difficult to make estimates that factor in all of the many elements that pull a business this way and that. Therefore, project plans are based on an optimistic assumption known to be false from the beginning.

[B]   Work Packets

A WBS work packet is a task small enough to estimate the amount of labor and materials required to complete it. It may be impossible to estimate the time and cost of installing a facility-wide wireless network, but it is possible to estimate the time and cost to install a single wireless access point in a specific location.

There is no set rule for how small or large a work packet can be. Typically, a work packet is between 4 and 40 hours of labor. This is a manageable level of effort without micromanaging the process. Work packets of less than four hours result in efforts that are more like task checklists than project plans.

A WBS should not have more than 250 work packets. At that point, the project is too large to manage effectively. It should be broken into subprojects, each possibly with its own project manager.

A packet must conclude with some sort of deliverable to the project manager. It is much easier to manage to a deliverable than a percentage of task completion. An important part of the packet description is to describe what this deliverable should look like and how it will perform.

[C]   Documenting an Identified Task

A considerable amount of time will elapse between WBS creation and when someone begins work on one of the activities. Once the WBS identifies a task, the information about it must be captured as the team discusses it. To avoid re-analyzing each task, write down the main points while it is still fresh in the team's minds.

The project manager should consider using a packet documentation form like the one shown in Exhibit 3-1: Task Identification Checklist.

A work packet should contain:

- Task description—an explanation of what this task involves and what might be required to complete it.

- Task deliverables—a description of the final deliverables of the task. If the deliverable from this module was described in the project definition, then they are attached.

Exhibit 3-1: Task Identification Checklist

Project Name:	
Task Name:	WBS Number:
Task Description:	Reference Document:
Deliverable:	

Estimate: Critical: _____　　Optional: _____
　　　　　　Optimistic: _____　Pessimistic: _____
　　　　　　Standard: _____　　Realistic: _____

Item	Reference Document
1. Task measurable goals and deliverables	
2. Task assumptions and constraints	
3. Criteria for resource requirements	
4. Critical tasks and their critical activities	
5. Skills criteria	
6. Contingency criteria and requirements	
7. Funding requirements	
8. Communications requirements	
9. Procurement policy and procedural requirements	
10. Quality control and verification requirements	
11. Training requirements	
12. Documentation requirements	
13. Risk management concerns	
14. Miscellaneous comments	

Assumptions:
-
-
-

Risks:
-
-
-

- Assumptions—any assumptions unique to this task. Do not include assumptions common to large parts of the project.

- Specific risks—any risk unique to this task. Do not include risks common to large parts of the project.

- Required resources—an estimate of the materials, equipment, and skills required to complete this task. Do not include any standard items, such as workstations or standard software. An example would be if this module used a technology new to the team and training was required.

[D] WBS Verification

When a WBS is first drafted, things may be overlooked. In the rush to get something on paper, the focus is on the straight path to project completion and not on all of the other activities essential for a successful project. Once the WBS is completed, it should be reviewed in its entirety with the team. If possible, include several other project managers. The goal is to identify gaps, unstated assumptions, and anything else that might be missing from the WBS.

> A time saver is to begin the WBS analysis with a WBS from a previous, but somewhat similar project. Even though every project is unique, portions may be similar, such as the testing steps, installation of a new firewall, or orientation of new team members.

[E] Form a Team

With a project manager assigned and a clear vision of the project's objective, begin charting a course for the project's completion. Based on an evaluation of the project goals, determine the technical expertise necessary to complete the project successfully and invite representatives from affected areas to a project planning meeting. Included with the invitation should be a copy of the project's approved goals and scope. The people invited may be the ones who will work on the project or they may be subject experts who will help to define the skill set needed for the project. A representative of the people who will be using the end product should always be invited.

If the WBS development technique is new to any of the team members, schedule a "premeeting" to explain how it works. Run a few exercises with team members to illustrate the process. Otherwise, they will hold back the rest of the team during the analysis process.

The planning meeting follows a simple format:

- Review the approved project definition.
- Review the selected WBS technique.
- Provide copies of previous similar WBSs.
- Assign someone to record WBS activities identified by the team.
- Assign someone to record the final WBS.

> Invite someone from the information security team to assist with the WBS development. Data that may seem innocent to the team may have security implications. Involving an information security technician provides them with project background in case security issues arise.
>
> Likewise, someone from the business continuity team should review the system design to determine if it changes the support requirements for a critical system or is itself a new critical system.

§ 3.03   WBS TECHNIQUES

Now is the time to start building a WBS! It is a long journey from a blank piece of paper to a well-considered project plan. The first step is to build a framework for action and to fill in as many activities as possible. Once the initial WBS is on paper, the remaining details can be identified.

There are many ways to do this. Consider the following basic approaches to drafting an initial project plan.

[A]   Brainstorming

This is useful when the project flow is not immediately obvious, when major parallel efforts obscure a clear vision of the plan, or when the project is something the company has never done before.

One effective brainstorming method is to use stick-on notes and a large whiteboard. Each stick-on note is equal to a task on the project plan. Anyone can call out an action necessary to the plan, such as "build the data entry screen," "identify field edits," or "coordinate with the database administrators." The tasks do not need to be in any particular order. One person is assigned to capture the ideas and attach them to the whiteboard as they are called out. A second person moderates the discussion and keeps it focused. All ideas are posted and none are criticized.

When the team runs out of ideas, it is time to select category names by which to group the tasks. The team reviews each task and assigns it to a group. Duplicate or overlapping tasks are consolidated or clarified.

Consider a five-block diagram where each block represents a phase of the project: "Design, Analyze, Code, Test, and Implement." Under each block list the actions required to achieve these project goals. Always maintain a focus on the project's deliverables. Refer to Chart 3-1 "WBS by Phase."

Finally, the tasks and groups are organized into a logical process flow from the beginning of the project to the end. The flow infers which processes are predecessors to which tasks and represents the initial project plan. Write down all of this information and/or enter it into project management software.

Examine each of the phases for completeness of the task list and to root out duplicates. Often duplicates are discovered while documenting each of the activities.

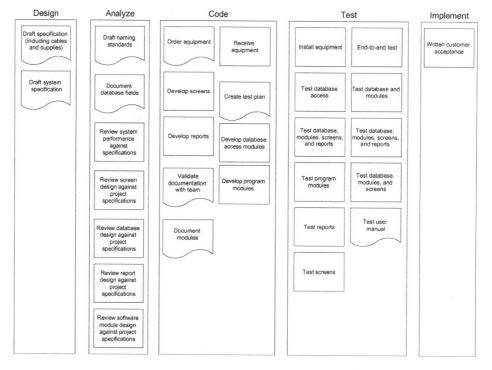

Chart 3-1: WBS by Phase

[B]   Left-to-Right Block Diagram

If the project is for something the team is familiar with, a list of tasks from start to finish can be made. Left to right means that the tasks will be identified in the approximate order in which they will appear on the plan.

This approach is focused on the project deliverables. Identify each deliverable for the project. Break down each deliverable into the activities necessary to complete it from beginning to end.

After all of the activities have been identified, review the WBS in its entirety. Look for duplicate or missing tasks. Add a lane for the project manager's tasks, milestone reviews, quality reviews, etc.

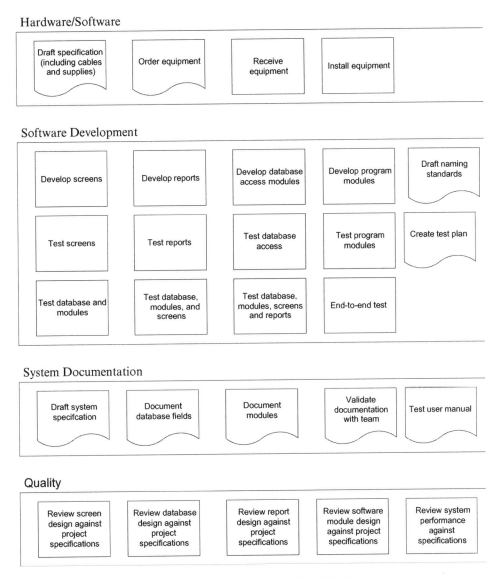

Chart 3-2: Left-to-Right WBS

[C]   Top-Down WBS

This approach starts with the project definition and then breaks it down repeatedly until the lowest level tasks are identified. This approach is useful when the project's objective is new to the team and is similar to peeling an onion, since the project is broken down one layer at a time.

> "Layers! Onions have layers! Ogres have layers! Onions have layers. You get it? We both have layers."
>
> "Oh, you both have layers. Oh. You know, not everybody likes onions. Cake! Everybody loves cake! Cakes have layers."
>
> "I don't care . . . what everyone likes. Ogres are not like cakes."
>
> —Shrek and Donkey, in Dreamworks' *Shrek*

Break down the project definition into its major areas. This may correspond to IT work teams such as database, network, etc. Then break down the project definition into what each of these areas must do to complete the project.

§ 3.04   NUMBERING FOR FUTURE IDENTIFICATION

With so many work packets, names are bound to overlap. A packet named "quality control assessment" might occur several times, each within a different phase of the project. To avoid confusion, a WBS uses a hierarchical numbering system to uniquely identify each packet. Refer to Chart 3-3: Top-Down WBS. Each of the activities is numbered.

Beginning with the first level, the number is "1.0." This is broken down into three lower-level activities called "Hardware," "Documentation," and "Software." Their numbers reflect being one level lower (1.1, 1.2, and 1.3, respectively). As the WBS further breaks down tasks one level at a time, each level is indicated by a period and that task's sequence within that level.

For example:

1.0
   1.1
      1.1.1

WBS numbers remain with a task throughout the project. Even if the task is moved to another part of the structure at a later date, the number originally assigned to it follows the task.

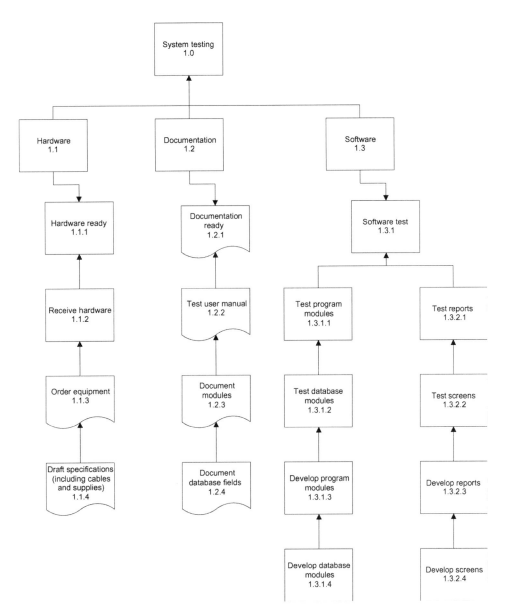

Chart 3-3: Top-Down WBS

[A] Put the Team to Work!

When developing work breakdown structures, take the time to solicit expert advice from the team. They may have additional insights into the resources required to achieve a task, and how much time a task should require. The team is assembled so that their expertise can be applied to developing a more realistic project plan. The best time to adjust a plan is in its development stage prior to its presentation to the sponsor for approval.

Another valuable team activity is to step through the sequenced activities one at a time and validate that they are all present. The group will have a broad background in other projects and in their own area of expertise. This discussion and plan review provides the psychological bond between the team members and the plan, which begins to make it "their" plan. This connection is important later when questions arise about the estimates and sequencing.

[B]   Scope Verification

A work breakdown schedule is useful for verifying the project's scope. Anything not contained in the WBS is out of scope. By breaking down the deliverables and determining what is needed, it reveals what is not needed.

Once the team finalizes the WBS, review it with the project's sponsor. Usually they consider this a bit of the "techie stuff" that project managers do and likely will not follow its detail. The important part of this meeting is to confirm with the sponsor any additions to the project scope. This is usually caused by hidden tasks. These tasks may increase the project's duration and cost.

At that meeting, also review any changes to the project's assumptions. Likely, the WBS development process raised many assumptions to validate. Each assumption has a corresponding risk that the assumption may be false.

[C]   WBS Quality Check

Before publishing the WBS to the project team, verify that everything has been accounted for.

- Is each task clearly and completely defined? This could cause a considerable amount of problems later. Without a clear and complete definition a task cannot be reasonably estimated for labor, skill required, or cost. Over time, people forget what was said or what was meant. Time spent now, clearly documenting each task, saves a lot of confusion later.

- Are packets within the range of acceptable size—not too small and not too large?

- Are all deliverables accounted for? Use a notation to indicate each one in the WBS so their supporting tasks can be reviewed in light of this objective.

- Have packets been included for testing components as they are completed?

- Are packets included at each milestone for the project manager to review the project with the sponsor and peers?

- Are milestone packets set up for updating the risk assessment?

- Is user training included in the WBS? If team training is required for this project, ensure tasks are included in the appropriate phases.

- Are work packets for documentation included where appropriate? System documentation, end-user documentation, and help desk "tip" sheets should all be included in the WBS.

§ 3.05   SUMMARY

A work breakdown schedule is a powerful tool for reducing a large project definition into "bite-size" work packets. A WBS is normally developed together with the resource plan and the project timeline.

A work packet is typically between 4 and 40 hours of labor. It must be just small enough to allow for reasonable time and cost estimates. Further detail is left to the person executing that task. A work packet should conclude with a project deliverable. It might be a piece of code, a report, or something whose existence indicates that the task is complete.

Project managers can select from different WBS techniques. Most select the approach most familiar to them or their team. Whatever approach is followed, the resulting work packets are numbered hierarchically to identify the packet even if it is moved.

A thorough WBS acts as a scope verification for the project definition. If uncovered activities materially alter the project budget, then the sponsor must be informed. In some cases, the project may then be scrapped.

When the WBS is complete, a quality check must be completed to ensure that all of the essential information was captured. Work packet size and descriptions are checked and all required deliverables are accountable in the activities.

Chapter 4

Resource Planning

§ 4.01　INTRODUCTION

A resource is anything that supports a project. It could be technical skills, equipment, materials, time, or money. A project manager is a resource, as is a workstation or even an office. The quality and quantity of resources available to a project team have a direct bearing on productivity. A project manager is responsible for ensuring the team has adequate resources for completing the project on time and within budget. If a project management office is available, then they can assume much of the resource scheduling responsibilities.

> Companies expect project managers to be good stewards of the resources entrusted to their use. Resource planning maps the resources required to their use during the project. The plan includes the resources' final disposition once the project is completed, as it has a direct bearing on what is purchased.

The degree of resource planning required by a project depends on:

- Its size and complexity,
- Expected duration, and
- If it is internal to an organization or run by an external organization.

Develop the resource plan in concert with the work breakdown schedule. Many resource questions will be the same as the ones developed for the task plan. Both are baseline project documents. The guiding rule is that the activity or task needs to be defined before its resources.

> Whenever working with issues involving people, always consult with the organization's personnel department. They have policies on approximately anything dealing with people, and it is better to deal with the personnel clerks at leisure instead of during a crisis.

§ 4.02   BUILD A PLAN

Resource problems are hottest at the beginning of a project. Office space, work-stations, supplies, and a wide range of things must be ready before the project team appears. Often these resources need a lead-time in which to prepare that the project schedule does not have.

Project managers, as a group, are optimists, often underestimating the resources needed to complete a project. They look at the project plan, focus on the goal and, at times, lose sight of the many little details necessary for a successful project. This goal-focused vision is a good thing, but in the beginning of the project, what is needed is a focus on the resources.

[A]   Creating a Resource Plan Checklist

Exhibit 4-1: Resource Plan Checklist is a "parent" form for resource management. The project manager establishes the assumptions and constraints for resource esti-mates. Resource estimates affect both cost and time estimates. A cost estimate may become invalid because of resource padding. A time estimate may become invalid because the resource's duration was estimated as too little or too much. The keys to the form are two necessary actions:

- There must be three estimates for each resource: pessimistic, realistic, and optimistic.
- Define each resource as critical, optional, or standard.

One of the most common mistakes in project management is only to have one estimate, whether it is cost, time, or resource. Each estimate must have a range, with the criteria for the range defined by the project before any resource definition. For example, in the program evaluation and review technique (PERT), a criterion is that an event will or will not happen once in 20 times.

> Minimize padding by using three estimates. Convert padding to a known contingency. An obvious example of padding is the situation where a manager states that a task needs four people rather than the realistic two. An optimistic scenario might be one person, while a pessimistic might be four. Each scenario needs its own cost and time estimates.

Exhibit 4-1: Resource Plan Checklist

Organization:		Date:	

Resource type:	

Estimate type: Critical ❑   Pessimistic ❑
                   Optional ❑   Realistic ❑
                   Standard ❑   Optimistic ❑

Resource description:

    Hardware ❑   Software ❑   Skill ❑   Support ❑

    Consultant ❑   Available ❑   Not Available ❑

Source:

Measurable objectives:

Training required: ❑   If checked, describe:

Documentation required: ❑   If checked, describe:

Time estimates with measurable criteria:

Cost estimates with measurable criteria:

Dependencies:

Events:

Hardware:

Software:

Skills:

Support:

Consultant:

Training:

Learning curve:

Exhibit 4-1: *(Continued)*

Documentation:
Timing:
Standards:
Benchmarks:
Performance level:
Contingency:
Quality control:
Effectiveness:
Efficiency:
Variances:
Risk analysis:
Special issues:

Instructions for Resource Plan Checklist

General Instructions

- Cost and time estimates for resources should include the following five situations:
    1. Resource descriptions
    2. Links

Exhibit 4-1: *(Continued)*

    3. Impacts

    4. Usage criteria

    5. Change requirements

- You should identify not only resources for operational and administrative activities but also their utilization and availability constraints and assumptions.

- You should identify any resource based on required skill level rather than by a headcount. You need three skill resource definitions for pessimistic, realistic, and optimistic.

- When not included specifically in the checklist, you need to consider the how, why, when, where, who, and what of any response.

- You should give measurable criteria for critical resources.

- You should state measurable criteria for estimating resources.

- You need to list measurable criteria for strategic, tactical, and operational resources.

- You need to state measurable criteria for any training or documentation requirements for the use of resources.

- You should list the measurable criteria for any potential risk that may impact resource acquisition.

- You should give potential impacts of the availability of resources on the project's success.

- When required, you need to note Quality Control requirements.

- When there is no applicability to a given answer on the checklist, state "There is no applicability."

- You should relate resources to cost, time, and activity estimates.

- You should relate the project scope definitions to resource estimates.

- You should show any critical resource relationships.

- You should show any critical effects of the cost parameters on resource estimates.

- You should give the impacts of departmental milestones on the resource estimates.

- You should give a control system to manage resources and any changes.

- You should identify when possible procurement policies need to be followed.

- You should not use an available resource to define activities unless it is critical to project goals.

Resource Identification Process

Before filling out the checklist, you should take the following steps:

1. Make a list, as specific as possible, of required resources.

2. Identify mandatory resources.

3. Identify resources as belonging to a pessimistic, an optimistic, or a realistic scenario.

4. Identify resources that belong to a contingency plan (based on a pessimistic scenario).

5. Group resources by project phase—planning, designing, developing, testing, or implementing.

Exhibit 4-1: *(Continued)*

6. Order the resources by priority—you need to define what you mean by priority.

7. Group resources by users—can be by administrative unit or individual.

8. Group resources by impact—this means as mandatory or optional such as the resource has to be available before X activity or task.

9. Group resources by availability—full-time, part-time, have to buy, have to rent, and so forth.

10. List resources by training requirements.

WARNING

All criteria (standards, benchmarks, and goals) and skills should be measurable. You would not have a resource skill definition such as, "An XML programmer is required." What are the measurable deliverables from the programmer to achieve a specific project goal?

Specific Instructions

- Each resource requires three forms for each of these scenarios: pessimistic, realistic, and optimistic.

- Internal source includes responsible estimator, title, phone number, organization unit, e-mail address, and any other special personal identifiers.

- External source should include all internal source data plus company address, and the name of the responsible company representative for the project.

- Date should be in the form of mm/dd/yyyy.

- Estimate type should include explanation of critical or optional in the last section of the form, "special issues."

- Resource description should be included as an attachment with the form. A description should be written in the context of the key definitions given in the chapter. For example, a resource description for a piece of hardware would include company name (part number), general use name, when required in the project, who is to use it, when and where it is to be used, what project goal it is for, present availability, procurement requirements, a permanent acquisition or a temporary lease, duration of use, and skill-level requirements for use.

- Objectives should include the associated project goal. When appropriate, you should give related procedural standards and performance benchmarks, which justify the requirement of the resource.

- The training description should include availability, why required, what the training is to achieve, when and duration of the training, and where the training is to be given. The names of the students should also be given as an attachment.

- The documentation description must include availability, why required, what the documentation is to achieve, when it is to be used, and who needs the documentation.

- Time estimates are one of the three major reasons for project failure. The description used is measurable and precise. Any estimate should take into consideration all these instructions.

- Cost estimates have the same impacts as time estimates.

Exhibit 4-1: *(Continued)*

- A dependency is a must requirement before a given project event (task) can be started or completed. For example, a person must acquire a certain level of knowledge before beginning the task (learning curve and training).

- The standard description should include name, organizational source, date, version number, where it can be located (may be a URL), pertinent paragraph numbers, and relevant Quality Control considerations.

- The benchmark description should be similar to the standard description.

- The performance description should be measurable and should include the source for the performance level.

- Contingency is not padding. A contingency is a factor based on pessimistic or optimistic measurable criteria.

- Quality Control descriptions should include information that can be integrated into a Quality Control program.

- The risk analysis description should be based on the estimate type of the form: pessimistic, realistic, or optimistic.

- The special issue should include any special considerations to clarify any prior descriptions on the form.

With a set of forms that fulfill the second requirement, sorting can be done quickly to identify resources that have to be used in defining a critical path. A critical path is a document that gives the required activities (the critical resource list is a constraint) and the least amount of time (duration) to achieve a project goal.

The availability of resources flagged as critical is known. A checkmark indicating the unavailability of a resource is a flag for a potential risk. By knowing this in advance, plans can be developed to eliminate this bump in the road.

Because there is a trend to use software to handle resource management, this form should give the data type information required to do the necessary input. When a management application is used, at a minimum, the following information is needed to ensure an adequate resource database:

- Identify calendar data
- Identify cost (when and specific amount) of resources
- Identify criticality of each resource
- Identify links between resources
- Identify links to tasks and people
- Identify locations of resources
- Identify physical amounts of each resource

- Identify resource scenarios: pessimistic, realistic, and optimistic
- Identify types of resources (hardware, software, skills, or materials)
- Identify usage of each resource

Exhibit 4-1: Resource Plan Checklist points directly and indirectly to all these requirements.

§ 4.03 VISUALIZE WHAT IS NEEDED

A tool for identifying resource requirements is the versatile fishbone chart. It is a handy visualization of everything required. Do not feel that a fishbone must fit on a standard size sheet of paper. The model can be as big as needed. In some cases, break each of the individual fish "ribs" into its own chart.

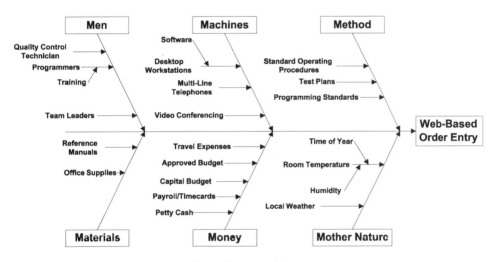

Chart 4-1: Fishbone

Often one resource (such as people) brings to mind the requirement for other things (such as office space, workstations, etc.) A fishbone diagram is useful for digging out the many resources needed for the project. Review the WBS and note the resources needed on the fishbone chart. A resource plan should have at least six sections:

- People—the most important project resource. List them by their technical skills. If using internal resources, include names on the slots.
- Equipment—the tools used by the skilled workers to create something. Slow and unreliable equipment wastes time.

- Material—all of the other things necessary to keep a project running. Most of this is never thought of until something is missing. This includes office supplies, blank forms, extra cables, etc. Don't let small things become big time wasters!

- Processes—standardized actions improve team mobility and provide a more consistent end product.

- Working environment—is an important productivity factor. Just because the boss' office is comfortable does not mean the workers are likewise satisfied.

- Cash—is included in the budget, but is mentioned here as an important resource to keep the project moving forward and to address emergencies.

[A]   Expand the Fishbone into a Checklist

The next step is to convert the fishbone information into an action plan. The fishbone brought out a list of what was needed. The resource plan adds detail to the needs.
    Using the same categories as the fishbone, the plan details:

- What is needed
- The WBS tasks it supports. This provides a lot of the detailed specifications and justification.
- If it is obtained internally to the company or externally through a supplier
- Source of the resource
- Any additional equipment use that particular resource implies
- What to do with the resource when the project no longer needs it

---

Why projects lack resources:

- Sometimes project managers underestimate resource requirements to obtain project approval. Although this may make the boss happy for a moment, it could lead to months of agony for the team.

- Some projects execute in great uncertainty. Important resource requirements may not be apparent until later in the project.

- Over the years, executives have browbeaten project managers about their time and cost estimates. Project managers are punished if they exceed their estimates, so they are padded with contingency time and costs. Then the same complaining executives cut the budget and timeline while keeping the scope the same. Each level of management approval cuts the project budget deeper. By the time the project

---

> budget is signed, it is trimmed far too close. This is the time for the project manager to act firmly to get the needed resources back into the budget. If getting more money looks hard now, it will be much harder later in the project.

Obtaining resources (and even more later) requires a bit of political finesse. Among their many skills, project managers need to establish and maintain good relations with all sources of project resources. Crises occur in their own good time and a "friend" who can loan something to a project in a pinch is a true friend. Establish these good relations as soon as possible. This cannot be done in an emergency.

> The skill level of the team members determines the resources required. A technical expert can get by with minimal tools. They just know how to do the job with less. However, a novice needs all of the help he or she can get and may seem immobile without the latest technology.

Resource Planning Chart					
Project: _____ Prepared by: _____			Date Prepared/Revised: _____		
Resource	**WBS Tasks**	**Internal/ External**	**Source**	**Equipment Required**	**Disposition at End of Project**
People					
Project Auditor	5 & 8	I	PMO	None	Return to Department
Java Programmers	1.3.1.3	E	Shady Joe's Software Shack	Workstation	Hire
Security Analyst	1.3.1	I	Information Security		Return to Department
Disaster Recovery Analyst	1.3.1	I	Business Continuity Team		Return to Department
Network Support	1.1.4	E	Shady Joe's Software Shack		Release
Quality Control Technician	1.3.1.3	E	Shady Joe's Software Shack		Hire
DBA - Oracle	1.3.1.4, 1.3.1.2	I	Database Administration Manager		Return to Department
DBA - SQL	1.3.1.4, 1.3.1.2	I	Database Administration Manager		Return to Department
Equipment					
High Speed Laser Printer	1.1.4	I	Desktop Support	Network cable	Pass on to Customer
Workstation - Desktop	1.1.4	I	Desktop Support	Electrical and Network Connections	Pass on to Customer
Workstation - Notebook	1.1.4	E	Shady Joe's Software Shack	2 GHz CPU/ 80 GB Disk	Release
Material					
Office Supplies		I	Facilties Manager		
Blank CDs		I	Facilties Manager		
Processes					
Programming Standards	1.2	I	Applications Manager	Binder	Pass to IT Manager
Status Reporting Standards		I	PMO Manager	Binder	Return to PMO
Expense Reports		I	Controller	Blank Template	Return to PMO
Standard Equipment List	1.1.4	I	Desktop Support	List	Return to PMO
Programming Quality Standards	1.2	I	Applications Manager	Binder	Pass to IT Manager
Working Environment					
Shared Printers	1.1.4	I	Desktop Support	Printer	Return to Desktop
Network Ports	1.1.4	I	Desktop Support		Return to Desktop
Cubicles		I	Facilties Manager	1 per Programmer	Release
Offices		I	Facilties Manager		Release
Conference Room		I	Facilties Manager		Release
Fax Machine		I	Desktop Support		Return to Desktop
Copier		I	Desktop Support		Return to Desktop
Cash					
Petty Cash		I	Plant Manager's Secretary		
Capital Budget		I	Controller		
Operating Budget		I	Controller		

Chart 4-2: Resource Planning Chart

§ 4.04   TEAM MEMBERS REQUIRED

The primary resource of an IT project is people. Just not any person will do. The project manager leads a team of artisans who possess the skills needed. Therefore, most resource planning starts with the project team.

> The productivity ratio of an expert versus a novice is about 10 to 1.

All team members must:

- Be skilled in their technical field

- Possess strong problem-solving skills—technical people tend to be problem-solvers, but they must recognize and admit when they are not making progress.

- Be goal oriented—workflow is rarely even and some weeks will be long, while others will be light. Project managers need people who will work to the schedule.

- Possess high self-esteem—egos must be big enough to share credit and admit failures. For some, their self-esteem is enough so that they are not threatened by admitting errors.

[A]   Internal Team Members

Internal team members are employees of the sponsor company loaned to the project for its duration. For a very long project, they may be loaned full-time. In most cases, team members will work on the project on a part-time basis. The problem is that the project manager is trying to attract the best people to the project. However, the manager providing the people for the project does not want to lose the best team members for an extended length of time, so the manager sends the team's "less productive" people to the project.

Another problem with using internal resources is that the project manager lacks the authority to promote or increase the workers' pay. The workers' "home" department holds that authority. Therefore, whenever the "home" department calls to have something done, the project is set aside until it is completed.

To attract the best internal candidates, the project manager must do a little advertising through informal informational channels. He must "talk up" the project and the skills needed for it. He should explain the importance of the project and the interesting technologies or challenges it will tackle. The goal here is to encourage the people to ask to be on the project.

Workers appreciate a manager who keeps their interests in mind. An important long-term action is to ensure that at the end of every project, the project manager provides recommendations and letters of appreciation to the departments that loaned the resources. This is to ensure everyone's goodwill. The next time that the project manager needs team members, they will be easier to recruit. However, the best people will avoid poor project managers.

[B]   External Team Members

Contract resources or employees of other companies or independent contractors also have their challenges. Good people are expensive and no company can afford for them to sit around for long. Expect people provided by a contract organization to fall into several categories:

- Their current project is wrapping up. This group is more likely to be skilled and ready to work. Unfortunately, it depends on the previous project ending as scheduled. Obtain a firm start date from the contract company, with financial penalties. If their previous project runs long, this forces the contract company to provide the support as promised.
- On the bench—this group is sitting around waiting for work. They can start right away. They may be fine for the job, but beware of people filling in on jobs for which they are not qualified to work.

Interview contract workers just as if they were being hired as an employee to join the team. Never accept anyone sent by a contract company without personally checking their skills and work habits. Project managers and team members invest time orienting new team members to the workplace, the project, processes, etc. Do not waste this effort on someone who should never have been admitted to the team to begin with.

> Never assume that companies providing contract technical workers are an endless supply of technical talent. In most cases, these companies must post advertisements and hire people like any other company—which takes time. Provide these vendors with at least four weeks of advance notice of project requirements.

Two other important things about working with contract resources:

1. When the project ends, these people are out of a paycheck so they are always watching for their next opportunity. When their part of the project is ending,

they are prone to jump for the next job. If it fits in the budget, offer a bonus to keep them on the project until its end. Contract companies promise this, but they have limited ability to deliver.

2. Once someone is accepted for the project, do not let the contract company switch them out. It is a common practice for a company to show off their best talent to gain the contract only to deliver someone else.

For a large project, consider what ratio of novice-to-expert worker is needed. Do not waste the time of experts on trivial work easily handled by a novice. At the same time, a novice would not be expected to shoulder an expert's workload. Some projects use a 5-to-1 novice/expert ratio. If the ratio is too high, then the expert spends too much time mentoring the novices.

[C] What Skill Level Is Needed?

When identifying skills needed for a task, some project managers use a junior programmer/programmer/senior programmer approach. Each category also may be more specific about the skills expected from this person, such as a number of years of experience in IT overall and a number of years in the specific skill desired. This corresponds to one/three/six years of experience. After developing a skills description for each category, the project manager can assign people to tasks and budget the expense accordingly.

Projects flow more smoothly when highly skilled people are employed. Experts are efficient and complete tasks more quickly, but they are expensive. However, not all tasks need the best and the brightest. Some tasks are relatively mundane and bore "experts" to the point of driving them away. It is wasteful to pay expensive technicians for routine work easily done by cheaper labor. These tasks are not time-critical and can be used for staff development.

When estimating the duration of a task, the time allotted is based on a specific person (and his or her skill level). This can be tricky if that person is not under the project manager's full-time direction. As the project schedule slips, the carefully planned time when the person must be available also changes and uncertainty begins to grow as to whether he or she will be available when needed. By using the three-level job description approach, the project manager can begin the process of identifying alternates in case the desired person is not around.

[D]   Project Process Skills Required

The secret of a successful team is finding the correct size and skill mixture. It is not the number of people that is important, but skill interplay. Following are some of the mental criteria for being a successful team member.

- Accepts change
- Accepts customers as a part of the effort
- Is able to compromise
- Is able to work within an organization
- Is comfortable with details
- Is technologically comfortable, but able to recognize that this is a business effort, not a place for hacking
- Can be a player on a team
- Has proven ability to accomplish given tasks
- Is a specialist, not a generalist

[E]   Clarify Skill Levels with a Job Description

A job description, as the name implies, describes a job. However, some managers try to shortcut the process and substitute vague documents. This is a big mistake. A well-written job description details the type of tasks that the employee is expected to perform. It communicates an expectation from the employer to the worker as to the skills and duties expected for that position. Job descriptions are also the foundation for setting a position's pay range.

How detailed should a job description be? Some will argue that more than one page is too much detail. Much of the description can be "standard," but some should be specific. For example, the "standard" part might be a description for a C++ programmer. Essentially, this class of workers has about the same technical skills. The "specific" part of the description may be details about the business skills, such as knowledge about materials management or payroll systems.

Some managers do not like a detailed job description. They feel it hinders their flexibility when assigning work. This is not true. Assign work as required. Well-written job descriptions include a final statement that the person will perform any additional duties as assigned.

[F]   What's in a Job Description?

Primary responsibilities are those that justify the existence of this staff position. This list is the determinant of who will be chosen for the position, so it must be carefully written. The primary responsibilities detail the skills and level of experience that is required. Exclude from consideration any candidate who does not meet each of the primary responsibilities. Because the primary responsibilities narrow the list of potential candidates, it should be a list of ten items or fewer.

> Do not start from scratch. Use the company's job descriptions or see if there is something available on the Internet.
>
> For example, a primary responsibility may require that the candidate possess at least "five years of project management experience." Just asking for project management experience could open the position to someone with insufficient background. Often more specific experience may be required, such as "Web software design project management."

Evaluating technical skills may be the same as for other positions within the department. An example might be two Java programmers sitting side by side with different business knowledge requirements. When listing skill requirements, think specifically about this person's assignments rather than generic tasks. This might include coding access to a nonstandard database, or interfacing with antique equipment or software, or it might require extensive travel.

Sometimes skill levels are indicated by professional certifications, such as PMI's Project Manager Professional or Microsoft Certified Systems Engineer. Certifications indicate an understanding of specific technical principles, but are not a reliable indicator of the person's ability to translate these principles into action.

Secondary responsibilities are the noncritical functions assigned to the employee. Evaluate candidates by how well they fulfill these requirements. Lacking a secondary skill should not disqualify someone from consideration. There may be expertise with technology outside of the normal responsibilities that would be handy for the department. Such an expertise might be knowledge of a specific foreign language or experience working for the government.

§ 4.05   EQUIPMENT (MACHINES)

The most common piece of equipment in an IT project is a workstation. Every team member will need one. In many cases, the worker will bring one with him or her.

The specifications for any workstations, servers, peripherals, etc., purchased for the project will depend on who will receive the unit. If the customer receives the machines, then they must conform to their standard unit list. This will allow the customer to easily add them to their service agreements.

If the equipment is to remain with the consulting company, then the company can use whatever works best. However, good practice is to always develop something on the same machine with the same configuration as the user will have, if at all possible. This eliminates the possibility of a subtle difference disrupting the final product.

If internal resources are used for the project, try to obtain a dedicated server for development. This contains the damage if the development efforts "crash" the server.

When setting up the team's offices, a few pieces of equipment should be considered. If there are remote team members, include a video conferencing system or dedicated teleconferencing numbers. These tools allow remote workers (team members who must travel) the chance to participate in meetings.

§ 4.06 MATERIALS

Small things like office supplies may not seem important, but without them, work can slow down. They are like bumps in the road in that the journey continues, but is much less comfortable.

Most companies maintain a small office supply room and order what they need for next-day delivery. This keeps inventory small. Select a locking cabinet for the team's office supplies or arrange with a nearby team to use their supplies.

Other useful materials include toner for printers, blank CDs for backups, paper for printers, etc. A few of the standard types of cables and some small tools round out the supplies inventory.

If reference materials are needed, such as a programming manual, then consider who is to receive it before purchasing it. If its cost is low, then it is offered without cost to the customer. If its cost is high, then the customer may be billed for its purchase.

§ 4.07 PROCESS (METHOD)

Projects are normally unique endeavors. If they are conducted entirely internally to a company, then the process portion of resource planning is simple—just use existing procedures and standards.

If the project is conducted for the benefit of another company, then these processes and standards must be identified and prepared for the team's arrival. Again, if the final product is software that will be supported by the customer's staff, then the development team must use the customer's development standards.

An important resource to secure before the team arrives is a set of team SOPs and IT development standards. Team SOPs cover administrative details like expense reports, status reporting, time reporting, absence policies, team meetings, naming conventions for the team share drive, etc. The more processes that are identified before the team forms, the fewer processes that will be thrown into the breach and become de facto practices.

IT development standards detail a consistent format for structuring new software, for naming fields, and for handling data throughout the entire software system.

§ 4.08   ENVIRONMENT

A nice, quiet, clean working area helps to keep a team focused on its efforts. A noisy, dirty, and dispersed work area costs the team time through distractions and infrequent communications. One of the project manager's first duties is to ensure that the team is provided with an adequate workspace.

[A]   Offices or Cubicles?

Offices versus cubicles are a tough tradeoff. Cubicles allow for informal conversations. The negative side is that informal conversations and telephone calls are all distractions to workers trying to concentrate. In the end, some people will work better in quiet offices and others (social creatures) will work better in cubicles. Never assign an office as a status symbol—it is just a tool for completing the job. However, if the team will be working with confidential information, then office space that can be locked is essential.

[B]   Sit as a Team

Try to get the team to sit as close together as possible. This will help the members to think as a team and to facilitate the quick exchange of bits of information. It will also improve morale. When team members are dispersed over a wide area, communication becomes difficult. Space requirements are a function of the number of people on the team, the amount and type of equipment, and the staffing schedule.

Another important tool is a conference room dedicated to the project. A dedicated conference room can be used to post the status of the project. Sharing a conference room means cleaning it up after every use. A large whiteboard is helpful when brainstorming solutions to difficult problems.

Other useful work area requirements include a dedicated computer lab. This provides quick access to the development server for loading data or software. Be sure that the server is properly backed up and the media stored off site.

§ 4.09 PLANNING THE END-GAME NOW

All things end, including projects. The time for resource planning a project's close is at the beginning. The end of a project can be a busy time. Customers toss out last-minute changes, budgets run dry, time runs out, team members resign for their next position, etc. Some time spent early in the project anticipating and planning for these risks will reduce some of the chaos later.

Early in the project, the WBS specifications are used to buy resources—hardware, software, peripherals, all sorts of things. At the end of the project, this equipment and material must go somewhere. Customers do not want to support nonstandard equipment. The contracting company does not want to absorb the expense of unwanted devices. Before buying anything, know what will be done with it at the end of the project.

[A] People

At the end of a project, people must be released. Internal team members simply return to their work areas (which they likely never left) and consultants are released for another assignment.

The problem with releasing team members is that the project may run longer than the timeline. Last-minute customer changes, problems in system testing, reluctance of the customer to sign the acceptance memorandums all conspire to keep the project hanging on and on.

The people, however, are anxious to move on. Consultants are expensive and the moment they are no longer needed, they are released from the project. If they already have their next assignment lined up, they may leave before a project extension is over. Given these problems, it is important that as the project begins to wind down, the project manager updates all team members weekly on the estimated end for the project.

As the end of the project nears, the project manager controls the departure of team members by scheduling their last day on the project and then protecting that departure time from change. In this way, the team can make an orderly transition to their next (or previous) work situation.

[B] Equipment

Some IT projects use existing hardware and software. Others require additional hardware. Examples of new hardware that may be required are servers to run new software, additional network equipment for external access, or even new software tools such as an ERP system.

At the end of the project, software licenses must be transferred. Usually, it is easier for the organization that will be the eventual recipient of the license to purchase it in the first place. This avoids an issue over license restrictions about transfers.

[C]   Materials

Materials are typically covered under miscellaneous expenses. If this is an internal project, excess materials are returned to the supply room. The trick is to pick a cut-off point and stop routinely buying office supplies. Materials can still be purchased, but in a controlled manner that questions how many more will be needed before the end.

[D]   Method (Process)

At the end of the project, collect the team for a lessons-learned session. Each of the SOPs and standards used are reviewed and updates are recommended. Any other practices documented by the team are reviewed and passed on to the IT manager for consideration.

The team must also gather the documents accumulated during the project for use by the people who will maintain the product after the project concludes. These memos will include design discussions, tradeoffs, why certain features were coded the way they were, etc.

[E]   Working Environment

Contact the facilities team to see what they want left and where. Be sure that each team member cleans up his area. Some large trash containers help maintain order as piles of files are converted to trash.

Some of the equipment, such as copiers and fax machines, may have a monthly rental on their use. If the facilities department knows when these items will become available, they can better manage their costs.

[F]   Money

As the end of the project approaches, work with the accounting manager to track the status of unpaid bills and outstanding purchase orders. Materials may be needed up to the last minute (such as printing boxes or user manuals), so beware of closing the project accounts too soon.

§ 4.10 MANAGEMENT INVOLVEMENT

The sponsor reviews the resource requirements. It is usually corporate policy for an executive to review capital spending. This manager might be able to add justifications for the resources in the context of corporate goals. A resource might be required for a long-range effort rather than just for the short-range effort of the project. The executive should support any procurement effort in a timely fashion.

It is the responsibility of the project manager to provide the IT director with realistic requirements and detailed justifications for resources needed. Use the scope plan as the starting point. The customer's needs should be the core for the utilization of any resource, not only for technical justification.

Project managers need to consider alternative solutions to resource requirements in order to achieve the project goals. Achievement is not less than the goal or more than the goal; it *is* the goal. Resources should be used to meet defined measurable goals.

Here are some of the actions required of an operational manager for managing the resource plan:

- Balance project resources
- Be able to justify the why and how of a resource's utilization
- Consider customer needs in acquiring resources
- Consider whether there are alternatives
- Develop a formula for the availability of people for your group
- Emphasize the need for skills rather than headcount
- Procure approved resources
- Support the tactical manager with justifications for the resource plan
- Work with the tactical manager to identify resource links
- Work within the constraints and assumptions of the scope plan in identifying resource requirements
- Brief sponsor—discuss money, timing, and general assumptions
- IT direct—discuss resources needed and when ID contractor is needed

---

Project Planning Versus Business Planning

Project managers and business managers may work in the same company, but they have distinctly different requirements. Here are ten

---

differences between project planning and business planning involving resources:

1. Project planning requires a place for contingency planning, while business planning does not.

2. Project planning maximizes the use of resources, where business planning seeks to minimize them.

3. Project planning cannot plan easily for peak periods, while business planning can more easily recognize peak periods such as holiday sales or end-of-quarter requirements.

4. Project planning needs skills, while business planning considers headcount.

5. Project planning does not necessarily have to consider long-term benefits, while business planning does.

6. Project planning usually requires highly skilled personnel, while business planning can smooth out the skill requirements.

7. Project planning usually has limited financial histories to use as an estimating tool, while business planning has at least last year's budget to use for planning.

8. Project planning cannot survive on underplanning, while business planning might.

9. Project planning is concerned with achieving goals, while business planning is concerned with profit.

10. Project planning relies on contract services more than business planning.

§ 4.11 SUMMARY

Resource planning is important. Once the WBS is in place, there is a great rush to form the project team and move forward. Although that is necessary, it is also important to identify the resources required and ensure the team has a decent place to work.

A resource planning form seems like a lot of paperwork but it helps to break down WBS tasks into their requirements. Either time is spent planning early in the process or everyone scrambles to do the planning after the team arrives.

A fishbone diagram is useful for brainstorming all of the resources necessary to get the project off the ground. Although the WBS contains considerable information about team member requirements and skill sets, it lacks other resource information such as shared equipment, etc.

Purchase hardware and software based on the requirements of the organization who will own it at the end of the project. This will minimize waste, improve vendor technical support, and avoid license transfer issues.

Take care of team members at the end of the project and they will be easy to recruit for future projects. Provide incentives to people to stay on the project until it is completed.

Exhibit 4-2: Resource Planning Questions Checklist

Project Name:	Comments
1. Are there alternate types of resources for unavailable ones?	
2. Are there resources that require capital funding?	
3. Have resources been closely related to cost estimates?	
4. Have skill-level resources been defined in measurable terms?	
5. Have the project scope definitions been used to plan resource estimates?	
6. How do resources relate to each other? (chart)	
7. What are the critical resources for the project?	
8. What are the effects of the cost parameters on resource estimates?	
9. What are the impacts of the milestones on the resource estimates?	
10. What are the impacts on the project because resources are unavailable?	
11. What are the specific resource requirements?	
12. What documents are required to control resources?	
13. What is (are) the range(s) for having an inadequate resource(s)?	
14. What is the control system to manage resources and any changes?	
15. What is the policy on changes in resource requirements?	
16. What is the policy on when resources are required?	
17. What is the resource allocation policy?	
18. What is the resource utilization policy?	
19. What procurement (contractors) policies have to be followed?	
20. Who defines the resource requirements?	

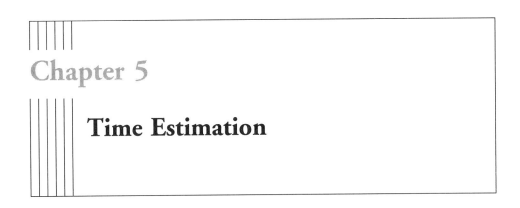

Chapter 5

Time Estimation

§ 5.01   INTRODUCTION

Time is an essential part of project management. A viable project plan depends on the accurate time estimation of its individual tasks. Correct time estimates simplify the coordination of assets throughout the project's duration, and permit the accurate forecasting of labor expenses. In short, correct time estimates are the foundation of a smooth running project. Time estimating is a parallel event to activity sequencing, cost estimating, and resource estimating.

> "In forming the plan of a campaign, it is requisite to foresee everything the enemy may do, and be prepared with the necessary means to counteract it."
>
> —Napoleon I: *Maxims of War*, Maxim II

Project managers know that the estimation process is part art and part science. As experience is gained estimating tasks, the project manager moves toward the "science" side of estimating and relies less on the "art" side. One way to move from art to science is to recognize and avoid the common errors and biases that plague the estimating process today.

> Project management focuses on the maximum use of time, while business management emphasizes the minimum use of time.

§ 5.02   DEFINITION

Time estimation is the process of the project manager assigning time duration to each task in the WBS that reflects how long it should take. However, the project manager cannot possibly know everything about every technology used in the project. To create credible estimates, the project manager must refer to various sources for their opinions. However, the project manager selects the final estimate. It is understandable, therefore, that time estimates may be the core reason for the failure of a project. Bad estimates turn team members into firefighters. Time estimates affect a number of events in the project process:

- Cost estimates
- Activity sequencing
- Schedule
- Project benchmarks
- Resource planning

- Budget cycle
- Risks

Time Estimating Compared to Scheduling

When the initial project schedule is approved, it becomes the baseline for the project. All references to the project's progress are made in comparison to it. Some comparisons between time estimating and scheduling are:

Time estimates:

- are a consequence of analyzing; scheduling is a consequence of planning.
- are a component of scheduling; scheduling is an integration of sequencing activities, resource planning, cost estimating, and time estimating.
- are reviewed by managers, while the sponsor reviews the schedule.
- are inputs into project management software; scheduling is the automatic output.
- are concerned with an individual activity or groups of related activities, while scheduling is concerned with the complete project.
- are to the schedule as cost estimating is to the budget.
- may be thought of as abstract, while scheduling may be thought of as concrete.

And scheduling:

- is based on dependencies, the interrelationships of time, resources, and activities.

---

§ 5.03 TIME ESTIMATION GUIDELINES

The following is a checklist of requirements for time estimation.

- Use a consistent time unit throughout all estimates, such as hours, days, weeks, etc.
- The accuracy of the time estimate depends on the clarity of the activity description. Begin estimating a task by review constraints and assumptions noted in the WBS. Add assumptions made when estimating.

- Provide three time estimates for each task:
  - Optimistic—everything is ready to start on time, everything goes well, no problems encountered
  - Realistic—a few things were not ready; some problems encountered during the task
  - Pessimistic—prerequisites were not ready, task was difficult to complete, and testing uncovered many problems
- Estimate task duration based on work required plus time for administrative details.
  - The task duration estimate is the total elapsed time for the work to be done plus associated waiting time. Note each separately.
  - Full-time workers are not working on one particular task full time. Allow some time for administrative tasks such as attending meetings, drafting status reports, etc.
  - Estimate productive time as 80 percent of time spent on the task.
- Break large tasks into smaller ones to understand them.
- Ask other project managers to validate the estimates for adequacy and to root out padding.
- Project duration makes a difference:
  - Short projects—straight to the point, minimal overhead; something of a sprint
  - Medium projects—more structure and time spent system testing and debugging
  - Long projects—more administrative time is required as the team settles in for the long haul. As portions of the project are completed, they slowly require more and more time to keep them in line with the latest work and assumptions.
- Base time estimates on the productivity of the average skilled person. Separate tasks into those that must be done by an expert, those that are suitable for a novice, and all of the rest. Estimate the third category, which is the most common, for a worker of average expertise.

"He who gains time gains everything."

—Benjamin Disraeli (1804-1881), *Tancred*, iv, 3

[A]   Sources of Time Estimates

There is no need to invent time estimates in a vacuum. There are sources of information that can provide insight into the tasks and problems encountered before. When practical, use more than one method to create the estimates and another to validate it. Typical sources of information are:

- Historical records—some part of this project *must* have been done before
- Expert opinion—ask someone who knows how to do it
- Team members—let the person who will do it say how long it will take
- Vendor guidelines—the steps and how long each requires for installation
- Industry standard values for specific types and units of work
  - Lines of code
  - Function point analysis
  - COCOMO

[B]   Refer to Historical Records

The first stop should be the archive for the project management office. Has this type of project ever been attempted before? Look for the same or a similar project. The more recent it is, the more it will apply to the current situation. Perhaps a subset of the project was already done, such as installing a firewall in a remote office or rolling out existing software to a new office.

The WBS, risk assessment, etc. from the previous plan will all be very useful. At this time, however, focus on the time estimates for the tasks. In particular, look at the variation between the estimates and the actual times. Are the same tasks included on the new plan or are they different? How the work is broken into tasks impacts their time estimates.

[C]   Ask Advice from an Expert

Project managers are not all-knowing beings. There is much they have never encountered and do not understand. Technology constantly changes and a clear understanding of networking issues five years ago may be of little use today. When facing a new technology or any area that the project manager is not familiar with, he should consult a local subject matter expert. This is not a place to cut corners. Hire a consultant if necessary.

Estimating tasks without understanding all they involve is pure guesswork, and a formula for an erratic project schedule. Task estimates should be within plus or minus 10 percent accuracy.

One expert who a project manager can ask is the project manager of the previous similar project. It is hard for some people to confess to making mistakes, but project managers deal with errors all the time. If the previous project manager is willing to help, then time estimation will move quickly.

Technical experts can provide a considerable amount of information about a task. The challenge of using a technical expert, however, is that they tend to estimate time they require to do a task and not for a typical technician. Still, they can explain the underlying assumption for each time estimate. Include these in the documentation for use when assigning that task.

One area of expertise is the technical support department of the vendor that has a product needed to achieve a project goal. The department should have historical data as to the amount of time it took to install and configure their product into other systems. If the vendor does not have this type of data, then immediately look for a different vendor.

[D]   Ask the Team Members

This early in the planning process, it may be obvious who will be on the project team. However, if some of the team members are available, ask them to estimate the time for tasks within their skill portfolio. Asking team members for their opinion helps to secure their commitment to the estimated time.

When asking team members for time estimates, use a structured format to collect the information.

- Read the task title and its supporting information from the WBS
- Confirm constraints, risks, or assumptions in the WBS notes
- Add constraints, risks, or assumptions used to determine the time estimate
- Note any specific experience performing a similar task on a different project

Typical pitfalls of this method are:

- Overly optimistic estimates by team members too proud of their skills
- Team members padding the task times to ensure they can make them
- Team members focused on minute details instead of the big picture; work for the sake of work instead of focused on the goal
- Record the estimate, and ask these questions:
  - Why do you think this is the correct estimate?

- What factors about this activity were the main determinants of the time estimate? (Maybe the task is defined with features of limited value to the customer that could be removed.)
- How confident are you that this estimate is "real"? (Is there some rule of thumb they are using to create an estimate? This may improve the project manager's comfort level and increase the participant's commitment to meeting the timeline.)
- What could be changed or removed from the activity that would reduce its uncertainty? (Often the uncertainty of one or more features or factors drives the time estimate high.)

A team concern will be that one person has added padding for their tasks while everyone else is held to tight timelines. To avoid this, wait until all team members have turned in their estimates and adjust them as a group.

> The expected quality level of the final product has a considerable bearing on the time required for tasks. Six Sigma–level quality will require longer task development time for module testing. System testing will likewise be extended.

[E] Estimating by Lines of Code

An early measure of programmer productivity was to count the lines of source code they created in a given amount of time. Using lines of code (LOC) as a metric is a classic example of "Beware what you reward." In a programming culture of compact efficiency, using a metric that favors verbosity focuses efforts in that direction.

Counting the lines of code has many advantages and disadvantages. The primary advantage of this metric is that it is easy to use. Its primary disadvantage is that it is easily manipulated.

[1] How It Works

There are two types of "lines of code," physical and logical. A physical line is a line on a source code listing. A logical line is a single command that may be spread over multiple physical lines.

A physical line in COBOL might be:

IF x = TRUE then Y = 0 else next sentence.

This same command is written using a more readable standard COBOL format:

IF x = TRUE
Then
Y = 0
ELSE
Next Sentence.

Even though it is five physical lines, it only counts as a single logical line. In this case, it is easy to see the connection between one line of logical code and how it equates to five lines of print.

The rules for counting the LOC vary among languages. For example, in COBOL it might count noncomment lines as any statement that ends with a period. For C it might be any statement that ends in a semicolon.

Lines of code can be easily manipulated. Imagine a table containing the valid abbreviations for the 50 states. A COBOL statement can be coded to use subscripts to validate the entry against the table. This would be a single logical line of code. The same end result could be provided by 50 "IF" statements. By the rules, this credits 50 lines of code. However, which approach is easiest to maintain or the most efficient to execute?

In this case, a series of rules can be crafted for counting lines of a language, but this eliminates the key advantage of counting LOC—simplicity. For this reason, the LOC method is normally not used by itself.

[2]   Problems with Using Lines of Code

There are several problems with using LOC as a unit of measure for software. Consider two applications that provide the same exact functionality (screens, reports, databases). The number of function points would be the same, but the amount of effort required to develop the application would be different (hours per function point). With this in mind:

1. The number of lines of code delivered is dependent upon the skill level of the programmer. In fact, the higher skill level of the programmer the fewer lines of code developed per function.

2. There is an inverse relationship between level of language and work output (when work output is lines of code). High-level languages such as Visual Basic™ need fewer lines than low-level languages, such as C, to provide the same function point.

3. The actual number of LOC is not known until the project is almost completed. Therefore, lines of code cannot be used to estimate the effort or schedule of a project.

4. What constitutes a "line of code"? Is it a physical line on a page? Is it a logical statement (which COBOL ends with a period)? How many lines is a complex SQL statement versus one that queries, builds a temporary data set, then queries again, etc. Are lines of comments counted? They take time to create/maintain as well.

5. Most programming mixes several languages in a module. For example, a program written in one language that uses a different language for an embedded database query may be employed.

6. An individual's programming style will directly impact line count.

7. Code generation programs speed productivity but can quickly generate many lines of code with a click of a mouse.

8. GUI programs (such as Visual Basic™) can create lines of code by dragging and dropping objects and cannot use this metric.

§ 5.04 FUNCTION POINT ANALYSIS OVERVIEW

Project managers of software development projects have long puzzled as to the best way to estimate the amount of time required to develop a piece of software. Historical information was useful, but the technology advanced steadily and productivity factors change. Often it is just a guess made by the programmer before beginning that module's detailed analysis.

[A] Background

In the late 1970s, Allan Albrecht of IBM developed a standard measurement based on the size and complexity of a software module, which he called function point analysis (FPA). FPA breaks software requirements into its smaller components for analysis. The FPA process has evolved over the years and is now recognized by the International Standards Organization™ (ISO) as an international standard for functional sizing.

Function points are a unit of measure for software. Think of it like a yardstick or speedometer. The primary use of function point analysis is to determine the level of effort required to create a piece of software. This can be done during the project analysis phase, for a company to bid on a contract, or for a project manager contemplating expanding a project's scope.

An important additional use of FPA is as a project and product metric. Once a system's function point score is determined, the same information can be used over time to determine:

- Defects per function point—When a module is delivered for component testing and again at system testing, this metric indicates the quality of craftsmanship by the programmers.
- Productivity—The number of function points completed per worker. This is a useful way to rate workers for future assignments.
- Cost per function point—Divide the monthly cost of individuals or the team to provide a useful estimating tool for estimating scope expansion.

A useful thing about function points is their independence of any particular technology. Function point analysis can determine the most productive environment or language to use in a given situation. Although function points do not correspond to any physical attribute of a software system (such as lines of code or the number of subroutines) it is a relative measure for comparing projects and measuring productivity.

[B]   Counting Function Points

Function point analysis recognizes two basic types of elementary processes: data in motion and data at rest. Data in motion has the characteristic of moving data inside to outside the application boundary or outside to inside the application boundary.
FPA measures:

- Inputs
- Outputs
- Files
- Inquires
- Interfaces

It categorizes components as simple, average, or complex. These values are scored and the total is expressed in unadjusted function points (UFPs).
Complexity factors described by 14 general systems characteristics, such as reusability, performance, and complexity of processing can be used to weight the UFP. Factors are also weighted on a scale of 0 (not present), 1 (minor influence), to 5 (strong influence). The result is a number that correlates to system size.

Once a final function point score is completed, it can be used to estimate time for a task. First, the organization's historical productivity values are calculated. Once this number is recorded, it is used to gauge future efforts, such as:

Historically, database administrators average 15 function points per month. Apply this to a 42-point project:

$$42 \text{ FP} \div 15 = 2.8 \text{ months of effort}$$

Next, translate the months of effort into cost. If the database administrators averaged $10,000 per month (salary plus benefits), then the cost for this task is:

$$2.8 \text{ months} \times \$10,000 = \$28,000$$

[C] Function Point Analysis Is a Six-Step Process

There are six identifiable steps to function point analysis.

1. Identification of the subsystem boundaries between the target and external applications.

2. Identification of the data functions (internal logical files and external interface files). The first three components are external inputs, external outputs, and external inquiries. Each of the components adds, modifies, deletes, retrieves, or processes information contained in the files and, hence, are called transactions.

   • Transactions that bring data from outside the application domain (or application boundary) to inside the application boundary are referred to as external inputs.

   • Data at rest is maintained by the application in internal logical files.

   • Data at rest is maintained by another application as external interface files.

3. Identification of transactional functions (external inputs, external outputs, and external inquiries). The other two components are the system's internal logical files and external interface files.

   The primary difference between an internal logical file and an external interface file is that an external file is not maintained by the application being counted, while an internal file is. The relative functional complexity and number of internal logical files and external interface files determine the contribution of the data functions to the unadjusted function point count.

4. Calculation of the unadjusted function point count.

   Once all the components in the application have been classified as one of the five major components mentioned above, they have to be rated as low, average, or high. Ranking is commonly based on file types referenced, data element types, and record element types.

5. Determination of the value adjustment factor.

The value adjustment factor is based on 14 general system characteristics that rate the general functionality of the application. The degrees of influence range on a scale of 0 to 5, from no influence to strong influence. The general system characteristics are:

- Data communication—the number of communications facilities for transferring data with the application

- Distributed functions—the way that distributed data and processes are handled

- Performance—use of specified throughput or response time performance objectives

- Heavily used configuration—how heavily used is the platform where this application will reside?

- Transaction rate—frequency of transaction operation (daily, monthly, etc.)

- Online data entry—percent of online entry

- End-user efficiency—application is designed for end-user efficiency

- Online update—files updated by online entry

- Complex processing—extensive logical processing

- Reusability—developed to meet the needs of one application or for many

- Installation ease—difficulty converting existing application to the new application

- Operational ease—number of automated administrative features

- Installation sites—installed at one or many

- Facilitate change—application designed for easy future enhancement

6. Calculation of the final function point count.

The final function point count (adjusted function point count) is a combination of both unadjusted function point count (UFP) and the general system characteristics.

[D]   When Not to Use Function Points

Function points are not a very good measure for estimating the complexity of maintenance efforts. Repairing software requires a great deal of detective work. In addition, the skill of the people making the repairs varies widely. Criticisms of FPA include:

- Counts are affected by project size and complexity
- Difficulty converting logical files to physical files
- Cannot compare function points between companies owing to variations in how they are calculated
- The validity of the FPA weights and the consistency of their application are questionable.

§ 5.05 COCOMO

COCOMO was published in 1981 as a tool for estimating the time required for a software project. This name came from the first two letters of each word of constructive cost model. It was later changed to COCOMO 81. This version reflects the programming practices of the 1980s.

COCOMO is an open model. Companies can easily adjust it to suit their local preferences and technical environment. It is useful for testing the impact on the schedule of various strategies. COCOMO's calculations are based on estimates of a project's source lines of code defined as:

- Delivered source lines of code—test and support software are excluded.
- Code from applications generators is excluded.
- Only logical lines of code count.
- Comments are not counted.

[A] COCOMO and COCOMO 81

Basic COCOMO provides rough estimates of software costs, but its accuracy is limited. It is heavily dependent on the evaluator's subjectivity. The algorithm uses ten steps:

1. Decompose the project specifications into its lowest level of modules.
2. Estimate the size of each module, and then roll the modules back up into subsystems and estimate the size of the entire project.
3. Determine effort multipliers for:
   - Level of personnel
   - Size of project
   - Reliability

- Development environment (complexity of the technologies)
- Module complexity

4. Apply the effort multipliers to each module.

5. Identify the effort multipliers for the subsystems, in addition to the previous module multipliers.

6. Roll up the module estimates along with the subsystem multipliers to create a combined subsystem estimate.

7. Roll up the estimates to a systemwide estimate.

8. Review all factors for interactions between subsystems and add to the estimates for this.

9. Add in additional costs not included in the system estimate.

10. Use an independent source to validate and adjust the estimates.

The official COCOMO Website is *http://sunset.usc.edu/COCOMOII/ cocomo.html*. It contains detailed information and free software tools for calculating a project estimate.

[B]   COCOMO II

Over the years, nighttime batch processing has given way to real time, Web-based database interaction. COCOMO II improves on COCOMO 81 by factoring in advances to software projects.

COCOMO II estimation algorithm uses "object points" to estimate the number of labor months required. The output of this calculation is adjusted using 17 "effort multipliers." Following is the object point estimation procedure:

1. Estimate object points in the application. An object point is a report, a file, a screen, etc.

2. Classify each object point's complexity (low, medium, high).

3. Determine the complexity weight of each.

4. Add all of the weighted objects into a single number.

5. Estimate the amount of reuse in the project.

6. Determine the number of new object points per person, per month.

7. Compute the estimates per number of months.

$\S$ 5.06 ADD ADMINISTRATIVE TASKS TO THE PLAN

Additional tasks are required for administrative actions that support, but are not directly indicated by, the project goal. Most of these tasks occur around the milestone reviews. Longer projects will have more of these and short projects may only use a few at the conclusion.

- Quality reviews of product and its configuration
- Customer review of product and project progress
- Tasks for holding contingency time and management reserve
- Customer reviews at milestones
- Lessons-learned sessions after a difficult task
- Peer review of project efficiency with other project managers

---

Employee Availability

A tricky action is the determination of employee work-hours. Working full time does not mean being available 100 percent of the time. A typical work year for a full-time employee is:

- There are 52 weeks in a year with 40 work-hours per week. This means a total of 2,080 hours of work.
- An employee gets at least two weeks' vacation a year. We need to subtract 80 hours from the yearly total, so we now have 2,000 hours available.
- An employee may be sick five days a year, so another 40 hours is removed from the total, leaving 1,960 hours.
- The company has ten holidays a year so there goes another 80 hours, leaving 1,880.
- An employee will probably be involved in miscellaneous activities such as attending meetings (consider 20 percent of the year for these activities). This comes to 416 hours, so we now have 1,464 hours.
- Each employee gets five days of training a year, so we now have 1,424 hours available for work from a full-time employee.

---

§ 5.07   TIME ESTIMATION PITFALLS

1. **Wishful thinking.** Project managers are optimists. They depend on this optimism to motivate the team to make the project a success. Unfortunately, this optimism is reflected in their time estimates. Project sponsors often apply pressure to keep estimates low, which, combined with optimism, sometimes creates estimates that have little basis in reality. The person estimating the time required for a task must not be caught up in excessive optimism when sizing up a task.

2. **Focusing on the best case.** This is a variation on wishful thinking. Bad things occur during a project that delay task completion. The longer the time estimate for a task, the more likely that something will occur. This situation arises when the project manager is either ignorant of the project's subject or if he or she is intent on satisfying the sponsor. Team members will exert themselves to help a troubled project, but they will not bother to work the extra time to bail out unrealistic estimates. An example of this pitfall is to expect every task to be completed correctly the first time.

3. **Overlooking a task.** The WBS tries to identify everything to put in the plan, but it is far from a perfect process. A perfect job estimating individual tasks is ruined if tasks have been overlooked. The project's sponsor focuses on the milestones, and an overlooked task is not that person's business. During the time estimation process, ask different sources to look over the WBS and suggest tasks that may have been omitted.

4. **Basing time estimates on a predetermined budget.** A project sponsor can try to limit project cost but he cannot get a mansion built for the price of a shack. Time estimates should never look at the project budget. That is done only when all of the tasks are rolled up and the sponsor either wants to proceed or not.

5. **Managing estimation biases.** People have patterns in their work. Most of these are automatic and never thought about. An example is a project manager who automatically adds 20 percent onto each time estimate, etc. Typical biases:

   - Believing the team is as motivated to complete the project quickly as the project manager is. (They are not. They believe that completing it early makes the project manager a hero, but there is no reward for them.)

   - Overestimating team member skill levels. A part of optimism is to think the best of people, and this leads to overestimating the capability of team members to perform.

- Owing to the project manager's limited perspective, he or she sees tasks as much simpler than they are.

- Overestimating a project task based on bad experiences on previous projects. This may also be due to an unwanted person being assigned to the team.

[A]   Management Involvement

At times, estimating time seems more an art than a science. When the project manager works hard to understand the details of a task before offering an estimate (science), executives may still arbitrarily cut the timeline (art) to suit their budget.

Everyone looks at the schedule as a commitment when it really is not; rather, it is a visual presentation based almost completely on some type of estimate. Time estimating is a major component used in developing the schedule. The chain is only as strong as its weakest link. The project manager ensures that the time-estimating process is consistent with other time-estimating processes in the company. Basic tactical actions of the project manager include the following:

- Ensure there are criteria for defining time estimates, such as:
  - Define estimates against project goals
  - Define estimates to average capabilities
  - Do not factor in overtime or possible part-time efforts
  - If possible, the person who will do the activity should estimate it
  - Define time measurements (hours, eight-hour days, or 20-day work months)
- Gather time estimates
  - Collect all estimates before doing a total overview
  - Set daily project priorities to manage time-estimate issues
  - Include time estimates for quality control and assurance
  - Use project management software to assist in evaluating time estimates
  - Factor procurement requirements into appropriate time estimates
- Analyze resource and time interdependencies
  - Analyze time estimates to see possible impacts on skills, resources, and materials needed for project
  - Determine how time estimates may influence acquisition of outside resources
  - Determine how time estimates impact costs (each operational area probably has its own cost per labor-hour)

- Determine how budget cycle might affect time estimates, especially those in the fourth quarter of the fiscal year
- Communicate
  - Use technical support of vendors to define any installation or configuration time estimates
  - Determine with operational managers what risks might develop with changes to time estimates
  - Document issues and discuss at meetings
- Clean up the estimate
  - Resolve a too-large total of time estimates for the project by beginning with the smallest and working to the largest
  - Resolve time issues such as getting a required resource well in advance of required date
  - Look for "forgotten" activities that need time estimates such as meetings, training, and documenting
  - Finish the time-estimate process before attempting to do the scheduling process

§ 5.08   SUMMARY

Time estimates are the foundation of project management. Accurate estimates enable the smooth coordination of resources as they enter and leave the project throughout its duration. Poor estimates leave the project team in a constant crisis mode, scrambling to complete some task to keep the project on track. The project manager is responsible for the quality of the project estimates. Projects plagued by poor estimates require the project manager to stop progress until the defect is corrected.

There are various ways to estimate time. Expert opinions can provide quick estimates, as can historical information. Asking team members to estimate their tasks invites their buy-in on the value of the project but watch out for extensive padding.

Three processes for estimating software projects were reviewed. The more accurate the desired result, the more time required to analyze the project and estimate the time. Both function points and COCOMO require training in the many details prior to use.

Some companies use lines of code as a measurement of project complexity. They measure the lines of similar completed projects and project these values onto a proposed project. This is a poor tool to use. Most companies use lines of code as a post-project evaluation of productivity.

Function points can be used to size software applications. Since function points use a unique and consistent method, different people measuring them will give almost the same result with very little margin of error. A nontechnical person can easily understand function points, which helps in communicating the same to the end user effectively and easily.

COCOMO is another widely used tool for estimating projects. It has evolved over the years to include lines of code and function points as descriptors of the project. COCOMO has many free online tools to help calculate estimates.

Exhibit 5-1: Time Estimates Checklists

	Attachments
Time estimates by scenario	
Pessimistic	
Realistic	
Optimistic	
Criteria by scenario	
Pessimistic	
Realistic	
Optimistic	
Impacts by scenario	
Pessimistic	
Realistic	
Optimistic	
Estimates by project goals	
Source ID	
Critical estimates	
Procurement tasks	
Skills development	
Resource tasks	
Material gathering	
Support tasks	
Training tasks	

Exhibit 5-1: *(Continued)*

Documentation tasks	
Production tasks	
Planning	
Design	
Development	
Testing	
Defined assumptions used	
Defined constraints used	
Deliverables accounted for	
Adequate duration	
Schedule requirements used	
Deadline criteria	
Quality	
Control	
Assurance	
Validation	
Field testing	
Resource procurements	
Equipment	
Internal	
External	
Materials	
Internal	
External	
Skills	
Internal	
External	
Project management tools	
Internal	

Exhibit 5-1: *(Continued)*

External	
Development tools	
Internal	
External	
Facilities	
Internal	
External	
Logistics	
Internal	
External	
Training requirements	
Internal	
External	
Documentation requirements	
Internal	
External	
Communications requirements	
Internal	
External	
Risk management	
Project administration	
Special time estimate criteria	
Duration	
Production time	
Wait time	
Calendar days	
Period/effort	
Dependency	

Exhibit 5-1: *(Continued)*

End-start	
Start-end	
Start-start	
Lag time	
Lead time	
Slack time	
Tradeoff considerations	
Part-time staff	
Full-time staff	
Other	
Special variants noted	
Consistency to	
Scope plan	
Activity	
Resource plan	
Manager's approval	

Instructions for the Time Estimates Checklist

This checklist assists the project team in writing the project activity plan, the project schedule, and the project budget. It is used by each operational manager to draft these documents at a group level or departmental level.

Time estimates by scenario: All project time estimates must be given in three forms: pessimistic, realistic, and optimistic. Actual format instructions come from the project team. The estimates should reflect items given in this checklist. A confidence level should be included with each estimate.

Criteria by scenario: There should be objective data to support the three types of estimates. The sources for the criteria include standards, benchmarks, historical records, or project team requirements.

Impacts by scenario: There should be explanations for each of the estimate types. For example, the estimate is pessimistic because no one is immediately available at this time with the skill level to do the task in less than three months. Another example is if the pessimistic estimate happens, then "X" risk may happen by affecting other estimates.

Exhibit 5-1: *(Continued)*

Estimates by project goals: Estimates should be linked to the project's goals as found in the project scope plan.

Source ID: Identify the person responsible for writing the time estimates, including title, e-mail address, and telephone number. If an external source, also include company information.

Critical estimates: For the listed items, give the justifications for being designated critical.

Defined assumptions: Use the assumptions from the scope plan to develop estimates.

Defined constraints: Use the constraints from the scope plan to develop estimates.

Deliverables: Give links to project deliverables for each estimate.

Adequate duration: Give the criteria for task duration that includes both production and wait times.

Schedule requirements: Use the project schedule requirements as defined by the project team.

Deadline criteria: Use deadline criteria as defined by the project team that is based on the scope plan.

Quality: Give any possible estimates that you consider relevant to the listed areas that might be required for product validation or field testing. Justification should be included, such as reference to a standard or benchmark.

Resource procurements: If a resource (hardware, software, skill, or support materials) has to be acquired from an external source, give estimates for the procurement tasks, such as negotiation and administrative times.

Risk management: Consider if a pessimistic scenario breaks down, the possible time required for correcting.

Project administration: Based on the project team requirements, give estimates. In addition, consider time estimates for giving status reports to the operational team by either e-mail or status presentations.

Special Time Estimate Criteria

Each of the following items is of a technical nature to assist you in writing a time estimate:

Duration:

Production time: Actual days of work.

Wait time: Actual days when work is not being done, such as weekends and holidays.

Calendar days: Use the Gregorian calendar.

Period/effort: A period is an amount of time, while an effort is the amount of work to complete a task.

Dependency:

End-start: An activity or task must end before another can start.

Start-end: An activity or task must begin before another can end.

Start-start: One activity or task must start before another.

Lag time: The time between two activities or tasks because of the nature of the activities.

Lead time: The overlapping time of two activities or tasks.

Slack time: The difference between earliest and latest (start or finish) times for an activity or task.

Tradeoff Considerations:

Part-time staff: State plainly, such as, one hour per day or once a week. Justify the use of a part-time staff over the use of a full-time staff.

Full-time staff: Give impacts of having full-time over part-time staff. Justify the use of a full-time staff over a part-time staff.

Other: Identify whether there is a need for a consultant or any other outside staff.

Special variants noted: Give any additional information that might assist the project team in its responsibilities and minimize further discussions.

Consistency to: There should be links in the justifications or impacts to the listed documents.

Scope plan: The strategic view of the constraints and assumptions of the project as developed by the project team.

Activity plan: A set of definitions for efforts required to achieve measurable results. At the operational level, you consider activities, at the project level, tasks.

Resource plan: Establish support requirements for a project as to costs, availability, start date and end date (length of time for use plus duration), and technical specifications.

Manager's approval: The manager should be of an appropriate management authority to agree to the time estimate.

Exhibit 5-2: Time-Estimating Questions Checklist

Project Name:	Comments
1. Are the time estimates based on skill types and levels?	
2. Are there specific time estimates for handling risks?	
3. Are there time estimates for communicating?	
4. Do the time estimates reflect the requirements of procurement policies?	
5. How do changes in time estimates affect project results?	
6. Is there a validating methodology for time estimates?	
7. What are the criteria for associating cost and time estimates and potential changes?	
8. What are the criteria for a time-estimate formula?	
9. What are the criteria for time measurements?	
10. What are the impacts of procurement policies on time estimates?	
11. What are the impacts of the resources on time estimates?	
12. What are the time increments for time estimates?	
13. What is the financial impact of expanding or shortening a time estimate?	
14. What is the impact of the quality control and assurance processes on time estimates?	
15. What is the policy on notifying team members of project time changes?	
16. What is the procedure for associating time estimates with people, and equipment and people acquisition?	

Exhibit 5-2: *(Continued)*

17. What is the project's duration?	
18. What is the quality control and validation process for time estimates?	
19. Who determines the time estimates that are used to establish the schedule?	
20. Who should have inputs into or be notified of time estimates?	

Chapter 6

Schedule Development

§ 6.01   INTRODUCTION

A schedule is a visual presentation of time-oriented project tasks. It projects all of the tasks onto a timeline as a blueprint for the project and its resources. The schedule is the baseline for gauging project progress and performance. It is to time as the budget is to cost.

> "Planners are always conservative and see all of the difficulties, and more can usually be done than they are willing to admit."
>
> —Franklin D. Roosevelt

Scheduling has two primary steps. First, it sequences the task from the work breakdown schedule (WBS) into a logical order. Second, it resequences the original order to accommodate limited resources and the required delivery date, and to shorten the critical path. The creation of an effective and efficient project schedule is the essence of project planning.

A schedule reflects the viewpoint of the project at a given point in time. When planning a six-month project, it is difficult to guess what the company's business situation will be when the project is in the later stages. As the project progresses, more information is obtained. Assumptions can be proved true or false and risks can be identified as real or imagined. The closer to the present that an estimate is made, the more likely it is to be accurate. The expectations for an IT project are:

1. Significant technical design and development
2. High degree of technical complexity
3. Intolerance for failure
4. Performance as the major criterion for success
5. High potential for risks

Two tools at the end of this chapter assist with the creation of project plans. The first is Exhibit 6-1: Schedule Planning Questions Checklist. This checklist helps project managers think through the schedule development process so that all pertinent information is included in the schedule.

The second tool determining the adequacy of the assembled schedule is Exhibit 6-2: Checklist for Creating a Project Schedule. It probes deeper into the aspect of task breakdown and areas that must be included somewhere within the project plan.

§ 6.02   LINKING TASKS

A schedule is a series of tasks linked together in a specific sequence. In its simplest sense, it is a series of sequential tasks. A sequential project plan is easy to understand, but requires more time to finish than a customer is willing to wait. It also wastes the time of the various team members as one of them works while the others are idle.

Instead, to maximize resources and reduce project completion time, examine the various tasks and have as many of them as possible run concurrently. The dependencies between tasks are examined as they are placed in order. The basic types of task dependencies are:

- The start-start dependency is when one activity must start before another activity may start, usually for concurrent activities. For example, all of the "estimating" project activities usually start together and run concurrently. Activities of the start-start dependency type can be grouped together in the project phases:
  - Design
  - Development
  - Testing
  - Implementation
  - Validation

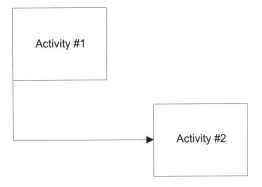

Chart 6-1: Start-Start

- The start-end dependency is when an activity must begin before another activity can end. An example of this is completing the initial procurement process before hiring a consultant. When the consultant is hired, the first phase of procurement is over.

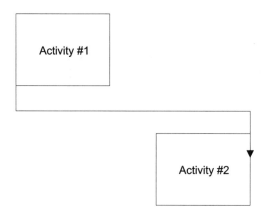

Chart 6-2: Start-End

- The end-start dependency is when an activity must end before another can start. This is the most common dependency. An example is coding that must be completed before implementation, but not before testing.

Chart 6-3: End-Start

- The end-end dependency activity cannot end until another activity has also ended. This is the least common dependency type. The obvious case is that testing cannot end before coding has also ended. An activity that has a distinctive problem because of this type of dependency is documentation.

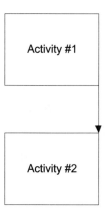

Chart 6-4: End-End

§ 6.03 DEVELOPING A SCHEDULE

The primary emphasis in scheduling is to piece together the tasks into a sequence that delivers the desired result in the shortest amount of time. Essential tools for creating a schedule include:

- Defined project scope and objectives
- Work breakdown schedule
- Activity costs
- Time estimates for each task
- Resources defined, including any special requirements and the time estimates for procuring them
- Essential milestones defined
- A list of assumptions, risks, and constraints and the tasks to which they pertain

The local policies and procedures ultimately determine the form of the schedule. The schedule could be based on calendar time or on a critical path where the completion of a given event or set of events is important to the completion of project goals.

[A] Reverse Planning

Reverse planning begins with the date that the project must be completed and then works backward to the present. It is the best way to plan a project schedule when time is short or when the final product is very new to the team. Reverse planning can be used to focus the team on the fewest tasks possible.

This type of planning is common to meet customer deadlines, legal compliance issues, or a firm delivery date. It is used extensively by the military.

[B] Forward Planning

Use forward planning when the goal is clear and the project team has an idea on how to achieve it. It begins with the present situation and charts a path to the future. It begins with where we are today, and then planning the next step, then the next, etc. It focuses the team on what is possible in the near future. The end goal serves as a distant target that the team marches toward like a beacon.

[C]   Considerations for Schedule Development

As the schedule is created, consider the following:

1. How can the company's budget cycle affect the schedule, especially in the fourth quarter?

2. How can the project manager ensure that the schedule realistically reflects the training and documentation requirements?

3. How should resource leveling be used?

4. What are the criteria for ensuring that the quality management schedule is appropriate?

5. What are the risk criteria that can affect the schedule?

6. What lag-time and lead-time relationships were defined?

7. What project management tools will be used to manage the scheduling process?

8. When were estimates defined to average capabilities?

9. Where in the schedule are events that can be impacted by procurement policies?

10. Why should issues be documented and discussed at meetings?

§ 6.04   MILESTONES

A milestone is a marker along the road. It indicates the distance from the last town and the remaining miles to the next. In the project sense, it is an event that signifies the completion of some major portion of the schedule. It is accompanied by a project-wide review of the progress to date. It also updates the upcoming schedule to include changes in the project environment. Milestones can be based on a variety of things, such as the following:

- **Calendar**—one milestone wrap-up every month. Use this for long projects where the project sponsor must report on progress to the executives. It is awkward for the project manager as it is based on a calendar event and not on progress. Therefore, the report will include many works-in-progress tasks.

- **Project phase**—one milestone at the completion of each event. There are five phases in a typical project. Each is a logical point to pause and reflect on project performance, and to contemplate the future. The phases are:
  - Design
  - Analyze
  - Develop

- ○ Test

- ○ Implement

- At completion of major components—when an important part of a large project is completed, such as completing the environmental controls of a new data center, completion of customer facing Web pages, etc.

- At the start and finish of a project. Every project has a milestone when it starts, and when it completes. At the beginning, the milestone is all of the activities to plan the project and to obtain customer approval. At the finish, it is to deliver the final product and obtain sponsor approval.

During a milestone review, the project manager is busy wrapping up the details from the completed tasks and focusing on the upcoming ones. Include these tasks at every milestone review to ensure adequate time is set aside to complete them:

- Project administrative time

- Risks and assumptions

- Customer review

- Quality control review

- Management contingency time

- Lessons learned

§ 6.05 PROJECT ADMINISTRATION TIME

There are many milestone administrative activities to complete. The first is to gather documentation for the tasks completed. This includes notes that indicate design decisions made and the logic behind them. Also, include meeting notes that detail scope clarification made with the sponsor (which was not included in a formal scope change). Forward-looking activities include:

- Updating the project plan. Based on what is known today, how will the schedule change between this point in time and the next milestone? It is always easier to estimate time that will occur sooner rather than later. The schedule estimates for the near future are easier to estimate than the distant future. At each milestone, adjust task times to the next milestone to improve accuracy.

- Review each change to the schedule for risks, assumptions, and constraints.

[A] Risks and Assumptions

Risks are guesses that certain negative actions will occur. At each milestone, review every risk and determine if it still exists. If it does, then review its mitigation plan for actions to include in the project plan. For example, a risk may have been that the database administrators will not be ready when needed. At this milestone, if there are plenty of administrators without a lot of experience, the risk is the time required to complete the project will be longer. The mitigation plan is to start sooner and ensure an expert mentors the administrators.

Some risks apply only to a specific milestone of the project. For example, the risk that a customer will not approve the final technical specification applies to a single task. When that task is completed, its associated risk is no longer valid. Move it from the active risk list to the archive list.

Assumptions are statements about the future that are possibly true. Treating them as facts allows planning to proceed. At each milestone review the list of assumptions to identify any that are no longer needed. Move these to the archive assumption list along with what actually occurred.

[B] Quality Control Review

There are two types of quality control to examine at a milestone. The quality of the product or service created must meet customer expectations. The sooner that a variance is discovered, the cheaper it is to resolve.

The second type of quality is the efficiency of the project's management. Everyone can improve and project managers are no exception. Normally the project management office evaluates project performance to gauge project managers and to update their personal development plans.

[C] Customer Review

Milestones typically include a meeting with the customer (or project sponsor) to review progress to date. This is a formal briefing about the schedule, budget, and product configuration. Milestone briefings are the time to raise concerns about the upcoming milestone.

[D] Lessons Learned

Before everyone forgets what has occurred, sit the team down and walk through the recent project tasks. First, review what went well so as to recognize areas of team excellence. Next review what did not go well. The team then can discuss what happened, what should have happened, and possible steps to avoid future problems of this type.

Capture these discussions for use by other teams. Sharing best practices and experiences is a powerful tool that should be encouraged by project management offices.

[E] Contingency Time

Tasks are estimated for average time to completion. This means that if estimation was perfect, half of them will complete sooner and half will complete later than the estimate. In theory, over the life of the project, the overruns and underruns should cancel each other out.

In reality, tasks do not finish sooner because people will slow down if they feel there is extra time available for a task. Project managers watch for this but it is tough to detect. To protect the scheduled milestone date, project managers add 20 percent on their timeline as a contingency against late tasks.

Some theorists recommend spreading this buffer among the tasks. Others recommend keeping it for use at the end of the milestone. The choice is a personal preference or a project management office policy.

§ 6.06   CALENDAR

A calendar lays some part of information against a timeline. This allows the reality of time to shape the sequence of tasks. Calendars are easily managed using project management software. There are several calendars to consider. Each has its own use.

- Task schedule calendar
- Resource requirements calendar
- Budget calendar

[A]   Task Schedule Calendar

Once the tasks are sequenced, they are placed against a calendar to see when the project will complete. This calendar must be set to normal workday length. All holidays blanked out as non-work-days.

This becomes the initial project plan. Often the end date shocks the sponsor so the project manager examines the task sequences to shorten the duration by scheduling tasks in parallel. Near-term time estimates are typically more accurate, so the more tasks that can be pulled closer to the beginning of the project, the more accurate the time estimate and the quicker the project is completed.

[B]   Resource Requirements Calendar

The resource calendar details the days and hours when specific resources are available to help with a project. A calendar description of each resource must be set up in the project management software. Part-time resources must indicate the days they can work on the project, or the number of hours per day.

The primary resource of a project is skilled people. Often they join the project for short periods and then assist with other company efforts. The resource calendar indicates the days and times that persons will be available to assist. It is common for a critical task to sit idle awaiting the availability of a critical team member.

Team members have lives outside of the project. The days they are not available for the project must be indicated. Vacations, training days, and other excused absences must be added to the calendar.

Once everything is included in the resource calendar, the resources must be "leveled." Up to this point, tasks have been added to the plan irrespective of the resources required. Project management software will indicate those times that resources are overcommitted to multiple tasks at the same time. A considerable amount of time will be spent rearranging the sequences of tasks to provide the balance of the shortest project time without resource conflicts. This is when it may become evident that additional skilled resources may be needed.

[C]   Budget Calendar

Projects exist within a company's financial environment. There are times when spending is delayed or denied. A project manager must understand the financial calendar for the sponsoring company. For example, most companies defer further purchases during the last two weeks of their fiscal year while they balance their various accounts. This delay is often extended through the first week of the new fiscal year. Therefore, project managers must plan their purchases to account for this.

If a major purchase is pending during the end of the fiscal year, check with the finance manager. The company may feel it makes better financial sense to incur the expense now rather than later.

§ 6.07   GANTT CHARTS

A schedule is a planning tool that helps a project manager to complete a project. If the schedule is not flexible, then the schedule, rather than the project manager, controls the project. Project schedules are an expression of the intention of what and when the results will be accomplished. If a project manager could predict project task durations with 100 percent accuracy, his task would be easy. In reality, a schedule is a "best guess" based on information available at the time it was developed.

A Gantt chart shows planned and actual progress for tasks displayed against a horizontal timeline. Gantt charts are easy to build and are a display feature in most project management software.

These charts are visual tools. Often they are displayed as a poster so interested stakeholders can see the project status. Gantt charts are excellent to preview a visual presentation or an overview of project timelines in the horizontal bar mode. They provide an easy-to-understand communications tool for the team. Gantt charts are suitable for simple projects, but because they do not illustrate activity relationships, they are weak for complex projects. They can, however, be used to compare the project's actual progress against the original definition.

Henry Laurence Gantt, an American engineer and social scientist, developed this technique at the turn of the twentieth century for presenting project tasks.

[A] Basic Features and Functions of a Gantt Chart

The first step in building a Gantt chart is to assemble the tasks in a network, which indicates the predecessors for each task. Computer-generated Gantt charts use a horizontal line connecting the end of one task to the beginning of the next. The Gantt chart uses this structure to indicate when a task may begin (such as task Z cannot begin until tasks X and Y are complete). The first column is tasks, while the other columns are dates.

The activities are listed by priority and sequence. The period of an activity is represented by a bar with its start and end dates as the parameters. The bars usually come in two colors. Use a light color to represent percentage of activity completion.

Other features to include within a Gantt chart are:

- Milestone symbols
- Overdue indicators
- Legend to note details, such as review type
- Notes

> Depending on the version of Microsoft Excel, there might be a limit to the number of columns available if you were to do a column for each day of the project. Check the product documentation for exact details. In addition, how do you handle the dates for weekends unless the project activities run seven days a week?

In all cases, the Gantt chart should be easy to comprehend. For example, a chart for a project lasting a year might be broken up into monthly increments (sections) for presentations rather than having one long chart.

If a Gantt chart is created using Microsoft's Project, there are many opportunities for modifying the "standard" style to accommodate local preferences. Some of the possibilities include the following:

- Editing
  ○ Text
  ○ Headings
  ○ Bar height
  ○ Bar style (color, shape, or pattern)
  ○ Link line appearances
- Formatting
  ○ Text and heading styles
  ○ Activity (task) categories
  ○ Bars
  ○ Time scales
  ○ Gridlines
- Sorting a view
- Copying
  ○ Graphics between Gantt charts
  ○ Graphics from other Microsoft products
  ○ Graphics to other Microsoft products

When a Gantt chart is used effectively, it can, in a simple manner, display the means for tracking the three areas of interest of the customer and of management:

schedule, performance, and cost. As to the schedule, the chart displays start and end dates for major activities. The performance as to percentage of work is displayed through the shading of the bars. Cost status is indicated through milestone symbols.

[B]   Constructing a Simple Gantt Chart

There are nine steps in constructing a simple Gantt chart in an Excel worksheet.

1. Starting with the second column, place the project timeline across the first row (days, weeks, and so forth).

2. Beginning with the second row, list the tasks (major tasks could be made bold and subtasks light) in the first column.

3. Using the color option, format the rows to represent the durations of tasks in a dark color (update using a light color). Also, consider placing the name of the group team or person in charge of completing the task for easy future reference.

4. Select the cell or cells you want to format.

5. Click Format on the Menu bar.

6. Click on Cells.

7. Click on Patterns.

8. Under Cell Shading Color, click colored box of preference.

9. Click on OK.

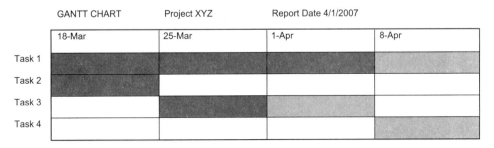

Chart 6-5: Sample Gantt Chart in Excel

§ 6.08   PERT/CPM TECHNIQUES

Program Evaluation and Review Technique (PERT) was developed for the U.S. Navy's Polaris submarine project. The Navy established four requirements for PERT:

1. Rules to establish events and activities in logical sequence

2. Clear visualization of activities

3. Three basic time estimate levels:
   - Optimistic
   - Probable (most likely)
   - Pessimistic

4. Ability to compute critical path and slack time (CPM)

The time estimates used in PERT have been given statistical definitions. Optimistic time (o) improves only 1 in 20 while pessimistic time (p) exceeds this ratio. Probable is the most likely value of occurrence (m). A common formula for determining an activity's mean duration (d) is:

$$d = (o + 4m + p)/6$$

Every IT project has at least four activity interactions to manage:

1. Activities are interdependent.

2. Some activities are performed at the same time.

3. Some activities must be completed prior to others.

4. All activities require some type of resource (skills, equipment, or materials).

From this logic comes the idea that some activities are more important, or more critical, to the timely completion of the project than are others. Knowledge of this critical path's activities and duration can control and manage the project's direction.

PERT is beneficial in developing scenarios for evaluating project changes, or risk analysis. The project manager may, for instance, do performance and resource trade-offs to identify potential project bottlenecks.

A statistically oriented person can determine the probabilities for meeting activities at a given milestone. Statistics assist in smoothing out uncertainty.

PERT, as a visual presentation, can assist in discussions with customers and project team members about apparent issues on the project. It becomes a standard of communications. What is necessary is an acceptance of all parties to use this technique.

[A] Negative Side of PERT/CPM

Following are some negative aspects that have occurred since PERT's introduction:

- Early forced federal government compliance
- Early software based on linear principles
- Needed resource extensions (1962)
- Introduction of the "earned-value" concept (1963)
- Labor-intensive
- Need for customer orientation definition (1990s)
- Too complex
- Too rigid
- Technique that may produce too much detail

[B] Basic Features and Functions of PERT/CPM Techniques

PERT and CPM each have a unique definition of duration. PERT uses ranges of durations. CPM uses averages of durations based on historical data.

Slack time is the difference between earliest and latest (start or finish) times for an activity or event. Total slack is the amount of time that can be lost without delaying the project's overall schedule. There is no slack time on the critical path. Four basic functions are available with any PERT/CPM software:

- Calculate earliest and latest dates.
- Plot network activity diagrams.
- Print out reports.
- Recalculate data based on new input.

CPM uses one of two methods for representing activities and events. The method to use is a matter of preference, and both may be used. The two methods are:

- Activity on arrow
- Activity on node

Both use circles and arrows. With the activity-on-arrow method (AOA), the activity is represented by the arrow, while the circle represents the event. With the activity-on-node method (AON), the activity is represented by the circle, while the arrow represents precedence between the activities.

A variation of the activity-on-node method is to use boxes to identify network precedence. This method is becoming more common in CPM software.

[C] Basic Terminology of PERT/CPM Techniques

The terminology of PERT/CPM techniques is expressed visually in symbols. In Chart 6-6:

- Circle represents an event.
- Arrow represents an activity.
- Number in circle represents event number.
- Text above activity arrow represents duration.

In Chart 6-6, event A has to be completed prior to the completion of event B. The events are numbered without necessarily meaning sequence. It takes two weeks to complete customer documentation after testing is completed.

Chart 6-6: Basic PERT Terms: Event and Activity

As shown in the following figures, one activity might flow into another activity; however, there are two other scenarios: Two or more activities flow into one another, or one activity flows into two or more activities.

The PERT term for the first scenario is "sink," while for the second it is "burst." (See Charts 6-7 and 6-8.)

One of the weaknesses of a Gantt chart is that the relationships among events cannot be shown. This is possible with PERT. Chart 6-9 is a simple Gantt chart with just the bars and event numbers. Charts 6-10 and 6-11 show this Gantt chart converted to a basic PERT activity diagram with potential relationships. Durations between activities are omitted. Note that Chart 6-11 is the same as 6-10, but with the critical path shown with bold arrows. Charts 6-10 and 6-11 both clearly show the start-start and end-start relationships not discernible from Chart 6-9. Chart 6-12 is a Gantt chart created using Microsoft Project, to give you an idea of what one looks like.

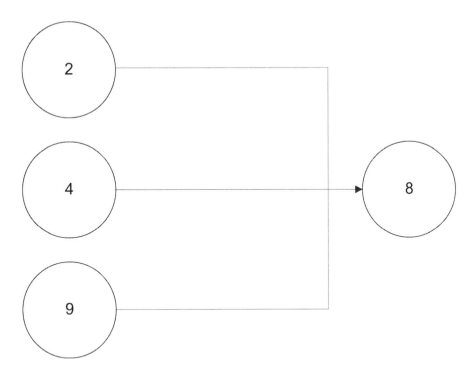

Chart 6-7: Sink Scenario

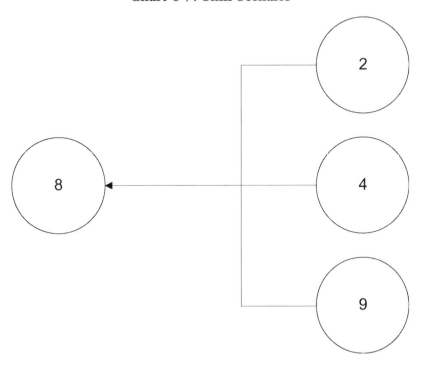

Chart 6-8: Burst Scenario

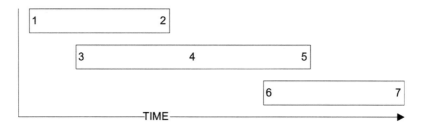

Chart 6-9: Basic Gantt Chart

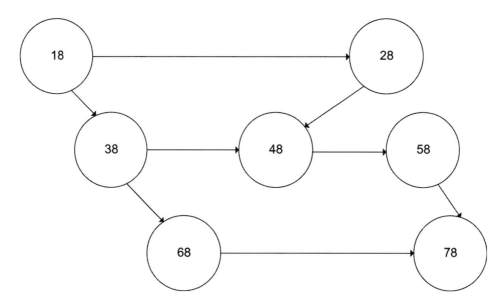

Chart 6-10: Gantt Chart Converted to a Basic PERT Chart

[D] Determining Slack Time

For every task in the schedule, identify the earliest day it can start and the latest day it can start without delaying the project. This will take some time, and experienced project managers will let the project management software do it for them.

To identify the earliest start date, begin with the first task in the project and identify the earliest that each task can begin. The first task starts on day #1 and its end date is its estimated duration plus the start date. Work through each leg of the network and begin each task as soon as its prerequisites are ready.

To identify the latest start date, start with the last task in the project network and work backward. As each task is encountered, identify this as its end date. Subtract the duration from its end date to determine its latest start date. Work through the entire project network in this way.

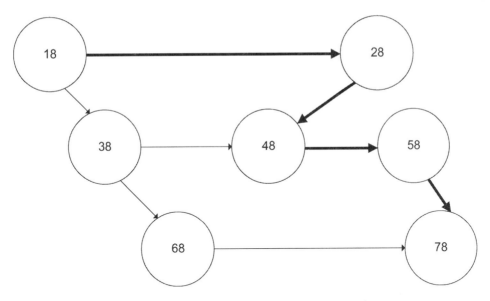

Chart 6-11: Critical Path on a PERT Chart

ID	Task Name	Duration	Start	Finish	31, '06							Jan 7, '07							Jan 14, '07							Jan
					M	T	W	T	F	S	S	M	T	W	T	F	S	S	M	T	W	T	F	S	S
1	Task 1	2 days	Wed 1/3/07	Thu 1/4/07																					
2	Task 2	4 days	Mon 1/8/07	Thu 1/11/07																					
3	Task 3	6 days	Tue 1/9/07	Tue 1/16/07																					

Chart 6-12: Gantt Chart Using Microsoft Project

Most tasks will have longer time available to complete than is required by the time duration estimate. This is slack time. The path of the tasks through the project plan with zero slack time is the critical path (both its early and late start dates). Anything that delays a task along the critical path will lengthen the time duration of the entire project. Conversely, this is where the project manager goes to shorten the project. However, shorten one critical path and expect another to appear elsewhere in the project.

§ 6.09   REFINING A SCHEDULE

"It is a bad plan that cannot be altered."

—Publius Syrus (1st century B.C.)

A project schedule is an important communications tool between the project manager and the various stakeholders. What is the best way of presenting integrated activities with a timeline so that it communicates clearly the expected outcomes?

Schedule completion checklist:

- Have the who, what, where, and how been clearly defined and placed in the schedule? This activity also includes the when.

- Have the people who can have an impact on or approve the schedule been identified? The schedule should indicate when people come into and leave the project.

- Have the project's milestone start and end times been confirmed? Have expected deliverables been identified?

- Are the essential scheduled milestones realistic? Consider the stated assumptions, constraints, and risks to estimate the amount of contingency required for each milestone. The more uncertainty there is about task durations, the greater contingency time that is required.

- Have the quality control events been included at the appropriate milestones?

- How will the schedule and its changes be communicated to the customers? Someone may be depending on the project completing no later than the original schedule date.

- Can resources be acquired on time? Is there historical data available to determine adequate resources? The schedule should have the flexibility to handle the procurement of outside resources (skills, equipment, and materials). There should be time in the schedule to complete any required procurement.

- Sometimes the use of historical data can be important in establishing a schedule. For example, the project management office may have kept records on how long it took to do the configuration for various applications in an intranet. The figure(s) can be used as a benchmark(s). A better set of figures, of course, would include information on what skill level was required to do the configurations.

[A] Aligning the Schedule

Collect all of the individual task duration estimates before creating the schedule. After the sponsor hears the projected completion date, the sponsor often demands to shorten the time to complete the project. Since all of the individual tasks are included in the schedule, changes consider all areas. Consider these seven actions for shortening a schedule:

- Work with the customer to see how concrete the end date is. If the customer is going to lose a large sum of money because of project failure, then it is no-go. Compare the potential loss to the cost of adding resources to rush the project.

- Check with the customer about completing the project in segments. Determine how critical timing is to achieving the project goals. Perhaps a basic product can be delivered and then nonessential features added to a later version.

- Consider reducing functionality. Identify the critical and the nice-to-have features. Focus the project on the critical functions.

- Consider adding people. The customer needs to understand the effect on the price. Adding people adds time for coordination and training. If the project is in the late stages, this will take more time than it will save.

- Consider subcontracting some of the functionality. This is a variation on adding people.

- Waive organizational standards. Consider (with higher management's approval) ignoring organizational rules, such as adjusting staff members' hours or limiting paperwork requirements.

- Work on more tasks in parallel. Examine the project for tasks that can be moved from the critical path. Instead of starting documentation after the product is finished and tested, begin writing it as modules are completed. Instead of waiting for a radio frequency (RF) network to be completed before training on RF scan guns, set up a single RF node and train users in advance. A quick brush-up at installation time will shorten the project rollout.

If none of the seven possibilities works to realign the schedule to the customer's satisfaction, there is one more option: just say no. The customer will consider the project manager has more integrity than if the schedule was attempted and failed. It also forces the customer to reconsider the options.

[B] Correcting a Schedule

This four-step approach can be used to make corrections:

1. Analyze the schedule from end to end to identify inconsistencies, omissions, or implausible values.

2. Determine the course of action to make the correction.

3. Revise the areas that require correction.

4. Evaluate the new schedule for impacts.

Some activity is going to come in late. There are two types of slippage, the expected and the unexpected. The expected slippage is known before the due date. The unexpected slippage is reported after the due date. The project manager can manage the first, while the second is a no-no on the part of an operational manager.

Prevent the second type through open discussions at status meetings. Discuss this type of failure in private with the offending manager. The project manager finds out why no one told them before the problem occurred. Consider an unexpected slippage as worse than being late. Not to be informed that a programmer who was expected to work on a project activity quit and a suitable replacement has not been found is a significant example of an unexpected slippage. Actions to resolve a slippage include the following:

- Consider extension of the schedule.

- Consider overtime as a last resort; the budget quickly overruns and the people will eventually burn out.

- Negotiate a reduction in the affected project goal; have supporting data.

- Correct in private, but be firm.

- Discover the extent of the slippage's impact; it may be minimal.

- Do not throw more resources at the project to correct the slippage; there is a learning curve to consider.

- Look for shortcuts or different approaches to accomplish the activity.

- Use project management software to develop various scenarios for possible solutions.

Use overtime for occasional catch-up of a task. Working continual overtime will only cause the people to slow down. In essence, more time is spent to achieve the normal 40 hours of result. If the team members wear out on the project, further time is lost training their replacements.

---

§ 6.10   SUMMARY

A schedule is a visual presentation of time-oriented project tasks. It is the baseline for gauging project progress and performance. It is to time as the budget is to cost.

The schedule is supported by a series of calendars. These are projections of resources, tasks, and significant company dates against the calendars that represent the days that a project exists.

All managers have an interest in the use of Gantt charts. A Gantt chart can be a simple tool that displays activities in comparison to timelines, or spending activities in comparison to cost estimates.

PERT, as a visual presentation, can assist in discussions with customers and project team members about apparent issues on the project. It becomes a standard of communications. What is necessary is an acceptance of all parties to use this technique.

Remember that software only speeds up the opportunity to do scenarios. It does not manage the project. In addition, remember to remind higher-level managers and customers that data must be entered before the software can be used effectively. The secret of success will always be experience.

Exhibit 6-1: Schedule Planning Questions Checklist

Project Name:	Comments
1. Is historical data available to determine adequate resources?	
2. Are the essential scheduled milestones realistic?	
3. Are the timelines consistent and coherent?	
4. Can resources be acquired on time?	
5. Have the people who can have an impact on or approve the schedule been identified?	
6. Have the quality control events been included at appropriate milestones?	
7. Have the start and end times been confirmed? Have expected deliverables been identified?	
8. Have the whos, whats, and hows been clearly defined and placed in the schedule?	
9. How are the budgetary procedures going to affect the schedule?	
10. How can the formulated schedule impact the outcome of integration?	
11. How will the schedule and its changes be given to the customers?	
12. Is the schedule based on a pessimistic, realistic, or optimistic view?	
13. Is the schedule based on the scope definition?	

Exhibit 6-1: *(Continued)*

14. Is there a change notification process for the schedule?	
15. Is there a quality control and validation schedule?	
16. Is there a requirement for a critical path?	
17. Is there a timeline for acquiring skills, equipment, and materials?	
18. Is time allocated for risk management?	
19. What are the criteria for changing the schedule?	
20. What type of timeline is required (calendar, flowchart)?	

Exhibit 6-2: Checklist for Creating a Project Schedule

	Attachments
Scenarios for each task	
Pessimistic	
Realistic	
Optimistic	
Critical path	
Duration	
Production time	
Wait time	
Lag time	
Lead time	
Dependencies	
Start-start	
Start-end	
End-start	
End-end	

Exhibit 6-2: *(Continued)*

Slack time	
Calendar structure	
Tasks	
Resources	
Spending	
Procurement	
Training	
Documentation	
Links to:	
Resources	
Skills	
Responsible people	
Project scope plan	
Measurable goals	
Assumptions	
Constraints	
Design and development plan	
Activity plan	
Resource plan	
Task relationships	
Major milestones	
Deliverables	
Milestones (Gates)	
Deadlines	
Communications milestones	
Logistics	
Location	
Milestones	
Reviews	

Exhibit 6-2: *(Continued)*

Quality events	
Control	
Assurance	
Budget	
Vendor	
Status presentations	
Schedule characteristics	
Readable	
Usable	
Reliable	
Consistent	
Coherent	
Manageable level of details	
24 × 7 mode used	
Resource leveling	
Aligned	
Graphics to highlight events	
Colors	
Icons	
Note indicators	
Company requirements	
Customer requirements	
Gantt chart requirements	
Estimates versus actual report	

Instructions for a Project Schedule Checklist

This checklist is used to assist the project team in creating the project schedule. It is to be used by each operational manager to prepare a schedule at a group or departmental level.

Exhibit 6-2: *(Continued)*

When the word "activity" is used, the reference is at the operational level, while "task" is used in reference to the project schedule. When "event" is used, it is in reference to a point in time at the start date for an activity or task for a milestone.

The core question for the design, development, and implementation of any schedule is "What is the most logical method of presenting integration tasks based on reliable estimates with a timeline so long that it communicates clearly the measurable project goals?" The essential principal in responding to this question or these instructions is to keep it simple.

The project schedule needs to be approved prior to refining the cost estimates and developing the project budget.

Task by scenario: The task-level detail used must be manageable in that the schedule has to be readable, useful, and reliable. Any detail must be given in three forms: pessimistic, realistic, and optimistic. This means if you have a start-end block, then you must have three sets of dates. The ordering of the scenario is a local issue; however, it must be consistent throughout the schedule and departmental schedules. Another possibility is to have three separate schedules when using a simple linear graphic.

Critical path: A path is critical when there is no available time for the slippage of the activity or task (no slack time). The critical path method (CPM) in its simplest form is selecting the "must" activities and tasks, doing them in the shortest possible amount of time, and covering the shortest duration. A critical task is a task that is not so complicated that it results in project failure.

Duration: The schedule is the duration of the project. It is the total involved time of an activity or task that is production time plus wait time. A project's duration is the total number of calendar days involved from start to end, including the project manager's activities in closing the project.

Production time: Since a schedule should use the 24×7 mode, production time at any activity level can be stated in hourly or daily increments.

Wait time: The duration minus production time.

Lag time: The time between two activities or tasks because of their natures.

Lead time: The overlapping time of two activities or tasks.

Dependencies: A dependency is an event. An event is a point in time such as the start or end of an activity or task.

Start-start: One activity or task must start before another.

Start-end: An activity or task must begin before another can end.

End-start: An activity or task must end before another can start.

Slack time: The difference between the earliest and latest (start or finish) times for an activity or task.

Calendar structure: A schedule must be related to the Gregorian calendar in contrast to using effort.

Sequence integration: The most important activity or task sequence is, of course, the critical path. All other sequences should be related to it.

Exhibit 6-2: *(Continued)*

Tasks or activities: Task sequences are used at the project schedule level, while activities are used at the operational level.

Resources: Use the icons as determined by the project team plus a note indicator. The icon is a visual clue, while the note indicator permits text to be placed in a supplemental document such as details for the resource plan. There may be a number of icons such as critical hardware, software, materials, and skills.

Spending: As resources.

Procurement: As resources.

Training: As resources.

Documentation: As resources.

Links to: Use note indications and a special link icon as determined by the project team.

Resources: Resources are the tactical ones such as hardware, software, and support materials (do not forget the pencil and paper).

Skills: The link must reference the skill type and its level to a person.

Responsible people: This group includes the customer representative, corporate manager for the project, the project manager, the project team members, the operational manager, and consultants.

Project scope plan: The strategic view of the constraints and assumptions of the project as developed by the project team.

Measurable goals: These goals are from the scope plan.

Assumptions: Predictions that something will be true; an event that ensures project success.

Constraints: Parameters, limitations, or boundaries for the project.

Design and development plan: Drives the project integration plan that captures all major design and development deliverables and milestones for management tracking and reporting.

Activity plan: At the operational level, an activity plan is a set of definitions. A definition includes the activity's constraints from the scope plan. At the schedule level, the definitions are for tasks.

Resource plan: The source document for identifying all the assumptions and constraints for the use of all the resources.

Task relationships: Relationships can be either between different organizations or within one organization.

Major milestones: Use the icons defined by the project team.

Deliverables: Clearly defined project results, products, or services; outcomes.

Milestones (Gates): A milestone is a clearly defined date of start or 100 percent completion. A gate is another term for milestone of a major project team.

Deadlines: Absolute dates; the critical sequence dependencies.

Communications milestones: The critical points in the process of getting the correct information to the correct location at the correct time. No indicators should be used to reflect

Exhibit 6-2: *(Continued)*

the specifics of the event such as a project management review. It is a regularly scheduled performance review.

Logistics: The process of getting the correct resource to the correct location at the correct time.

Reviews: All dates or events for management and technical reviews should be noted.

Quality events: The schedule quality events should be in two sequences. The control sequence includes the events for gathering and distributing information for or about the project. The assurance sequence includes the events for validation and testing based on performance.

Budget: Identify critical funding or spending milestones based on the finalized budget. This possibly is the final act to be completed in the project schedule, beyond updates.

Vendor: A vendor has a product, while a consultant has information or services.

Status presentations: These include the customer, upper-level management, and the team.

Schedule characteristics: These characteristics may be abstract; thus, agreement as to meanings should be by consensus of the project team.

Readable: The level of detail should not be so broad that an event cannot be identified easily.

Usable: The schedule should be so useful that it is the basis for status presentations.

Reliable: The time estimates must be valid.

Consistent: The use of icons and colors should be the same, whether on the project schedule or on operational schedules.

Coherent: Events and task sequences should be synchronized.

Manageable level of details: Details at the project schedule level should be tasks, while at the operational level the details are based on activities.

24 × 7 mode used: The schedule should be given in a 24 × 7 mode because some of the logistic events may occur at any time. In addition, critical tasks such as customer presentations may be identified in hours rather than 6 days.

Resource leveling: This technique is used to smooth out peaks and valleys for the employment of resources.

Aligned: Alignment is another form of leveling, except absolute dates are used.

Graphics to highlight events: Graphic standards are determined by the project team. However, red and green should be used only to highlight a negative or positive situation.

Colors: The colors are determined by the project team. Do not use red or green except to highlight significant negative and positive events.

Icons: The icons are determined by the project team. Icons are an excellent way to distinguish between types of links.

Note indicators: As determined by the project team.

Company requirements: Based on a company policy or standard for a schedule's format.

Customer requirements: A special schedule might be done based on the customer's specific requirements. The requirements are a measurable goal of the project.

Exhibit 6-2: *(Continued)*

Gantt chart requirements: A Gantt chart is a visual presentation, a horizontal bar chart, of activities or tasks against time. A histogram is the opposite of a Gantt chart because vertical bars are used to represent values.

Estimates versus actual report: This report should be updated at milestones and prior to any briefing with the customer or upper-level management.

Chapter 7

Budget Development

§ 7.01   INTRODUCTION

Project sponsors typically do not understand the technology that they are paying for. They cannot judge if the project is advancing sufficiently or if it is faltering. The two things they can understand are the project schedule and the budget. For most sponsors, a schedule is either ahead or behind. They do not understand the technical reasons for this. However, a budget is something they deal with regularly in their business. Since it is a part of management they understand it, and they focus on it almost exclusively.

> "With many calculations, one can win; with few one cannot. How much less chance of victory has one who makes none at all! By this means, I examine the situation and the outcome will be clearly apparent."
>
> —Sun Tzu (6th century B.C.), *The Act of War*

Another reason project sponsors emphasize budgets is that their bosses have approved it. If the budget is inadequate for the project, then the sponsor must explain why they did not ask for enough money to run the project. They would rather pressure the project manager to cut corners and stay within the approved financial boundaries. If the project manager has diligently worked on the project estimates, then the sponsor will avoid many budget problems.

Creating a budget is easy once the tasks are estimated. The individual numbers are recorded and applied to a timeline. The result is a report detailing the cash requirements for the project, per month. During its existence, a project could have three different budgets:

- The initial budget is an estimate created along with the project proposal to provide an idea of the expected project costs. The estimate is based on some historical measure of cost and the project's scope plan. It provides the project sponsor with the general magnitude of the expense. The goal of the initial budget is to be within 25 percent (plus or minus) of the final cost.

- The project baseline budget is approved at the beginning of the project. It is the "official" amount to be paid for the project. All future efforts will be judged compared to the amount originally approved. If a thorough analysis of the project uncovered all hidden issues, then this budget should be within 10 percent (plus or minus) of the actual amount required.

- The project operating budget is the "working" budget for managing the project. It began as the baseline budget. During the project, it expands to include approved changes to the baseline budget and budget variances (plus *and* minus). Management reports compare this budget to the baseline budget to determine if the project will require additional funding.

§ 7.02   BUDGETS BEGIN WITH COST ESTIMATES

Cost estimates establish the amount to be set aside for a task based on constraints and assumptions. The cost of a task is typically the labor (hourly rate times the estimated effort) and materials (such as a new server, cables, etc.) required. Most project plans apply overhead (the project manager, etc.) to the plan as a whole and not to individual tasks.

Cost estimates are for an average amount. If each activity's budget estimate is made for a 99 percent accuracy rate, then the budget will be heavily

> padded and probably there will be those inclined to spend every penny of it. If the money is not wasted away, then when the next project is started, the percentage of the money turned in from the previous project will be deducted from the new one!

Cost estimates consider both tangible and intangible costs. A tangible cost is using known rates (hourly, weekly, monthly, or fixed) for the services of people involved in the project. A related intangible cost is the impact of the skill levels of the same people. An expert costs more in the long term than a novice. If the expert is paid $100 per hour and a novice $20 per hour, the expert would have to produce at a rate five times as fast as the novice does. The intangible is the quality comparison; an expert who produces a higher-quality product may well be worth the extra cost. Therefore, it is very important to compare tangible costs against potential intangible costs.

[A]   Basic Cost-Estimating Approaches

Four basic approaches for creating a budget are as follows:

- The person assigned to perform the task should provide an estimate and the details of what drives the cost. This is known as the bottom-up approach. Its virtue is that the "expert" who will be working the problem is the one providing the estimate. If multiple experts are available, use a consensus approach where each person provides an estimate and the group selects one. This approach smoothes out the optimistic and pessimistic estimates.

- The analogous approach uses historical data to create estimates based on what was used before. It is used when there is a limited amount of information about the project, such as in the early stages of working with new technology. It relies heavily on expert judgment. It is less expensive and time consuming to use, but also less accurate. Analogous estimation has the advantage of identifying the cost of resources actually required instead of creating an estimate. Of course, each situation is unique, so the historical information requires some interpretation.

- A parametric modeling approach is based on industry standards—for example, a line of code costs a set number of dollars and a program of this type typically has a set number of lines. Although its imprecision is immediately obvious, it still provides a better basis for estimating than a simple guess does.

- Top-down budgeting is where executives estimate the cost of a project based on similar projects conducted by the company. Of course, what sounds the same to them can be a very different animal in reality. This approach should have a large contingency fund to account for variables of opinion.

Cost estimates can fail due to unrealistic time estimates. No business manager or customer ever believes a project will cost as estimated. When confronted with a negative response to project cost estimates, respond with strong supporting justification.

If an estimate is excessive, find out why. Check other tasks estimated by that person to see if they were estimated in the same way. Making a single large correction to the budget is easier than many small ones.

> Budgets enable the accounting and finance departments to project the cash requirements for a given month. These groups are charged to not spend more money than the company has (thereby generating a need for a loan) or allow idle cash to pile up. It can be annoying when these organizations push back on budget requests. By understanding a bit about their work environment, the project manager can present a more persuasive argument for funding project budget shortfalls.

[B] Cost Estimating Versus Budgeting

Some comparisons worth noting between cost estimating and budgeting are as follows:

- Cost estimates are inputs into budget, while budget items are inputs into the table of accounts.

- Cost estimating is a component of budgeting; budgeting is the formal structuring of many activities that include activities of the project at one level of the corporate budget.

- Cost estimating is a consequence of analyzing; budgeting is a consequence of planning.

- Cost estimating is concerned with an individual activity or groups of related activities, while budgeting is concerned with the complete project.

- Cost estimating is to the budget as time estimating is to the schedule.

- Cost estimating uses the duration of a single activity or a group of related activities, while budgeting is the method used to frame the spending plan within a calendar usually based on monthly increments and accounting categories.

One final point about cost estimates: *Never give a casual one*. A project manager may find later that such an estimate has been considered a commitment and he or she may be held to it.

§ 7.03 CREATING COST ESTIMATES

When developing cost estimates, there are six principles to making cost estimating more methodical. The following is a list of these principles that might assist in this activity.

1. Carefully review personnel costs. If the organization uses internal chargeback for personnel, ensure that only people with the appropriate skill sets and skill levels are assigned to the project. Too low skills will hamper the project. Too high skills will cost too much.

    If internal personnel costs are high, do not hesitate to use outside personnel instead. This will not make the project manager popular with other company managers, but it will keep the project within its budget. Often a credible threat to use outsiders will soften internal chargebacks to the same price range. Also, a fixed bid for outsiders to complete a task provides a number to negotiate with internal sources.

2. Base cost estimates on average production. The human resources department should have data on the average hourly cost for a labor classification such as for programmers. This also sets a minimum expectation when a better-than-average worker is available.

3. Before cutting the budget, complete all the task cost estimates, and then total them. In this way, people will not feel that all tasks were considered equally for reduction. This will maintain a sense of fairness on the project team.

    Revise cost estimates from the least to the largest. Challenge the higher estimates after the lower estimates are changed and there are no significant results. When judging a cost, focus on the factors that drive that cost.

4. Factor in the possibilities of the price increases in developing the original cost estimates. Until they actually occur, anything can happen, but once the budget is set, it is difficult to reopen it for negotiation.

5. Use knowledgeable and objective people to conduct cost-estimate reviews. Reviews of the cost estimates should be by knowledgeable people who are not a part of establishing the original numbers. This team should be looking for "padding."

6. Collect all contingency amounts together in one place. If there is padding, it should be an up-front activity and be labeled as a contingency fund. Padding individual activities tends to create a use-it-or-lose-it mentality, and money is spent for dubious reasons. In addition, extracting such resources from individual tasks and concentrating the resources into a project-wide fund makes the contingency funds available where needed. Once the budget is included in the

company's financial projections, it is hard to increase, so ensure contingency funds are included in the initial budget.

> Executives do not like to approve contingency funds. They are concerned that the money will be used to cover up errors and that later audits will hold them responsible for how the funds were used. However, this fund greatly eases project administration. Without it, there will be numerous small requests for additional funds. This "death by 1,000 cuts" reflects poorly on the project manager.

§ 7.04   REFINING COST ESTIMATES

[A]   Using a Cost-Estimates Checklist

Invalid cost estimates are a major cause of project failure. However, the source of the failure may be because of two factors: invalid time estimates and the assumption that costs are discrete data; that is, a range of costs is not needed. Use Exhibit 7-1: Cost Estimates Checklist to consider both of these problems.

Even when there is a single piece of hardware with a "fixed" catalog value, there has to be a cost estimate that includes the pessimistic, realistic, and optimistic scenarios. The pessimistic estimate includes the effects of not having the hardware, while the optimistic considers having an even better piece of hardware if it is available.

> The first assumption for the design and development of the checklist and its instructions is that there must be a separate project budget, even if in actuality the various budget items are "hidden" within the IT group's budget because of corporate constraints. Use a separate management document to control the financial issues and to demonstrate the project's efficiency.
>
> *Warning*: Shoddy cost estimates hit the project budget in the same manner as inferior time estimates impact the project schedule. However, upper-level management tends to view a schedule as a management tool, but a budget is a document that is set in stone.

Exhibit 7-1: Cost Estimates Checklist

	Attachments
Cost estimates by scenario	
Pessimistic	
Realistic	
Optimistic	
Criteria by scenario	
Pessimistic	
Realistic	
Optimistic	
Impacts by scenario	
Pessimistic	
Realistic	
Optimistic	
Estimates by project goals	
Source ID	
Critical path estimates	
Procurement	
Hardware	
Software	
Consultants	
Special materials	
Skills	
Training	
Procurement	
Internal resources	
Support tasks	
Documentation tasks	
Production tasks	
Planning	
Design	
Development	
Testing	
Noncritical path estimates	
Procurement	
Hardware	
Software	
Consultants	
Special materials	
Skills	
Training	
Procurement	
Internal resources	
Support tasks	
Documentation tasks	
Production tasks	
Planning	
Design	

Exhibit 7-1: *(Continued)*

Development	
Testing	
Defined assumptions used	
Defined constraints used	
Deliverables accounted for	
Budget requirements used	
Deadline criteria	
Time estimates inputs	
Quality	
Control	
Assurance	
Validation	
Field testing	
Resource cost tools	
Equipment	
Internal	
External	
Materials	
Internal	
External	
Skills	
Internal	
External	
Approximate headcount	
Project management tools	
Internal	
External	
Development tools	
Internal	
External	
Facilities	
Internal	
External	
Logistics	
Internal	
External	
Training cost totals	
Internal	
External	
Documentation cost totals	
Internal	
External	
Communications cost totals	
Internal	
External	
Travel	
Risk management	
Project administration	
Links to time estimates	
Incremental spending periods	
One time	
Monthly	
Quarterly	
Vendor pricing	
Fixed	

Exhibit 7-1: *(Continued)*

Variants from fixed	
Dependency	
Project goals	
Project milestones	
Task milestones	
Learning curve	
Special event	
Tradeoff considerations	
Cost-benefit analysis	
Part-time staff	
Full-time staff	
Other	
Contingency plan	
Special customer support	
Special variants noted	
Consistency to:	
Scope plan	
Activity plan	
Resource plan	
Project plan	
Business justification	
Commercial specification	
Design/Development plan	
Market analysis report	
Trial (Beta) strategy	
Request for proposal	
Funding source approval	

Instructions for a Cost-Estimates Checklist

Cost estimates by scenario: All project cost estimates must be given in three forms: pessimistic, realistic, and optimistic. Actual format instructions come from the project team. All the estimates need to reflect items given in this checklist. A part of this task is to get a draft set of estimates. Second, these estimates are refined using outside assistance, if necessary. Third, refine the estimates to determine if they are affordable for the customer. As a part of the refinements, a confidence level should be stated for each one.

Criteria by scenario: There should be objective data to support the three types of estimates. The sources for the criteria include standards, benchmarks, historical records, or project team requirements.

Impacts by scenario: There should be explanations for each of the estimate types. For example, the estimate is pessimistic because no one is immediately available at this time with the skill level to do the task in less than three months. Another example is if the pessimistic estimate happens, then "X" risk may happen by affecting other estimates.

Estimates by project goals: Estimates should be linked to the project's goals as found in the project scope plan.

Source ID: Identify the person responsible for writing the time estimates, including title, e-mail address, and telephone number. If an external source, also include company information.

Exhibit 7-1: *(Continued)*

Critical path estimates: For the listed items, give the justifications for being designated critical.

Noncritical path estimates: For the items listed, give the formulas and their sources, plus relevant standards or benchmarks for estimates.

Defined assumptions: Use the assumptions from the scope plan to develop estimates.

Defined constraints: Use the constraints from the scope plan to develop estimates.

Deliverables: Give links to project deliverables for each estimate.

Budget requirements: Use the project budget requirements as defined by the project team. Check for rules of aggregation of cost estimates.

Deadline criteria: Use deadline criteria, as defined by the project team, based on the scope plan.

Time estimates inputs: There should be objective data to support time estimates. If the duration of a realistic estimate for a linked task is too short or too long for your function, what are the potential impacts? For example, if "X" training course is more than two weeks in length, there will be serious impacts such as "Y."

Quality: Give any possible estimates that you consider relevant to the listed areas that might be required for product validation or field testing. Justification should be included, such as reference to a standard or benchmark.

Resource cost totals: If a resource (hardware, software, skill, or support material) has to be acquired from an external source, give estimates for the procurement tasks (such as negotiation that includes travel and direct administrative costs). Internal costs may have to be budgeted to another corporate functional group such as training or documentation.

Travel: Give costs as to airplane, hotel, meals, and car rental. Justify requirements based on data given earlier with this form.

Risk management: Consider if a pessimistic scenario breaks down, the possible time required for correcting.

Project administration: Based on the project team requirements, give estimates. In addition, consider time estimates for giving status reports to the operational team by either e-mail or status presentations.

Special Cost-Estimate Criteria

Links to time estimates: Define links as they relate to costs. In addition, give links as appropriate to the project schedule.

Incremental spending periods: You must give spending increments based on the project schedule. Quarterly can be defined by the project team as either a three-month period of the project's duration or a calendar quarter.

Vendor Pricing:

Fixed: Justify the reasons a price is fixed for such items as hardware or training courses. Determine if the vendor is "buying the job."

Exhibit 7-1: *(Continued)*

Variants from fixed: Give the justifications for cost for a lesser item and a better item. In addition, consider the cost impacts of not getting the product.

Dependency: When appropriate, give the dependency requirements for the listed items. An example is a goal that must be completed before spending is required. A second example is spending that must be done before a milestone or event can be started. Give the cost impacts if a learning curve shortens or lengthens the time.

Tradeoff Considerations:

Cost-benefit analysis: When appropriate, work with the marketing group to do an analysis that serves as a standard for the estimate.

Part-time staff: State such as one hour per day or once a week. Justify the use of a part-time staff over the use of a full-time staff.

Full-time staff: Give impacts of having full time versus part time. Justify the use of a full-time staff over a part-time staff.

Other: Identify whether there is a need for a consultant or any other outside staff.

Contingency plan: Give justifications for including a contingency amount and the potential requirements. This plan formalizes padding.

Special customer support: Include the possible "hidden" costs for corporate training; including travel.

Special variants: Give any additional information that might assist the project team in its responsibilities and minimize further discussions.

Consistency to: There should be links in the justifications or impacts to the listed documents.

Scope plan: The strategic view of the constraints and assumptions of the project as developed by the project team.

Activity plan: A set of definitions for efforts required to achieve measurable results. At the operational level, you consider activities, at the project level, tasks.

Resource plan: Establish support requirements for a project as to costs, availability, start date and end date (length of time for use plus duration), and technical specifications.

Project schedule: Formalizes the time estimates within a calendar structure. It is an integration of sequencing tasks, resource planning, cost estimating, and time estimating.

Business justification: The general rationale for making the financial investment.

Commercial specification: An evolution of the business justification. It identifies the market need and gives adequate requirement and limitation data for the design and development group(s).

Design and development plan: Drives the project integration plan that captures all major design and development deliverables and milestones for management tracking and reporting.

Market analysis report: Documents and verifies market opportunities and justifies the features, services, and applications for the project goals.

Exhibit 7-1: *(Continued)*

Trial (Beta) strategy: Identifies the software and hardware elements in the project that are a part of any trial.

Request for proposal (RFP): Ensure there is a contingency between the requirements of the RFP and the vendor's response. Ensure that response adheres to the requirements of this checklist.

Funding source approval: The funding source(s) must give a written agreement to the cost estimates.

§ 7.05   CONVERTING ESTIMATES INTO A BUDGET

A project budget is the estimated financial plan for a project, for which funding is required. This document includes both a list of expenses expected to be incurred during the project, as well as any income that may be generated during the project. A well-crafted budget can add significantly to management's understanding of the project.

The project budget could become important historical and benchmark data. It is recommended that any technical upgrades to the company's information system should be included in the IT operations budget (and not charged to the project). An IT project is an activity intended to support a customer's needs, not to support operational needs. Avoid mixing project expenses with those of the day-to-day operations.

> Some projects generate cash during execution. For example, a project to replace existing desktop units in a company may earn cash by selling the old units instead of sending them to the landfill. Although this is far less than the cost of the project, the cash inflow should be reflected in the budget.

[A]   Project Budget Versus Business Budget

Every project needs its own budget. An unfortunate practice is to enter individual project budget items as one combined item in the IT group budget or in the formal budget of each participating group of the project team.

Because of the differences between the perceptions of a project budget and a business budget, discuss the project budget outside the general budget reviews.

The project should be considered as an external or separate corporate effort. The differences between a project budget and a business budget are as follows:

- A project budget cannot easily determine unpredictable peak periods, while a business budget can be created to manage peak periods such as holiday sales or end-of-quarter requirements.

- A project budget cannot survive on underplanning, while a business budget might be able to (reason for third- and fourth-quarter reviews of budgets).

- A project budget does not have to consider long-term benefits, while a business budget usually does.

- A project budget is concerned with achieving goals, while a business budget's focus is profit.

- A project budget needs money to maximize resources, while the business budget baselines for minimum resources.

- A project budget needs to reflect skill requirements, while a business budget considers headcount.

- A project budget relies on contract services more than a business budget does.

- A project budget requires a place for contingencies, while a business budget usually does not.

- A project budget usually has limited financial histories to use as an estimating tool, while a business budget usually has at least last year's budget to use for planning or financial histories with similar functions.

Beware of the parasites! Unscrupulous team members, accounting clerks, and managers will charge their expenses to other projects. This is more likely to happen if the project manager is known as someone who keeps poor records! Monitor the project's monthly expenses, or by the time the project is far behind, it will be impossible to identify those who sank the project's budget.

The essential assumption of the checklist in Exhibit 7-2: Cost-Planning Checklist is that there must be a separate project budget. It does not necessarily have to be a part of the formal budget structure of the company, but it would make project management—and perhaps even the managing of IT financial issues—much easier if it was.

Exhibit 7-2: Cost-Planning Checklist

Project:	Date:			
Preparer:				
		YES	NO	EST.
PROJECT/SYSTEM LABOR COSTS				
Definition				
Design				
Impact on legacy infrastructure				
Software integration				
Documentation				
Training				
Tool support				
Configuration				
Quality control				
Support				
HARDWARE COSTS				
Planning				
Capital				
Training				
Installation				
Maintenance				
Legacy implications				
SOFTWARE COSTS				
Planning				
Operating system				
Installation				
Documentation				
Training				
Maintenance				
Legacy implications				
Support applications				
COMMUNICATIONS COSTS				
Planning				
Capital				
Equipment				
Installation				
Maintenance				
EXECUTION COSTS				
Travel and living				
Consultants				
Training				
Office supplies and materials				
CLIENT COSTS				
Team member involvement				
Meetings				
Training				
IMPLEMENTATION COSTS				
Travel and living				
Staff support				
Labor costs				
OTHER				

The checklist assists in the design and development of a budget. Always use the company's approved budget format. A project budget gives a visual financial status of the project and supportive evidence in a set of documents. It includes the source of funds, the amount to be spent by major task groups, and the month in which it is to be spent. If the financial components of a project are "hidden" within single or multiple lines of an IT budget, it is a struggle to keep matters correct.

> "The budget should be balanced. Public debt should be reduced. The arrogance of officialdom should be tempered, and assistance to foreign lands should be curtailed, lest Rome become bankrupt."
>
> —Marcus Tullius Cicero (106–43 B.C.)

§ 7.06   REVISING A BUDGET

Questions for cost estimating should be based on identified benchmarks—that is, a measurable activity or task—whenever possible. These questions need to reflect managing of actual, specific expenses (costs) against planned costs (budget).

The responses to the following questions should be based on the goals and deliverables for the project, and the activities or tasks necessary to achieve them. Think in terms of both an optimistic cost and a pessimistic cost, and then determine a reliable median cost. Cost estimates should be a range rather than a single value. This principle can reduce padding and help create a realistic financial contingency plan.

The following questions reflect the general cost-estimating process:

- Who is going to fund the various project activities? Is there a reporting system that links the appropriate people to the project costs and to the people with budgetary control? Always think of linkages in terms of cost estimates and budgets that should reflect these costs. Some people may confuse the daily IT costs as being a part of the project process.

- How do cost estimates reflect final project expectations? Ensure that the total of the estimates is not greater than the customer's cost expectations. Identify what can be done as to functionality and service expectations within cost constraints.

- To what degree are cost estimates based on reliable, defined time estimates? Cost estimates should reflect time estimates and should indicate the type of time measure used. If the time estimate formula uses plus or minus measurements, the cost estimates should also reflect this type of formula.

- Should resources be internal only? Cost estimates should reflect skill levels rather than headcount. When cost estimating, use the basic categories of resources: skills, equipment, and materials. First consider cost estimates against labor classifications (such as a Java programmer) rather than against a skill level. This gives a baseline salary range for establishing a cost estimate for a given skill level.

What To Do about Minimal Funding

Projects with too-tight budgets cause their own problems. Minimal budgets lead to hiring cheaper (less skilled) people, which extends the timeline and often exceeds the personnel budget amount. Another problem is that penny-pinching budgets hurt morale, which in turn lowers product quality and team productivity.

The team quickly realizes that the tiny budget can be achieved if they hide problems for the inevitable "second version." This reduces short-term costs, but provides a minimal or ineffective product.

Extreme circumstances call for radical action. Projects with tight budgets and timelines have the best chance for success if they are separated from the rest of the organization. One term for this type of operation is a "skunkworks." A separate operation provides many benefits:

- Minimizes interference from management and internal politics
- Establishes minimal policies which encourages innovation and agility
- Minimizes formal reporting through use of periodic informal updates
- Allows the project manager maximum flexibility to address issues, with a focus on results

---

[A] Basic Questions for Resolving Budget Issues

A budget is an itemized plan of revenues and expenditures to implement the original project goals. A project budget can be linked to other budgets and it is important to define those linkages. The answers to the questions should be relevant to the project budget and these other budget links.

- **In whose budget (chart of accounts) do the cost estimates go?** Know the organizational structure of the budget to determine where the cost estimates are going. It is possible to have several different types of budgets.

- **How are various budgets interrelated?** The important links are the cost estimates to budget lines or items. It is also important that budget expenditures and revenues reflect the timeline of the project cycle.

- **Does the project cover more than one budget cycle involved?** Projects that cross a company's fiscal year boundary must ensure that adequate funds are available in the next fiscal period.

- **How are project cost estimates to be allocated?** Cost estimates can go into one budget line or many. The resources of the project can usually be divided into salaries, equipment, and materials. Keep the project budget as granular as possible.

For each budget item, record the calculations done to arrive at a dollar figure for each item. These can be essential when remembering how the numbers were developed to discuss it with project sponsors.

[B] Refining the Budget

The project manager has provided reliable cost and resource estimates. The customer and upper management say the budget is too high. The project manager thinks, "they agreed to the cost and resource estimates!" The project manager's task is to do a budget alignment similar to a schedule alignment. Six areas the project manager analyzes in this process are:

- **Capital spending:** Have project managers accepted a capital cost that really belongs to the customer? If the equipment is to be turned over to the customer, then you need to treat this situation as a flow-through and not as a budget item.

- **Cash flow:** Adjust customer payment milestones so their frequencies cover outgoing costs. The cash inflow must equal or exceed the cash outflow.

- **Contingency funding:** Analyze the contingencies for emergency travel, consultants, and training. All of this funding should be overt, not covert.

- **Expenses:** Evaluate extraordinary expenses such as travel or special supplies. Do reports really need to be bound and in four-color? Consider lower-cost alternatives.

- **Overhead:** Consider if certain costs can be paid for by other company funds rather than the project. Say, for example, a person needs to be trained to assist on some specific project activity; however, after the project the person's training will be used in long-term operational tasks. Perhaps the operational group should be paying for the training.

- **Staff charges:** For staff charges, reduce rates per hour as much as possible. Perhaps a certain activity needs a novice employee, but the operational manager has placed a top runner on the job and is charging accordingly; try to negotiate a lower staff charge.

Exhibit 7-3: Checklist for Project Budget Items

	Attachments
Budget methodology	
Corporate budget requirements	
Table of accounts	
Item locations	
Item aggregation	
Spending increments	
Input requirements	
Reporting structure	
Reporting requirements	
Funding sources	
Customer	
Internal (IS)	
Other	
Scenario type	
Pessimistic	
Realistic	
Optimistic	
Link types to estimates by:	
Pessimistic	
Realistic	
Optimistic	
Milestones:	
Pessimistic	
Realistic	
Optimistic	
Links to project goals	
Links to deliverables	
Source ID	
Critical path items	
Procurement	
Hardware	
Software	
Special materials	
Skills	
Training	
Procurement	
Internal resources	
Support tasks	
Documentation tasks	
Production tasks	
Planning	
Design	
Development	
Testing	
Contingency	
Noncritical path items	
Procurement	
Hardware	
Software	
Consultants	
Special materials	
Skills	
Training	
Procurement	
Internal resources	
Support tasks	

Exhibit 7-3: *(Continued)*

Documentation tasks	
Production tasks	
Planning	
Design	
Development	
Testing	
Links to assumptions	
Links to constraints	
Deadline impacts	
Time estimates inputs	
Quality items	
Control	
Assurance	
Validation	
Field testing	
Resource items	
Equipment	
Internal	
External	
Materials	
Internal	
External	
Skills	
Internal	
External	
Headcount equivalent	
Project management tools	
Internal	
External	
Development tools	
Internal	
External	
Facilities	
Internal	
External	
Logistics	
Internal	
External	
Training cost totals	
Internal	
External	
Documentation cost totals	
Internal	
External	
Communications cost totals	
Internal	
External	
Travel	
Customer support	
Training	
Data gathering	
Time requirements	
Vendors	
Functional	
Goal	
Deliverable	
Time requirements	

Exhibit 7-3: *(Continued)*

Payment requirements	
Dependency links	
Project goals	
Project milestones	
Task milestones	
Learning curve	
Special event	
Risk management	
Project administration	
Special variants noted	
Consistency to:	
Scope plan	
Activity plan	
Resource plan	
Project schedule	
Business justification	
Commercial specification	
Design/Development plan	
Baseline plan	
Change management	
Update requirements	
Slippage rules	
Links to other budgets	
Funding source approval	
Estimates versus actual report	

Instructions for a Project Budget Checklist

This checklist may be used during the general estimating process; however, it cannot be completed until there is an approved project schedule. Time has costs.

There is one question for project budget design: "What method should I use so the project's budget is minimally impacted by the business budget cycle?" This checklist is the framework for answering this question.

There is a major assumption for project budget design. It is that there should be three budgets: pessimistic, realistic, and optimistic. The realistic budget is the project budget. The other two budgets are the bases for change and contingency management.

A second assumption of the project budget is that it is more than a list of budget items and the times when they will be funded. There must be a set of support documents. Unfortunately, the project manager or an essential player might be lost from the project and there are no written parameters for managing the budget.

Use this checklist to keep track of the documents you need to create the budget. In the "Attachments" column, name the document that contains the information for the item listed in the first column.

Budget methodology: Use the "bottom-up" approach if budgeting can be done at the task level. However, if fund allocation is tight, then use the "top-down" approach to allocate funds at the functional level.

Corporate budget requirements: Before designing your own budget, check for special corporate requirements and exceptions. In particular, check the listed items. If there is a requirement for the formal project budget to be a part of the corporate structure, ensure you can define as many separate project budget items as possible from IS group budget items. You still need to create a set of informal project budgets.

Reporting requirements: It is important to know corporate, customer, and project team requirements for information. These requirements affect the level of detail (table of accounts) for the budget.

Funding sources: When possible, each source should be identified on a separate budget line. "Other" means such things as the training group pays for customer training because of a marketing agreement.

Scenario type: Unfortunately, the basic attitude is that you have only one formal budget. Changes and updates can require a large amount of effort. By having three budgets up front, it saves administrative time during the project's duration.

Link types to estimates by: There needs to be a document that gives the source or responsible person for the cost estimates.

Milestones: Milestones help determine when there is to be funding and spending and what the incremental amounts will be.

Links to project goals: Each budget item should have a link to one or more project goals as found in the scope plan.

Links to deliverables: When it is appropriate, there should be links from budget items to deliverables; this includes training and documentation.

Source ID: Identify the person responsible for writing the budget item, including title, e-mail address, and telephone number. If an external source, also include company information.

Critical path estimates: The budget items for the critical path determine the fundamental design of the project budget. When there is no expenditure for a listed item, then $0.00 should be given on the checklist. It may be necessary to break down the list further, such as production or testing hardware.

Contingency: The rational preparation for change. A contingency plan is the preparation for a pessimistic scenario to become reality.

Noncritical path estimates: These items can be changed or possibly can even be deleted without risk to the project. If this assumption is incorrect, then there needs to be a supporting document as to the possible amount of change or the impacts of deleting the budget item.

Links to assumptions: Use the assumptions in the scope plan and in cost estimates to determine a budget item and when amounts will be funded or spent.

Links to constraints: Use the constraints in the scope plan and in cost estimates to determine a budget item and when amounts will be funded or spent.

Deadline impacts: When amounts will be funded or spent is absolutely affected by deadlines because they are given absolute dates.

Time estimates inputs: These inputs are used to determine when amounts for a given budget item will be funded or spent. You never take a budget item amount and divide it by the monthly increments or the project's or task's duration.

Quality items: Budget items for quality tasks should be divided by at least the four listed items. When there is only one line, it is difficult to determine impacts. In addition, the tasks by different groups may be either internal or external.

Resource items: Amounts for various resource types should be detailed when possible, especially if there is more than one funding source. If there is no expenditure for a listed item, then $0.00 should be entered on the checklist.

Training: Integrate appropriate items in the training group's budget into the project budget. In addition, create special budget items for training done outside the training group.

Documentation: Integrate when appropriate in the related documentation group's budget items into the project budget. In addition, create special budget items for training done outside the documentation.

Communications: Budget items such as cost to communicate with the customer about the project's status would be here. Travel might be included here or under the travel budget item.

Travel: Budget items for travel should be broken down into at least four categories.

Customer support: This item might be here or under communications. You should also include car rental, hotel, and meals.

Training: Use only if customer training is given in a project goal.

Data gathering: There may be a special requirement to go to a vendor's location. In this case, the budget item can be here or located under budget.

Time requirements: If there is a direct cost, amounts should be defined. Indirect costs are never put in a budget. The costs for direct and indirect administrative efforts are one item in a standard budget. The corporate financial group usually states for a given head or a certain type and level, the budget factor is $175 per hour. This amount covers all the various administrative tasks and travel time, say, of a manager or programmer.

Vendors: The budget items can be broken down to function or deliverable. A budget support document should state the goal, the time for funding or spending, and payment requirements.

Dependency links: When appropriate, a document should be written that includes the appropriate listed items.

Risk management: There needs to be a budget item for potential risk corrections. This amount is a contingency, a known padding factor. An amount not spent might be moved to another budget item that had slippage if required when not spent during the month. A slippage is a form of risk.

Project administration: If there is a corporate rule that certain administrative activities or tasks are to be considered direct, then this budget item should be in the project budget. For example, your costs for being a project manager might be here, and your costs for being an IS manager would be given in the IS budget.

Special variants: Give any additional information that might assist the project team in its responsibilities and minimize further discussions.

Consistency to: There should be links in the justifications or impacts to the listed documents.

Scope plan: The strategic view of the constraints and assumptions of the project as developed by the project team.

Activity plan: A set of definitions for efforts required to achieve measurable results. At the operational level, you consider activities; at the project level, tasks.

Resource plan: Established support requirements for a project as to costs, availability, start date and end date (length of time for use plus duration), and technical specifications.

Project schedule: Formalizes the time estimates within a calendar structure. It is an integration of sequencing tasks, resource planning, cost estimating, and time estimating.

Business justification: The general rationale for making the financial investment.

Commercial specification: An evolution of the business justification. It identifies the market need and gives adequate requirement and limitation data for the design and development group(s).

Design and development plan: Drives the project integration plan that captures all major design and development deliverables and milestones for management tracking and reporting.

Baseline plan: The initial approved point from which any deviation will be determined using standards and benchmarks.

Change management: The procedure for changing the budget should be documented.

Update requirements: The procedure for updating the budget should be documented.

Slippage rules: The procedure for managing a slippage should be documented in order to better track when a budget item is overspent.

Links to other budgets: Rather than including the training group's budget items that directly affect the project, there can be a support document that lists these items.

Funding source approval: The funding source(s) must give a written agreement to the cost estimates.

Estimates versus actual report: This should be done after the financial group sends an update of funding and spending. No review briefing should be held with the customer until this report is completed. The exception to this is that budget issues are not on the agenda.

All the managers should ensure there is a process in place to get the most reliable estimates possible for any activity duration, resource requirements, and potential costs. The budget should reflect money for the critical support functions of quality control, risk management, training, and documentation. All managers should be aware that any spending that is reflected in the project budget is for:

- Deliverables as specified in the project plan; no "hidden" add-ons such as "the customer will really like this feature"
- Invoices reflecting the vendors' commitments
- Resources defined in the project plan and other project documents, such as third-party commitments
- Reasons for delays in spending for their particular area of concern
- Overspending for a particular month; that is, a delay from an earlier month or an overage that might be in a future month's allocation or a real overspending.

Poor strategic managers will avoid asking for additional funds by robbing them from other approved projects. This shuffling of funds may appear to them to be pragmatic, but it prevents a project's financial performance from being measured accurately.

§ 7.07   SUMMARY

An attitude seems to exist among business managers that anyone can do cost estimates and it really does not take that much effort. In fact, many feel that it can be done casually. However, the budget is a complex activity. As the old saying goes, "Garbage in, garbage out."

Each management level should be involved in the defining of reliable cost estimates. Everyone looks at the budget as the truth when it really is not; it is actually a formalized visual presentation based on estimates. The budget format comes from a set of evolved accounting rules, experiences, and the need of the highest level of management to comprehend the bottom line quickly.

Cost estimating is the major activity used in developing the budget. The budget is structured in the context of corporate marketing goals. The chain is only as strong as its weakest link.

Consider the information needs of each of the project stakeholders. Each has their own view of what the project budget should contain. When reporting budget information, provide an explanation of the project's status to set the budget results into context. Detail the issues recently overcome as well as any impending obstacles.

When project budget performance is used to determine bonuses, the budget must be broken into the groupings of controllable and noncontrollable expenses. This allows the budget results to reflect actual performance.

The project manager should not consider a project budget a commitment, but rather a plan. The manager should try to get from higher management an acceptance that the project budget is a separate management tool and should not be treated the same as the operational budgets are during quarterly reviews. This is especially true if the project is to resolve a customer's needs more than a specific corporate need.

One of the issues of the corporate world is that business managers forget that an estimate is a guess, not a fact. They also tend to forget that a budget or a schedule is a plan, not a commitment. There is a major contrast between the thinking of business managers, who think in terms of commitment, and project managers, who tend to think in terms of plans. Many project issues can find their origins based on these contrasting viewpoints.

Exhibit 7-4: Budget Questions Checklist

Project Name:	Comments:
1. Are there budget lines for support functions such as documentation and training?	
2. Are there separate budget lines for quality control and verification?	
3. Has the quality process been cost-estimated and budgeted?	
4. Have links between the project's budget and any other budgets been defined?	
5. Have potential threats and opportunities been factored into the budgetary process?	
6. How and to whom is financial information given?	
7. How are internal and external resources budgeted?	
8. How are project cost estimates allocated?	
9. How are various budgets interrelated?	
10. How do I organize project cost estimates into a formal structure?	
11. How many budgets are affected by this project?	
12. In whose budget (chart of accounts) do the cost estimates go?	
13. Is the budget consistent with the project's goals that reflect the customer's needs?	
14. Is there a procedure for handling the payments for outside resources?	
15. Is there a procedure for handling the project's budget cycle when it impacts another budget over several of its cycles?	
16. Is there a procedure for making changes and updates to the budget-reporting system as relevant to the project?	
17. Is there a separate budget line for risk management or an identified component of another budget line?	
18. Is there a statement on which budget lines are impacted (complex budget)?	
19. What are the impacts on the budgetary process for outsourcing activities?	
20. What is the defined duration of the project?	

Chapter 8

Risk Analysis

§ 8.01   INTRODUCTION

Project managers swim in a sea of uncertainty. Business managers loathe uncertainty. It annoys executives who ask if the project is on schedule for a project manager to say, "I think so." Yet there are so many unknowns in a project. How can anyone say with complete certainty when a project will be completed and at what cost? So many things might occur to delay one task or another. At best, the entire project plan is a series of guesses. Anything that might cause a deviation to the plan is a risk. Managing these risks are the reasons project managers exist.

Luck—a force that brings good fortune or adversity

The outcome of any decision depends on both the actions of the decisionmaker and the environment in which he operates. It also depends on "luck," that element of randomness that permeates our existence. Even if all other factors are controlled, a random event can always slip past and create a crisis. In this case, the environment includes the many external things that can affect a project. If the decisionmaker had perfect knowledge of all things that could happen, and complete control of the environment, then a value could be assigned to each course of action and they would be able to select the situation that provides the greatest return.

The reality of life is that a course of action can be planned, but no one can control every factor that can alter its outcome. Guesses can be made about factors that might interfere with the project, and this will still not identify all of the things that may go wrong with a task. Inaction is not an option, so pressing forward is the best that can be done. This is decisionmaking under uncertainty. Uncertainty can take several forms:

- Uncertainty about the time estimates and cash required for tasks

- Uncertainty about the outcome of the project (what will the finished product really look like?)

- Uncertainty about the people working on the tasks—their expertise, productivity or availability

- Uncertainty about the side effects of the completed project

§ 8.02   RISK DEFINITION

A "risk" is any factor that may adversely affect the successful completion of the project. A risk has the dimensions of likelihood, impact, and warning. A risk is only the potential of a problem occurring. It does not mean that it *will* occur; only that it *might*. Essentially, a risk is anything that may happen that could create an adverse effect on schedule, costs, quality, or scope of a project. With an endeavor as complex as a project, this could be many things. All projects (and for that matter, everything in life) entail risks. The key is to identify the risks in advance and then manage them. Project managers proactively manage risk to eliminate it or to reduce its impact on the project.

> Imagine a project with just three sequential tasks called A, B, and C. The project manager assigns a time to complete each of them to within 90 percent accuracy. We can compute the possibility of the entire project completing on time by multiplying 90 percent × 90 percent × 90 percent for a 73 percent chance of the project completing on time. Consistently estimating a task's duration with 90 percent accuracy is superb for project planning. Now imagine a project with hundreds of tasks each estimated with a 90 percent change of accuracy and it is easy to see why a project's completion date is just a big guess.

"Risk management" is the ongoing action of monitoring risks and proactively addressing them before they occur. It is an essential part of project management and successful project managers try to resolve risks before they occur. The risk management project consists of risk identification, analysis, quantification, and mitigation. These processes are applied continually throughout the project's "life."

Some project managers are uncomfortable with examining risks as they are, by nature, optimistic people. However, by detecting risks, the project manager can contain and resolve them with less effort than if the project had simply blundered along. Ignoring the risks confronting a project is like driving a car at night with the headlights off, dealing with obstacles only as they are encountered.

Some risks are reducible almost to the point of elimination. A hospital could install a backup generator system with the goal of ensuring 100 percent electrical availability. This will protect them against the risk of electrical blackouts and brownouts. It also introduces new (or consequential) risks, such as the generator failing to start automatically when the electricity fails. Further, it also does not protect the hospital against a massive electrical failure internal to the building.

> Not all risks become reality. There is much potential in our world that does not occur. Driving to work today, I saw dark clouds that indicated the potential of rain. Dark clouds do not denote a certainty of precipitation, but they do indicate a greater potential than a clear sky. I perceived an increased risk that I would get drenched on the long walk across the company parking lot, so I carried an umbrella with me. The odds were that it would not rain. The meteorologist said the clouds would pass. I could even see patches of blue sky between the massive dark clouds. Still, to reduce my risk of being soaked, I carried an umbrella.

Some risks are unavoidable, however, and the project manager can only take steps to reduce their impact. If the facility is located on the ocean with a lovely view of the sea, defenses can be built against a tidal surge or hurricanes, but the bad events cannot be prevented. The damage from them can only be minimized. For example, an important team member cannot be prevented from leaving the company in the middle of a project, but all work can be well documented, so that the next person will be able to pick up the work faster.

> "Project Risk is an uncertain event or condition that, if it occurs, has a positive or negative effect on a project objective. A risk has a cause, and if it occurs, a consequence."
> —Project Management Body of Knowledge, Project Management Institute (www.pmi.org)

There is one risk that all project managers experience. Business managers tend to consider risks seriously only when they occur. Project managers must reduce the risk of misunderstanding by business managers by:

- Documenting all risks and plans for mitigating them
- Keeping business management informed
- Educating management about risk management at every opportunity
- Presenting measurable recommendations
- Making sure management comprehends the consequences of risk
- Keeping a neutral position by never saying, "I told you so"

> "The pessimist sees difficulty in every opportunity. The optimist sees opportunity in every difficulty."
>
> —Winston Churchill

§ 8.03   RISK AND OPPORTUNITY ARE TWO SIDES OF THE SAME COIN

A risk has an adverse effect on a project—a potentially disastrous one. An opportunity is a significant positive result for the project that improves the company's bottom line. A risk or an opportunity can each begin as a ripple and turn into a tidal wave. Manage both of them. For every risk, there may be a matching opportunity. The danger, of course, is the possibility that an opportunity is a disguised risk.

Many opportunities or "positive risks" can occur during a project. The price of hardware or software may decrease due to sharp negotiations or from market pressure. New technology may be easier to master than scheduled, and perhaps shorten the development time. A particularly difficult section of code may be easier to complete than estimated.

Therefore, the list of possible opportunities can be as long as the list of risks. The only difference is that risks will delay a project or cause a budget over-run. Both of these have negative consequences for the company, which may have set aside a certain amount of money to complete the project or which may have other business activities tied to the completion of the project. An opportunity may reduce the financial burden of a project or its length. Both a reduction of the financial burden or a shorter completion time are disruptive to the company. Therefore, while opportunities should be maximized, the project manager's focus should be on managing the risks.

Include budget items and time estimates for risk management reviews and mitigation in each phase of the project. If there are few risks to the project in a given phase, an opportunity then emerges to use these resources elsewhere.

§ 8.04   DEVELOPING A RISK MANAGEMENT PLAN

A risk management plan makes the entire project more likely to succeed in terms of final product, completion date, and budget. Its purpose is to examine a plan, to identify what might go wrong, and how to address it before the failure occurs.

A project's risk management plan begins as soon as the project definition phase is completed (asking if this project's objectives are achievable) and continues until the final file is closed at the end of the project.

Developing a risk management program involves four functions:

1. Identifying the potential risks

2. Evaluating their likelihood, impact, and warning

3. Developing mitigation plans for the most serious risks

4. Reviewing and monitoring risks throughout the project

The approach to assembling a risk management plan is to have the project team perform the risk analyses together. The team's collective knowledge of such things as the time and budget estimate for a task and the certainty of assumptions will make these reviews move quickly. The team will also be invaluable when determining the impact on the project should a risk become a reality.

Risk management is an important tool in the project's quality assurance program. Quality assurance uses the risk management plan to incorporate actions in the project plan to avoid risks when possible, or that include contingency actions to minimize the impact of likely risks. Quality assurance guides the project plan toward the more certain courses of action and away from the risky ones. After the initial risk management plan is completed, the mitigation actions identified in the plan are included in the main project plan as task items.

Small projects can fit their risk plan onto one or two sheets of paper. As a project's scope grows in complexity, length, terms of multiple teams' involvement, and, depending on new technology, the value of a risk plan skyrockets.

> "A good plan executed today is better than a perfect plan executed at some indefinite point in the future."
>
> —General George S. Patton, Jr.

[A] Identifying Risks

Use the risk management plan spreadsheet ("Risk Plan.XLS"). Begin with the three leftmost columns entitled "Risk ID #," "Phase," and "WBS #/Description" to identify risks to the project.

- Risk ID #—a unique number assigned to ease the tracking of the risk

- Phase—the part of the project to which the risk belongs
- WBS #/Description—the work breakdown schedule number and a verbal description of this risk

[1] "Standard" Risks

The first step is to identify all of the things that could go wrong with the project. The usual approach is to list *everything* that could go wrong and then edit the list for likely problems. Skip risks that seem remote and stand little likelihood of remaining on the list. For example, imagine the risk to a project under way in Montana being delayed by a hurricane. It may somehow be possible, but probably not in our lifetime. Skip the trivial and focus on the significant, few risks. Consolidate some of the risks triggered by the same event or mitigated in the same fashion.

> Project managers can calculate the risks for those things that they know or are aware of, but they cannot plan for things which they do not know. Often, people do not know what it is that they do not know.

Standard risks may apply across the entire project. They might involve inaction or negative action by the key stakeholders, inaccuracy in the mission statement, changes in the company environment, or changes in the business climate. Some "standard" or "global" risks that apply to all projects are:

- Project-wide risks
  - Sponsor changes jobs
  - Sponsor loses interest
  - Stakeholder opposition or ambivalence
  - Funding cut
  - Major scope change
  - Project manager change
  - Key technical expert not available
  - Material (hardware or software) delivery late
  - Business environment changes drastically
  - Legal environment changes drastically
  - Weather delays
  - Natural disasters

- ○ Working in a foreign country
- ○ New technologies of any type
- ○ Under- or over-estimating a task
- Source documents useful for identifying risks
  - ○ List of assumptions
  - ○ Stakeholder analysis
  - ○ Mission statement
  - ○ Project charter
  - ○ Legal constraints on the business
  - ○ Previous projects
- Ask the team!
  - ○ Explain to them how to recognize a risk and how to fill out the form
  - ○ Provide a survey and permit anonymous submissions
  - ○ Assemble the suggestions into a random order
  - ○ Review each risk with the team

Another way to identify risks is to consider them by category. Ten common categories of risk are:

1. Customer
   —Financial support becomes unavailable
   —Not participating in agreed-upon reviews
   —Refuses to sign acceptance documents
   —Geographically dispersed
   —Long time to respond to questions
   —Unilateral re-interpretation of goals
   —Key resources not available when needed

2. Delivery of project's product
   —Product does not meet functional requirements
   —Product has incompatibility issues
   —Product has interoperability issues
   —Product's requirements exceed available capacity
   —Product's response time is inadequate

3. Equipment

   —New technology for a company

   —Does not meet specifications

   —Material is difficult to obtain in desired quantity

   —New vendor on project

   —Unstable technology or changing industry standards

   —Key component (server, compiler, or database) upgrade in middle of project

   —Price increases or hidden costs

4. People

   —Lacking in skills required

   —High cost of skilled workers

   —Geographically dispersed

   —Not available at time required

   —Insufficient number of skilled people available when needed

   —Not available because of job change

5. Physical

   —Inadequate facility

   —Critical computers or hardware fail

   —Poor working environment

   —Facility lost through fire or other catastrophe

   —Virus infects some critical data

6. Scope

   —Customer identifies the need for additional effort

   —Major scope change late in the project

   —An operational area introduces new functionality without approval by the project manager

7. Technology

   —Key technology is in flux; changing standards

   —Technical assumptions are not factual

   —Technical constraints cannot be overcome

   —Technology is not understood clearly

—Technology is too new and not stable

—Technology is too complex for a particular company to execute

—High number of technical interfaces required

—Technology will not interface with existing systems

8. Information security

—Project requires handling sensitive data

—Vendor must touch sensitive data for final testing and conversion

—Vendor subcontracts to foreign companies

—Data collected by new system violates company policies

—Data is governed by laws not previously applicable to the company

9. Vendor

—Financial failure or lack of financial stability

—Not participating in agreed-upon reviews

—Failure to deliver goods on time

—Response time to questions not timely

—Unilateral re-interpretation of goals

—High price of scope changes

—Skill resources not available when promised

—Foreign outsourcing time zones complicates project coordination

10. Natural disaster

—Severe winter weather that closes the roads and delays work

—Wide area disasters, such as earthquakes, hurricanes, and flooding

—Structural fires that destroy part of project product

[2] Risks Unique to the Project

Standard risks are useful for examining the project scope documents to date and identifying potential risks with the project. Every project is different. After identifying the standard risks, step back and look for specific risks to the project. These could be coordination points where skilled experts must be available or outside materials received.

It could be situations where the project team must coordinate actions with another project team to build interfaces. To identify additional risks due to the specifics of the project, refer to the work breakdown schedule, list of assumptions, and stakeholder analysis completed so far.

Review the risk to the project created by stakeholders in a separate stakeholder analysis. Machines behave in relatively predictable ways but people do not. Computers, driven by software, should provide the same results time after time given a consistent operating environment. People are much more complex and unpredictable. The environment they exist in is far out of the project manager's control and ability to monitor. It is often unclear what really motivates a stakeholder to pursue a specific course of action.

A skilled project manager establishes a positive, respectful relationship with each stakeholder in an effort to build up a "bank" of goodwill. When the project hits on hard times, as it eventually will, this goodwill may cushion the tension between the project manager and the various stakeholders. Goodwill, like respect, is so very hard to build and so very easy to lose.

[3] Risk Interactions

They say that trouble comes in threes, and on occasion, this is true of risks. Sometimes risks will combine and hit the project from several directions at once. If the project manager believes that certain risks can combine, then list the combination as a separate risk item. The likelihood of the risks coinciding is the product of the likelihood of the individual risks.

Examples of combined risks are:

- A cut to the project budget hitting at the same time as a software license increase
- A change in the legal requirements for a product at the same time that the timeline was cut

[4] Project Quality Assurance Risk Checklist

Use the following checklist to see if anything may have been overlooked:

1. Have all operational activity sequences been identified?
2. Have all training activity sequences been identified?
3. Are there any pending legal changes that will disrupt the project?
4. Have all documentation activity sequences been identified?
5. Have all quality assurance and control points been identified?
6. Are there standards or benchmarks for comparing activity durations?
7. Have operational cost estimates been identified?
8. Have indirect cost estimates been identified?
9. Are all of the revenue dates identified?

10. Have skills availability been identified?

11. Have deliverable dates been identified?

12. Have status report dates been identified?

13. Has a critical path been established?

14. Have critical equipment/materials requirement dates been established?

15. Have software infrastructure benchmarks (configuration, compatibility, etc.) been identified?

16. Have hardware infrastructure benchmarks (interoperability, portability, etc.) been identified?

17. Have the dates, equipment, and resources been entered from all vendors and consultants?

18. Have skill level benchmarks been identified?

"Don't be afraid to go out on a limb. That's where the fruit is."

—H. Jackson Browne

---

§ 8.05 CATEGORIZING RISK

Review the project's list of risks for commonality and overlap. Some risks will logically appear in multiple categories, such as the risk of a budget cut or a major scope change. The concern is if the mitigating actions for the overlapping risks begin to conflict and make managing the risk management plan too awkward.

Risk management requires a regular review of the identified project risks throughout the life of the project. Risks no longer relevant need to be shuttled aside to prevent obscuring the ones requiring attention. Keeping all risks on the "active" list can make things a bit long to handle. The risk plan is easier to follow if risks are categorized in some fashion. One way is to identify the risks by project phase. Group risks according to any common characteristic. Use the grouping that makes the most sense for the project, the team, and the company's culture.

One way to categorize risk is to make one copy of the risk plan spreadsheet for each phase or milestone, plus a separate sheet for risks applicable to the overall project. This is useful for grouping risks since risks unique to the design phase would not be applicable when working on the implementation phase.

[A]   Risk Analysis Score

Risk analysis is a technique for assessing quantitatively or qualitatively (or both) the impact of a potential risk. It applies a value to the characteristics of the risk to generate a score, which can be used to prioritize the risks to be managed. The analysis indicates which risks to manage closely and which to acknowledge without taking further action.

Risk analysis is a big field. Insurance companies spend a considerable amount of time slicing and dicing numbers to quantify a risk so they can set an insurance rate for it. Project managers do not have time to do that. They must analyze risks using the broad-brush factors of likelihood, impact, and warning time.

The entire team should be actively involved in the risk analysis process. If there are too many people to conduct an orderly analysis, then appoint representatives from each organizational component. The team's collective experience will provide a well-rounded perspective on what to address, and the most effective way to do it.

A key goal of any risk analysis tool is its clarity. Many people with a wide range of backgrounds will be reading this document and ease of use is essential for them to gain the greatest benefit from it. The clearer the document is, the greater its credibility will be among the stockholders. Use the plan shown in Chart 8-1.

[B]   Rating the Risks

Refer to the risk analysis worksheet. By now it should contain the list of risks identified thus far, grouped according to whatever categories have been chosen by the project manager. In this step, add values under the "quantification" section. The quantification section is where a "score" is developed to determine which risks require mitigation plans and which ones can be accepted but nothing can be done about it until a later time.

[1]   How the Risk Analysis Spreadsheet Tool Works

The quantification section has four columns:

- *Likelihood* is an estimate of the probability that the risk will become a reality. Some risks are very real but very unlikely to occur. A risk of lightening striking a key team member is real but extremely low.

- *Impact* is how badly the event would damage the project's scope, budget, or timeline if it occurred.

- *Warning* is how much warning the project manager would have before this event occurred. In the case of a hurricane, the weather reports could be monitored as it moves closer and plans can be shifted accordingly. In the case of an earthquake, there would likely be no warning before it struck.

| WBS # / Description | QUANTIFICATION | | | | Damage | | Trigger | Risk Event Status | Actual Results | Mitigation Actions | Assigned To | Date | Comments |
	Likelihood	Impact	Warning	Score	$ At Stake	Time at Stake							
				0									
				0									
				0									
				0									
				0									
				0									
				0									
				0									
				0									
				0									
				0									

Chart 8-1: Project Risk Management Plan

- *Score* is a numeric risk score based on the previous three values.

The scales for likelihood and impact are from 1 to 10, with 1 as extremely unlikely and 10 as a sure thing. Use any consistent numbering system for the scores, but if a zero is used as a value, then score that entire risk as zero. Some companies establish a range for each value:

- Likelihood
  - 1 to 3 is very unlikely
  - 4 to 5 is unlikely
  - 6 to 8 is possible
  - 9 to 10 is very possible.
- Impact (to the scope, budget, or timeline)
  - 1 to 3 is little negative impact—a nuisance
  - 4 to 5 is some negative impact—a disruption
  - 6 to 8 is definite negative impact—serious impact
  - 9 to 10 is severe negative impact—a project-threatening crisis

Score the warning column the reverse from the other two. It is also rated from 1 to 10. A risk typically accompanied with a lot of warning would be rated very low. Rate a risk that would occur with little or no warning as high since the project manager would not have time to react. Some companies establish a warning range for each value:

- Warning (signals the risk is about to occur)
  - 1 to 3 gives lots of warning—can see it coming far off
  - 4 to 5 builds over time—sufficient notice to implement mitigation
  - 6 to 8 gives little warning—short notice before it strikes
  - 9 to 10 is a sudden event—no notice before the risk strikes

Now move the risk analysis from dealing with the many, to addressing the critical few. A risk's score is determined by multiplying the three columns together. The higher the score is, the greater the attention that must be paid to that risk. The score is the key to the analysis. After scoring the risks, sort the entire spreadsheet on this column in descending order. This brings the risks with the highest score to the top.

Review the sorted risks. At some point in the list, draw a line across it. Monitor anything below this point, but take no further action about it. This focuses attention toward addressing the key risks. As the project progresses, review the risks below the line every milestone or month, to see if they should be moved up the list or dropped altogether.

[C]   Identifying Likelihood, Impact, and Warning Values

There are several ways to establish a score for the likelihood, impact, and warning fields for each risk.

a. Do it yourself. The easiest way is for the project manager to sit down and fill in whatever values the situation warrants. This is quick, but it depends on a single person's perspective. A project is a team effort and if the team does not participate in its development, they may lack ownership in its execution.

b. A better way is to use risk assessments from previous projects to see the score for these risks and how closely the score was reflected in what occurred during the project. Although this project exists in a different time, with a different goal and with a different team, there may be enough similarities for this research to be useful.

c. The best way is to use team scoring along with a review of historical information. Assemble the project team and discuss the list of risks to the project along with any pertinent historical data. Distribute a score sheet listing each risk item to the team members and ask them to score each risk as to its likelihood, impact, and warning. This step typically raises many questions about the risk descriptions and is useful for clarifying them. Clear risk descriptions are important since many of the stakeholders may refer to this list.

Next, collect the sheets and average the scores for each item. Redistribute the sheets for the participants to score again, but this time around, indicate the average value from the first pass through. Average the values for the second pass, and then average the average value from both passes together.

Redistribute the risk sheets with the revised numbers and ask the participants to speak up for any value they feel is more than 10 percent too high or too low. The discussion will either answer the person's questions or allow the person to raise issues about a risk's score that others may not have considered before.

§ 8.06   WORKING THE CRITICAL RISKS

With the project's risks listed and grouped, it is time to address the critical few. Begin by filling in the remainder of the form for each line on the risk management spreadsheet. The team approach is the best way to accomplish this. It is also useful to consider historical information from previous projects.

[A]   Damage

If this risk became reality, what would its impact be on the project? Divide damage into two types, financial impact and timeline impact.

- **Money at stake**—How severely would this risk damage the project budget? For example, if the risk was that the task might overrun its schedule and incur additional costs for contracted programmers, how much would this be? Should lost revenue be included in this amount if the overall project is late? Are there legal penalties to pay or bonuses lost for being late?

- **Time at stake**—How long would this risk delay the project's completion? Use the same unit of time as used by the project plan (days, weeks, etc.).

These two factors describe the damage in various ways. For example, if a task not on the critical path is late, it may not damage the project in either category, unless a change in the plan suddenly elevates that task onto the critical path. Some companies establish a risk guideline that the most a risk can declare is financially at stake is the budgeted cash outlay for that task.

[B]   Trigger

The trigger column is where events that would enable the risk to occur are identified. It alerts the project manager that the conditions are right for the risk to arise. For example:

- A task becomes at risk of being late only after it has begun.

- The project is at risk of losing a sponsor's support if that executive is replaced, or if the project falls significantly behind the plan.

- A financial report by the company indicating excessive losses may signal an upcoming budget cut.

- Equipment installation is only at risk of being late after it has been received.

When monitoring risk during the project's progression, the trigger column provides a quick tool for the project manager to focus on the risks significant at that moment.

[C]   Risk Event Status

The risk event status column indicates if this risk is past, active, or in the future. This column is useful for a quick review of risks looming on the horizon. The risk analysis spreadsheet is a valuable historical tool to review whenever new projects are started. This column allows valid risks to remain on the document even after they pass.

Valid values for this column are:

- **Past**—The task at risk is completed and can be ignored.
- **Active**—The task at risk is in process or about to start.
- **Future**—The task at risk is far into the future.

[D]   Actual Results

Actual results is the outcome of the risk once it has occurred or passed. Pull valuable project documentation for lessons learned and historical purposes from this column. Did the risk occur? Were the triggers useful or incorrect? What was the impact? Which mitigation steps were the most effective or were the least useful?

This column is a gold mine of information for future projects if time is taken to fill in the details. Make the column as large as needed or use it to refer to a detailed document in the project files.

[E]   Mitigation Actions

Mitigation actions are tasks to eliminate a risk or reduce its impact. They are key steps in proactive management of the project. These actions may be added to the project plan. The primary mitigation actions are avoidance, diminishment, transference, and acceptance. It is always cheaper to mitigate a risk than to repair the damage after it occurs.

Some examples of mitigation activities follow:

- Critical contract labor
  - Hire them to join the project earlier than needed. If they are idle, arrange something useful for them to do that the project manager can control so they can be redirected to the project when needed.
  - Schedule them to remain longer than needed in case the project runs longer than expected.

- Materials
  - Arrange for materials to arrive early enough for a reshipment in case they were damaged in transit.
  - Insure shipments to cover the expense of a prompt replacement for damaged goods.
  - Ship materials on a dedicated vehicle to avoid stops along the way.
  - Purchase backup equipment at the same time, but ensure it is shipped separately.

> One author witnessed a project where all of the money for personal computers was spent at the beginning of the project to ensure the funds could not be cut. Unfortunately, it was 15 months before all of the units were installed and the warranty only covered the first 12.

[F] Assigned To

Assigned to is the name of the person designated to monitor the risk. Instead of the project manager scurrying from desk to desk trying to monitor risks, they can be assigned to team leaders or the person working on that task. Although the project manager has the ultimate responsibility for the project, effective delegation spreads the workload around the team. The team member working on a task is close enough to it to see if the risk is becoming reality. If the team member is too close to the work to see the problems, then assign the risk to the team leader.

[G] Date

The date the risk was assigned to a person to monitor.

[H] Comments

Comments are anything that would clarify the risk, its triggers, or its mitigation actions. When this risk is added to the list and analyzed, many details can be captured. Adding some notes here will be useful when monitoring the tasks weeks later. This also provides valuable historical information for future projects. If the spreadsheet cell is too small to hold the pertinent comments, then refer to a detailed document. Again, this type of historical information is very valuable to the project's lessons learned and is helpful input to future projects.

> "Risks come from not knowing what you are doing."
>
> —Warren Buffet

§ 8.07   RISK MITIGATION

Managing risk is a proactive job. A skilled project manager does not sit back and hope for the best. The project manager constantly works to drive out the uncertainty surrounding the project plans. One step toward this goal is to develop mitigation plans for the project risks monitored by the risk management plan.

Risks can result in four types of consequences:

- Benefits are delayed or reduced
- Time frames are extended
- Expenses are advanced or increased
- Output quality is reduced

When planning the scope of a project, think of risks as potential threats. However, the project manager might be one of those unique people who sees a way to turn a situation into an opportunity. Perhaps it takes six months to develop a product, and then someone has invented a utility that shortens the time in half or less. Does this affect the project? Of course it does. Just think of the example of the utilities that can be used to create a Web page in hours rather than days. Are they as simple as the vendors say they are?

An interesting aspect of risk is that the mitigation action taken to reduce a specific risk to the project may create another risk somewhere else. Speeding the purchase of hardware to avoid a budget cut avoids the financial reduction, but introduces the risk of material damaged in storage. Writing a subsystem of a program several months in advance to save time introduces the risk that the scope requirements will change before the project reaches this stage and the program code must be reworked. These are known as consequential risks and begin the risk analysis cycle anew.

With all of this background in mind, let us get specific about mitigation planning. Once the project's risks have been identified and ranked, the project manager examines each critical risk to determine if its impact can be minimized, if the risk's likelihood of occurrence can be reduced or avoided, or if its detect ability can be improved.

[A]   Avoidance

Avoidance is the best risk mitigation approach since it eliminates the risk. However, it is not always possible, and may add new risks to the plan. Avoidance is changing the project plan to eliminate the condition under which a risk would occur. This reduces the level of uncertainty associated with the plan by eliminating the risk. Avoidance is the preferred action because the risk goes away, but unfortunately, this is not always possible. We can avoid all project risk by canceling the project, but add a new risk to the company of not fulfilling an important business need.

An avoidance mitigation action might be to use proven technology instead of leading-edge technology to develop the product. In that case, eliminate the uncertainty surrounding the new technology by using the older, more familiar technology. However, the old technology introduces a new set of risks including the impending obsolescence of the system!

Avoid risks to the project's success by minimizing the features included in the project scope. The fewer the tasks attempted, the less the chance of failing at one of them. Another avoidance action is to use proven contractors on the project instead of hiring a new company. The old company provides some measure of predictability missing from bringing in a new group.

[B]   Diminish Risk Impact

Some risks are impossible to avoid. For example, there is the risk that the primary network engineer will not be available when needed through illness, other assignments, etc. Diminish the impact of this loss by ensuring there is a trained backup network engineer available when needed. There is still the impact of the primary person being gone and the backup person may not be as productive. In this way, the risk occurred, but its impact on the project was minimized. The added cost of the second network engineer is the price paid for greater project certainty.

[C]   Transference

Transference shifts the impact of the risk to a third party; usually through insurance. For example, if a shipment of critical equipment is lost or damaged in transit and this would place the project in serious jeopardy, then insure against the event to recover some of the financial loss of the occurrence.

A common example of transference is a fixed bid contract. This transfers the risk of major cost overruns to the contractor. It also forces them to operate efficiently.

[D]   Acceptance

Sometimes, there is no way to reduce the likelihood or impact of a risk. The project manager accepts it and hopes it does not become real. Accepting a risk does not mean surrender. Develop a fallback plan to execute if the risk occurs. Risk triggers may detect that the conditions are ripe for the risk to become real and alert the project manager to dust off a contingency plan or to roll it out immediately. Monitor accepted risks for any change in their likelihood. A commonly accepted risk is the weather. Severe winter weather may close the roads for days and heavy ice can down power poles. All of this delays a project.

§ 8.08   MANAGING RISK

Managing risk is a proactive function. Waiting until a crisis erupts before taking any action is damage control, not risk management. It is the responsibility of the project manager to control, manage, and mitigate risks. In addition, it is the responsibility of the sponsor to support the need for risk analysis and management across corporate divisions.

Once the project plan is established and the project begun, the project manager continuously monitors the risk management plan to see which trigger events are impending. In addition, complete a risk assessment at every major project phase or milestone.

Although a risk can come roaring out of the sidelines; there are not enough hours in the day to monitor everything that might happen. Instead, project managers note which risks are along the critical path or are on the secondary critical path. These risks merit the closest watch—just do not completely forget the others!

> A skilled project manager manages the project's risk in a positive manner. Always state the question as "How can we resolve this risk if it happens?" Avoid stating the question as "What can go wrong?" The word "wrong" implies a moral decision. Instead, use the word "incorrectly" since it implies a potential measurable standard or benchmark.

Many of the risk mitigation plans and risk triggers identified in the plan will involve people. These people may be key stakeholders, team members, department managers, or a wide range of others. Communicating with these communities prior to a problem occurring will make communicating with them after it occurs much easier.

As the project progresses, there should be periodic reviews of the risk plan into which these groups should be brought for evaluation and discussion.

Throughout the project's life, the project manager must evaluate potential risks and define new ones with the use of risk-analysis tools and techniques. The project manager detects, controls, and manages risks through:

- Team meetings
- Informational conferences with the strategic manager and customers
- Project status reports
- Risk-analysis tools to develop solutions to potential risks

[A]   Keep a "Rainy Day" Fund

A common project planning action is to establish a contingency reserve, which includes amounts of time, money, or resources for known and unknown risks. Often calculated as a percent of the total budget, the contingency fund covers overages without requesting additional funds.

[B]   Proactive Risk Management

Every week, print the list of project risks and highlight the ones on the critical path. Review the triggers for these risks frequently. Add a column to the risk plan to indicate risks that are on the critical path, but keep in mind that updates to the project schedule may change the critical path itself.

The essential actions of the project risk management are:

- Keep the risk management plan up to date.
- Discuss risk potentials at all scheduled meetings.
- Assign team members to correct and perform quick technical analyses of risks.
- Ask key customers to assist with risk evaluations and crises.
- Ensure that risk management has adequate time in the schedule.
- Ensure there is funding in the budget for risk management, distinctive from the quality assurance and control functions.
- Ensure there is a contingency fund to handle significant risk issues.
- Assist the quality group in the analysis and evaluation of any identified risk.

[C] Documenting Risks and Opportunities

An important part of project documentation is a running account of what happened, when and why. This information feeds into the project's lessons learned file for use in later projects. The risk management plan supplies this information in several ways:

- Original risk assessment and how it changed over time to track with the project's progress and challenges
- Major revisions to the risk assessment plan, usually at milestones or after a major scope change
- Comparison of risks and triggers to review how well the trigger signaled an impending risk
- The effectiveness of the mitigation actions planned and actually executed

File this information in the program office for all project managers to review. Remember to screen out all personal references in the documents, especially those pertaining to obnoxious executives.

§ 8.09 SUMMARY

Project managers have a tough job. Everyone expects them to look into the future and guess, with perfect certainty, how much and how long a project requires to be completed. This is an unrealistic, yet not unmanageable expectation. At best, the entire project planning process is a series of guesses.

The key to managing the uncertainty of a project is to identify the things which might go wrong—the risks to each task or goal. Once the primary risks are identified, they are analyzed to estimate their impact, likelihood, and probability of occurrence. The fallacy is that as people, we do not know what we do not know. For example, if the project manager is unaware of an impending sale of an important vendor and its impact on the project, then he or she cannot plan for the risk.

After the more important risks are identified, plans can be laid to minimize their impact on the project. Some risks cannot be avoided or mitigated and must be accepted. Monitor those risks to see if they are likely to become serious problems.

Managing risk is a proactive function. Waiting until a crisis erupts before taking any action is damage control, not risk management. It is the responsibility of the project manager to control, manage, and mitigate risks. In addition, it is the responsibility of the sponsor to support the need for risk analysis, management, and mitigation.

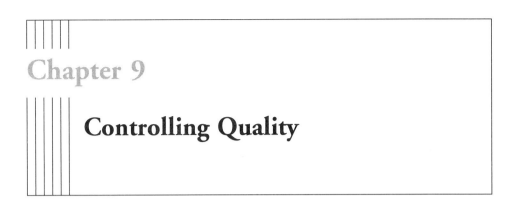

Chapter 9

Controlling Quality

§ 9.01   INTRODUCTION

Customers, either internal or external to the company, purchase a product to solve a business problem for them. In exchange for money and some of their time, the project relieves them of that problem. The extent that the product succeeds in this area is the degree of customer satisfaction. Quality is always defined from the customer's perspective.

> "It is quality rather than quantity that matters."
>
> —Lucius Seneca (5 B.C.–65 A.D.)

Quality management issues can be viewed as either a cost center or profit maker for any business. It is costly because expensive technicians must be hired to do the work. However, an active quality management program can bring sizable savings by identifying serious errors in products or services prior to their release. A quality program that maintains a high standard for products or services is profitable because it brands the company as highly competent.

Quality inspection exists only because there are defects in the product or process. The real goal is to eliminate the need for expensive inspection and rework. If specifications were complete and the design was thorough prior to beginning the effort, then the quality is built in instead of stuffed in later.

Leaders set the tone for the project's quality efforts through their actions. If they pay close attention to the steps for ensuring quality, then so will the team.

§ 9.02   QUALITY PROCESS DEFINITION

The two basic types of quality process are assurance and control. In most projects, the same team member who is dedicated to quality analysis evaluates both. In a large team, there will be a person for each function because the focus is different.

Quality has been defined by some as "conformance to specification." Another way to state this is that it seeks to minimize performance errors. Quality efforts also strive to ensure the final product is fit for use.

Quality assurance and quality control are concerned with two general aspects of the project:

- Quality of the product or service created
- Quality of the project execution

Project quality focuses on three areas:

Prevention—Evaluate the project processes and design to stop errors before they occur. Success in preventing problems will improve the project's budget performance and reduce testing time.

Inspection—Test and review peers to catch a problem with the product before the customer sees it. Inspection locates problems and tracks them until they are resolved.

Lessons learned—Conduct periodic reviews to spread the solution to issues among the rest of the project team to prevent similar errors elsewhere.

[A]   Quality Assurance

Quality assurance encompasses all of the things done to ensure the project has the best tools, materials, and a clear description of the deliverables before the project begins. In essence, quality assurance means that it takes good things into the project to get good things out of it. Its goal is to anticipate and prevent problems before they occur. An effective quality assurance program saves money by minimizing rework of completed products. Quality assurance principles are applied to every task throughout the project even before it begins. Some of the areas where quality assurance is applied follow:

- **Tools**—Ensuring the team's tools (such as compilers, workstations, or even work areas) are reliable and suitable for the purpose allows for the work to flow smoothly. Reliable means that unstable software development tools or hardware are not passed to the team "just because they are convenient." Suitable to the purpose means that the team's tools provide adequate performance and are easy to use. Again, just because 300 MHz desktop units are "free" to the project (saving expense), does not mean that they should be used.

- **Processes**—Providing the team with essential efficient processes means that work flows smoothly. This defines performance standards, and the process for measuring and evaluating project performance against these standards.

- **Design and analysis**—The greatest savings from quality is in the design and analysis part of the project. The project manager must resist being rushed by the sponsor to "do something" which would bypass the quality assurance steps. Scope and design verification are the key to minimizing product rework:

  - Ensuring the customer and/or project sponsor fully understands what problem they are trying to solve.

  - Verifying the project scope, including everything necessary to solve that problem.

  - Ensuring that all deliverables are clearly defined and objectively measurable.

  - During execution, comparing the project plan to the vision to ensure it includes the necessary steps to fulfill its mission.

  - When appropriate, using prototyping of customer interfaces to verify everything required is in the project definition.

  - At the design point where subsystems integrate, obtaining written agreement on passing control, data, and any other dependencies.

[B]   Quality Control

Verifying the results of completed work is the duty of quality control. Quality control compares the product or service created to the documented scope and specifications to ensure it meets the stated customer expectations. Errors are always cheaper to repair closest to where they occur. The quality control function minimizes the negative budget impact of errors.

An old management maxim is, "There is never enough time to do it right, but there is always time to do it over."

Quality control acts as the project's gatekeeper. Before judging a task as complete, the quality control technician verifies that the finished piece meets all of the deliverables identified for it. Errors that evade detection here will be much more difficult to repair once they are embedded deep within the product.

Heavy industry learned long ago that inspecting quality into a product is a long and expensive process. The goal is to design the process, tools, and specifications so the result is consistently right the first time.

[C]   Product Quality

Projects exist to create something—usually a product or service. The primary focus of the project's quality initiative is to ensure the product fulfills customer requirements. The ultimate goal of product quality is customer satisfaction. Customer satisfaction is improved by diligently monitoring all of the customers' expectations in the design phase and then tracking them as the project evolves to modify the scope so that the final product meets those expectations. Characteristics of customer satisfaction with a quality product include the following:

- Quality demonstrates an awareness of customer needs. In one sense, the quality of the specifications means that the product does what the customer desires.

- Quality is measurable. When a customer uses the product, the customer can validate functionality against product specifications.

- Quality is support for the effort even when there are disagreements. A single person cannot accomplish the project and the team is only as strong as its weakest link.

- Quality means there is communication between the project manager and the customer. Communications can establish a bond of confidence.

- Quality requires metrics. Analysis can determine the degree of success. When the customer knows there are product metrics, it establishes a sense of product integrity.

- Quality revolves around coordination. Integrate all project stakeholders into a team with a shared vision of the project's desired outcome.

[D] Quality of Project Execution

Projects are themselves a process. An inefficient project will overrun its timelines and budget. Both of these circumstances irritate customers. Most project managers are reluctant to create a mechanism that will question their decisions. Companies with project management offices or a project sponsor normally ensure that the project execution is itself evaluated in terms of quality assurance and quality control.

Monitoring the quality of the project's execution is one way that an impending problem can be identified. If the project manager is juggling timelines and budget items to hide internal project problems, then the quality check will uncover this. Some of the areas of project execution quality to review include the following:

- Accuracy of the time and budget estimates
- Accuracy of the project's scope when compared to the finished product (or work in progress)
- Ability to issue timely project reports and notices
- Speed with which issues are resolved
- Speed with which scope changes are addressed
- Efficient use of budget—is money wasted on express deliveries or late charges?
- Quality evaluations are spread throughout the project schedule and not just at the end of milestones.
- Minimize project performance errors by providing the right skill at the right place, at the right time.
- Quality is commitment. It is the obligation of any project team member to state when an activity as defined cannot be accomplished.
- Quality means avoidance of cost for things unnecessary. This does not mean turning out a cheap product, but focusing spending on only what is required.

The quality of execution is a valuable personal development tool for a project manager. Everyone has areas of personal excellence and areas that could be improved.

Properly applied, the quality evaluations of how the project is conducted can be used to identify areas for personal development of the project manager.

Remember to review the quality of the quality implementation for the project. It is false security to provide a sham quality program just to fulfill an unwanted project requirement. This is often done by an outside organization for very large or troubled projects.

[E] Measuring Quality

Before a project can deliver "quality," it must know what the quality is. Every technical specification in the scope of work must include a description of how to measure it. Measurement indicates the degree of conformity of the delivered product.

For example, if the specification says to include a way to securely enter credit card information into a Web page, this might be measured with a Yes/No answer (the feature exists or it does not). However, if the specification is to validate the credit card number (as not stolen) within 1.25 seconds after the customer submits their information, then there is a measurable deliverable. The quality delivered is the degree to which it achieves or surpasses the 1.25 seconds during peak usage.

During the development phase, keep close to customers whose "second thoughts" on the project definition will surface. Sometimes this is due to changing business conditions or different ideas of what the finished product should look like.

There are three basic types of quality measurements:

1. Objective measurements (the preferred type). Objective measurements are measurable in some way. When an objective measurement is assigned to a product specification, a description of how it is to be measured should be included. This is normally done during the project definition phase. It is easier to obtain customer agreement on how to measure something during its definition. Examples of an objective measurement is a "GO/NO-GO," or a number on a scale, such as the response time example mentioned above.

2. Subjective measurements (opinion based). Project managers avoid these since a person's opinion can vary from day to day. How can a time estimate be created

for a task whose completion is subject to a whim? An example of this type of measurement is a requirement to provide a "visually pleasing" Web page.

3. Task measurement. Everything can be measured in some way even if the project manager must creatively invent a measurement. Perhaps the module's performance can be inferred from the performance of some other module. The most common result from this type of quality description is a "GO/NO-GO" criteria (it exists or it does not).

When possible, ensure that each task's quality measurements are objectively measured. This reduces arguments at the end of the project. This means that as scope changes are made, the corresponding quality measurement is also updated. Example software metrics include the following:

- Availability—number of minutes in a day the software system is operational. Nonavailable time would be when it is down for data backups, service to hardware, service to intervening network devices, etc.

- Recoverability—how long it takes to reload the software and data in case of a disaster. Software can be designed for recoverability through frequent database checkpoints, by journaling the data to an offsite location, by identifying the minimal components for operation that restore basic service until the full system is reloaded. This is important when designing company-critical systems.

- Usability—how long it takes a user to learn it. Is it intuitively obvious or must a manual always be within reach? A data entry screen can be quickly thrown together, but one that is easy to understand, where the data is logically linked and that provides clear messages of edit failures takes a long time to complete.

> "Quality is the result of a carefully constructed cultural environment. It has to be the fabric of the organization, not part of the fabric."
>
> —Phil Crosby

[F]   Quality and the ISO

The International Organization for Standardization (ISO) is a consortium that sets quality standards in a variety of areas. ISO standards provide an internationally recognized collection of best practices dedicated to customer satisfaction. (The ":2000" following each standard is the year of the standard's approval.) The following ISO standards are important to the project's quality program:

1. ISO 9000:2000 is a quality system standard for any product, service, or process.

2. ISO 9001:2000 is a quality system standard for design, production, and installation of a product or service.

3. ISO 9004:2000 is a set of quality management guidelines for any organization to use to develop and implement a quality system.

> The use of external appropriate benchmarks or standards for project activities and for evaluation of the end goal would make the project more valid to the world. This would be valuable to a product sold on the open market.

The ISO's purpose is to facilitate international trade by providing a single set of standards that people everywhere would recognize and respect. ISO focuses on eight areas:

1. The customer—Understand the customer's requirements and strive to exceed them.

2. Provide leadership—Identify a unity of purpose and set the direction for the organization. Create a positive work environment that helps people to achieve the company's goals.

3. Involve the team—Help people to develop and use their abilities. Involve all management levels in the quality process, in everything they do.

4. Use a process approach—Examine, document, and improve the processes throughout the organization.

5. Use a systems approach—Most company processes are interrelated, yet are managed separately. Ignore internal organizational boundaries and manage systems as a unit.

6. Encourage continual improvement—Businesses are pressured by a wide range of environmental forces. These forces change small and large aspects of the company processes. Strive to maximize this through the continual improvement of processes.

7. Get the facts before deciding—Gather and analyze data about processes and their results. Use the data to identify the root cause of problems and address them.

8. Work with suppliers—The business between the project and the supplier binds the two futures together. Work together as partners to improve customer satisfaction, to everyone's mutual benefit.

Two other important sources for IT quality assurance and control information are:

- Institute of Electrical and Electronics Engineers (IEEE) at www. ieee.org
- American Society of Quality (ASQ) at www.asq.org

---

§ 9.03   CONTROLLING THE QUALITY EFFORT

As with everything else in the project plan, the quality effort will have a plan of its own. It may be in the form of a section of the project's definition or a large annex to a major project. The basics of a quality plan do not change very often, so the easiest way to develop one is to copy one from a similar project previously completed for that organization. With a small amount of adjustment, it may provide satisfactory guidance.

In large projects, track the quality effort separately on the budget and project schedule. This measures the time and expense associated with quality. If the quality assurance effort is highly effective, it will show that much of the quality control time and expense was not used. On the other hand, if the product has many problems, it will show where the time for quality work was shortchanged.

Do not assume that corporate and IT quality groups will address the project's quality issues without direction. These groups know their jobs, but the project quality plan sets expectations for every team member to fulfill.

"Quality means doing it right when no one is looking."

—Henry Ford

[A]   Quality Plan Requirements

Complete the quality plan before finalizing the project specifications. This plan identifies the quality standards applied to the project. These may be the customer's policies, industry standards, or some mutually agreed to standards. The plan defines quality assurance, quality control, and continuous improvement aspects as they apply to the project.

Quality is measured against the project's stated characteristics—conformation of the final product to the specifications. Creating a quality plan in the beginning of the planning process sets an expectation in the minds of the team members that results must match the plan.

Whoever will be using the results of the project should be a part of the project team. Provide them with opportunities to review project progress during the design, development, implementation, testing, and validation phases. Customers typically prefer to assist only in the testing and implementation phases. This is when the unspoken expectations of the customer that were not included in the writing of the measurable project goals appear.

Quality control considerations are universal to all activities. Whenever a quality problem is detected, corrective action must be prompt. Log and track all quality issues through to completion in the same way as a risk or assumption. This will provide useful historical information for later projects.

The project's quality plan does not end on paper. It makes no difference to the customer if fault was due to a contractor or an employee. The quality plans for all critical contractors or suppliers must also be considered in the final plan—or each must adopt the same one as used by the project. If a contractor has its own quality plan, then review it to ensure that it essentially conforms to the project's plan or better.

[B]   Quality Audits

A quality audit is an independent review of a process to verify that it conforms to the quality plan. A quality audit can be done at any time. It verifies how closely the project conformed to the published quality plan and company policies. The degree of conformance provides feedback on the effectiveness of processes to support the project.

The focus of an audit must be on identifying and correcting those actions which will save money and time. They should never be punitive. If they are, then time during the project will be wasted while team members raise defenses against them.

Sometimes an audit is needed because a project has major problems with the product development, project schedule, or budget. Much of the audit is spent identifying where the problems arose, what actions the sponsor and project manager took, and the steps necessary to correct the problem.

The quality audit also verifies that:

• The project used approved tools and practices. Any new tools created or modified to address specific situations should be reviewed for acceptance by the project management office.

- The accuracy and completeness of project metrics. These metrics gauge project progress and efficiency. Knowledge of a potential audit inhibits a project manager from disguising project problems by misreporting metrics.

- The quality of the product created as compared to the current scope and criteria for success. Did the project deliver the form, fit, and function requested?

- How well the project manager's actions conformed to the published schedule and how effectively the project manager utilized assigned resources.

- The project as a whole and individual tasks within it, along with the actions taken by the project manager, for the likelihood or impact of adverse events.

Another quality function is to randomly audit portions of a project. Do this carefully since audits may create delays in an otherwise on-schedule effort. The goal of a random audit is to detect problems before they become major issues. Narrowly focus random audits on such things as issues tracking, financial reporting, or risk management. This helps to determine the quality of the project management effort with a minimum of disruption.

[C] Using a Quality Management Program Checklist

Like anything else, if the project manager wants people to use something, it should be made easy for them to use. Exhibit 9-1: Checklist for a Quality Management Program and its instructions assist in integrating the quality functions into these efforts.

Use a quality management checklist to identify the intangible effects on the IT infrastructure and the project's results. These intangibles include innovation, interoperability, reliability, scalability, stakeholder satisfaction, and production quality. When these intangibles are ignored, there is the potential for long-range effects beyond the project's duration with the IT group. In addition, all forms of information gathering should be considered: formal technical meetings, review briefings, reports (paper, e-mail, and bulletin boards), and—perhaps the most powerful form of information gathering—hallway conversations.

Imagine a carpenter who was building a cabinet. What would the finished product look like if the carpenter kept reworking the material to repair mistakes made in the creation? An artisan knows to measure twice and cut once. Compare this to IT technicians who build things and then spend time testing, reworking, and testing again to get it to work. If it were built correctly the first time, all of the extra effort would not be needed.

§ 9.04 CONTINUOUS IMPROVEMENT

Quality actions cannot be viewed as one-time measures that are "someone else's" responsibility. They must be a part of the project team's culture. Nurturing this culture of quality falls squarely on the project manager. It is based on the project manager's responsibility to enforce the quality plan of the product as well as on the quality of the project.

[A] Project Team Members Are the Key

Continuous improvement means every team member assists in improving the product quality and the quality of the project's execution. If the team member's opinion is valued, then he or she will offer it. If it is ignored, then valuable continuous improvement information will be lost.

The following are used to evaluate the process.

- Critique project processes—What processes and tools have been provided to the team and are they adequate for the job? Are the processes heavily burdened with busy work that adds no value? Are there ways to meet project requirements while reducing time and expense?

- Critique pending tasks—Look ahead on the project plan to see if the estimates and detail of specification are adequate. Although the workers may have been involved with the original estimates, they may feel differently about them now that they have worked through some of the project's other tasks.

- Critique problems and incidents—Look back, what could have been done differently to avoid some of the problems that arose during previous tasks.

[B] Peer Reviews

Beyond the traditional quality assurance and control group is the use of peer reviews. Team members examine deliverables and project issues to offer recommendations. Peer reviews are an important part of an organization's continuous improvement program where everyone shares best practices and lessons learned from errors.

Peer reviews can address quality assurance, quality control, or project quality issues. Each peer review should result in written recommendations covering the following:

- Quality assurance
  - Adequacy of consultant and vendor quality plans
  - Capacity plans

- ○ Coding techniques applicable to the current project
- ○ Documentation
- ○ Implementation plan
- ○ Internet working plan
- ○ Project plan
- ○ System design
- ○ System development
- ○ Testing plan
- ○ Training
- • Quality control
  - ○ Does it meet corporate benchmarks and appropriate standards?
  - ○ Does it technically fulfill project goals?
  - ○ Does it meet operational requirements?
  - ○ Does documentation correctly state technical requirements?
  - ○ Have training courses been developed to address technical issues?
  - ○ Does it meet functional, protocol, and security requirements?
  - ○ Does the help function assist the customer in resolving technical issues?
- • Project quality
  - ○ Do the project policies make sense given the current work environment and project?
  - ○ Are the tools provided efficient and effective?
  - ○ Is the project budget fairly apportioned among the tasks based on their requirements?

Management (this includes the project manager) should be absent from peer reviews, so the discussion does not turn into an individual performance review.

---

§ 9.05 SUMMARY

Project managers are concerned with both the quality of the finished product and the quality of project execution. Project quality programs must be tailored to the unique aspects of the project. If the organization benefiting from the project has a quality program, use their standards, processes, tests and reports. Another source is industry benchmarks, such as ISOs.

The project sponsor ensures that there is an effective quality assurance and control effort for the project. Although the project manager can recommend actions, there is an implied conflict for the project manager to both do something and then evaluate its performance.

The key to any project quality process is the attitude of its leaders. No matter what they say, their actions tell the team what to do. When times are tough, if the first thing they drop are the quality steps, then so will the team—a short-term gain exchanged for a long-term problem.

Exhibit 9-1: Checklist for a Quality Management Program

	Attachments
QUALITY CONTROL	
Source ID	
Document identification	
Scope plan	
Activity plan	
Resource plan	
Schedule	
Budget	
Standards	
Benchmarks	
Verification	
Testing	
Time estimate criteria	
Cost estimate criteria	
Resource estimate criteria	
Skill criteria	
Technical procedures	
Technical policies	
Procurements policies	
Communications	
ISO standards	
PMI standards	
Customer satisfaction criteria	
Critical path criteria	
Identify skill criteria	
Pessimistic	
Realistic	
Optimistic	
Establish tasks criteria	
Planning	
Design	
Production	
Testing	
Task-sequencing criteria	
Determine reviews requirements	
Time estimates	
Cost estimates	
Resource estimates	
Project administration criteria	
Assumptions	
Criteria	
Validation criteria	

Exhibit 9-1: *(Continued)*

	Attachments
QUALITY CONTROL	
Constraints	
Criteria	
Validation criteria	
Determine field test criteria	
Identify training criteria	
Validation	
Testing	
Identify quality support tasks	
Variances criteria:	
Time	
Cost	
Resources	
Variance-reporting criteria	
Risk management criteria	
Specify random inspection criteria	
Equipment	
Materials	
Skills	
Project management tools	
Development tools	
Facilities	
Logistics	
Training	
Documentation	
Communications	
Specify audit criteria	
Equipment	
Materials	
Skills	
Project management tools	
Development tools	
Facilities	
Logistics	
Training	
Documentation	
Communications	
Vendors	
Assist writing RFPs	
Gather performance history	
Gather validation criteria	
Gather testing criteria	
Dependency identification	
Project goals	
Project milestones	
Task milestones	
Learning curve	
Special events	

Exhibit 9-1: *(Continued)*

	Attachments
QUALITY CONTROL	
Consistency determination criteria	
Scope plan	
Activity plan	
Resource plan	
Project schedule	
Project budget	
Business justification	
Commercial specification	
Design/Development plan	
Baseline plan	
Field introduction	
Gather change management criteria	
Identify update requirements	
Describe slippage rules	
Contingency plan criteria	
Resource leveling assistance	
Gather logistics criteria	
Gather modeling data	
QUALITY ASSURANCE	
Source ID	
Review viability responses	
Confirm project administration criteria	
Analyze skills	
Pessimistic	
Realistic	
Optimistic	
Validate document usage	
Scope plan	
Activity plan	
Resource plan	
Schedule	
Budget	
Standards	
Benchmarks	
Verification	
Testing	
Time estimate criteria	
Cost estimate criteria	
Resource estimate criteria	
Skill criteria	
Technical procedures	
Technical policies	
Procurements policies	
Communications	
ISO standards	
PMI standards	
Customer satisfaction criteria	

Exhibit 9-1: *(Continued)*

	Attachments
QUALITY CONTROL	
Authenticate tasks criteria	
Planning	
Design	
Development	
Production	
Testing	
Assist in the field test	
Validate training performance	
Verify documentation	
Customer	
User	
Technical (IS)	
Reports	
Do quality support tasks	
Validate and test assumptions	
Validate and test constraints	
Assist in reviews	
Time estimates checklists	
Cost estimates checklists	
Resource estimates	
Task identification checklists	
Task sequencing	
Critical path	
Contingency plan	
Approve risk management criteria	
Do variance reports	
Perform random inspections	
Identify variances and causes	
Time	
Cost	
Resources	
Equipment	
Materials	
Skills	
Project management tools	
Development tools	
Facilities	
Logistics	
Training	
Documentation	
Communications	
Perform audits	
Identify variances and causes	
Time	
Cost	
Resources	
Equipment	
Materials	
Skills	

Exhibit 9-1: *(Continued)*

	Attachments
QUALITY CONTROL	
Project management tools	
Development tools	
Facilities	
Logistics	
Training	
Documentation	
Communications	
Project management process	
IS procedures and process	
Manufacturing	
Other support groups	
Vendors	
Review RFP responses	
Analyze performance history	
Confirm validation process	
Confirm testing process	
Confirm dependency usage	
Project goals	
Project milestones	
Task milestones	
Learning curve	
Special event	
Consistency validation	
Scope plan	
Activity plan	
Resource plan	
Project schedule	
Project budget	
Business justification	
Commercial specification	
Design/Development plan	
Baseline plan	
Field introduction	
Validate change management process	
Validate update process	
Validate slippage usages	
Do feedback reports	
Assistance resource leveling	
Analyze logistics criteria	
Assist in model development	
Validate and test deliverables	

Exhibit 9-1: *(Continued)*

Instructions for Checklist for a Quality Management Program

Quality management is the process that seeks to prevent risks and if a risk occurs, minimize it. The quality plan defines the tasks of quality management's two functions, control and assurance, in all phases of the project process.

It is the purpose of this checklist to assist in the writing of the plan.

The guiding principle for responding to this checklist is that quality control creates the map, while quality assurance drives a route based on the map.

This comprehensive checklist should be used to the level of detail that produces an effective and efficient quality management for the project.

Quality control: It is the quality management component, which considers the system or the development of a project's processes. It has tasks used to gather performance information requirements, that is, standards and benchmarks.

Source ID: Identify the person responsible for writing the budget item, including title, e-mail address, and telephone number. If an external source, also include company information.

Document identification: Results in a distributed document that identifies the location of listed documents and the methods of acquisition. There should be brief descriptions of the relevance of documents to the project. Two optional project process documents sets are the ISO and PMI standards. The International Organization for Standardization (ISO) is a consortium that sets process standards in a variety of areas. The Project Management Institute (PMI) is a professional organization that studies and promotes project management through its standards. The standards should be more than technical; they should include the requirements for stakeholder satisfaction (customer, management, and team); financial variances; and the impacts of innovation on the project and on the IS infrastructure as to interoperability, reliability, and scalability.

Critical path criteria: A critical project task means that if it is not completed, there is a potential project failure. The task is to identify criteria for the meaning of critical. Second, the task is to assist in the design and development of the critical path. Third, the task is to distribute the path criteria as required by the project team.

Identify skill criteria: Gather information so there is consistency in the method of defining skills on three levels (pessimistic, realistic, and optimistic).

Establish tasks criteria: Develop criteria that distinguish between a task and an activity for the project schedule for the listed project phases.

Task-sequencing criteria: Gather information to ensure that task sequencing is done in a consistent manner so project goals are completed.

Determine reviews requirements: Gather objective criteria and any special customer, company, or project team requirements to ensure that the three major types of estimates meet any relevant standards or benchmarks.

Project administrative criteria: Define administrative criteria to ensure that the project process used a systematic and sequential set of tasks of the project manager, the project team, and the operational managers. One of the project management techniques that must

Exhibit 9-1: *(Continued)*

be considered in the development of criteria is the program evaluation and review technique (PERT). It combines statistics and network diagrams.

Assumptions: Predictions that something will be true, an event that ensures project success. This task assists in defining any criteria (pessimistic, realistic, and optimistic). Second, it establishes the criteria that are used to validate or test project components as to performance or results. Third, these assumptions and their validation requirements are organized into a document and distributed as required.

Constraints: Parameters, limitations, or boundaries for the project such as the project schedule or the project budget. First, this task assists in identifying any constraints (pessimistic, realistic, and optimistic). Second, it establishes the criteria that are used to validate or test project components as to performance or results. Third, these assumptions and their validation requirements are organized into a document and distributed as required.

Determine field test criteria: Gather data for the trial (beta) strategy that identifies the software and hardware elements in the project that are a part of any trial. Also the where, when, why, how, and whom should be included. This provides a clear identification of the testing requirements, plus the extent of the resources and capabilities for a trial.

Identify training criteria: Gather data for doing validation testing of defined project goals and results for formal and informal training. It includes identifying required skill levels to training events.

Identify documentation criteria: Gather data for doing validation testing of defined project goals and results for customer, user, and technical support documents. IT includes identifying links to project goals.

Identify quality support tasks: Are any special tasks directly implied from the project goals or by the project team not given in this checklist?

Variances criteria: Gather the criteria for determining normal and risk variances. A variance is any deviation from the planned work, whether it is cost, time, or resources.

Variance-reporting criteria: Gather data on methods for writing variance reports. Other data to be included would be: when they should be completed, why they should be written, and for whom they should be given.

Risk management criteria: Gather the benchmarks for determining risks and potential scenarios that foreshadow them. A risk is a performance error that can have a significant or disastrous impact on the success of a project or major activity. It is not just a problem. A scenario is a set of possibilities that could happen to cause a risk.

Specify random inspection criteria: The criteria are for an independent evaluation or test of a part of listed project components by qualified personnel. Independent here means evaluation by with QA or an outside consultant. The criteria should be distributed as required by the project team.

Specify audit criteria: The criteria are for an independent evaluation or test of one of the listed project components by qualified personnel. Independent here means evaluation by either QA or an outside consultant. The criteria should be distributed by the project team.

Exhibit 9-1: *(Continued)*

VENDORS

Assist writing RFPs: Ensure a request for proposal is consistent with related project goals and milestones, technical performance requirements, quality process, skill-level requirements, and competitive position.

Gather performance history: Performance as used here means that there are objective data that demonstrate that the vendor can act at the level of work required by the RFP.

Gather validation criteria: Identify methods for validating information from vendors against project goals.

Gather testing criteria: Identify methods for testing information from vendors against project goals.

Dependency information: Dependency means that a task has to be completed before or after another one. For example, coding has to be completed before code testing can be completed. Less obvious is that a code test has to be written before code testing. A document should be a collection of dependencies for at least the listed items and distributed in accordance with the project team's instructions.

Consistency determination criteria: Identify the data links between the listed documents so that what is stated is the same sequentially throughout the documents.

Baseline plan: The initial approved point from which any deviation will be determined using standards and benchmarks.

Field introduction: Assist in the writing of the trial (beta) strategy.

Gather change management criteria: Classify the parameters required to make changes to the project estimates, in particular those that directly affect the schedule and budget as to who, what, why, where, and how.

Identify update requirements: Here parameters are described as to which are required to make updates to the project estimates, in particular those that directly affect the schedule and budget as to who, what, why, when, where, and how.

Describe slippage rules: Define a potential schedule or budget slippage and how and when it should be reported. Budget slippage happens when a budget item is overspent. Time slippage is expected when you know about it before the due date, while it is unexpected when you learn about the fact after the due date.

Contingency plan criteria: Here a document is prepared of potential causes and solutions using pessimistic scenarios or worse, with the potential that they will become a reality. In addition, the document identifies time and cost estimates that have a contingency value.

Resource-leveling assistance: Do leveling; that is, the technique of smoothing out peaks and valleys for the use of resources in a project schedule.

Gather logistics criteria: The criteria should ensure that the logistics process gets the correct resource to the correct location at the correct time. The criteria should be published as required by the project team.

Gather modeling data: Define the data requirements for doing models or simulations to ensure theoretically that process results as defined by required project goals can be validated

Exhibit 9-1: *(Continued)*

prior to project completion. However, more preferable is validation before project development begins.

QUALITY ASSURANCE

Source ID: Identify the person responsible for writing the budget item, including title, e-mail address, and telephone number. If an external source, also include company information.

Review viability responses: Assist the project manager in the responses for the project viability process before any review by upper-level management.

Confirm project administrative criteria: Validate the defined administrative criteria are being used to ensure that the project process is systematic and sequential to achieve the project's measurable goals. The validation includes the project administrative tasks of the project manager, the project team, and the operational managers. While this checklist does reflect the more specific tasks of the project management process, a broad set of project administration areas needs to be monitored and evaluated. The areas include planning, organizing, systematic processing for nontechnical areas (financial, communications, change, risk management), and control management (resources, cost, and time).

Analyze skills: Analyze the skill requirements and the demonstrated abilities of the person holding the skill.

Validate document usage: This task should use inspections and audit to determine if project stakeholders are adhering to criteria relevant to the project as found in the listed documents.

Authenticate tasks criteria: Here tasks are authenticated that drive the project-level processes, while activities drive the operational-level processes.

Assist in the field test: Ensure that the process in the trial (beta) strategy is followed. In addition, the task includes determining when technical expertise is available to give support until the completion of the test.

Validate training performance: Validate that formal and, when possible, informal training meets the project goals and that it produces the required skill levels to achieve realistic estimates.

Verify documentation: Validate that the listed document types are written in accordance with project goals and requirements.

Do quality support tasks: Do any special tasks implied from the project goals not given in the schedule.

Validate and test assumptions: First, the task randomly validates and tests any critical assumptions. Second, this task confirms the assumptions for validating or testing project components as to performance or results. Third, the results are organized into documents as required and distributed.

Validate and test constraints: First, this task validates and tests critical constraints. Second, it determines how the criteria are being used in the project process. Third, the results are organized into documents and distributed as required.

Exhibit 9-1: *(Continued)*

Assist in reviews: For the listed times, the task is for quality assurance to review a member that determines that estimates, tasks, and plans reflect the project goals as stated in the scope plan.

Critical path: Assist in the review of the critical path plan. Report to the project team on negative and positive deviations from the critical path.

Contingency plan: This task gives assistance in reviewing the document. Second, it validates the need for a particular part of the plan to go into effect.

Approve risk management criteria: Here benchmarks are analyzed for determining risks and potential scenarios that foreshadow them and for determining if all goals have been covered. In addition, the task includes verifying the project process against the benchmarks.

Do variance reports: Complete reports for the project team on variances of standards and benchmarks as found in inspections and audits. This task uses the data gathered by quality control as to the method for writing variance reports. Other data would include when they should be completed, why they should be written, and for whom they should be given.

Perform random inspections: An independent evaluation or test for part of a project's component by qualified personnel. It is a partial audit. The task includes using quality control criteria and doing this task before milestones or critical events.

Identify variances and causes: Any time this task is performed; all related estimates (time, cost, and resources) have to be considered.

Perform audits: An independent evaluation or test of some component of the project by qualified personnel. It is more complete than an inspection. An audit is accomplished at a milestone or major event for the listed time.

Identify variances and causes: Any time this task is performed; all related estimates (time, cost, and resources) have to be considered.

Other support groups: Examples of other support groups are marketing and human resources. These groups are only audited as to their performance based on the scope plan.

VENDORS

Review RFP responses: Assist in the analysis of any RFP response as to how it reflects the stated requirements and criteria in the RFP.

Analyze performance history: Analyze performance data to ensure that the vendor has demonstrated at the level of work required by the RFP.

Confirm validation process: Verify the vendor's stated validation process from the RFP response.

Confirm testing process: Verify the vendor's stated testing process from the RFP response.

Confirm dependency usage: Validate or test stated dependencies.

Consistency validation: Ensure that what is stated in any documents is used consistently through the other listed documents. The baseline in all cases is the scope plan.

Baseline plan: The initial approved point from which any deviation will be determined using standards and benchmarks.

Field introduction: Assist in the process as given in the trial (beta) strategy.

Exhibit 9-1: *(Continued)*

Validate change management process: Validate the change process as to how it is being managed in accordance with the defined project standards and benchmarks.

Validate update process: Validate the update process as to how it is being managed in accordance with the defined project standards and benchmarks.

Validate slippage usage: Validate the slippage management process as to whether it is being managed in accordance with the defined project standards and benchmarks.

Do feedback reports: Provide feedback on any task listed in this checklist as required by the project team or relevant quality standards.

Assistance resource leveling: Provide assistance in using leveling to smooth out peaks and valleys in the use of resources in a project schedule.

Analyze logistics criteria: Validate that the criteria are being followed so that the logistics process is getting the correct resource to the correct location at the correct time.

Assist in model development: Use the criteria established by the quality control to assist in modeling or simulation.

Validate and test deliverables: Ensure that all deliverables as defined in the project goals are as promised in the scope plan. Any deviations are to be reported to the project team.

Exhibit 9-2: Activity Audit

Project Name:		Date:	
Preparer:		**Activity:**	

Core Evaluation:

Performance:	ON	ABOVE	BELOW	(circle one)
Budget:	ON	ABOVE	BELOW	(circle one)
Schedule:	ON	ABOVE	BELOW	(circle one)
Overall Status:	Positive	Negative		(circle one)

Factors:

Things done above standards/benchmarks:

Things done below standards/benchmarks:

Recommendations:

Additional comments:

Exhibit 9-3: Quality Control and Deliverables Questions Checklist

1. Have the quality standards been made consistent?	
2. Has a comprehensive quality control program been defined, including standards and benchmarks?	
3. Has the quality process been cost estimated and budgeted?	
4. Have the quality control events been included at the appropriate milestones?	
5. What are the criteria for documenting quality control activities?	
6. What are the quality control procedures that need to be in the activity plan?	
7. What are the standards and benchmarks for quality control?	
8. What is the necessary time for quality validation?	
9. What quality control policies, benchmarks, or standards have to be followed?	
Questions on a Deliverable	
1. Does the documentation correctly state technical requirements?	
2. Does it meet appropriate standards?	
3. Does it meet corporate benchmarks?	
4. Does it meet functional requirements?	
5. Does it meet operational requirements?	
6. Does it meet protocol requirements?	
7. Does it meet security requirements?	
8. Does it technically fulfill project goals?	
9. Does the help function assist the customer in resolving technical issues?	
10. Have training courses been developed to cover technical issues correctly?	

Chapter 10

Managing Stakeholders

§ 10.01   INTRODUCTION

> "Be sincere. Be brief. Be seated."
>
> —Franklin Delano Roosevelt

Projects involve many people. Imagine a project to resurface a busy roadway. Everyone who uses that road has an interest in how quickly it will be completed, how smooth it will be, and how long it lasts before needing replacement. Other interests include the highway department's concern about quality and cost, nearby businesses' worry about lost sales, etc. Each of these is a stakeholder with some interest in the timely completion of the project. Some stakeholders expect periodic updates about aspects of the job, while others simply wait for the orange barrels to come down.

So how does this apply to an IT project? Consider a project to replace all of the payroll time clocks in the facility. How many stakeholders are affected? Is the payroll department anxious? How about the employees? What would happen to the project execution if all of them began shouting complaints and concerns at the same time?

Identifying the interested parties and reporting on the progress of a project is an important project management responsibility. The goodwill of the interested parties is essential to a smooth project execution. Stakeholders want information: factual, timely, and succinct. If the project manager, the person with the most accurate information, does not provide this when desired, then they will resort to other, less accurate information channels. They may also listen to their worst fears and attack the project. Some benefits of a stakeholder management plan are as follows:

- The opinions of the most powerful stakeholders can shape the project in its early stages. This provides the dual benefits of making the project "their own" and improving the quality of the project.

- It identifies stakeholders who are friendly and unfriendly toward the project with the goal of winning over the unfriendly ones.

- Risks to the project from disenfranchised or angry stakeholders are reduced.

- It forms the foundation for the communications plan.

§ 10.02   STAKEHOLDER PLANNING

A project stakeholder is any individual or group that participates, benefits, or is injured by the planning, initiation, execution, or completion of the project. The interest of stakeholders can be in the project outcome, the project execution, or both.

A project cannot move forward without stakeholders. They provide specifications for shaping the project's final product, equipment, information, or other resources that are critical to the project. Some stakeholders are involved with the project throughout its existence. Others are unique to a particular phase. Some are in daily contact with the work, and others pop in and out as needed. Stakeholders are everywhere!

Like everything else in the project, stakeholder planning takes time. Most of this planning occurs during the initial project phases. A stakeholder plan involves the following:

1. Identifying the stakeholders—the people and organizations with an interest in the project. Who are they? Why do they care? What is their motivation? Separate the curious from the significant.

2. Interviewing each significant stakeholder. Ask them about their views on the project, its goals, and method of execution.

3. Analyzing the interviews to separate the friends from the foes using a stakeholder assessment matrix. The matrix identifies each stakeholder's potential contribution (positive or negative) to the project.

4. Create a communications plan to identify information to provide to each stakeholder, and when.

§ 10.03 IDENTIFYING STAKEHOLDERS

A primary source of stakeholder information is the project charter. Some charters include a project organization chart and/or a list of the people on the project steering committee. Everyone listed in the charter is a project stakeholder.

Many of the stakeholders can be identified by answering some simple questions:

- Who will receive the deliverables of or benefits from the project?

- Who will work on the project, both from the project organization and from the customer organization? Does the project involve anything that touches the public?

- Who is the expert about different aspects of the project or solution?

- Does the project touch anything overseen by a government regulatory agency? (At a minimum, the answer is always, "Yes, OSHA.")

- Who serves as the project's champion in the customer organization?

- Who is paying for the project?

- Who will use the product created by the project?

Another useful stakeholder identification tool is a company's organization chart, which identifies positional authority. Job titles generally indicate who performs what tasks within a company. An organization chart also shows who reports to whom, which is useful in addressing negative stakeholders. For example, if the project involves installing radio frequency network points in the facility, then the facility manager is a team member since that person oversees the work of the team that will run the wires to the nodes.

However, an organization chart only shows the official lines of authority. It does not show the very important unofficial lines of influence. These "real power brokers" are as significant as the formal ones.

If the project is supporting a third-party client, then information is needed to identify their stakeholders as well. Examine customer newsletters, announcements, and published minutes from meetings. These may provide insight into the client's organizational structure, the roles and responsibilities of the client's staff, and their reporting methods, motivation, challenges and other items.

> "You don't have to be a 'person of influence' to be influential. In fact, the most influential people in my life are probably not even aware of the things they've taught me."
>
> —Scott Adams

§ 10.04   TYPICAL STAKEHOLDERS

All IT projects start with the same core set of stakeholders. There will be other stakeholders around the project, but this core group is the same on all projects:

- Project manager (of course)—The person who leads, plans, and controls the project. This involves a wide range of actions including monitoring, documenting, reporting, and reacting to issues as they arise. He or she is the primary contact for stakeholders and provides status reports as required.

- Sponsor—The sponsor is the person who approved the project. He or she provides authority, finance support, and advice. The sponsor shares responsibility for the project success with the project manager and minimizes "political" interference by other executives.

- Customer—The customer is the person or organization that pays for and/or uses the project result. Customers are broken down into those who will use the product and those who approve it. Customers who approve the final product are key stakeholders.

- Team members—The people assigned to the project team are the ones who transform an idea into action. They are very interested in all aspects of the project.

- Information security—Someone must identify the data elements created by or used by the project that must be safeguarded. These recommendations must be carefully considered.

- Business management—In some ways, all IT projects touch one of the business departments, such as manufacturing, sales, engineering, materials, or order processing. Keep them informed of the project's progress and successes even if they seem unconcerned.

- Accounting/Finance—Somewhere in the depths of the accounting department is a clerk who reviews the project budget and all spending requests. Establishing a positive relationship with this stakeholder keeps paperwork flowing smoothly.

- Human resources—This department supplies the team with personnel, both permanent and temporary. Human resources also assists with personnel problems throughout the project and the reassignment of staff when they are no longer needed on the team.

Large projects also consider the following groups as possible stakeholders:

- Executive steering committee—This is sort of a "super sponsor" made up of senior executives who monitor progress on projects that may significantly impact the organization, or whose budget represents a significant portion of the organization's expenses.

- Shareholders—This group expects results from the project to match what the company executives proposed to them. They are more concerned with the outcome, but become involved if the budget or schedule deviates significantly.

- Government agencies—Some government agencies, such as OSHA, EPA, and EEOC, touch every workplace and every project (although few project managers invite them to team meetings).

> "It is better to act quickly and err than to hesitate until the time of action is past."
>
> —Clausewitz

§ 10.05 MEET THE STAKEHOLDERS!

Early in the project, meet individually with the stakeholders to gauge their attitude toward the project. Use this opportunity to establish a positive working relationship with each one. This involves, among other things, determining the stakeholders' opinions as to the project's viability and goals, and their perception of how the project affects their own work environment. Plug this information into a project definition that key stakeholders will support.

Two common stakeholder complaints about projects are that "no one told me," and "no one asked me." Tell each stakeholder about the project and ask his or her opinion. These discussions reveal the stakeholder's level of interest in the project. Is his interest driven by an expected benefit from the project's outcome? Are there resources that the stakeholder must provide to the project? Will these resources be made available when needed?

Mixed in with the stakeholders' comments is their unspoken opinion about the project. This must be a part of the discussion. If a stakeholder has an issue to be addressed, now is the time to raise it. This may take many forms. Does the stakeholder have a conflict with one of the other stakeholders? Will this project diminish the stakeholder's stature in the company? Will this project place some of the stakeholder's data systems at risk?

During interviews, stakeholders should describe aspects of the project they believe need adjusting. These discussions are useful since they help to sharpen the project's scope and definition. Beware of raising a false expectation in their minds. Do not commit to changing the scope, but only to submitting the request to the project sponsor through the formal scope change process.

Organize all of this information into a stakeholder analysis. This information feeds into project strategies, procedures, and activities throughout the project management process. Its ultimate goal is to promote stakeholder support and minimize negative influence in order to ensure project success.

[A] Interviewing

For the interview, choose a quiet, neutral location such as a meeting room. The interview process is straightforward. Pose a question and get the interviewer talking. Follow-up on the responses with short, leading questions, such as, "Why do you feel that way," "What happened then," etc. This is not a police interrogation, but statements made about the project are often the result of underlying factors. Follow-up interview questions help to root out these factors so the project can avoid future problems.

As the conversation flows, the stakeholder may relax and gradually speak his or her mind about the project. Note his or her attitude and tone as he discusses people, processes, and the project goals. These unspoken factors may point to underlying issues that need to be explored.

Following is a list of goals of the interview process.

- Identify whether the interviewee is in favor of or against the project.
- Why does he or she feel that way? What are the significant factors of this opinion?
- What can the project manager do to make this person a positive, contributing member of the team?
- Discover other stakeholders with whom to meet.
- Uncover the unofficial lines of authority.

[B]   Create a Questionnaire

Draft a questionnaire to guide the discussions. Using a form during these interview discussions ensures that data are collected on the same critical questions. Each question should relate to a column in the analysis. Of course, as the discussions proceed, modify the form to target new issues as they arise. Use these questions as an agenda for the meeting so the stakeholders can prepare for the discussion.

An example is provided in Exhibit 10-1: Stakeholder Interview, located at the end of this chapter. Fill out page 1 during the meeting. Page 2 gathers the interviewer's confidential impressions of the stakeholder and any additional notes made during the meeting. Fill in page 2 after the interview ends.

[C]   Analyze the Results

Two tools make stakeholder analysis easy. They can be built with a spreadsheet and are based on the data collected during the interviews. Using a questionnaire ensures that information needed for the analysis is collected from each person.

[1]   Stakeholder Assessment

The first tool is a list of all of the stakeholders and information about them. This list is used to create the communication plan—that is, who gets what status report. Refer to Chart 10-1, Stakeholder Assessment. The goals of this assessment are to:

- Ensure everyone is included.
- Provide a rough score based on three criteria to separate the significant few stakeholders from the many others.
- Identify concerns for the risk analysis. This chart ties the risk to the person so the team can assist in its mitigation.
- Highlight areas to include in the project plan.

Role	Stakeholder's Name	Interest	Influence	Favorable Attitude	Impact Score	Key Wants	Key Concerns	Risk Tolerance	Win-Win Strategies
Sponsor									

Chart 10-1: Stakeholder Assessment

The fields for the matrix are:

- Role—What role does this person play on the project? Typical roles might be sponsor, steering committee member, department manager, team member, user of the final product, labor representative, purchasing agent, maintenance manager, government agency, public supplier, etc.

- Stakeholder's name—The person's name. If the person in this role changes, make a second entry, but do not eliminate the first.

- Rate the stakeholder's overall importance to the project

  - Interest—How interested is the person in the outcome of the project? Does it involve his or her department in some fashion, pass data to the person's files, etc? Use a scale of 1 to 10, with 1 being the lowest.

  - Influence—How much influence does this person have in the company or over this project? What is his or her ability to force project changes or cancellation? Use a scale of 1 to 10, with 1 being the lowest.

  - Favorable attitude—How supportive is the person of the project's goal, the project effort itself, or project management overall? In some cases, the lack of support deals with conflicts with individuals rather than issues with the project. Use a scale of 1 to 10, with 1 being the lowest.

  - Impact score—Tally the ratings for interest, influence, and favorable attitude to obtain an overall impact score. This score separates the key stakeholders from the multitudes. These numbers can be multiplied together or totaled. Sort the scores in a descending sequence, and select a cutoff point, below which stakeholders will not be actively addressed.

- Key wants—What are the significant few things this person is looking for before declaring this to be a successful project? Can this person be included in the project definition?

- Key concerns—What are the significant few obstacles this person sees facing the project? Should they be added to the risk assessment?

- Risk tolerance—What is this person's level of risk tolerance? How comfortable is he or she working in the midst of uncertainty? Stakeholders with low risk comfort require more frequent status updates with little detail.

- Win-win strategies—What actions can be taken to ensure that this person's key wants are included in the project scope and key concerns are addressed in the risk management plan, so that this person may be kept as an ally to the project?

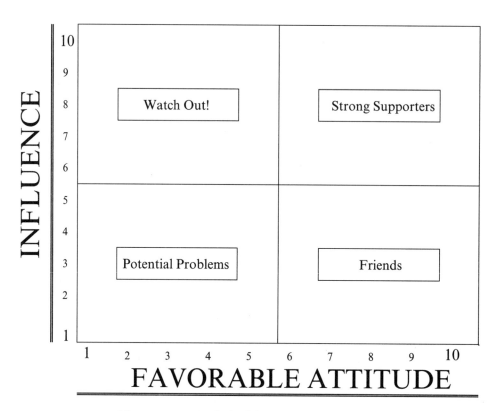

Chart 10-2: Stakeholder Support Matrix

> Throughout the stakeholder analysis process, many observations are made about the motivations, personality traits, and work ethic of the various stakeholders. Beware what is written as it may surface at inconvenient times and destroy all of the positive things built up around the project.

[2] Stakeholder Support Matrix

Build a visual tool to illustrate how the stakeholders stack up to the project. Refer to Chart 10-2: Stakeholder Support Matrix. This matrix plots the stakeholder's influence score along the "Y" axis and the favorable attitude score along the "X" axis. Where these points come together, write that person's name on the chart. For example, if someone has an influence score of 7 and favorable attitude score of 8, then write his or her name at that point on the matrix. The person is in the "Strong Supporters" quadrant.

As is quickly obvious, this matrix should be held from general distribution as people may take offense at their rating. However, for the project manager, it provides a handy, quick reference. The goal is to build a plan that moves all key stakeholders toward the right (more favorable) attitude. Someone's position on the grid shows the project manager how to work with the person:

- "Strong Supporters"—High influence, high favorable attitude: these are the people to fully engage in the project and make the greatest efforts to satisfy.

- "Watch Out!"—High influence, low favorable attitude: identify ways to persuade them to increase their support of the project.

- "Friends"—Low influence, high favorable attitude: keep these people adequately informed, and talk to them to ensure that no major issues are arising. These people can often be very helpful with the details of the project.

- "Potential Problems"—Low influence, low favorable attitude: monitor these people, but do not bore them with excessive communication. Their attitude often flows with the prevailing political wind.

"The herd seeks out the great, not for their sake but for their influence; and the great welcome them out of vanity or need."

—Napoleon Bonaparte

---

§ 10.06 STAKEHOLDER COMMUNICATIONS

An important responsibility of the project manager is to report the progress made on a project toward completion of its goals. Regular, factual reports are essential for building confidence in the project's management and for maintaining sponsor support. A tool for identifying the various reports required and the data they must contain is a communications plan. (An example is found in Chart 10-3: Stakeholder Communications Plan.) This plan uses information gathered during the stakeholder analysis interviews.

Each type of stakeholder has his or her own interest in project information, the method by which he or she prefers to receive it, and in a format easiest to digest. These preferences are shaped by the work environment, the amount of information thrown at him or her, and the priorities of the moment.

No one likes to hear bad news. If there is bad news to announce to a stakeholder, the project manager should ensure that the person is the first to know and not hear about it through office gossip channels. If possible, deliver it personally so that questions can be answered immediately. This increases the project manager's credibility and reduces the stakeholder's reliance on the informal communications channels.

§ 10.07 KNOW THE AUDIENCE

[A] Executives and Sponsors

Executives and sponsors may have a short attention span. In their eyes, they have passed responsibility for the project onto the project manager. They only want to know briefly if the project will meet its scheduled completion date and budget. If the expenses or schedule are significantly over what was originally scheduled, they may be interested in the team's challenges and how they were overcome and the reasons for delay or cost overruns.

Project status reports include a recap of the project's schedule and budget performance followed by major successes and problems encountered since the last report. Include any significant changes to the scope (approved or in process). If possible, keep the report to a single page. If more detail is required, the stakeholder will ask for it.

Executive reports are typically provided in written form along with a follow-up face-to-face briefing to answer any questions. Executives' time horizons are generally long term and they will typically ask for reports every month.

Sponsors will need to know more information and expect a report once per week. In this way, they can detect trends toward exceeding budgets before they overstep accepted variances.

> Take care of what is said, and how it was said! The project manager's word is the official word. A piece of information may be a rumor or it may be common knowledge but whatever the project manager says becomes the "official statement," since he or she is the one person most "in the know" about all aspects of the project.

[B] Team Members

Team members are involved with the day-to-day tasks. They want information on what has occurred in the last two weeks and what is coming up in the immediate future. Communications are usually made through a weekly team meeting. Structure the meetings around an agenda with time limits on the discussion of issues. Conduct longer discussions as needed in a separate forum focused on the specific problem.

An important tool is an issues log reviewed at every team meeting. Team members want to know details about current tasks, upcoming work, pending scope changes, current risk mitigation actions—everything that affects their work environment.

[C]   Other Stakeholders

This group needs to be generally aware of the project's progress so they can consider its impact on their future. Their information requirements vary. The accounting department wants a report on expenses past and pending; the human resources department is only interested in pending headcount changes, etc.

Keep in mind that the culture of the organization influences the reporting mechanisms used. For example:

- Do stakeholders prefer formal or informal communication? Do they prefer face-to-face, telephone, or written communication? Paper or paperless?

- Which delivery mechanisms (e.g., e-mail, Web pages, MS project) are preferred?

- If this project is to deliver a result for a paying client, then the reporting structure must consider both the supplying and the client organizations.

§ 10.08   STAKEHOLDER COMMUNICATIONS PLAN

Build a visual tool to illustrate how the stakeholders stack up behind the project. Refer again to Chart 10-3: Stakeholder Communications Plan. This matrix illustrates who needs what status information and when. Not everyone wants the same information at the same time. Some want information weekly, some monthly, etc. Some reports may contain information that the company wants closely held, such as headcount changes, actual project expenses, etc. Use this matrix to keep everything straight! The columns on Chart 10-3 are allocated as follows:

- Stakeholder—Use the list of people from the stakeholder assessments.

- Reports—Which reports are sent to this person (the weekly status report, updated information security risk assessment, etc.)?

- Amount of detail—Do the stakeholders want a summary or all of the dirty details?

- Best format—How does the stakeholder want to see the information (charts, lists of numbers, PowerPoint presentation, or formal written report)?

- Frequency—How often is this information needed? This might be weekly, or the first Friday of every month, etc.

- Delivery—What is the best way to deliver the information? This might be in person, by e-mail, or in a formal written report.

Stakeholder	Reports	Amount of Detail	Best Format	Frequency	Delivery
Sponsor					
Team Members					
Project Management Office Manager					
Finance Manager					
Human Resources Manager					

Chart 10-3: Stakeholder Communications Plan

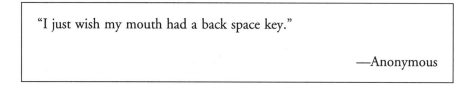

"I just wish my mouth had a back space key."

—Anonymous

§ 10.09   SUMMARY

An important factor in a successful project is the good opinion of the key stakeholders. If they are supportive of the project, especially when serious problems arise, then the project manager can focus more on the issues and less on the political repercussions. On the other hand, if key stakeholders oppose the project, then the vultures swoop in at the first sign of trouble.

Therefore, a project manager should never neglect stakeholders. The most efficient way to manage them is through a careful program of gathering their interests, accommodating as many as practical, and keeping them informed during project execution. They may not like what they hear, but a negative stakeholder may turn into a neutral one.

Most of all, stakeholders want a steady stream of factual information about the project's progress. Most of them understand that projects surge ahead and fall behind. So long as they stay within the company's acceptable variation level (usually 15 percent), they stay at arm's length.

Exhibit 10-1: Stakeholder Interview

Name: _____ Date: _____ Time: _____

Location: _____

Others in attendance: _____

THE PROJECT

What do you see the benefits of this project to be? _____

_____

What problems do you foresee for this project? _____

_____

Has this ever been tried before? _____

- What was done well? _____

- What could have been done better? _____

- Who was involved with this? _____

THE PEOPLE

Who are the key people who should be involved in this project? Why?

_____

_____

Can you think of anyone who may be opposed to the project? Why?

_____

What sort of assistance can you provide to the project? How?

_____

ISSUES

What would you like to see included in this project? _____

_____

What would you like to see avoided in this project? _____

_____

COMMUNICATIONS

What sort of information would you like to hear about the project?

_____

What is the best way to send this?

_____

Exhibit 10-1: *(Continued)*

Page 2 of stakeholder form

How often would you like to hear about it?

_____

Name: _____ Date: _____

Additional notes:

Favorable attitude:	1 2 3 4 5 6 7 8 9 10
Interest in the project's success:	1 2 3 4 5 6 7 8 9 10
Impact on project:	1 2 3 4 5 6 7 8 9 10
Level of competency:	1 2 3 4 5 6 7 8 9 10
Influence on project:	1 2 3 4 5 6 7 8 9 10

Reports to:

Controls key resources:

Instructions for Completing Stakeholder Interview Form

Page 1

At the top of the form is some basic information identifying the stakeholder and when the meeting occurred. Note any other people in the room during the meeting, as sometimes the stakeholder's comments made to the interviewer were intended for the other parties.

- **The Project**

What do you see the benefits of this project to be? This is the stakeholder's opportunity to identify something positive about the project. Compare this response with the project's scope to ensure the project delivers the good thing the stakeholder is expecting. If it does not, determine if the stakeholder's desire should be included in the scope.

What problems do you foresee for this project? This gives the stakeholder an opportunity to state their reservations about the project. Determine if the obstacles are in the project's path. Include these obstacles in the risk analysis.

Has this ever been tried before? The responses to this question may surprise you. Sometimes the project has been tried before and failed. There may have been a similar effort elsewhere in the company. This is a great time to find out what happened, to whom, and when. (Make a note to talk to these people.) Impressions are fine but facts

Exhibit 10-1: *(Continued)*

and names are important tools for uncovering what really happened. These issues will also go into the risk analysis and may alter the project's scope.

- **The People**

Who are the key people that should be involved in this project? Find out who they believe are the key people to involve with the project. This may uncover the unofficial lines of authority in the office. It also identifies subject matter experts in the end-user ranks.

Can you think of anyone who may be opposed to the project? Someone with an objection to the project should be counted as a stakeholder. Add him or her to the interview list to see if he or she really opposes the project, and why. Often these people just want to be heard and be kept informed about what is going on in the company. Perhaps they see a big obstacle in the path of the project that no one else will acknowledge!

What sort of assistance can you provide to the project? Some stakeholders can assist by providing resources such as people or information. Some would occasionally like to express an opinion. Document what this person expects to provide. This is also a time to mention what may be needed from them and their department for the project's progress.

- **Issues**

What would you like to see included in this project? Take care not to raise the stakeholders' expectations that this conversation is a commitment to include these changes to the scope. Explain the scope change process and offer to write up these suggestions for them. Asking their opinion about the project is a positive action that will somewhat flatter people. Most people have their own opinions and their ideas may be valuable.

What would you like to see avoided in this project? Check for risks not yet identified. These may be issues to avoid in the project scope.

- **Communications**

What sort of information would you like to hear about the project? Now that the stakeholders feel like part of the team, how can you best communicate project news to them? This is important if they are to provide a resource to the project so they can gauge when it might be ready.

What is the best way to communicate this? How would the stakeholder prefer to hear about the project's progress? Each person is different. If his job includes wading through a large list of e-mails every day, he might prefer a simple voice-mail.

Exhibit 10-1: *(Continued)*

How often would you like to hear about it? Some people only want an occasional update. Others may have a keen interest in the project and want to know more, and hear it more often. This may change over the life of the project.

Page 2

At the top of the form is the stakeholder name and the date of the discussion in case this form is separated from page 1.

Additional notes is a recap of any additional notes made during the meeting. Often the discussion brings out issues that do not seem to fit on page 1.

Favorable attitude is a scoring system of 1 to 10, with 1 being most negative, 5 is neutral, and 10 the most positive. Some people use -10 to $+10$; 0 being neutral.

Interest in the project's success is scored on a scale of 1 to 10, with 1 being total disregard and 10 being highly dedicated to its success. This indicator is a gauge of how much the interviewer feels the stakeholder is committed to the project's success.

Impact on project is scored on a scale of 1 to 10, with 1 being no impact and 10 being a key player in the project's continuing existence.

Level of competency is scored on a scale of 1 to 10, with 1 being little competency in their field and 10 being a recognized expert. When discussing project objectives and requirements with someone, do not assume he or she is the expert you thought, based on job title or responsibilities. If he or she is incompetent, then he or she should not be depended upon for advising the project.

Reports to is the name of the person to whom the stakeholder reports. If the meeting was with a group, then list his leader's name.

Influence on project is scored on a scale of 1 to 10, with 1 being of little influence on the project and 10 indicating he or she has some "full."

Tolerance to risk is scored on a scale of 1 to 10, with 1 being total disregard and 10 being highly dedicated to its success.

Key resources controlled is a recap of resources controlled by the person that the project needs for its completion. For example, end-users to test the product or to assist in detailing screen layouts.

Chapter 11

Project Management Office Processes and Tools

§ 11.01   INTRODUCTION

> "The task of the leader is to get his people from where they are to where they have not been."
>
> —Henry Kissinger

A project management office (PMO) is a competency center that coordinates projects for the IT department or, in some cases, for an entire company. It provides a framework of management tools and practices to ensure consistency of effort and results. This consistency allows team members to move easily between projects, saves time when initiating new projects and facilitates team communication with common processes and defined deliverables. The PMO's standard processes create a shared project management vocabulary throughout the organization, which reduces misunderstandings when discussing project-related work.

PMO control of all IT projects ensures that projects, both in process and under consideration, remain focused on the company's strategic goals. This control can identify overlapping project objectives, duplicate objectives, or occasionally projects with competing goals. For example, a project to save money by consolidating facilities seeks the opposite goal from a business continuity project to create separate and redundant facilities.

A well-run project management office saves the company money in several ways. An immediate savings comes from optimizing the use of project managers and other project resources over a broader range of projects. Schedule and cost estimations may be more realistic, projects experience fewer interruptions and company management saves time since each project presents the same "face" to the customer.

What company does not feel pressure to reduce overhead costs? The PMO helps by consolidating and reducing the administrative overhead common to all projects. This may include consolidating status reporting, managing shared project resources and qualifying new project requests. This frees time for individual project managers to focus on their projects.

A PMO promotes consistency in processes among both new and experienced project managers as it provides common processes through training. This training exposes project managers to aspects of project management that they may not have previously encountered. PMO training also reaches out to sponsors and team members to explain their responsibilities as part of the project team.

Another important PMO service is to collect and store historical documents of all projects in a central library. These documents provide information that may be valuable when planning or estimating future projects. Project documentation often forms the basis for ongoing system maintenance. If these documents, which often detail design decisions and resource requirements, are not retained, the maintenance effort must begin by tediously recreating the same information.

§ 11.02 HOW TO DO IT

Establishing a project management office is like campaigning for any other cultural change in a company. An executive sponsor is essential. Often the sponsor is the executive to whom the PMO will report. A PMO cuts across department boundaries and shifts the control of individual project managers from various departments to a central office. Resistance to this shift in control is minimized if the sponsor has sufficient executive stature to compel the change. Consolidating project managers under a single manager is essential to the PMO's exercise of strategic oversight of projects.

The shift to a PMO eases workloads for all. (See Charts 11-1 and 11-2.) Instead of dealing with individual project managers, each supporting department (e.g., accounting, purchasing, facilities and human resources) can refer to a single place when providing services. For example, instead of creating separate status reports for each concerned executive, project managers can submit a single document to the PMO, who distributes reports to the interested parties.

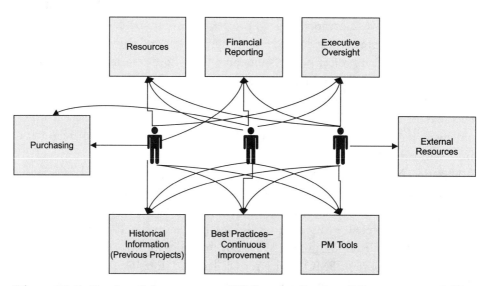

Chart 11-1: Project Management Without a Project Management Office

Chart 11-2: Project Management with a Project Management Office

A new PMO develops several fundamental documents to establish the scope of its actions and its strategy for implementing the office. Properly written, these documents will define an expectation of where the PMO fits into the company's organization and the value it adds to the bottom line.

A. Mission statement—a general statement that outlines what the PMO does, how it is to be done and who the customers are. It establishes the scope of the PMO's authority within the company, such as IT-only, company-wide, or support for a particular site.

B. Strategies, or high-level directions, on how the PMO will fulfill its mission statement and align with the company's business goals. Strategies provide an overall framework for creating objectives as well as an anchor for PMO policies and procedures.

C. Objectives—a clear statement of what the PMO intends to achieve over a defined period. Objectives should be specific, measurable, achievable and identify a specific time duration. Typical objectives are:

   1. To hire and manage qualified project managers and support staff.

   2. During weekly project status meetings, to ensure that all customer commitments are documented and tracked to completion.

   3. On a biweekly basis, to track and maximize the use of resources (labor, cash, time and equipment) for the greatest benefit of the company.

   4. To provide clear, summary information on project status in a timely manner, on a scheduled basis or upon request from senior management.

   5. To provide mentoring, training and assistance in the career development of the PMO's project managers.

D. Deliverables that will be created or offered by the PMO. These may be products or services. PMOs add value to the company through the combined application of their products and services.

"So much of what we call management consists in making it difficult for people to work."

—Peter F. Drucker

[A] Appointing a PMO Leader

The appointment of a project management office leader is very important. This person's work style and quality standards will permeate the PMO. In effect, this person will personify the PMO. Customer impressions of the PMO leader will color their perception, for good or bad, of the project management office.

The PMO leader is in both an administrative and a leadership position. As an administrator, the PMO leader will create and maintain many documents, such as templates and examples. Large PMOs may include an administrative assistant to reduce the project leader's administrative workload. The PMO leader also ensures that the PMO library is maintained. As a leader, the PMO supervisor motivates, encourages and assists the project managers in completing their projects.

The PMO leader serves as a buffer between the project managers and the stakeholders. The PMO leader's goal is to minimize the administrative demands on the project managers. To accomplish this, the PMO leader may work with the company's departments to provide them with accurate and timely information on each of their projects through the normal status reporting process.

The PMO leader's duties include:

- Guiding the project managers to ensure they understand and follow the PMO-published processes

- Coordinating resource allocations between the teams providing resources and those using them

- Reassignment of resources at the conclusion of projects

- Establishing and maintaining positive business relationships with the various company departments (e.g., accounting, human resources). The PMO leader monitors relationships between the project teams and these departments to proactively address issues before they become problems

- Acting as the primary face of the PMO to company executives

- Ensuring that project status reports are clear, accurate and free from excessive detail

- Identifying administrative requirements and consolidating them as effectively as possible to minimize the project managers' workload while satisfying stakeholders' needs

- Acting as the primary cheerleader for project management throughout the company, losing no opportunity to educate coworkers on project management principles and to highlight the successes of the project management office

- Randomly auditing projects in process, any projects in trouble and all projects during project closeout

- Establishing and maintaining PMO processes and tools
- Developing an ongoing training and career development plan for each project manager

[B] Establish a Tool Set

The heart of the project management office is comprised of its tools and processes. These are variously called its "toolkit," methodology, or standard operating procedures. They promote the flow of projects through the organization. Some of the tools are:

- Estimation guides for judging the time and expense of completing a task
- Resource requirement projections to reserve technical resources for specific periods
- Standards for project scheduling and knowledge management to ensure others can assist with or take over a project
- Information about procurement procedures
- Scope and budget change processes to ensure control of these critical functions
- Consolidated status reporting to present one "face" to executive management

Standardized project management processes also make it easier for the PMO to provide oversight and mentoring of project managers. Also, by using the same processes and tools for every project, team members can become acclimated and thus require less time to get up to speed on new projects.

> "You don't concentrate on risks. You concentrate on results. No risk is too great to prevent the necessary job from getting done."
>
> —Chuck Yeager

[C] Resource Management

Ensuring that the right people will be available when needed is an important ingredient for project progress. Project managers use resources (e.g., skilled people, special tools and money) to advance a project toward completion. The more scarce or expensive these resources are, the more difficult they become to schedule, since the company cannot afford to leave them idle for long. Also, the more time a project requires to execute, the more difficult it is to accurately estimate when a resource will be needed. The PMO provides tools for project managers to use in estimating the timing of their resource requirements, consolidating them into a central requirements file and resolving conflicts between projects.

To optimize resource utilization, the PMO must be established as the primary customer for these services. This allows the PMO to request specific units of resources to support all projects and ensure their proper utilization. For example, the PMO might request 60 hours per week of Java programming support for project development. Instead of bombarding the Java programming team leader with requests from various projects, the team leader can identify the resources available and allocate the programmers to the projects that need them.

At the end of a project, there may be furniture, computers, or skilled people to reallocate or be sent on their way. The PMO leader's view over all projects makes the reallocation of resources easier and more efficient. If this action is left to the very end of a project, skilled resources and expensive equipment may be idled, adding to company costs.

[D] Ensure the Company Sees the PMO's Value

Project management offices, like all departments, exist only as long as they demonstrate value to the company. In the annual ritual of departments building budgets and fighting over corporate resources, the department that demonstrates the greatest benefit often has the easiest time securing resources. Therefore, the PMO leader is responsible for an ongoing program to identify, record and publish the department's successes.

An early goal for a new PMO is to assess the company's project management environment. This assessment may entail a combination of interviews and surveys across all parts of the company. It should detail barriers, past project successes, customer attitudes, skill levels, standards, and overall corporate culture. This establishes a baseline of performance (based on past projects) and a baseline of resources (employee skills and company culture) for comparing PMO performance to the previous year.

PMOs add value through improved scope management. Carefully controlling the scope of projects ensures alignment with the customer's expectations. This allows the addition of tasks to the plan that will improve the credibility of project completion on schedule and on budget. The PMO also adds value through the reuse of project management tools and experience gained through the completion of other projects.

A major PMO value is the improvement of communications between stakeholders and the project team. This is a result of the combination of a consistent tool set, standard processes, and time available for the PMO to focus on stakeholder information requirements. Improved communication always results in higher satisfaction and reduced friction between stakeholders.

Finally, and most importantly, the PMO leader adds value to the team of project managers by buffering them from the many distractions provided by executives seeking "immediate" status reports and detailed explanations for routine decisions as well as other departments seeking to push their own agendas. A PMO will never reach its full potential if the PMO leader cannot intercept, block, and eliminate these distractions.

> "Time is the scarcest resource and unless it is managed nothing else can be managed."
>
> —Peter F. Drucker

§ 11.03 PROJECT PORTFOLIO MANAGEMENT

An important function of the project management office is the control of projects. In times past, each department of the company might include in their strategic plans various types of projects to meet their business objectives. These isolated projects were rarely coordinated to maximize resources. Sometimes they worked at cross-purposes or consumed resources for nonstrategic objectives.

A PMO brings all pending and current projects together under a single office's control. The PMO leader can then examine all projects side by side to identify and resolve areas of overlap to the company's advantage. This framework optimizes the use of resources and minimizes mutually exclusive project goals.

[A] Executive Steering Committee

To manage the project portfolio, many companies create steering committees of senior executives. This group reviews the progress of in-process projects to ensure they remain on track and focused on the company's strategic direction. Any projects that fall behind can be identified and corrective action can be taken.

Companies have long used the steering committee for governing shared departments. In the case of the PMO, the committee provides executive perspective from a range of departments to ensure the PMO benefits everyone.

The steering committee reviews new project proposals to ensure they add value in proportion to their costs. The appropriate level of funding for a project requires executive support. The steering committee's approval for a project not only approves the funding, but also provides approval for the project. Along with funding, the committee assigns a priority to the project.

An important steering committee function is to set the overall priorities for the PMO and all projects. This is often a clearer restatement of the company strategy, such as cost reductions, IT strategic direction for hardware or the promotion of specific business practices. The PMO's relationship with a powerful steering committee provides it with a strong organizational position when overcoming internal resistance to good project management practices.

Steering committees are not a project's sponsor. The sponsor is an executive who has a direct interest in the project and is often the person who requested it. Where the broad exposure of the steering committee is useful for guiding project selection, the sponsor is closer to the issues at hand and should be the one to make judgment calls on major changes in project scope or budget. Committees are useful, but tend to be less decisive than a sponsor who has a personal stake in the project's outcome.

[B]   Project Portfolio Prioritization

A common PMO challenge is selecting which project to work on first, and which ones to continue. To do this, the PMO must regularly evaluate all projects, pending and active, to determine priority of execution. Business climates and marketplaces change. Projects already in action must be reviewed to revalidate the reasons for their approval. This process is known as project portfolio management.

Portfolio management seeks to maximize the value of the projects in the portfolio. (Note that a company may value several different things in a project.) Not every project is worth doing. Each PMO must determine how it will evaluate projects to select the best mix to work on. Some of the various selection goals might include:

- Support the company's strategic initiatives
- Provide the maximum financial payback
- Ensure optimum use of available resources
- Manage risk

There are several easy-to-set-up tools that support portfolio management. Consider Chart 11-3, Portfolio Management Matrix. This matrix creates a weighted score for each project in the portfolio, active and pending. To build this matrix:

1. Identify the criteria used to evaluate the projects. In this example, the criteria are categorized as "Strategic, Technical, Financial." Under each category are several areas to rate projects.

2. For each of the rating criteria, assign a weight for its importance. For example, if the company's cash flow is low for this time of year, then use a low weight for project cost, or a high weight for cost reduction.

3. List each project along the top of the matrix as column headings.

4. Rate the projects according to each of these criteria from 0 to 10 in terms of the following areas:

Strategic

- Strategic alignment—How well does this project's goals align with the company's stated strategies?

- Marketplace enhancement—Does this project improve an existing product, or create a new product that protects or enhances market share?

- Core competencies—Does this project emphasize core competencies or does it require new expertise?

- Business risk—Overall, how uncertain is this project's outcome? Does it involve a new market segment, a new technology, or even something outside of the company's traditional business?

Technical

- Resource utilization—How well does this project maximize use of the company's resources, and minimize reliance on external resources?

- Technical risk—How risky is the technology involved? Is the technology proven but new to the company, or is it leading edge? Some companies prefer a mix of high-risk and low-risk projects.

Financial

- Project cost—How expensive is the project?

- Financial payback—What is the potential payback for the investment? This may be ROI or net present value.

- Cost reduction—Does this project reduce operating costs?

5. Score—Multiply each criteria's rating of 0 to 10 by its weight and sum the scores across that row. Sort the scores in descending order so the highest scores move to the left of the list.

	Project	Weight	(Project 1)	(Project 2)	(Project 3)	(Project 4)			
Strategic	Strategic Alignment								
	Core Competencies								
	Marketplace Enhancement								
	Business Risk								
Technical	Resource Utilization								
	Technical Risk								
Financial	Project Cost								
	Financial Payback								
	Cost Reduction								
	Score		0	0	0	0	0	0	0

Chart 11-3: Portfolio Management Matrix

There are some limitations to this matrix.

- It assumes that the financial projections for cost and payback are reliable. Often, such estimates are within +25 or −10 percent.
- The true risk of each project is a guess, especially if it is a new technology or product.
- Projects such as legal compliance or contractually required efforts are "trumped" to the top of the list.

[C]   Bubble Charts

Sometimes it is easier to restate the project portfolio visually. A common tool is a bubble chart, as shown in Chart 11-4.

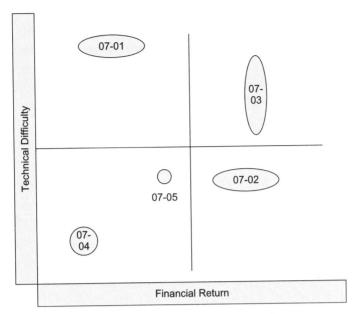

Chart 11-4: Portfolio Bubble Chart

In this visual report for management, the horizontal axis indicates the estimated payback for a project and the vertical axis is the technical difficulty. Each project is labeled (for example, 07-xx for 2007, project number xx). The size of the bubble indicates the potential estimation error. A bubble that is oval shaped from left to right indicates that the financial return estimate has a high degree of uncertainty while the estimate of technical difficulty is relatively certain.

In this example, Project 07-01 has a high estimated technical difficulty for an uncertain, but low payback. Project 07-02 looks like a project with moderate technical difficulty with a high payback. Given a choice between the two, Project 07-02 would win.

Bubble matrices can be in any format. The axis can reflect project score versus risk, or any desired combination. Often the portfolio management matrix and the bubble chart are used together when discussing portfolio options.

[D]   Standardized Project Initiation

A PMO is a lightening rod, attracting all project requests into a central place for executive review. Proposals pass through the PMO's project proposal process. This ensures a consistent data basis for steering committee review and same-to-same comparison with other projects.

[1] Keeping Track of Requests

Large PMOs usually use basic service request software as a tracking tool to ensure that requests are not lost in the shuffle of "hot projects." This is the same type of software help desks use to track service requests except that the purpose is to ensure that requests keep flowing through the PMO bureaucracy. Service request management software provides metrics on:

- how long each step in the process requires
- an indication of on whose desk the requests' documents are resting
- a measurable indication of the volume of requests

Small PMOs can adequately track requests on a spreadsheet. Even small offices have a backlog of projects, so some sort of ordered list is useful. PMOs that do not track outstanding projects will eventually find themselves reanalyzing the same rejected project requests time after time.

[2] Return on Investment

Upon receipt of a project request from a competent authority (generally someone authorized to spend the company's money), the PMO assigns a project manager to review the proposal's costs and benefits. Few people requesting a project have a clear idea of how long a project will take or what it will cost to implement. In general, their experience has been to see or use the external aspects of the result, with little experience of the essential background effort or materials required. (If the project already has a complete and approved feasibility study, then base the ROI analysis on that information.)

The PMO creates a standard format for gathering the essential elements of a project. This includes a clear business case, a concise scope statement, a list of success criteria, anticipated costs and benefits, required completion dates, and a list of actions required to complete the project. Taken together, a reasonable bottoms-up cost estimate can be made for completing the project. However, the longer the project runs, the wider the tolerance for resource estimation must be. Estimates supporting a 90-day project should vary much less than estimates for a year-long project.

At this point, a minimal amount of time has been spent obtaining specific cost information. This analysis approximates a project's costs since most equipment and services quotes expire in 30 days. A complete costing of the project requires considerable analysis and this will be lost if the project is not promptly approved. Cost estimates at the "approximate cost" stage should be within ±25 percent.

With the cost estimate in hand, conduct an analysis of the project's benefits. As described by the project requestor, the project benefits can be inflated as much as the costs are deflated. Verify claims of project benefits. Labor savings is a particularly difficult area to calculate.

> If labor savings are included, they must adhere to the company's labor accounting practices. For example, in most companies, a project cannot save one-half of a person. Either it eliminates a position and someone is discharged (which reduces the company's payroll) or it does not. If no one leaves the company, then no payroll savings exist—even though hours in the week are now available for other uses.

Project savings claimed for equipment departing the company is a different issue. Leased equipment may incur a penalty for early return. Equipment freed up as the result of one project's completion does not become a "free" asset available for use elsewhere in the company. For a project to claim a savings for eliminating a device, that equipment must exit the premises.

Along with proposed ROI, the analyst will assess the risks surrounding the project. The risk of failure, that resource costs will skyrocket, of technical obsolescence, and all other risk dimensions must be included in the report. Some PMOs detail specific environmental and resource risks to address in a proposal.

A variation of ROI is the cost of noninvestment (CONI). CONI measures how much not doing a project will cost the company. This is common with legal compliance issues, such as mandatory environmental controls for air pollution, water pollution, or disposal of toxic wastes. In some instances, the cost is measured in time instead of dollars—jail time!

[3] Proper Approval

After a project is approved and prioritized by the steering committee, the PMO adds the project to the pending project list. Review this list periodically with the PMO's executive steering committee to set and adjust project priorities and identify projects for immediate execution—even if outside project managers and resources are required.

Some projects are pre-approved executive mandates and an ROI is not required. However, if time permits, an ROI review will provide considerable insight into the project's requirements and the resources necessary for its success.

[E]   Project Backlog Management

Today's non-urgent project can become tomorrow's hot topic. The PMO consolidates new project requests into a single file. Review requests periodically to determine if project priorities might have changed.

The PMO monitors the projects in the backlog for opportunities to combine any of them with new projects. Opportunities also may arise to combine several of the backlogged projects into one. This would provide additional resource economies.

[F]   Metrics

A popular management maxim is that you cannot manage what cannot be measured. Create a consistent set of project performance metrics for executive oversight. Project metrics provide performance visibility to management in a common and consistent manner. It also permits the comparison of current project performance to historical levels. There are two primary types of project metrics:

1. Product metrics pertain to the result or product created by the project. How closely does the result conform to the published specifications? How much better is it in identified key quality areas, etc.? How does the customer rate the final product's quality?

2. Project management metrics deal with how effectively and efficiently the project was in creating the result. Were unnecessary steps included? Were resources efficiently utilized?

Metrics provide a source of feedback for the PMO's performance and customer satisfaction measures. They ensure decisions are based on facts. Metrics illustrate the result of changes made to processes and show areas for improvement. Since metrics use numbers instead of pass/fail, smaller changes can be detected, such as a trend toward greater resource efficiency. Examples of metrics to track include:

A. Schedule performance
   - The number of tasks completed on time
   - The estimated hours to complete the project (as a percentage over or under run)

B. Financial performance—Actual expenses compared to budgeted expenses (as a percentage over or under run)

C. Customer satisfaction as measured by end-of-project or end-of-milestone surveys

D. Percentage of tasks completed on time, sequenced by the resources used

[G] Project Audits

PMOs add value by auditing projects in process or recently completed. This audit verifies how closely the project conformed to PMO processes. The degree of conformance (quality) provides feedback on the effectiveness of processes.

Sometimes an audit is needed because a project has experienced major problems with the end-product development, the project schedule or the project budget. Since a project is already troubled, most of the audit is spent identifying where the problems arose, what actions the sponsor and project manager took, and what steps to take to correct the problem. The PMO project audit also verifies that:

A. The project used approved PMO tools and practices. Review any new tools created or modified to address specific situations for acceptance by the PMO.

B. The accuracy and completeness of project metrics. These metrics guide future PMO actions and their accuracy is important. Knowledge of a potential audit inhibits a project manager from disguising project problems by misreporting metrics.

C. The quality of the product created as compared to the current scope and criteria for success. In essence, did the project deliver the form, fit, and function that was requested?

D. How well the project manager's actions conformed to the published schedule and how effectively the project manager utilized assigned resources.

E. The project as a whole and individual tasks within it, along with the actions taken by the project manager, for the likelihood or impact of adverse events.

Another PMO function is to randomly audit projects in process to ensure proper management. Do this carefully since the time taken to address an audit may create delays in an otherwise on-schedule effort. The goal of a random audit is to detect problems before they become major issues. Narrowly focus random audits on such things as issues tracking, financial reporting or risk management. This helps to determine the quality of the project management effort with a minimum of disruption.

> "To introduce something altogether new would mean to begin all over, to become ignorant again, and to run the old, old risk of failing to learn."
>
> —Isaac Asimov

§ 11.04   PROCESSES AND TOOLS

Selecting a set of project management processes and tools is a critical decision in a project management office's development. The processes used must reflect the company's attitude toward work in general and project management in particular. Companies with a large percentage of unskilled workers might mandate tightly controlled project management processes with lock-step actions required of all projects at specific points in their existence. Highly technical companies with skilled workers often prefer a loose arrangement between the project team and the project manager. If the selected tool set does not fit the company's work ethic or corporate culture, then adapting it will require a time-consuming cultural shift before it is accepted.

Stakeholder requirements are an important factor to consider in PMO tool and process development. The budget department will require performance and expense projection reports. Purchasing will require specific authorizations and references before ordering materials. Executives will want to know specific information about projects at regular intervals. All of this is fed into the tool and process development program to determine the fewest materials that satisfy the greatest number of requirements.

> How important is standardization? Imagine that every time truck drivers crossed a state line they had to learn an entire new set of traffic regulations, practices, and what the highway signs meant. Since this is standardized across the country, a person in Montana can easily comply with the traffic laws in Texas. The same holds true for project management. The use of standard practices allows team members to move from project to project or project managers to float among projects and feel "at home" with the tools. This does not make every project identical, but similar enough so that someone can step up to help with a new issue with a minimum level of difficulty.

[A]   Make or Buy?

Some companies purchase their PMO processes and tools from a consulting company. This approach provides proven tools and processes. However, it is a rare situation where purchased tools exactly reflect a company's culture and merge well with its other working processes.

Sometimes it is easier for employees to buy into new processes if suggested by outsiders. This is similar to the dilemma many parents face with their children who seem to listen to strangers, but ignore the same good advice from their parents. If a company deadlock is anticipated over tool selection, then consider using external expertise.

"If the only tool you have is a hammer, you tend to see every problem as a nail."

—Abraham Maslow

To arrive at a methodology, a new PMO has three basic choices:

1. Buy it. Buying a methodology from a consulting company is attractive since the purchaser is acquiring a proven model. Consulting companies' ongoing financial success depends on properly-run projects. This approach is easier to justify if the consulting company has previously managed a few projects for the buyer.

   - The positive aspects of this are time and completeness.

     A. Time is saved during the PMO startup since the basic solution is already at hand. The tools are distributed and the PMO is operational.

     B. The selling company can provide training and mentoring in the nuances of the processes and tools to speed startup.

     C. The tool set will be more complete than a homegrown solution since the consulting company probably has a wider range of experience working in multiple environments and industries.

     D. Purchasing a tool set sidesteps office egos over whose project management approach to select.

   - Some negative aspects to this approach include:

     A. Cost—A consulting company will not part with the "heart and soul" of their operations very cheaply.

     B. If the consulting company's approach is too rigid or too loose, then extensive modifications may negate the benefits of the purchased package.

     C. The purchasing company may not know enough to identify major shortcomings with specific processes.

2. Build it based on collective experience. The company's project managers contribute their best practices and tools for review by a committee of their peers. The ones selected form the basis of the company's PMO toolkit. Clearly document each

process and place all templates in a shared directory for easy reference. Identify gaps and assign someone to create whatever is needed to fill out the tool set.

- The positive aspects of this are time and completeness.

    A. The methodology will reflect the corporate culture and collective experience of supporting projects for the company.

    B. The PMO team feels greater ownership of the tool set and the PMO itself.

    C. It is less expensive than purchasing processes and tools from a consulting company.

- Some negative aspects to this approach include:

    A. Startup time for the PMO will be longer.

    B. The methodology may be narrow since it is based on the experiences of a few project managers.

    C. "Strong personalities" in the group building the tools may narrow the usefulness of the tools designed.

3. Buy a methodology or portion of it and then adjust it to suit the PMO's needs. Buying a shell of a methodology can jump-start a PMO in the development of their tools. The "machinery" of a PMO is its people, and people rarely fit a "cookie cutter" approach. This works best if the consulting company's approach is similar to the purchaser's existing priorities. A variation on this is to hire a consultant to facilitate the assembly of the PMO's methodology using their experience to speed the development of tools and processes.

- The positive aspects of this are time and completeness.

    A. The tools will be more in tune with the company, its attitudes, and its approach to work.

- Some negative aspects to this approach include:

    A. Startup time for the PMO will be longer.

    B. The methodology may be narrow since it is based on the experiences of a few project managers.

    C. This approach has all of the cost of buying the methodology and all of the time delay of a homegrown solution.

[B]   Processes and Tools

Everyone has a preferred way to approach a task. In general, each approach reflects steps that have proven successful for individuals in the past. The issue is how someone identifies what is "successful." If these steps omit actions the PMO believes are useful or essential to task completion, then the task is not finished.

> "Adequate" task completion is a matter of a person's perspective as to what is sufficient effort for a task. For example, some project managers may feel that if their project requires software, their task is complete once the software is ordered. Other project managers would include additional tasks to ensure the order flows smoothly through the purchasing process, monitor its delivery date, ensure it is properly installed and configured, and ensure the invoice is correct and promptly paid. In the first case, the project manager is confident that once an order is submitted, the other company processes will flow smoothly to the desired execution. The second project manager feels that losing visibility of an important resource introduces a risk of failure into the project.

All PMO processes should be clearly documented and published to everyone on the project management office team. The instructions should detail the mandatory and optional steps. Often, a document or spreadsheet template will accompany a written process to aid in organizing the data. Examples of processes and tools potentially provided by the PMO include:

A. Time and cost estimation guides—These are based on historical data for performing that type of task or the productivity of using a specific resource.

B. Resource requirement projections—A process for predicting and reserving resources for assignment at some point during a project.

C. Standards for project scheduling—Creates a consistent "look and feel" for project schedules to permit easy comprehension by anyone working in the project management office.

D. Simplified equipment acquisition—The PMO locates suppliers, negotiates and ensures the proper purchasing paperwork is completed. While a project manager may do something only a few times a year, the PMO quickly gains experience by providing this service for all projects.

E. Change control procedures—Scope and budget change control processes include appropriate analysis for changes to the ROI, impact on the schedule, etc. and ensure they are properly approved. Customers will agree to anything until the end of the project when their memory fails and then they point to the original scope and budget documents. If a change is not written and signed by the customer, it must not be executed by the project manager.

F. Consolidated status reporting—There should be one person to deal with executive management. The PMO establishes a standard format for project status reporting. Project managers submit their status reports to the PMO, which combines them into a format for easy review. This simple format (often the traffic light of red (danger), yellow (behind), or green (on time) quickly conveys project progress. This focuses attention on projects behind schedule or over budget. These "standard" reports should support all of the core company departments (e.g., finance, budget, purchasing and facilities management).

G. Creation and maintenance of an issues log to ensure commitments to customers are tracked until completed—A consistent tool that allows easier sponsor oversight of progress in resolving issues.

H. Risk management—Processes and templates for identifying risks to a project or its product and specific actions planned or taken to mitigate the risks.

[C] Project Life-Cycle Management

"Project life-cycle" is a checklist of administrative steps to ensure that a project's requisite paperwork is completed. A life-cycle document is a checklist of actions required for most projects. These actions center on a project's proper start-up and closeout. Maintaining this checklist in a specific location allows the PMO to gauge a project's administrative progress.

A project has specific actions to address at various times in its "life." For example, a risk is cheaper to address during the project's planning stages than in the later phases of the project. (Note that these stages do not conform to the standard project life-cycle stages.) A few of the checklist items might be:

A. Start-up

1. The idea (scope) driving the project must be clearly defined (or the rest of the project will be a mess).

2. Spell out the criteria for success in detail. The project plan must address how each of these will be achieved.

3. Complete the ROI analysis. The project plan must ensure any savings claimed in the project analysis are realized, such as the timing for removing replaced data systems hardware.

4. Identify and note on the project schedule key project deliverables.

5. Key project documents must be completed (as required by the project); these may include risk assessment (possibly one for the project plan and one for the end product), communications plan, stakeholder analysis, quality plan and resource management plan.

B. Major milestones

1. Update all project documents (e.g., schedule, budget, risk assessment, assumptions and stakeholder analysis) periodically or at every milestone.

2. Conduct a project review with PMO leader, sponsor and interested stakeholders.

C. Testing

1. Specific test action for the product or interim tests for major components.

2. Stakeholder sign-off for completed product or components.

D. Closeout

1. Report open bills to the accounting manager.

2. Create and send final report to PMO comparing project planned resource usage and costs to actual resource usage and costs for all tasks.

3. Organize project files into proper reference format for storage in the PMO library.

4. Organize disposal of assets and redeployment of technical resources.

5. Conduct a formal appreciation party for the project team.

6. Transition product to the ongoing maintenance team.

§ 11.05 RESOURCE MANAGEMENT

When first planning a project, a project manager faces many unknowns: What tasks are required? What technical resources are required? Who should work on each task? How long is the lead time for new equipment? When will the resources be available?

To convert the requirements to a manageable schedule, the project manager solicits advice from others, refers to completed projects for actual duration, and states assumptions that answer questions that seem unanswerable. One key assumption during project schedule creation is that all resources will be available when needed.

In the past, project managers were on their own to locate resources, evaluate their skills, and schedule them into the project. This was very inefficient as resources drifted away and the project manager had to scramble to locate and secure new ones. Later, when the project again ran off schedule, the project manager repeated this process to verify the availability of resources for the new dates.

The PMO management of resources adds value by consolidating all of these requests and negotiating with the resource providers. This provides several key benefits.

A. Instead of the project manager negotiating with each department or technician, the project's requirements were provided to the PMO with the assumption that they would be met until told otherwise.

B. Instead of bombarding technicians and managers with requests for people from many directions, they can now plan vacations, training, and their own process improvement projects by providing the PMO with a steady block of time available to support projects.

C. By "owning" the resources, the PMO can allocate them based on availability and need. Requirement overages and under-runs are smoothed in cooperation with the affected project managers.

D. Identify critical resource shortages early so accommodations can be made to defer the schedule or obtain the resource from other sources.

E. Shifting project schedules necessitates a new requirements forecast, which the PMO can use to reallocate resources.

F. Compare idle resources to upcoming requirements. The PMO leader can assign idle resources to work ahead on project tasks.

G. The PMO's experience locating and negotiating with less commonly used resources can relieve the project manager from having to chase down a new resource with which he or she lacks personal experience.

At the conclusion of projects or at major milestones, the PMO meets with the project managers involved to hear their evaluations of the performance of various resources. The PMO uses these discussions when assigning resources to future projects. Report any technicians who performed poorly to their respective management. Use technicians who performed at a grade below their rating to fill lower-rated assignments in the future—no matter what level the company rates them. Identify hardworking and competent technicians and make them the first requested for future opportunities.

[A]   Resource Planning

A PMO manages the scheduling of limited and expensive resources. What is desirable depends on where someone sits. From the company's perspective, idle and expensive resources are wasteful. From the technician's perspective, sitting around is a waste of time when there is other work in the department to do. The project manager is sympathetic but needs the resource at the time and place dictated by the project. This might mean that the technician must wait on the sidelines until the task is ready to begin. Project managers know that a single missing resource can easily idle an entire project team, so a resource in hand is one less risk to worry about.

Unfortunately, while the project manager may have solved the availability problem, the company still loses use of the resource—that may be sorely needed elsewhere. Assigning resources to the PMO rather than to a specific project allows the PMO to float them among projects wherever it makes sense and enables the company to approach 100 percent utilization.

[1] What Is a Resource?

Resource planning begins by defining what each resource is. In IT, this might be the use of a network technician, a network security specialist, or even a telephony expert. A resource might be a piece of test equipment, a vehicle, a print server, or any other reusable item. (Strictly speaking, consumable materials are resources, but managed as purchased items and not a true "resource." Examples of consumables include network cabling, backup tapes, and bar code printer ribbons.)

One approach to defining people resources is to list a skill description in a way similar to a job description. Each description should describe the technologies and expertise level for each technology. (State this as functional capabilities rather than specific technical expertise such as certifications.) Resource management is easiest if the categories are broad. Resource descriptions should be general enough to meet the project's needs without unnecessarily calling in outside suppliers. These descriptions will be very important for finding outside technicians on short notice. Some of the resources on the list might include the following:

- C++ junior programmer—Less than two years with SQL experience
- C++ programmer—Between two and five years Java into hierarchical databases
- C++ senior programmer—More than five years' programming experience
- Network architect—Designs networks from scratch
- Senior Windows administrator
- Text database administrator

[2] Create a Process for Requesting Resources

Typically, a project schedule assumes that the required resources will be available when needed. Roll up and present the resource requirements for the draft schedule to the PMO. For example, a resource request might include a two-week requirement for a database administrator, use of a specific file server for two months, and a request that a network technician must be available from 8 a.m. to 9 p.m. daily for the upcoming week.

Write these requests in a specific format. Feed these requests into a software tool to total and analyze resource needs for specific periods. Resource projections are often displayed in spreadsheets.

[3]   Project Total Requirements

After receiving the resource requests from the project managers, the PMO should consolidate them into a single resource plan using an automated tool. These requests should be resubmitted periodically, usually every two weeks, and cover the upcoming 90- or 120-day period. They indicate the resource required, how long it is needed, and when in the calendar it must be present. Once these requirements are totaled across all projects for a given time period, this becomes the resource requirements for the PMO.

For example, Project A needs a senior network technician for 10 hours per week, for six weeks, beginning on June 3. Another way is to state the time as specific days. This might be necessary if the technician was involved only on weekends to install new systems.

To identify the gap between availability and requirements, the PMO must poll the technical teams to obtain the number of hours they have available, given their ongoing maintenance requirements, to support projects. This time should be compared to the total hours of support required for the network technician over the given time period. The result is generally a series of peaks and valleys of demand. With their "big picture" view of all projects, the PMO can work with the project managers to identify tasks that can be shifted between time periods to smooth out resource supply and demand.

[4]   Resource Forecasting Tool Example

Forecasting the resources for all of the projects in a PMO's active portfolio is an interesting challenge. Resources required within the next month are more of a firm requirement than those farther into the future. Yet this projection is what allows the PMO to line up resources and, if necessary, contract for additional ones. In short, the PMO needs to know how many of each resource is needed for each time period.

This process begins by identifying each factor.

A. Identify the time intervals to be covered, such as by the day, week, or month. The interval selected depends on the local work environment. Given the normal ebb and flow of a project, this example will use a period of one week.

B. Determine the unit of time to use within the period. This could be hours, days, etc. This is usually the same unit of time used by the project plan. For example, the projection may be for a telephone system technician to work on the project for 15 hours (unit of time) per week (projection period).

Telephone Tech	10	15	15	10		10		22

C. Develop a list of requested resources. The list should include minimal, yet sufficient detail, to identify the requirement. Too narrow a description of the skills required might unnecessarily complicate staffing. (Example, a requirement for a Java programmer versus a requirement for a Java programmer with a COBOL programming background.)

D. Resource projections should reach far enough into the future to allow sufficient time to bring in outside resources as required. Resources hired on short notice may be overpriced and underskilled. Typical lead time for locating and approving outside technicians is about two months.

E. Update resource projections as frequently as required to ensure a smooth allocation of resources. However, the more often this is done, the greater the time burden on the project manager.

A tool to aggregate resource requirements must address a three-dimensional issue. The PMO has multiple projects, each of which have multiple resources required and each of the resources are needed for multiple times. The easiest way to handle this is through a simple database application (see Exhibit 11-1).

Exhibit 11-1: Simple Database Application

Set up a multi-tabbed spreadsheet.

A. Use one tab for *each* resource supported by the PMO.

B. Identify each tab by its resource name, such as Unix Administrator, Print Room Operator, etc.

C. Set up the cells in each tab as follows:

This tool may support many projects, so the totals and calculations are at the top of the sheet. Formulas:

A. "Resource Shortfall" = Total Available − Total Requirements

B. "Total Available" is the number of times (hours or days) available for use by the PMO, as provided by the resource allocators.

C. "Total Requirements" is the sum of all rows starting with Project #1 as far down the sheet as the PMO wants to go, so long as it encompasses all of the rows.

Resource Shortfall	14	−3	1	−29	24	18	28	6

Total Available	32	32	32	32	32	32	32	32
Total Requirements	18	35	31	61	8	14	4	26

	1-Jan	8-Jan	15-Jan	22-Jan	29-Jan	5-Feb	12-Feb	19-Feb
Project #1	10	15	15	10		10		22
Project #2	8	20	8	35		4	4	4
Project #3			8	16	8			

The "Resource Shortfall," which is the primary focus of the analysis, is the difference between "Total Available" and "Total Requirements." If this number is positive, then those hours are available for use elsewhere. If it is negative, then this resource has a shortfall of labor compared to demand. To address this, examine the workload of the various projects to determine where this resource can start a task later or sooner.

[B]   Shuffling Key Resources

Actual project execution ebbs and flows. Sometimes a project races ahead—at other times a project may seem mired down in one issue after another. When the PMO detects a resource issue, the PMO leader proactively works with the project manager involved to determine the impact on the project and the resources. Any variation of a project schedule disrupts the timing of resource requirements. Shuffle tasks within the project to address this. Other times, resources lined up for an abruptly-halted project are released on short notice. Before returning this labor or equipment back to its originating department, the PMO should use a "big picture" perspective to locate opportunities for reallocating the resources.

Reallocating resources serves several important purposes. First, it respects the originating department by smoothing demands on their services. It helps project managers by offering resources early that may speed completion of tasks off the critical path. Finally, it helps the resources themselves by reducing the number of "panic" assignments they receive from project managers.

As a central clearinghouse of resources, the PMO can provide information about specific resources that have successfully completed project tasks in the past but have not been assigned to the normal service departments. This might be a programmer who is now a database administrator or a network technician who previously programmed and debugged telecommunications equipment.

[C]   Supplier Management

The PMO adds value by coordinating the external acquisition of resources. Instead of each project manager locating and hiring his or her own resources, the PMO concentrates the company's buying power on a few vendors and negotiates the best prices. Another disadvantage of decentralized purchasing is a lack of accountability from the vendor. Poor service can be disguised by moving an underperforming resource on to the next project. By consolidating external resource acquisition through the PMO, service performance records are available from a readily accessible central point.

PMOs must remember that external technical talent providers are vendors and not partners. Monitor them and focus their performance on completing tasks; they must not be allowed to stretch out tasks. The sure knowledge that the PMO is monitoring service will discourage vendors from cutting corners.

§ 11.06   PROJECT STATUS REPORTING

The bane of all project managers is status reporting. Stakeholders seem to want to know every small detail on short notice with a comprehensive explanation of every decision, just so they can nod thoughtfully as if the technical details mean something to them. Everyone appreciates the need of project sponsors to monitor the progress made on their important and expensive projects; however, the demand for individual and duplicate status reports from a range of executives often seems to consume a project manager's every waking hour.

Status reporting is a vital project management task. The project's sponsor has entrusted the project manager with accomplishing an important task and often with considerable company finances. Status reports are the primary communications tool between the project manager and all interested stakeholders. Therefore, one of a project manager's primary responsibilities is to nurture and enhance these communications. Breakdowns in communications are easy to detect, such as when the sponsor begins to drown the project manager with an endless stream of status requests out of concern for an impending project failure.

If the sponsors are satisfied with the project's progress, then they will be supportive regarding problems, budget issues, or scope changes. However, if the project manager does not keep the sponsor fully informed and office gossip highlights the project's shortcomings (and never its successes), the sponsor may become nervous. The PMO leader should monitor the company rumor mill and determine whether the rumors have any basis before they spin out of control. Sponsors expect the PMO to know what is going on with all projects. One poorly run project that spins out of control may tarnish their opinion of all of the others in process.

For all of their value, time spent creating a status report is time spent away from addressing project problems. Project managers depend on the PMO to screen status requests to minimize the hours required to research and write reports. The PMO does this by meeting with the various executives and project sponsors to identify and qualify each data element on which they require status information. The PMO should negotiate with each requestor to minimize the number of items to collect, and to establish a reasonable frequency for the report. The PMO should make a single status request of the project manager, who will then provide the data once per reporting period to a single place. The PMO can then distribute the pertinent data elements to each interested stakeholder.

As a key communications tool, the PMO should ensure that status reports strike a balance between completeness and the amount of time required to complete them. The PMO adds value by negotiating with the various executives to identify the essential information elements they want to see and the format in which they want to see them. Translate the data into a standard status report format. This allows the project manager to arrange paperwork to facilitate obtaining these pieces of information from the very beginning of the project.

Remember, the PMO is the project management department's face to executive management. Make it a good one. The PMO leader is the key to demonstrating the value of project management and the project management office to executives. How successful the PMO leader is at achieving this goal will determine how good the department's relationship will be with company leaders.

[A] Creating the Standard

How do the critical stakeholders want to receive project status information? Under the old model, each project manager provided whatever information they could in whatever format they chose to follow. This required each stakeholder to adjust to the various report layouts. There also may have been conflicting underlying assumptions that made up each calculation or data item. In the end, the management stakeholders were just as worn out interpreting the various reports as the project managers were creating them.

A "standard" report means a consistent report. The same information is located under the same heading for every project. Again, in the days before the PMO, each supporting department requested information from each project manager. Even if a department provided a form to each team, the project manager may have used a different basis to derive each of the data elements. To improve data consistency, the PMO should work with each of the supporting departments to identify essential elements of information and create a format that is easy for project managers to fill in and easy for the requester to find what he or she is looking for. The PMO also should ensure the information presented is based on consistent criteria.

Begin by identifying all of the data elements requested by executives. This includes schedule variances, expenditures to date, and estimated time to complete the next milestone. Unequivocally define the criteria for each data element. The variables used in every formula must indicate the same project characteristic across all projects.

A subset of this step is to confirm the need for each item requested. Is a management stakeholder trying to micro-manage projects? Does the request require an extraordinary amount of effort to satisfy for very little return? Sometimes stakeholders ask for information just because their predecessor did, but they have no use for it. Do not be afraid to challenge requests outside of the ordinary. Another variation is the "busybody" stakeholder who wants to know everything about anything so as to be able to criticize it later. Send these requests to the sponsor.

With the required information identified and the format for the information secured, the PMO should concentrate on easing the work required to gather the information. First, the PMO should check to see how much of the information already exists in the PMO tools and processes methodology. Normally, the tools contain everything needed to address schedule and financial variances. If the project manager is reliable, then the issues log also will be current. Altogether, this will likely contain everything needed for the reports. Adjust the PMO tools to include any new items needed. (Data collected for the status report provide an ideal opportunity to gather items required for PMO metrics.)

Once the project manager has the tools to gather all of the data elements required for the reports, the total status report data can be collected and passed on to the PMO leader. The PMO leader should then review the data and follow up with the project manager to fill in any gaps or to explain variances. Explanations are prepared for all problem areas. Present this background information in the context of what the issue means to the company's business. Save tedious technical explanations for those projects that request them.

The PMO leader should use the collective status information to format the reports for the various management stakeholders. Although "news" about a project may be interesting, each stakeholder needs to receive information in a format and communications medium that is easiest for them to use. The financial team may want the PMO to detail the project financial requirements and roll them up for an overall PMO total. The preferred medium may be a spreadsheet that can be acted on instead of rekeying numbers from printed reports.

Some executive sponsors may prefer a short verbal report in a specific format. Others may prefer to hear about projects that exceed a certain threshold (perhaps 10 percent over budget or schedule) that may require their attention. Detail this in the project's communications plan, which should list stakeholders, the essential information they require, and the best way to communicate it.

Not all status reports should flow through the PMO—only those routine reports where the PMO can add value by saving everyone time. Reports that are specific to a project and sent to a stakeholder outside of the usual executive stakeholders move directly from the project manager to the requester.

[B]   Organization-Wide Reporting

Most executives want to focus their attention on troubled projects and leave the well-run ones to continue on course. To simplify summary status reports, the PMO leader should establish a PMO-wide summary overview of each project for quick executive review. The exact format should reflect the balance of what is needed for an overview and what information will be asked for next. For example, if a project is significantly behind schedule or over budget, the next question will be "What is being done to bring the project back on course?" In this case, the project manager should be required to provide additional information, whereas a project on schedule and on budget would not require any additional information.

A commonly used analogy is a project's "traffic light." This easy-to-understand approach assigns project values for green (on course), yellow (drifting off course), and red (danger of failure). Traffic lights allow for a quick executive review. Projects drifting off course or in danger of failure must have the nature of the problem, its impact, and actions to move the project back into the green zone explained in their reports.

The PMO should organize status reports from all projects into one document. See Exhibit 11-2 for an example of a consolidated project report.

Exhibit 11-2: Consolidated Project Report

	Current Status			Projected Status		
	Schedule	Budget	Issues	Schedule	Budget	Issues
Project #1	Green	Red	Hired additional resources to meet schedule	Green	Yellow	Hardware costs less than budgeted
Project #2	Yellow	Green	Delayed start	Yellow	Green	Make up five days by working weekends
Project #3	Yellow	Red	Lack of critical resources	Yellow	Red	Hire outside workers

When using reporting indicators such as red, yellow, and green, the PMO must define what each indicator says about the project. Implied in these indicators should be items in the PMO methodology that automatically determine the variance for the schedule and budget. For example:

	Schedule	Budget
Green	±10%	±10%
Yellow	±15%	±15%
Red	±20%	±20%

A portfolio-wide report also lends itself to comparison against historical data or combination with other performance metrics. The PMO may refer to historical information where past projects supporting certain departments or depending on specific resources have been consistently over budget or behind schedule.

§ 11.07 TRAINING

Project management is a learned skill. Like all forms of expertise, it benefits from occasional refreshing. Successful project managers must master a range of skills in such areas as:

- Problem analysis
- Interpersonal communications

- Persuasion and conflict resolution

- Accounting and budgeting

- Technical skills for the areas addressed by the project

- Ever-changing legal issues

- Company procedures

Sitting in a classroom discussing these issues is only one part of a project manager's education. Placing these skills into action raises many more questions and highlights areas of shortcoming. This makes training an iterative process. Training introduces and explains the concepts but does not confer expertise. Expertise comes from applying the new techniques and converting concepts into skills. For this reason, there should be an ongoing requirement for training on emerging subjects, such as new technologies, as well as on the basics: team building, finance, and task estimation.

Training also is a way to establish an expectation in the mind of a person. An appreciation of project management processes and theories is useful to project team members, such as the sponsor, technical support, or even support staff such as administration or accounting. These expectations may include an understanding of the importance of timeliness or even an understanding of the normal business processes in a department.

A vigorous program of training will help the PMO to promote consistency in processes across the department. This is very important for new project managers joining the organization. Every PMO leader has a twist to "standard" practices to explain to new arrivals. Experienced project managers may have worked in several different company areas, but none has worked everywhere with everyone. Training also helps to refresh rarely used skill sets that may be essential in future projects.

As is obvious, new project managers have an ongoing requirement for training and a mentored break-in period. They need to understand how the local office conducts business, its standard processes, and how to meet the requirements of the supporting departments. The PMO is uniquely situated to gather this information and package it for presentation to the project managers.

PMO training also encompasses sponsors and team members, who may need training on their project team responsibilities. At times, team members believe the project managers speak a foreign language or have their priorities backward. Training the team to understand what and why a project manager is doing something makes it easier for the group to anticipate requirements and plan work, and may minimize friction among the team.

[A]   PMO-Based Project Manager Training

The PMO training builds core project management expertise. Training delivered by the PMO may be cheaper than using an outside organization and the PMO will be best able to provide training on organization-specific needs and expectations. Rather than sending project managers off to "canned" training sessions, the PMO can tailor the classes to address local issues.

[1]   What to Teach

Identifying which issues to include in a PMO training program is easy. In the course of a day, a successful project manager uses a variety of skills. Ways to identify training issues include:

A. Identifying gaps between PMO job descriptions and resumes.

B. Conducting a skills self-assessment of where the project managers feel they are and need to be.

C. Asking the project managers what areas cause them the greatest problems or confusion.

D. Noting any complaints about project management from sponsors, team members, or others.

E. Noting any complaints by project managers about supporting departments.

F. Identifying emerging technologies or legal issues.

Training need not require large amounts of time. Some companies tack it on to the end of each staff meeting, either as a short, focused session or as an open forum to discuss problems of common interest. Some companies provide training during "brown bag" lunches where employees provide their own lunches and the PMO provides a one-hour class. The key to training is to have a list of short topics available for presentation on short notice.

[2]   Project Management

Focus basic project management training on project rollout actions, including defining the scope, developing a schedule, and estimating resource requirements. Advanced subjects include quality management, risk management techniques, and project metrics. All project managers can benefit from refresher training. If they cannot— then they should be the trainers!

Project management is such a broad subject that the PMO can develop a long list of individual "short sessions" for review with the project managers. Later, the project managers can use the same focused training session with their own project teams, which will squeeze "double duty" out of a single lesson and reinforce it to the project manager.

A valuable but sensitive training session can be to examine troubled projects to discuss what happened and when, and how it could have been handled differently. Peer critiques can be very valuable if attention is focused on the issues and not the personalities.

[3] "Hard" Skills

Hard skills are specific technical areas of expertise that are useful to project managers. This might include budgeting, capital finance, or UNIX system administration. Often these are learned in traditional classrooms. PMO training in these areas should focus on those aspects specific to the worksite. Site-specific training is an ideal subject for one of the most skilled project managers to teach. The experience and insight added to the discussion will help to keep the training relevant.

In theory, any skilled project manager should be able to manage any project. In reality, without at least a basic understanding of the underlying technologies involved, the project manager cannot make judgment calls about schedule changes, allocation of resources, etc. For very technically-complex projects, it may be advisable to assign a chief engineer to make technical decisions. Team members may mislead project managers who do not understand the technologies they are managing and project efficiency will suffer.

[4] "Soft" Skills

Few project managers have full authority and control over their teams. They move the project forward by influencing the team's actions and, at times, by force of personality. Soft skills, such as interpersonal interactions, are difficult to teach in a classroom. Allot sufficient time to introduce a technique and then practice it.

Periodically refresh the team's soft skills. A PMO should conduct a series of soft-skill training sessions that repeat at least every two years. The instructor can vary class materials by converting some discussions into role-playing or lectures into discussions.

Soft skills will often include restatements of company personnel policies. Because perception equals guilt in many companies, project managers must be sensitive to how their actions or words could be perceived adversely.

> "There is small risk a general will be regarded with contempt by those he leads, if, whatever he may have to preach, he shows himself best able to perform."
>
> —Xenophon

[B] Lessons Learned

Sometimes projects are spectacular successes and other times humiliating flops. This was initially attributed to the talents of the project manager. Over time, however, companies discovered that a degree of this success was due to the tools and practices used by the more successful project managers.

At the end of every project or major milestone, the PMO should conduct a lessons-learned meeting to elicit feedback on processes, team members, the project manager, etc. Gather these into a document of "best practices" for use across the PMO. Each project attempted or completed will turn up something new. This could be a new challenge, a new work-around process, or even a stellar performance by a resource. Whatever happened—good or bad—share the experience with other project managers so everyone can benefit from the great idea or watch out for the problem. The PMO should zero in on repeated problems and address their root causes.

Lessons-learned meetings should include everyone who worked on the project team at any time, key stakeholders, and, as time permits, other project managers. This will provide a range of perceptions. The challenge for the moderator is to encourage quiet people to speak up without fear of retribution. The moderator also must keep the discussion focused on the project and not on a person. Project managers are present as observers and to learn from the successes and failures of other projects.

Lessons-learned meetings should center on five broad questions. The PMO schedules the meeting within a week after the milestone or project is completed. The PMO should act as a moderator to keep the discussions focused.

A common format for a lessons-learned discussion is for the moderator to pose five open-ended questions concerning an event or the project as a whole:

1. What happened?

2. What should have happened?

3. What went well?

4. What could have gone better?

5. What will be done differently next time?

In addition to these general areas, sometimes the moderator must discuss all areas of the project. If the conversation begins to lag or move in an undesirable direction, the moderator steers it back to the issues by asking about any of these specific areas:

A. Project schedule

B. Time allotted for tasks

C. Adequacy of tools and supporting resources provided

D. Project budget

E. Clarity of project scope

F. Clarity of task assignments

G. Major work distractions

H. "Heroic" work efforts

I. Quality of project manager support

J. What did you do that you were glad the project manager did not know about?

A successful discussion will bring to the surface many issues, including some pertaining directly to people, the quality of their performance, etc. When conducting the meeting, a scribe maintains a record of all discussions to capture the issues as they arise. After the meeting is completed, consolidate the meeting notes into a report. Include the following points:

A. General information about the project

B. Specific information about the project or resources

C. Actions to consider in future projects

Conduct a separate lessons-learned meeting between the project manager, the project sponsor, and the PMO. Although this meeting should be free form and can address any issue, it also should focus on the project management process, the tools used, areas of friction, etc. Review the report from this meeting with other project managers to identify opportunities to improve their own projects.

[C]   Industry and Professional Trends

Companies struggle forward in a whirlwind of business advances, legal mandates, market forces, and a range of other factors. Project managers must understand the issues driving their project sponsors and team members if they are to remain effective. Instead of each project manager individually seeking out this information, the PMO adds value by monitoring the ever-changing business environment and then passing it on to the department.

The PMO team must constantly monitor the trade press. As new or revised processes or tools become available, the PMO should look for opportunities to deploy them in the organization. As technologies evolve, new ways of applying them will become available or commonplace.

Changes in the legal landscape often require training project managers on the appropriate actions. Changes in customer privacy, employee privacy, and data retention can come from all directions. The PMO can collect this information and act as a clearinghouse to distribute relevant pieces to project managers.

[D] Training the Team

Everyone on the project team has a role to play, responsibilities to fulfill, and expertise to offer. To maximize the participation of the team members, they need to understand the parts they play in moving a project forward.

Train the project sponsors so they understand their contribution to a successful project team. The PMO is the logical group to lead this effort. The result will be a set of sponsors who understand the tools, techniques, and challenges of project management and who use a common terminology.

Conduct team training during project orientation. The project manager describes the role of the team members and their place in the project schedule. This sets an expectation in the minds of the team members about what they should be doing and what other individuals should be doing. This will reduce the initial friction among team members.

[E] Peer Mentoring

Even experienced project managers face unusual challenges. They may lead a difficult project, a difficult team, or combination of the two. The PMO can provide assistance in the form of mentoring. Mentoring provides personal advice from a senior project manager to a less-experienced team member or even to a peer. Unlike formal training, mentoring is more personal and targeted toward a specific issue.

The PMO also can provide a forum where project managers can explain a particular situation they are experiencing and solicit advice from their peers for possible solutions. If a project continues to slide toward failure, assign a senior project manager to assist and mentor the project manager until the project gets back on track. Managing projects can sometimes be a lonely job and it may help project managers to be able to discuss issues with their peers.

> "Management is doing things right; leadership is doing the right things."
>
> —Peter F. Drucker

[F] Raising Company Awareness

Project managers move their projects forward through their ability to persuade others to assist them. It is rare for a project manager to have the authority to mandate everyone take a specific course of action. A positive working relationship takes time to develop. However, project managers must often work through people they have never met before. Many people are reluctant or slow to react on directions from a stranger. A tool that can lower resistance is a company-wide, general education program about the benefits of project management.

Project management has a positive story to tell and it is easily understood by other employees. Who has not been involved with major company initiatives that are doomed from the start? Who has not been disgusted by obviously mismanaged efforts that cost precious company funds when pay raises are frozen "due to financial constraints"? An outreach program that explains basic project management principles and introduces the PMO team is an easy concept to "sell."

How should the PMO go about this? The first step is to realize that this is a distance race—not a sprint. A steady stream of small success stories and tips on how to use project management practices in daily work can go farther than a single news story splashed across the company newsletter. Excellent communications media include:

A. The company newsletter is *always* hungry for well-written, short articles pertinent to the company. This is an excellent place for short tips, success stories that highlight employee contributions to the project, and progress on highly visible projects.

B. A handy tool (with considerably more PMO control) is to establish a PMO Web page on the company intranet. Unlike the newsletter that comes out periodically, the Web page is changed whenever the PMO wants it to be. In addition, the PMO will have control over the content, whereas the newsletter editor may alter the story to fit the space or to change its slant.

C. If a project is pending for an area of the company, the PMO should visit the staff meetings for those departments, introduce themselves, and explain how the company runs projects. This also is an excellent way to make more contacts throughout the company because a project manager never knows what may arise in a project. It is far easier to call even a passing acquaintance than a total stranger.

§ 11.08 REFERENCE LIBRARY

Projects create many documents. These documents detail thought processes, failed tests, and discarded options. All of this is useful in the future. Before this wisdom can be applied later, it must be collected from the projects, cataloged for easy reference, and safely stored. The PMO is uniquely positioned to gather documents from all projects and manage their central storage.

[A] What to Collect

Which of the myriad of project documents should be collected for future value? As always, the answer is to ask how the information will be used. Some examples of useful documents are:

- Project charters and scope change documents
- Project schedules along with actual hours used for each task
- Project issues logs and risk assessments
- Stakeholder analysis
- Project budget reports
- Minutes from meetings where major design decisions were made
- Test scripts used to validate software modules
- Reports from lessons-learned meetings

Estimating the tasks, time durations, and risks associated with a new project can require a considerable amount of work. Yet some tasks will still be overlooked, some risks underrated, and some time estimates way off the mark. A valuable resource for planning new projects is the experience gained from managing completed projects. Every project is unique, yet there may be similarities in situation, requirements, environment, key stakeholders, etc. All of these provide useful information during the project-planning phase.

During the closeout phase of every project, the PMO gathers all documents of value, such as plans, analyses, charts, correspondence, and anything else that pertains to the project, and stores them in the project management experience center. This material should be organized and made available for quick reference.

[B] How It Will Be Used

A great use of the reference library is as an estimation resource. Identifying project tasks and estimating the resources required for each project is difficult. Historical documents can provide the raw data for the development of a resource-estimate template. The template can provide a historical perspective of the average amount of time that a particular class of tasks requires, such as to build a database, write a data entry screen, or to install a network hub.

Another resource estimation tool is resource efficiency. When explaining a task to a particular resource, and having that resource provide an estimate of time to complete the task, how accurate has this been? Do the members of the telephone support team regularly complete their tasks on time without padding their estimates? Do the database administrators (DBAs) frequently underestimate tasks assigned? An analysis of resource estimates (provided by the people doing the work) versus the actual cost can result in an adjustment figure to modify future estimates.

For example, if the DBAs estimate 100 hours to complete a task, the project manager may apply a 20 percent factor to the estimate to compensate for consistently late performance. (A cynical project manager would be sure *not* to inform the DBAs about the schedule adjustment in case they adjust their work intensity to complete their tasks 20 percent over the padded plan!)

Another use of the reference library is for future system maintenance—design considerations, test scripts, and names of team members who built the code are all valuable information to the person assigned to provide ongoing maintenance to a new piece of technology. We plan to deliver new systems with complete and accurate technical documentation. Yet the project documents will provide more depth to the analysis of future issues and fill in gaps in the technical manual. Other uses for the resource library include:

A. New project design. Has a similar project been attempted in the past? What happened? Reviewing similar projects may identify best practices to embrace and pitfalls to avoid. Although project environments change over time, reviewing old projects will provide insight into what to expect and what to avoid.

B. Project audits. Reviews of completed projects or milestones will allow the PMO to determine how efficiently the project was managed and how effectively the resources were applied. Hindsight is always sharper than foresight. When properly applied; this review can improve the performance of the project management team.

C. Historical metrics. The PMO office will need to measure how well it is performing compared to past projects. Over time, it should become more effective and efficient. However, the PMO leader will never know this unless critical metrics are consistently gathered and tracked. Documentation from old projects can provide a range of information for metric creation.

The PMO leader, or whoever is appointed to monitor the library, must ensure that personal comments about individuals are screened out of all material prior to its storage. Personal invective stored in the library might surface at an embarrassing time. Such comments only serve to fuel petty grudges and distract the team from the work at hand.

[C] How to Organize It

A simple way to organize the material is in chronological order for the project. Chronological sequence allows people to view information "in context" of the moment. This should reduce the rush to condemn a decision or action irrespective of the priorities and pressures of the moment.

Sometimes the material is searched for information on a specific subject. This includes resource utilization and meeting minutes with the sponsor. Cross-references can be created to indicate the location of key information, by subject.

Because the PMO uses a standard tool set, project managers should be able to quickly search through the material. Organize it just like any other project. True, some project managers are more fastidious than others for gathering information or for reporting, but still the resource calendar should be in a certain place, the project budget in its own place, etc.

> "Each morning sees some task begun, each evening sees it close; Something attempted, something done, has earned a night's repose."
>
> —Henry Wadsworth Longfellow

§ 11.09 SUMMARY

A project management office provides many useful services for an organization. By consolidating oversight tasks into a PMO, valuable project management time is freed to allow project managers to focus on their project work.

A PMO manages the company's project portfolio. This requires collecting estimates for the essential information elements used to approve projects and for arranging them hierarchically in the portfolio. An executive committee uses the portfolio to select projects for execution. As the business climate changes, the PMO manager may update the project information and priorities in the portfolio may change.

A PMO provides a consolidated resource management pool for project support. This pool ensures that as schedules change, the supporting lines of service are not surprised with critical new support tasks and that resources are not idle.

Chapter 12

A Balanced Scorecard Approach to Project Management

§ 12.01 INTRODUCTION

Company leaders have long struggled to find the best way to shape their organizations for improved performance. Although changes can be dictated from the top, real change only occurs when employees choose to adopt the new way rather than ignore it. Every enterprise has strategic goals. Through mission statements, company-wide meetings, and planning sessions, executives strive to encourage employees to fulfill these objectives.

Many companies have achieved change through a balanced scorecard program. This aligns an organization's strategy with its value chain—from the worker to the customer. It changes a corporate strategy from words on a page into marching orders for all employees using top-down communication for aligning employee activities toward meeting the company's strategic goals. Through its metrics, the balanced scorecard is also bottoms-up performance reporting to executives on progress toward achieving these goals.

The balanced scorecard process measures four key areas to focus employees on activities necessary to achieve the stated strategic goals. The value chain perspectives are:

- Learning and growth—Employees are the foundation for innovation and creativity. What must employees learn to innovate and achieve the strategic goals?

- Business processes—Skilled, creative employees question the status quo and work to improve business processes. To achieve the strategic goals, which processes must be improved and measured?

- Customer satisfaction—Improved processes lead to improved products and services for customers. What aspects of the customer experience is the company seeking to improve?

- Financial results—Satisfied and loyal customers lead to increased revenues. Establish financial objectives needed to accomplish that strategic goal.

Balanced scorecards are implemented throughout an organization and provide visibility and accountability for progress. Metrics replace subjective evaluations with verifiable data. Since the balanced scorecard reaches into all aspects of an enterprise, it must be tailored to the company's culture.

Balanced scorecards were developed in the 1990s as a way to convert a company's value drivers to a series of published metrics. This process was described by Kaplan and Norton in their book *The Balanced Scorecard*. The basic premise is that creative people are the real power within a successful business. With constant change in the marketplace, companies must hire the best people and continue to train them throughout their careers.

> For more detailed and comprehensive information on implementing a balanced scorecard program see *The Balanced Scorecard: Translating Strategy into Action* by Robert Kaplan and David Norton, Harvard Business Press, 1996.

A scorecard program is implemented at each organizational level from the top executives down to the individual workers. By articulating strategies and mandating data that are collected toward achieving them, the program serves to align the objectives throughout the organization. The scorecard program is both a strategic communication tool and a way to measure progress toward the goals. Instead of feeling like faceless cogs in a big machine, employees can now demonstrate their contribution to the enterprise. If the strategic goals are carefully selected and the metrics are accurate, then as company fortunes improve, employee teams can see how their efforts have improved company profitability.

By communicating company priorities up and down the management chain, the scorecard also promotes alignment between business units. Departments must move in sync as the business environment changes. Sometimes they have not communicated well between themselves. With the balanced scorecard, managers can examine the scorecard metrics and objectives for other departments when making their own strategic decisions.

> Beginning a balanced scorecard program is a lot like planning a project. It begins with what is to be achieved, and then breaks the program down into the tasks needed to do this.. The scorecard is used to measure progress toward identified goals, much as typical project metrics of timelines and budgets indicate the project's progress.

[A] Getting Started

There are basic measures used to describe the value chain: learning and growth, customer, business process, and financial. Each of these requires careful nurturing for the program to succeed.

[1] Learning and Personal Growth

Many companies (wishfully) assume employees already know all that they need to know to perform their jobs adequately. This philosophy overlooks the constant changes that occur in the workplace. Change is all around us in the form of new regulations, evolving industry standards, the implementation of new processes, the entrance of new employees, introduction of new technologies, reorganization of departments, etc. Some executives see training as a drain on profit with little direct return. The primary argument against more-than-minimal employee training is the time it requires workers to be away from their busy desks. This immediate cost in lost labor is seen as an exchange for a *potential* future return. The balanced scorecard ties employee skills development directly to the strategic goals that everyone is working toward.

Learning and growth must be mission-oriented. (In the case of the balanced scorecard, this mission is focused on the company's strategic goals.) Employee learning and personal growth stimulates creativity in an organization through knowledge gained. Hire the best people with the right skills and attitudes for innovation; and then mentor them throughout their career. An initial skills assessment establishes a baseline for gauging the effectiveness of future training. All employees are then nurtured through periodic assessments, an active training program, and collaboration in areas of interest.

Employee training involves more than having the employees sit in a classroom and learn how to run a personal computer. It includes mentoring of unseasoned employees by more seasoned ones. It also includes participation in lessons learned and peer reviews of work products.

[2] Business Process Improvements Are Usually the Result of Employee Suggestions

A business process improvement might take the form of an increase in the flow of transactions by reducing the steps required to complete them. It might be the application of technology to automate a step. Every company must encourage a steady flow of new ideas and innovation from all employees. Japanese automakers are far ahead of others in encouraging and adopting employee innovation. The results are clear for all to see.

People who perform a job are the most knowledgeable about it. The more employees know about the company, its processes, their industry, and technology, the more that this experience can be tapped for process improvement. Improved business processes provide better, faster, and/or cheaper products for the customer.

> Total quality management (TQM) is a process that holds that employees, as the most knowledgeable people about their work processes, should be empowered to make changes in their own area. Its goal is an endless stream of small improvements which, over time, adds up to big savings.

[3]   Customer Relationship Management—Know What the Customer Wants and Values

The balanced scorecard measures improvements in customer satisfaction. Improved customer satisfaction leads to more customers and a broader market for the company's goods and services.

Companies creating goods or services strive to strike a balance between the three product drivers: cost, quality, and speed of delivery. Changing any one of these automatically changes the other two. If a product is needed more quickly, then either more resources must be applied (cost) or quality is reduced. Conversely, if costs must be reduced, then fewer resources are applied and delivery time is lengthened. The ideal way to make a shift in equilibrium among the three product drivers is in innovation, which reduces cost or time to delivery without reducing quality (or increasing quality without increasing cost or delivery time).

Companies rely on market research to identify ways to improve their product drivers in the eyes of their customers. They look to see which areas delight their customers, which ones simply meet their requirements, and which ones dissatisfy them. Companies also run the same type of analysis on their competitors' products and services. From this, they can identify areas for improvement that will increase customer loyalty, market share, and profitability.

Kano analysis is a powerful tool for evaluating what characteristics customers value in a product. This is fed into quality function deployment's (QFD) House of Quality matrix, which ties a product characteristic to something a customer values.

[4]   Improved Financial Management Using Techniques such as Activity-Based Costing for Better Management Information

Financial performance must also be innovative to better identify costs, profits, and the success of a given project. Innovation does not stop at the product/service level. It must reach into all components of the organization, including the financial. Timely and accurate information for the cost per unit production (or service) is essential. Some companies adopt activity-based costing or other measures of effort-to-product analysis. The same customer requirements of better, faster, and cheaper apply to financial reports. Improvements in financial accounting and reporting generate benefits throughout an organization.

[B]   Strategic Linkage Model

A valuable tool for assembling a balanced scorecard program is the strategic linkage model. This is an illustration of the linkages between the company's goals and the various processes measured on the scorecard. The strategic linkage model cuts across all four of the perspectives at a glance. The arrows indicate the relations between actions and outcomes.

There is no one right strategic linkage model format. The key is to illustrate the relationships involved. In the example of a strategic linkage map shown in Chart 12-1, the project management office's sole strategic goal is to improve customer satisfaction with project processes. Most companies will strive to pursue four or five strategic goals at the same time.

One of the authors worked in a project management office, which required all of the project managers to use an automated project-tracking tool that many of the project managers found to be clumsy, slow, and occasionally defective. The customer quickly caught on to this and asked the PMO manager why the PMO's overhead costs for using a wasteful, slow, automated tool was passed on to them. They suggested fixing the tool, replacing it, or reducing their fees to compensate for suboptimal tools.

Refer to Chart 12-1: Example Strategic Linkage Map for a Single Goal. The map has four levels.

- Customer—What aspect of the customer experience is to be improved? In this example, the top goal is somewhat general, to "improve customer satisfaction with project processes." This might be explained as all of the frustrations the customer experiences with project administrative details, or that the customer perceives as wasted effort passed on as increased labor costs.

    A successful project is more than delivering a finished product or service. A successful project is also the journey—the project's progress from the beginning to the outcome. A project may successfully deliver its product yet be considered a failure by the customer because of problems encountered along the way. A skillful project manager addresses customer issues and expectations during the project to ensure satisfaction with the overall effort.

- Financial—What financial rewards will the PMO see as a result of these changes? The strategic map indicates the financial benefits of lower costs and no late

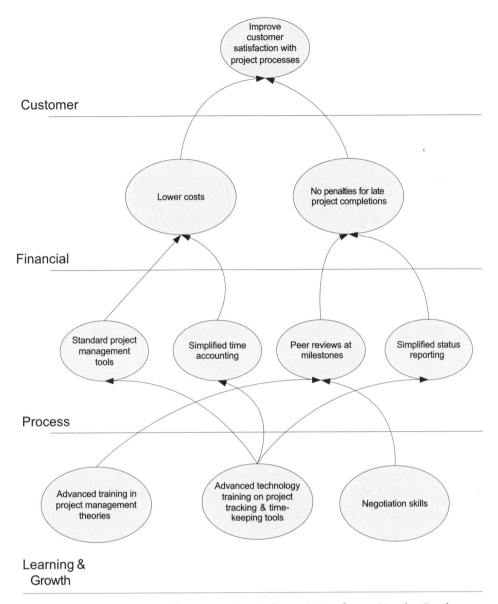

Chart 12-1: Example Strategic Linkage Map for a Single Goal

penalties for projects. If processes are simplified, then labor lost to overhead tasks will be reduced and more time will be available for completing the project's goals. Late penalties may be reduced by freeing the project manager's time to address other issues. The degree this is realized depends on the amount of wasteful overhead currently required of team members.

All overhead cost and labor is a drain on a project. However, some overhead is necessary to support the team and the project. Without someone handling the payroll, vacations, sick time, time accounting, office supplies, status reports, etc., a project will quickly grind to a halt. The trick is to minimize the amount of "drag" on a project's completion. However, this assumes that any time saved will be applied toward the project's completion and not used elsewhere.

- Process—What processes must be improved to achieve these goals?
  The four processes identified on the strategy map will improve productivity and lead to customer satisfaction and the financial goals desired. Each of them will have action items assigned to team members to complete.

  1. Standard project management tools—The PMO manager is to identify and obtain automated tools that meet the organization's requirements but are still simple and efficient. Train all members of the PMO and require them to use the same tools.

  2. Simplified time accounting—The goal is to reduce the amount of time lost by team members fumbling with a slow and unforgiving time accounting system. However, this tool must still fulfill the requirements of the PMO organization as well as any customer reporting requirements.

  3. Peer reviews at milestones—Reduce the amount of rework in a project by including other project managers in peer reviews of projects at every major milestone. The suggestions may identify previously unseen risks, and the managers can share expertise.

  4. Simplified status reporting—Reduce the amount of time gathering information and formatting it into a report to the stakeholders.

- Learning and growth—What training would be useful for achieving these goals?
  Three areas of training support these objectives.

  1. Advanced training in project management theories. This is a combination of training and mentoring designed to learn new and relearn old project management procedures and techniques. The instruction might be led by the PMO manager or outside instructors. It might involve certification by all project managers in their field or in the technologies they support.

  2. Advanced technology training on project tracking and time-keeping tools. This training will focus on the specific technology tools used by the project managers with the intention of increasing productivity. Training may also

encompass the more efficient use of electronic mail, word processors, presentation tools, etc.

3. Negotiation skills. People are a project manager's primary tool. The ability to focus team members on completing a project task directly affects a project's ability to keep moving forward. All project managers benefit from learning new techniques to improve their negotiation effectiveness. Often customer dissatisfaction during a project is due to their poor communication with the project manager.

Assembling a strategic linkage model can involve some tradeoffs. Process changes impact both customers and financials—some more than others. The question is what comes first, the financial impact or the customer impact? In general, the idea is that lower costs will result in improved customer satisfaction through reduced prices.

[C] Selecting the Metrics

Metrics are measures of something. For the balanced scorecard, the measures indicate the degree of progress made toward achieving a goal. For example, if the metric was for learning and growth, it might be the number of team members trained to use a new technology. Metrics fall into the two broad categories of leading and lagging indicators. A balance between the two types of metrics must be struck on the scorecard:

- Leading indicators are metrics collected prior to an event that indicate the likely result.
- Lagging indicators—usually financial—are collected after an event. They provide a historical record of what has occurred. The historical record is often used as an indicator of what future performance may be.

In order to make these measurements, a description of what to measure, how/when the data are to be collected, and their target values need to be defined. Following are some guidelines for selecting metrics.

1. Metrics must have a focus. They must be clearly defined as to what, how, and when to count. They also may include things to exclude from the count.

2. Do not select metrics based on ease of collection. Select metrics that are true indicators of the issue being addressed. Often this means creating new metrics to monitor processes. Repurposing existing metrics is unlikely to provide different results than were previously achieved.

3. Data collection and analysis take time. A business unit has a limited number of vital signs. The remaining indicators are useful but not vital. Consider limiting the number of scorecard metrics to 15 or less. The more data that are collected, the more overhead that the balanced scorecard program adds.

4. Roll out new metrics over time. It takes time for team members to understand the purpose of and process for collecting new metrics. Issuing too many of them at one time is confusing. A staggered metric collection rollout allows for successes along the way, which improves support for the program.

Metric selection is done as a team, and the goals and strategies to attain them are discussed as a group. Remember, the people doing the job are the local experts. They should be the ones to identify the metrics and the best way to collect them.

Meeting as a team:

1. Review the strategic problem to be addressed. Clearly identify the "what" that is to be accomplished. The team should discuss this to clarify in their minds the essential elements of the strategic goal.

2. Brainstorm and select a strategy to achieve the goal. This may be a process change, the addition of a new technology, etc. This is the "how" of what will be done. What will be done differently to achieve this goal? This step will identify the learning and growth goals for the department as well.

3. Brainstorm metrics that will measure progress toward meeting the strategic goal. By discussing the metrics as they are selected, the team is self-training on what actions they can take to influence the scorecard.

4. Review this plan with executives to ensure the scorecard is valid and coordinated with the remainder of the organization. The discussion should elicit explicit approval for the strategic goals, the changes made to meet them, and the metrics used to measure progress.

[D] Pitfalls

As with all processes that involve people, sometimes a balanced scorecard program can go awry. The key is careful planning, and of course, using a knowledgeable person to launch the program.

The critical people issue to overcome is fear. Managers and their workers tend to fear something that is new to them but will directly influence their work life. This intrusion into their comfort zone must be treated as a gradual cultural change that requires a long-term management commitment. The way that the output of the balanced scorecard is used will be a major determinant in the degree of opposition to its use.

In addition to fear, some other pitfalls or complaints from workers against this program may include the following:

1. Some companies tie balanced scorecard performance to compensation incentives. This has led to complaints that the balanced scorecard is simply a variation of management by objectives (MBO) which flopped in the 1970s. This is not the case. Properly implemented, the balanced scorecard is a holistic approach to the value chain from employee to customer. MBO fell apart because it was poorly implemented at most companies and because employees focused on the objectives they were accountable for, to the exclusion of others.

2. Executives will get what they measure. It is critical that the scorecard focus employees on the important points but not to the exclusion of all others. Selecting the wrong metrics may focus well-meaning employees away from the right things onto the wrong ones. This is why careful planning is important. Monitoring the effect of the scorecard on results felt by the customer is a good feedback mechanism to detect and correct this.

3. There may be a tendency to use the easiest metrics to collect (or re-use existing metrics), thereby missing the ones most important for monitoring value and progress.

4. If the scorecard is not refreshed often enough, what looked like an important goal in January may not be very germane in June.

5. Do not select too many metrics to monitor. This will make the program difficult to support and manage.

6. Managers have an irresistible urge to massage data as it is passed upward to "manage the message." This must not be permitted. The executive champion for the balanced scorecard must audit samples of the source data used to create the metrics to ensure this has not occurred.

§ 12.02   APPLYING A BALANCED SCORECARD TO A PROJECT MANAGEMENT OFFICE

In most companies, a balanced scorecard program is mandated from the top levels. The PMO is just one of the departments caught in its net. However, even if the company does not implement an enterprise-wide program, there is no reason why a PMO manager cannot initiate a program of his own.

Why would a PMO want to go through the time and expense of a balanced scorecard process? Simply put—survival! Business is a highly competitive arena. Internal PMO departments can be outsourced. PMOs provided under contracts can be replaced. For every well-run PMO there are likely several more that blunder forward day by day with no clear program for self-improvement. They display an attitude of, "What was good enough for last year is good enough for next year." A balanced scorecard program focuses a PMO team on specific areas of improvement with a corresponding improvement in customer satisfaction.

The balanced scorecard process can be easily applied to a project management office. Projects, by definition, are a series of unique actions with a defined beginning and end. Their operation includes a series of defined and repeatable processes that constitute what we think of as the profession of project management. A balanced scorecard identifies customer-oriented goals that a PMO might strive for by improving the execution of these repeatable processes.

The key customer experience areas to focus on are quality, profitability, and cost. Strategic goals should be few. A PMO can reasonably tackle only four or five at one time since so many processes directly or indirectly influence each of them.

Applying a balanced scorecard program to a PMO forces project managers and the PMO support staff to examine their own methods and interactions within the department. This focus can lead to identifying and removing obstacles to performance. Over time, the PMO emphasis shifts from just getting the project completed to completing it with customer satisfaction.

The key driver to a PMO balanced scorecard is, of course, the PMO manager. This person must believe in the potential benefits of the program and ensure that all team members incorporate these benefits into all projects. The PMO manager will find his task easier if the executive oversight one level higher is also a part of the balanced scorecard team.

Implementing a balanced scorecard requires a considerable amount of effort and thought. If an organization is not willing to change its culture, then the time spent on developing a balanced scorecard will be wasted. Most companies find the services of a consultant for implementing this culture change to be very useful. Consultants bring a fresh insight into a company's processes as well as in-depth understanding of the balanced scorecard process. Since the balanced scorecard method requires a substantial amount of up-front training, the consultant can provide ongoing mentoring of employees as the process is rolled out.

[A] Prepare the Team

The rollout process for the balanced scorecard follows the phases of inform, train, and mentor. Cultural changes occur over time. Rolling out a balanced scorecard program requires a careful preparation of the workforce that anticipates a gradual acceptance of the program.

During their tenure, employees gradually build up expertise in their functional areas. This provides a measure of stability and predictability in their lives. It also minimizes the fear of the unknown since they have some control over their workday through their expertise. Introducing change into this area stirs fears of the unknown—especially with the visibility of performance measures through a "scorecard."

Companies must accentuate the positive of the system. The champion should gently press the program forward through implementation, and should demonstrate early and frequent successes. To help pass on this positive message, train local champions in each department. These people can then answer questions and ensure any message is tailored to the local work situation.

In most companies, the greatest employee concern surrounds the scorecard itself. Using this tool introduces visibility of performance to higher management levels as well as to other departments. Few department managers (or their workers) welcome such open scrutiny. In most companies, pay is tied to performance and anything that introduces a new way to monitor performance introduces uncertainty into the workplace. This is partially overcome by including the workers in the scorecard development process.

[1] Inform

Begin the rollout by announcing the program to the PMO team and explaining how it will improve the company's performance. Beyond the upper management ranks, be prepared for a big yawn. Over time, many new things have been tried and most fizzle out in a year or so.

After the initial announcement, schedule information sessions for all employees over a period of time (perhaps a month). These sessions explain the program in detail and provide a forum for addressing concerns. As these concerns are raised and resolved, wrap up the solution into the next presentation of the program so that others can better understand what is being asked of them.

[2] Training

After alerting the PMO team to what is coming (and hopefully setting a positive expectation), begin training the employees. Training classes should use examples from the department. Apply the lessons for developing strategies and metrics to their own work. This allows the instructor to mentor the team through the process as they apply what they have learned.

[3] Mentor

Training provides familiarization, not expertise. As the teams apply the balanced scorecard techniques, someone familiar with both the scorecard process and the company's processes in general should mentor the team members. This assistance is to provide help over the rough spots and answer questions that arise. An active mentoring process should follow each team member for at least one year after the completion of training.

Mentoring is provided on several levels. The mentor should meet with the team at least once per month to review progress. During these meetings, the scorecard process should be discussed along with the department's progress toward meetings its goals as measured by the scorecard. This provides a forum to discuss issues and forces the team to update the scorecard at least monthly. Mentoring is also accomplished in one-on-one sessions, answering individuals' questions.

The key to a successful mentoring program is continuing executive support. As executives publicly review performance represented in the scorecards, employees see how their performance is considered and appreciated. Executive emphasis over the long run shifts employee priorities so that they make time for participating and succeeding in the program.

[B] Identify the PMO's Strategic Goals

Each PMO exists in a unique business environment. Some are contracted operations where every action results in some cost to the customer. Some are departments within a company that support only internal projects. Both environments have the same problems—the delivery of products and services in a timely, cost-effective manner to satisfy customer requirements. To the degree that they do this, they are considered competent. If they can accomplish this while generating a high degree of customer satisfaction, then they will be sought out for more work and be protected from replacement.

[1] What Do They Want?

The first step in a PMO balanced scorecard is to identify customer experience goals that can be improved. Areas of improvement can be identified through a wide range of sources. Complaints, customer satisfaction surveys, post-project reviews, and benchmarking against other PMOs are just a few of the places that strategic goals may come from.

Some of these goals might be:

- Percentage of projects (or major milestones) completed on time and on budget
- Client satisfaction as indicated by end-of-project customer surveys
- Number of scope changes/budget variances requested during a project
- Percentage of project proposals released to the customer by the agreed-upon delivery date
- Similarly, turnaround time between a request for a project estimate of time and cost, and delivery of that estimate to the customer

A variation on these goals is what constitutes a customer. Is it simply the person or organization paying for the work? Are there other interested parties, such as the accounting department, facilities and maintenance department, purchasing department, or others? Sometimes the greatest benefit is derived with the least effort by investigating the neglected support departments.

One way to identify areas for improvement is to examine the components used to create a successful project. A tool for doing this is a fishbone diagram. As shown in Chart 12-2, each major "bone" on the fish corresponds to one of the primary components of a project.

[2] Selecting Goals for the Scorecard

From the long list of customer improvement issues, select the ones that will provide the greatest benefit. This is tempered by the cost and time required to complete each one. Chart 12-3 is an example of a ranking list of potential strategic improvements.

- List the potential improvements down the left side.
- Rank the benefits of each in terms of cost savings (real cash) and customer satisfaction. This might be from 1 to 5 with 5 being the most valuable benefit. Using this scale instead of actual numbers will prevent a few large projects from overwhelming the statistics.
- Rank the difficulty of achieving each goal from 1 to 5 with 5 being the easiest and 1 being the most difficult.
- Multiply the ranking of the cost savings, the customer satisfaction, and the difficulty across the row and obtain an overall ranking score.
- Sort the table from high to low based on the overall ranking column. This should bring the highest-value goals to the top of the list.

Select up to five goals for the PMO to address, based on their ranking in the matrix. Many goals interrelate in some manner. However, trying to address too many goals at one time creates too large of a hurdle for rolling out a new concept.

It is possible that some of the strategic goals involve supporting departments, or even behaviors by the project customers. These are fair game for the scorecard. Be sure that these changes are achievable. In the short run, it is unlikely that an external stakeholder can be changed. However, over the long run, anything is possible.

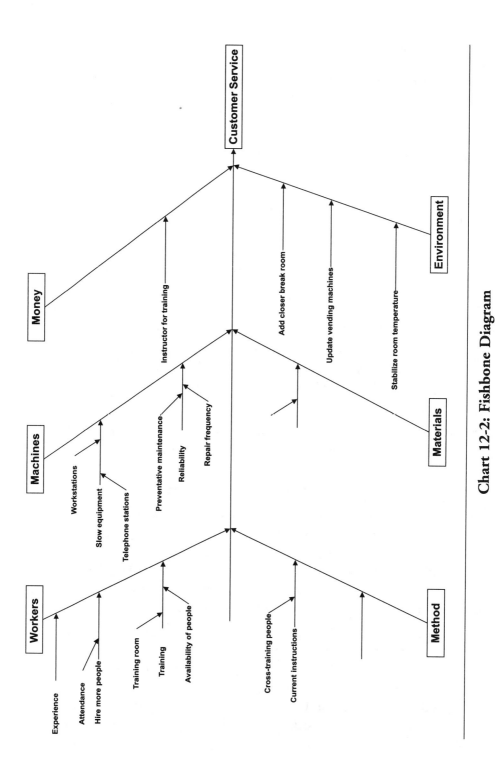

Chart 12-2: Fishbone Diagram

Process Improvement	Benefits		Difficulty	Overall Ranking
	Cost Savings	Customer Satisfaction		
Projects (or major milestones) completed on time and on budget				
Projects released to the customer by the agreed-upon delivery date				
Client satisfaction as indicated by customer surveys completed at the end of a project				
Number of scope changes/budget variances requested during a project				
Time between a request for a project estimate and delivery of estimate to the customer				

Chart 12-3: Selecting Goals

[C]   Identifying Processes to Improve

Strategic goals are fine, but how is the department going to realize them? What will the team do to achieve these goals? Fortunately, a PMO is well-equipped to tackle problems from analysis through solution. Achieving one of the strategic improvement goals is as hard as building a project plan and working it to completion!

First, the team must determine which existing PMO processes have a positive or negative impact on each of the goals. It is possible that some new processes are needed. The processes to add or change should initially be the ones that the PMO team has control over. This permits quicker action requiring the fewest external approvals.

Based on the strategic goals identified, meet with the team to discuss ways that these goals can be met. A balanced scorecard program is most efficiently run as a team effort and never as a one-man show. This is another place where a fishbone diagram can be useful for analyzing a process, since the diagram can be used to break down a process into its components (Chart 12-4).

Every business process involves one or more inputs that result in an output. For example, as shown in Chart 12-4, a project status reporting process would have the inputs from money spent, hours used, tasks completed, issues outstanding, etc. The single output (for this process) is a status report for the customer. A process improvement would be to improve the quality, cost, or speed of obtaining the output of this process. If it is determined that one of these inputs needs improvement, then the process that creates that input is the one upon which to focus.

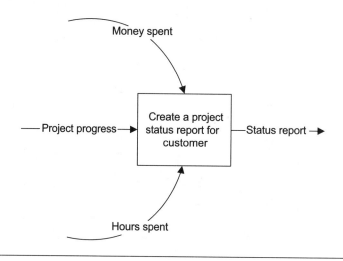

Chart 12-4: Process Analysis

Typically, a scorecard identifies between 10 and 15 process improvements to address in order to influence four to five strategic improvement goals. Identify a way to measure progress on each of the process improvements. The measurement describes the output. It should be easy to collect and update periodically. The numbers do not need to be "to the penny." They are indicating a trend as much as an overall value.

[D]   Map Objectives to Goals

To show which process improvements support which strategic goal, develop a "map" similar to the one shown in Chart 12-5, illustrating the relationships.

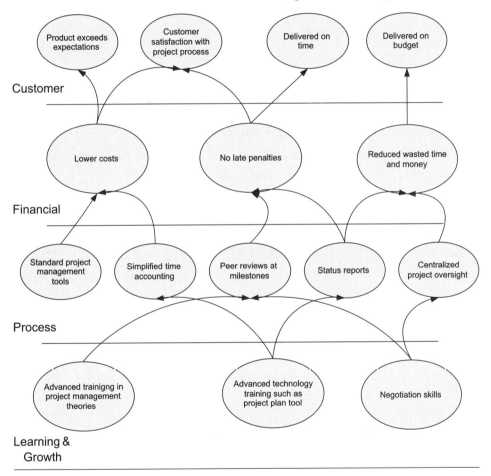

Chart 12-5: Mapping Objectives to Goals

[E]   Select Meaningful Metrics

Selecting useful scorecard metrics is a cornerstone of the entire program. The depth, breadth, and reasoning behind the PMO's metrics reflect the PMO manager's understanding of the department's operation. These numbers guide future business decisions. Focusing on the wrong numbers will send employees off on potentially expensive journeys in the wrong direction.

Once the strategic model is completed, the PMO team can brainstorm the metrics for measuring the progress made for each one. The proper selection of metrics is a major effort. During the selection process, balance metrics between leading and lagging indicators.

Assign each metric to a team member. That person will be the champion responsible for ensuring data are correctly collected and reported on time. They will investigate and report on significant variances in the results.

Describe each metric with:

- What it represents

- The units of measure being used (minutes, number of events, number of people, percentage of on-time documents, etc.)

- At what point in the process it is collected

- How it is collected in terms of the place and time. This would also include a description of formulas used to derive the values

- Who is responsible for collecting and reporting it

- How often it will be reported

- A target value that, once obtained, indicates the improvement is considered complete

The value obtained the first time that a metric is collected becomes its baseline quantity from which all future progress is measured.

[1]   Financial Perspective

Using the financial perspective from the earlier example, consider which metrics might meaningfully indicate the output from each one. In both cases, a line chart as shown in Chart 12-6 will indicate trends toward meeting the goals.

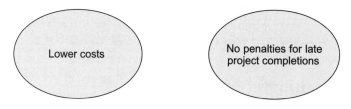

Financial

Chart 12-6: Financial Perspective

- Lower costs
  - Metric #1 might be to measure the cost per project. This is difficult since most projects are nonrecurring. However, it might be possible to measure the percent of labor from in-house sources used against external sources. Again, this depends on the mix of projects in play at a given time. It is influenced by the PMO manager's administration of the project portfolio to smooth out resource requirements. The metric might be reported as the percentage of variance between the budgeted and actual amount. Using a percentage instead of actual numbers would allow the comparison of large and small projects.
  - Metric #2 might be the percentage of costs spent versus budget, collected at each milestone. The goal is to reduce the variance between estimated and actual. Although the project manager can manipulate this at a milestone boundary, it would even out at the end of the project.
- No penalties for late project completions
  - Metric #1 might be the amount of money lost due to late fees.
  - Metric #2 might be the percent of projects that incurred late fees.

[2]   *Process Perspective*

Metrics for the process perspective in the scorecard would be a bit easier to identify (Chart 12-7).

Process

Chart 12-7: Process Perspective

- Standard project management tools
  - Metric #1 would be the number of standard tools in use versus the number of nonstandard tools in use. The key is to identify the standard tool set and then track its adoption by all staff members. Simply mandating that everyone use the same tools ignores the impact of a sudden change on productivity.
  - Metric #2 would be under the perspective of learning and growth describing the number of people trained on the use of each standard product.

- Simplified accounting
  - Metric #1 might be the number of sources for accounting information required in a status report with the goal to obtain all information from a single source.
  - Metric #2 might be the number of values required by the customer with the intent of minimizing the amount of information that must be calculated.
- Peer review at milestones
  - Metric #1 might be the number of peer reviews conducted in a given time period.
  - Metric #2 might be the number of project managers participating in the peer reviews.
  - Metric #3 might be a correlation between customer satisfaction surveys at the conclusion of projects that conducted peer reviews versus projects by the same project manager when peer reviews were not conducted.
- Simplified status reporting
  - Metric #1 might be the number of information elements required per report with the intent of decreasing the number.
  - Metric #2 might be a similar issue to metric #1 but only as pertains to smaller projects (less than 200 hours or some set cost amount). The idea is to minimize overhead on smaller projects where there is less time and expense to spread it across.

§ 12.03   SUMMARY

The collection and analysis of PMO metrics are essential for organizational improvement. Metrics must be carefully selected. Their goal is to focus workers on some aspect of the business. Poorly selected metrics will focus efforts on the wrong things and away from places where it is needed.

A tool for identifying and collecting data is a balanced scorecard. This process begins with identifying the organization's strategic goals. Then these goals are broken down into the four perspectives:

- Customer—What aspect of the customer experience is to be improved?
- Financial—What financial rewards will the organization see as a result of these changes?
- Process—What processes must be improved to achieve these goals?
- Learning and growth—What training would be useful for achieving these goals?

These four perspectives are used to formulate a balanced set of actions to achieve the strategic goals. From the PMO's perspective, a balanced scorecard can be implemented within its own department, whether the organization participates or not. The PMO often sets its own strategic goals and controls the processes for achieving them. The key is to create and roll out the program as the way to identify key areas and measure projects.

Implementing a PMO scorecard program takes planning and patience. People are naturally reluctant to embrace something strange and new that evaluates their work. With patience, the metrics can be identified and incorporated into the standard project structure. Take care that the metrics measure the things the PMO leaders want emphasized. Otherwise, everyone will be working on the wrong things.

Chapter 13

Project Documentation

§ 13.01   INTRODUCTION

> "The length of this document defends it well against the risk of its being read."
>
> —Winston Churchill

The term "documentation" is commonly used in IT practice to refer to a written description of something. It can be instructions on how to use a software system, the details of algorithms used to calculate something, or even the minutes of a meeting. This chapter focuses on the documentation essential to running a project, and some of the documentation created by an IT project. Small projects may need little documentation while large ones may require a great deal of it. Documents are tools and the project manager must select those tools that are useful to the project.

The value of any documentation drops substantially if it is unreadable. Documents critical to the project should follow a standard format to ensure they contain all of the essential information in a usable format. This will help the document users to share information quickly.

To organize all of these paper (and electronic) documents, the project management office maintains a library (PMO library). As projects progress, copies of critical documents are stored in the library. The PMO library is designed to provide quick reference to documents for project estimation and history. Some project documents, such as those created as artifacts of the software development process, may be stored in a tool designed to manage such artifacts. These documents are vital to the project and should be named or stored so that their association to the project is clear.

§ 13.02 PROJECT DOCUMENTATION ESSENTIALS

Projects generate a lot of paperwork such as product designs, status reports, change requests, etc. Much of this paper is of passing value, but some of it has persistent value and must be retained. The key is for the project manager to separate one type of document from the other. Otherwise, the useless will conceal the valuable amidst a pile of paper.

Using standard document formats organizes information for easy reading. Information is found in the same place in every document. A standard font size prevents authors from using tiny type to save on paper (at the expense of our eyes). Standard formats also make it easier to classify documents for storage and retrieval.

§ 13.03 DOCUMENTATION FORMAT

Most companies already have writing guidelines in place for preparing important documents. If not, consider the following basic guidelines.

A. Set the word processor to default to 12-point Arial or Times Roman font.

B. Each document should read from major topic to minor topic—or broad view to narrow view. The beginning of the document deals with actions that would affect the entire process, and then farther into the document, issues that are more specific are addressed.

C. On the first page, include a brief narrative overview of the business function that this particular process supports.

D. Be concise. Limit each sentence to less than 25 words, each paragraph to one topic, and each sentence to a single idea. This avoids swamping the reader's short-term memory. Concise text respects the reader's time and reduces ambiguity.

E. Write in a neutral tone and avoid humor, personal opinion, and popular slang.

F. Define any unusual technical or business terms that are used. Often, it is easier to write a bit longer statement and work around "insider" code words. Common technical or business terms are acceptable.

G. Use graphics to provide supporting information, not to repeat what has already been written.

H. Always write in the active voice. It is easier to understand than the passive voice.

Many technicians will say they are not "writers." (Of course, they were not technicians until they learned what to do, either.) Like any technical skill, writing needs a bit of explanation, a few examples to demonstrate the basics, and a lot of practice. In many organizations, professional technical writers take on the task of creating much of the project documentation, while others assume the responsibility for creating selected documents. Business process analysts, for example, may write a requirements document or use cases. For technical staff unaccustomed to writing, writing usable reference documentation should be no more difficult than telling someone a story. Good documentation is easier to read when written conversationally. Start at the beginning (where the process originates) and then explain the flow of data through to the end of the process.

Use simple, direct sentences and leave the large words for the dictionaries. Simple sentences are not an insult to anyone's intelligence. IT documentation is not fine literature; users appreciate finding what they want to know as quickly as possible.

Documentation must include a consistent way to identify documents. Using a word processor's header and footer function will do this with minimum effort. Most word processors will easily accommodate the following format steps.

A. Set the page footers to include a page number in the center, and the current date in the lower right corner. This date will help to indicate which files are the most current.

B. The header should also include the phrase "Company Confidential" on every page and, if possible, include a small version of the company logo. The logo identifies "which" company the document is confidential to. This reinforces the need to keep company data private.

C. Most documents over five pages long will benefit from a table of contents and an executive summary. The table of contents includes all section headings in the document. The executive summary provides a quick explanation of the document's contents.

D. Section headings group together similar information and assist the reader to quickly locate the topic he or she seeks. Use these guidelines when writing section headings:

1. Use a "level one" heading to start a broad subject area. Level one headings are typically generic titles, such as "Hardware," "System Justification," or "Immediate Actions for System Crashes." Level one headings should contain one distinct type of information subdivided by lower-level sections.

2. Use level two, level three, and level four headings to progressively subdivide information into easy-to-identify sections. The titles should succinctly summarize the information contained in that section.

3. Do not use more than four heading levels. Instead, subdivide the level 0 (zero) section into its major sections.

4. Try to have at least two headings within a section.

§ 13.04 PMO REFERENCE LIBRARY

Project documents detail the thought processes, failed tests, and options that were examined but discarded. All of this information has application in the future. It must be collected from the projects, cataloged for easy reference, and safely stored. The PMO is uniquely positioned to gather documents from projects and manage their central storage.

> Every company keeps some sort of documentation library today. In some cases, it is in a dusty bookcase. More often, manuals and system documentation are scattered around the various work areas and programmer cubicles. All of these documents vary in currency, accuracy, and usability. In many cases, no one knows what books a coworker may have on his shelves. Most hardware and software vendors would be very happy to provide their documentation electronically (on an optical disk or via an Internet link) since printing mounds of manuals only distracts them from what they do best.
>
> A well-maintained documentation library provides an IT team with ready access to the latest information, saves on storage space since fewer copies are floating around, and provides greater ease for responding to user problem reports.

[A] What to Collect

With so many documents pertinent to a project, which ones should be collected? As always, the answer depends on what the information is and how it will be used. Examples of useful documents are:

- Minutes from meetings where major design decisions were made

- Test scripts used to validate software modules

- Reports from lessons-learned meetings

- Project charters and scope change documents

- Project schedules along with actual hours used for each task
- Project issues logs and risk assessments
- Stakeholder analysis
- Project budget reports

This information provides invaluable material for planning or estimating future projects. Project documentation often forms the basis for ongoing system maintenance. If the documents that detail design decisions, resource requirements, etc., are not retained, the maintenance effort must begin by tediously recreating the same documents.

> Two factors that determine the number and size of documents are the requirements for data that come out of the pre-project preview, and the requirements established by the company for project documentation.

Estimating the tasks, time duration, and risks associated with a new project can require a considerable amount of work. Yet some tasks will still be overlooked, some risks underrated, and some time-estimates way off the mark. A valuable resource for planning new projects is the experience gained in managing old projects. Every project is unique, yet there may be similarities in situation, requirements, environment, key stakeholders, etc. Documentation from past projects can provide information useful during the planning phase of new projects.

The PMO is the logical place to gather this information. At the conclusion of every project, the PMO should gather all documents, plans, analyses, charts, correspondence, and anything else that pertains to the project and store it in the project management experience center. Organize the material for quick reference.

[B]   How It Will Be Used

A great use of the reference library is as an estimation resource. Identifying project tasks and estimating the resources required for each one is difficult. Historical documents, however, can provide the raw data for the development of a resource-estimate template. The template can provide a historical perspective of the average amount of time that a particular class of tasks requires, such as to build a database, write a data entry screen, or install a network hub.

Another resource estimation tool is resource efficiency. How accurate has a task estimation been? Do the members of the telephone support team regularly complete their tasks on time without padding their estimates? Do the Oracle database administrators frequently underestimate tasks assigned? An analysis of resource estimates (provided by the people doing the work) versus the actual cost can result in an adjustment figure to modify future estimates.

For example, if the database administrators (DBAs) estimate 100 hours to complete a task, the project manager may apply a 20 percent factor to the estimate to compensate for consistently late performance. (A cynical project manager would be sure not to inform the DBAs about the schedule adjustment in case they adjust their work intensity to still complete their tasks 20 percent over plan!)

Another use of the reference library is for future system maintenance—design considerations, test scripts, and names of team members who built the code are all valuable information to the person assigned to provide ongoing maintenance to a new piece of technology. New systems should be delivered with complete and accurate technical documentation. Yet the project documents will provide depth to the analysis of future issues and fill in gaps in the technical manual. Other uses for the resource library include:

A. New project design. Has a similar project been attempted in the past? What happened? Reviewing similar projects may identify best practices to embrace and pitfalls to avoid. Although project environments change over time, reviewing old projects will provide insight into what to expect and what to avoid.

B. Project audits. Reviews of completed projects or milestones will allow the PMO to determine how efficiently the project was managed and how effectively the resources were applied. Hindsight is always sharper than foresight. When properly applied this review can improve the performance of the project management team.

C. Historical metrics. The PMO office will need to measure how well it is performing compared to past projects. Over time, it should become more effective and efficient. However, the PMO leader will never know this unless critical metrics are consistently gathered and tracked. Documentation from old projects can provide a range of information for metric creation.

> The more clearly documentation is written, the closer it comes to achieving expected goals. Clear, concise documentation helps to eliminate hidden agendas and to maintain the project manager's control of the project.

[C] How to Organize It

A simple way to organize material is in chronological order for the project. A chronological sequence allows people to view information "in context" of the moment.

This should reduce the impulse to hastily condemn a decision or action regardless of the priorities and pressures in evidence at the time it was made.

Sometimes the material is searched for information on a specific subject, such as resource utilization and meeting minutes with the sponsor. Cross-references can be created to indicate the location of key information, by subject.

Because the PMO uses a standard tool set, project managers should be able to quickly search through the material. It is organized just like any of the other project. True, some project managers are more fastidious than others for gathering information or for reporting, but still the resource calendar should be in a certain place, the project budget in its own place, etc.

The PMO leader, or whoever is appointed to monitor the library, must ensure that personal comments about individuals are screened out of all material prior to its storage. Personal invective stored in the library might surface at an embarrassing time. Such comments only serve to fuel petty grudges and distract the team from the work at hand.

---

§ 13.05 POTENTIAL PROJECT DOCUMENTS

The number and type of documents used in an IT project depend on its length and complexity. Documents are simply another tool. As with any other job, the artisan picks the tools that make the job flow the smoothest toward completion. Here is a list of potential documents used to manage a large project:

- Business affiliate plan
- Business justification
- Business justification updates
- Commercial specification
- Communications plan
- Content agreement
- Customer documentation strategy
- Design and development plan
- End-user documentation
- Field introduction strategy
- Help desk documentation

- Initial budget estimate
- Initial funding requirements
- Market analysis report
- Organizational chart
- Project cost update
- Project manager's log
- Project proposal
- Project specification
- Project support plan
- Quality plan
- Risk assessment
- Schedule
- Technical documentation
- Third-party market agreement
- Third-party service plan
- Training strategy
- Trial (Beta) strategy

§ 13.06   PROJECT SCOPE AND DEFINITION PLANNING

Projects generate mounds of documents. Ideally, most of them are created during the thoughtful process of defining problems and creating the project schedule. However, some of these tools seem to be created during project execution as the final product takes shape. The documents in each category will vary by local preference, and small projects may use few of them.

[A]   Business Affiliate Plan

This plan provides information when the project is to be developed by a third-party organization. The plan can consist of the following:

- Explanation of the need for a third-party developer
- How the third party doing the development qualifies
- What part the third party plays in the marketing program

- Training requirements
- Documentation requirements
- Quality control system description

[B] Business Justification

This document is the financial investment rationale for doing the project. Some of the following questions should be answered to develop the initial justification.

- How do this project's goals affect already-established market policies and strategies?
- What are the impacts on existing systems?
- What are the requirements for success?
- What is the business (nonprofit) opportunity?
- What is the financial (revenue) opportunity?
- When must the goals be completed?

  The business justification may include:

- Competition data
- Concept (as compared to definition)
- Distribution strategy
- Impact on products
- Market need
- Market window
- Required functions and characteristics
- Return on investment (ROI)
- Cost of noninvestment (such as legal penalties if not done)

In order for upper-level management to be able to make decisions, a cost-benefit analysis should be included. It is important for the IT project manager to get necessary support, especially when the project crosses multiple business functions. Include a timeline that shows the cost of obtaining the product, the value of having it, and the cost-value (benefit) position.

The business justification further defines the features to include in the project scope. If time is short and the scope must be trimmed, this document can identify essential elements that must be retained in the design.

[C] Business Justification Update

This document provides the current view of any project's performance criteria. Projects exist in a swirl of uncertainty. The business justification is useful for reminding executives why the project exists, why it is important, and how it will benefit the company in the future. For most projects, this document is the best protection available against preemptory cancellation. The update may have a one or more year(s) view of:

- Revenues
- Maintenance costs
- Investment
- Return on investment (ROI)
- Customer impact

[D] Commercial Specification

The commercial specification is an evolution of the business justification and identifies the market need. The specification gives adequate requirements and limitations for the design and development group(s). There should be design flexibility to achieve expectations. The commercial specification describes the expected *what* for the project's goals.

The commercial specification describes in detail the project requirements and the targeted market. The key to a successful system could include:

- Application of the project
- Customer participation
- Customer verification plans
- Design constraints
- Distribution methods
- Project maintenance
- Enterprise support requirements
- Key performance requirements and features
- Life-cycle
- Market historical background
- Market window
- Portfolio information

- Special interfaces
- Standards
- Success criteria for the project
- Target costs versus revenues

This is a suggested, unordered list. A one-page spreadsheet for a very large project can be useful.

[E]   Content Agreement

This agreement is the written "contract" between the development group and the marketing group as to the content and functions of the deliverable. This should include the following:

- How end-users use the project's functional results
- Hardware requirements (availability status)
- Software features and requirements

[F]   Initial Budget Requirements

This document provides a view of the expected development costs. The estimate is usually based on the preliminary project specification. The document gives estimates for direct labor, indirect costs, and capital and expense requirements. The initial budget requirements might include a number of different types of cost estimates or parameters for developing these costs. Here are five possible cost types that might be considered in a project:

- General—rough estimates that could be in a -50 to a $+50$ percent range
- Definitive—clearly identified costs that could be in a -5 to a $+5$ percent range
- Capital—level defined by the corporation with costs in a -15 to a $+15$ percent range
- Feasibility—level determined by project size with costs in a -25 to a $+25$ percent range
- Appropriation—level determined by criticality of project with a -20 to $+20$ percent range

The goal of the cost estimates is to reduce the range of estimation uncertainty based on experiences, standards, and benchmarks.

A project budget exists only to implement a project plan. Link each budget item to a specific task in the schedule, which is tied to a project plan objective. If that objective is cancelled, then so are the associated budget and schedule items. If the task is delayed, then those budget items are easily identifiable for movement to the appropriate budget time period.

The initial budget estimate provides the financial baseline for measuring the project's performance (efficiency).

[G] Initial Funding Requirements

This document is for monitoring and reporting project costs at each major phase of implementation. There should be comparisons to the original funding document used to establish financial targets and expected milestones and deliverables. This document can also be included in the project cost update.

[H] Market Analysis Report

This report documents and verifies market opportunities. It sets the environmental context for using the finished product. A market analysis report can be global in nature or segmented into localized conditions. This report should be in agreement with the viability of project goals and include an explanation as to how the project is to be introduced into the marketplace.

The market analysis report identifies and justifies project goals for applications, features, and services. Base this input on such things as:

- Competition
- Customer needs
- Inferred commitments for special functions
- Market opportunities
- New governmental regulations
- Product surveys

The report should include adequate descriptions of the input so there is sufficient information to make design decisions. The report should also include potential revenue gains. The counter to this is a statement on potential revenue losses, if this project is not implemented.

The finished products produced by a project do not function within a vacuum. They are used by people who exist in an ever-changing environment. The market analysis identifies the primary forces that act on the users of this product and identifies key features the product must include.

For example, if the product is a new or revised payroll system, it must be flexible enough to readily change tax rates (external requirement), provide statistical management reports (internal requirement), and be extremely reliable (a marketplace expectation). The environment may require the addition of new taxes on short notice, require the creation of ad hoc reports, or require flexibility to link to the human resources system. All of this information applies whether the product is for internal use or developed for the benefit of a paying customer.

A life-cycle statement identifies the various stages of this version of the computer system's market cycle such as introduction, growth, maturity, and replacement. It explains impacts on existing products.

[I]   Project Proposal

This proposal is a formal response to the commercial specification that describes the requirements for a project. This proposal may include the following information.

- Commercial specification compliance
- Definition of preliminary functions
- Hardware requirements
- Installation requirements
- Maintenance requirements
- Software requirements
- Software strategy
- Summary of commercial information
- Target costs based on preliminary development definition
- Testing requirements
- Verification requirements

[J]   Project Specification

This specification is also a formal response to the commercial specification that outlines the requirements for a project. This specification may include the following types of information.

- Project definition from a technology (hardware and software) perspective
- Project definition from an external user's viewpoint

- Project estimated costs
- Project introduction strategy
- Project operational description
- Specific testing requirements
- Standards requirements
- Updates to the project proposal

Include a section on possible noncompliance. The section describes deviations from the commercial specification. It should be determined if noncompliance is permanent or temporary. When the noncompliance is permanent, note the changes in the design and development plan for a project through the change management process.

[K]   Quality Plan

This plan defines the role of quality control in all phases of the project process. It also defines the deliverables, functions, and specific activities required of quality control to ensure successful product completion. Quality procedures that are specific to each project goal should also be identified, possibly in an appendix.

The quality plan should include a set of quality metrics that defines the various measures by which the quality of the product produced by the project is measured, attained, and controlled. The quality plan also summarizes the staff, resources, and equipment required by quality control to perform specific activities and to support a new application. Update the quality plan before each major phase review to reflect changes.

The following five areas might be defined in separate documents, but can be included in the quality plan as appendices. The five areas are:

- Quality policy
- Quality objectives
- Quality assurance
- Quality control
- Quality audit

A quality policy states the "what," promotes consistency, gives a view for out-siders (important for ISO 9000 compliance), specifies guidelines, and provides methods for updating the policy. This document is usually written by experts in the area. However, a corporate policy could be modified for use by the project team.

Quality objectives have to be measurable, realistic, comprehensible, and specific as to deadlines. The objectives specify the policy. Quality objectives should advance the project's progress, not frustrate it.

A quality control program determines items or events to be controlled, establishes the standards, provides the measurement tools, analyzes the test results, monitors any measuring devices, and documents the results. Quality control is the formal set of activities that monitors the stated project process and ultimately is responsible for certifying that the process was successful.

Quality assurance is the formal set of activities that ensures that the stated project goals meet the stated quality standards and benchmarks. A quality assurance system identifies appropriate standards and benchmarks, seeks to eliminate risk through prevention, collects data for continuous improvement, maintains performance measures, and establishes criteria for quality audits.

A quality audit system identifies areas that can be improved, identifies that data collection is adequate, checks for product safety, and ensures all applicable laws are followed.

[L]   Risk Assessment

It is important that any risk assessment plan consider both threats and opportunities. At least representatives from each component (the project team, marketing, and project users) should review the risk assessment plan, and it should be updated at every major phase of the project.

Compare the risk assessment plan to established thresholds. An example of a threshold is that no action will be taken until a certain number of errors are found in a process.

A good source for risk management is the Department of Defense's Directive (DoDD) 4245.7-M. This directive provides a standard for identifying technical risks, especially during the transitional period from development to production. It gives methods for reducing risks.

Another recommended guideline is the Office of Naval Acquisition Support Pamphlet (ONAS P) 4855-X, "Engineering Risk Assessment." This pamphlet gives guidelines for appropriate managers to monitor risk corrections.

The risk assessment plan might include considerations for the following risk types.

- External risks
- Internal risks

[M]   Training Strategy

All IT products rely at some point on the people who use them. A full-featured, stable, and bug-free product is worthless if people do not understand how to use it. A training strategy is needed. It can have two components: internal requirements and customer (external) requirements. The strategy document should show how training is to be designed, developed, implemented, and verified. The emphasis of the strategy should be based on the customers' needs and expectations.

The strategy might include the following.

- Key activities
- Schedule
- Worker requirements
- Cost estimates
- Implementation process

> Do not forget to include a plan for ongoing software maintenance, especially if there is a lack of internal programming expertise.

§ 13.07   PROJECT EXECUTION

Several documents should relate to the executor of the project.

[A]   Communications Plan

A communications plan is a scheme for providing the right information to the right people in the right format at the right time. A project addresses a wide range of audiences, such as executives, team members, managers of the various company departments, and, in some cases, the public. Each audience has its own information requirements and each is most receptive if the information is formatted and delivered in a way that can be easily assimilated.

A communications plan is often in the form of a matrix that lists the people to receive the information down the first column and other column headings for frequency, format, and best method of delivery (e-mail, presentation, informal, etc.) on the other column. This plan should include as a minimum:

- People doing the reporting
- People who receive the reports

- Types of reports to be sent
- When reports are sent (specific dates or after an event occurs)
- How reports are sent
- Level of detail to include (summary, a running narrative, etc.)
- Types of information (financial, schedule, problems, etc.)

All the measurable data gathered and all the clearly defined activities and estimates will mean absolutely nothing if they are not communicated to the correct people at the correct time. The plan should cover formal and informal, written and oral situations. The direction of the communication can be lateral, upward, or downward.

There are also barriers to the communication process. Following are several important barriers:

- Communications skills
- Evaluation skills
- Feedback
- Listening skills
- Preconceived ideas

The method of communication also plays a significant role in the process. A visual presentation might convey something differently from a nonvisual one. One can reread a written presentation but not a spoken one. Different senses can have different effects on the communication process.

[B] Customer Documentation Strategy

This strategic document details how timely and quality project documentation becomes available. There really is a triad in quality: control, documentation, and training.

The strategy contains activities, schedules, and estimates that develop into a plan. The strategy is developed through negotiations among the product management group, the marketing group, and the development group. The strategy might include the following.

- Key activities
- Schedules
- Worker requirements

- Cost estimates
- Production process

[C] Design and Development Plan

The design and development plan drives the project integration plan that captures all major design and development deliverables and milestones for management tracking and reporting. The document may include the following items (if applicable):

- Project goals
- Project definition
- Project software structure description
- Project hardware structure description
- Project user definition
- Project market (summary from project specification)
- Risk assessment
- Responsibilities defined
- Resources defined
- Project milestones
- Verification dates

[D] End-User Documentation

End users are the key to a project's success. The old rule that perception equals reality is true. If the user has a difficult time using even the best made product, he or she will declare it (long and loud) as a failure. End-user documentation (even if it is very brief) should be included in all project plans as a component of the finished product delivery. This document is the basis for end-user training.

End-user documentation is a written explanation of what the person using the product should do to maximize its benefit to them. It must explain all of the options of every screen, the fields on every report, and the data edits embedded in the software. End-user documentation is the IT department's first line of defense against many small, time-consuming support questions.

The documentation must be written in terms familiar to the reader, and at a reading level the user can understand. Avoid technical terms and relate the product's use to the user's existing workstation instructions. The easier the documentation is to use, the fewer calls will be made for support.

[E]   Field Introduction Strategy

This document reflects the strategy and detailed plans to verify conformance to specification and functionality as defined in the project specification. This document should be concerned with such events as how the customers become users of the project's product.

[F]   Help Desk Documentation

Help desk documentation is the tool that the help desk team refers to, when users call for help. It is a cross between the user documentation (which is included with it) and the technical documentation. The help desk needs to understand enough about the technical side so that analysis can determine if they should call the network technician, the database administrator, the programmer, etc., to solve the problem.

   Well-written software documentation is the bread and butter of a help desk. When users call, help desk analysts can answer most questions if they have access to current user documentation. They can also research technical questions in the system documentation. The more information that is available to the help desk, the fewer distractions will be passed on to the technical staff. Oh yes, and the callers appreciate the quick answers to their questions!

[G]   Organizational Chart

A project team should have a formal organizational chart, along with a description of major project responsibilities. There must be a detailed statement of the project manager's responsibilities. All other responsibility statements should be linked to this description.

   An organizational chart is usually a center of political intrigue because some people consider it a flag for potential promotion when someone is labeled a "project leader" or an "operational manager." In the earlier days of project management, a tree-type organizational chart was used. Temporary relationships were identified that in some cases became permanent relationships after the project's end. This resulted in issues about titles and power. Perhaps the best chart is a circular one with all the team members situated on the circle, with a line drawn from each to their project responsibilities. Very few people will be working full-time on a project, even a large one. Consider broken lines rather than solid lines on the chart. The essential point of a project's organizational chart is to show dynamic relationships and potential responsibilities.

The focus of a project organizational chart is the project manager. This document needs to delineate the project manager's responsibilities, which include the following at a minimum:

- Prime position in the project
- Ability to resolve cross-functional conflicts
- Authority to cross divisional boundaries to manage and control the project
- Controller of project funds
- Final approval on project plan
- First in the project, last out of the project
- Participant in management decisions
- Prime liaison to customer
- Project team's voice
- Selector of subcontractors

[H] Project Cost Update

This document updates initial project cost estimates at each key phase of implementation with comparison to the initial budget estimate. The concern here is how the costs (actual expenditures) and revenues go into the budget (the financial plan). The costs are usually reported on a monthly basis.

[I] Project Manager's Log

The project manager's log is an electronic "to do" list. It can be as simple as a Word document with a set of dates, each with a priority. As action is taken, a comment about the action is noted, such as, "I talked to John Smith about activity X and he said it is on schedule." At the end of the day, that day's actions are moved to the bottom of the file so the latest date is always at the top of the list. Review the priorities for the next workday. Use the "find" function to check for any occurrence of "John Smith" or any other item of interest. This gives a historical record of administrative project duties, and can refer to other files such as conference minutes.

[J] Project Support Plan

This plan ensures that the project is supportable in a market environment. It includes a process for providing the level of customer support needed. The product support plan defines the logistic support requirements of the project. This is the plan for the product after development that requires maintenance, service, and support (technical, documentation, and training). At least nine areas need to be considered:

- Facilities
- Hardware support
- IT support
- Maintenance support
- Personnel
- Supply support
- Technical data (documentation)
- Training
- Transportation process

[K]   Schedule

A schedule is a tool, not a sacred document. It is based on time estimates using experiences that in some cases may only be opinions. The schedule and the budget that are seen by business managers are, in their view, written in concrete. A project schedule should be seen as written with a pencil that can be erased as necessary. The only certainty in a project schedule is that it will change!

The schedule can be as elaborate as required to implement the project. It should be easily understandable by the project team and all other stakeholders. An example of a schedule is a flowchart with milestones and times. There could also be links to key players and groups and their responsibilities to the implementation of the project goals. A schedule should include both the quality control and verification milestones.

One aspect of a schedule is the development of a critical path. One formal technique is called critical path method (CPM), which is usually used in conjunction with another scheduling tool, program evaluation and review technique (PERT). A highly simplified definition of a critical path is achieving the "must" requirements in a minimum of time. The critical path is a piece of concrete; it is a schedule in the truest sense in that it cannot be modified without approval by the customer.

[L]   Technical Documentation

Technical documentation provides a description of a system's internal workings. It is the starting point for the technical support staff to investigate problems or make changes to the system. This is best written while the system is being developed to capture a fresh understanding of how the system works. Without technical documentation, every debugging effort must start with a time-consuming analysis of how the system works, from where each data element originates, how data is manipulated, etc.

Technical documentation (even if it is very brief) should be included in all project plans as a component of the finished product delivery. During handover, the developers should walk the maintenance team through the document to identify gaps and explain the details.

For examples of some forms that are useful for project documentation, see Exhibit 13-1: Documentation Checklist and Exhibit 13-2: Project Report Form at the end of this chapter.

§ 13.08   VENDOR MANAGEMENT

Vendor management encompasses party agreement, plans, and strategies.

[A]   Third-Party Market Agreement

This agreement provides the plans where the project is to be marketed by a third-party. This agreement may include:

- Product content
- Delivery schedules
- Marketing strategy
- Verification strategy
- Documentation strategy
- Training strategy

[B]   Third-Party Service Plan

This provides the plan describing how the project is to be serviced by a third-party developer. The question is, "Will the third party do customer service?" The plan may include details on:

- Customer training
- Customer documentation
- Diagnostic tools
- Support process

[C] Trial (Beta) Strategy

This strategy identifies and locates the software and hardware elements in the project that are a part of the project trial. It specifies when and who should conduct the trial. This provides a clear identification of the testing requirements plus the extent of the resources and capabilities needed to test.

§ 13.09 SUMMARY

Project documentation is a tool for communications between the project manager and the many stakeholders. Projects create lots of paper. These might be agreements, records of performance, consultant invoices, etc. All of this is useful to future project managers who may work on projects with similar goals or that use the same resources. The project management office must capture copies of these documents so the information is available for future use.

One issue is to manage documentation requirements and standards across divisions. Many of the writers of the project documentation may be new to the project environment versus the business environment, and if also interested in project results, may be enthusiastic and cloud issues with details. Of course, the project manager might find the reverse and not be able to find the details because of high-level highlights. Distinguish between the support and the administrative types of documents and recognize when a document should be closed and another begun or continued.

The project sponsor should resolve cross-divisional issues for documentation. For example, the documentation or training groups might have policies contrary to the project's requirements, such as a different format for documents or for the method of training to be used.

Exhibit 13-1: Documentation Checklist

Document	Yes	No	Start Date	End Date	Source
Market Analysis Report	☐	☐			
Business Justification	☐	☐			
Commercial Specification	☐	☐			
Organizational Chart	☐	☐			
Project Proposal	☐	☐			
Project Specification	☐	☐			
Content Agreement	☐	☐			
Schedule	☐	☐			
Design Development Plan	☐	☐			
Initial Budget Estimate	☐	☐			
Initial Funding Requirements	☐	☐			
Quality Plan	☐	☐			
Trial (Beta) Strategy	☐	☐			
Field Introduction Strategy	☐	☐			
Training Strategy	☐	☐			
Communications Plan	☐	☐			
Risk Assessment	☐	☐			
Third-Party Documents	☐	☐			
Project Cost Update	☐	☐			
Project Support Plan	☐	☐			
Customer Documentation Strategy	☐	☐			
Business Justification Update	☐	☐			
Other	☐	☐			

Notes:

Exhibit 13-2: Project Report Form

Project			From Date:	
Preparer:			To Date:	

Schedule Status:	ON	AHEAD	BEHIND	(Circle One)

Any change to project goal:	Change Request by Customer/by Business:

Potential Issues:

Potential Impacts of Change	Approval Authority/Standard/Benchmark:
Time:	
Cost:	
Resources:	Steps required to make changes:
Performance:	
Other:	

Comments:

Chapter 14

Lean Six Sigma Applied to Project Management

§ 14.01   INTRODUCTION

In recent years, there has been a push to apply Six Sigma problem identification and resolution techniques to all sorts of process issues. This is unfortunate because these tools are not suited to all situations. The most successful operations gather their projects into a list and then assign them for action by the lean processes team, the rapid improvement team (Kaizen), or Six Sigma "Black Belts." In essence, the problem determines the tool to apply.

In general, a company should apply lean techniques to address the more obvious problems. Lean attacks process waste. This removes clutter from the workplace, reduces the amount of materials sitting around, and cuts costs while improving quality. No company is truly lean. They strive for continuous improvement, making their processes more lean as they go. An example of this process would be to review the project's change control process to reduce the amount of effort and delays in approving a change.

Some issues need immediate attention. Problem processes can be attacked over a short time period by a rapid improvement (or Kaizen) event. These events apply lean techniques in an intensive five-day rebuilding of a single process. An example is where a project installs a new technology and it brings the user's department to a halt.

Address stubborn problems through a Six Sigma project. Six Sigma techniques may take a long time to complete, but the root cause of a problem will be laid bare and a problem will be gone! An example might be that interaction of data among several systems makes system performance slow to a crawl, yet no one can identify what is causing this issue. Lean techniques can help to provide an answer and a solution.

Successful IT projects play close attention to the people element of the process. All IT technologies begin and end with people. To integrate technology smoothly into a process, lean techniques should be applied to simplify the user processes prior to adding them to the project's product.

The primary lean tools useful to a project manager include:

- 5S
- 8 forms of waste
- Value stream mapping

§ 14.02 LEAN PROCESSES DEFINED

Lean processes evolved from techniques developed by engineers at Japanese auto-makers. Lean is based on the principles of respect for workers, cost reduction, and emphasis on continuous improvement.

A lean process contains only the minimal essential action for a process and nothing more. It is lean because it contains the fewest possible steps. It seeks the shortest time to complete a process by eliminating waste, based on the concept that simpler processes are more resilient than complex ones.

Leaning a process increases the speed with which it is completed, and increases its quality. Lean uses a rigorous examination of every step to identify and eliminate the causes of non-value-added actions.

Lean process improvement tools are applicable to a wide range of locations from factories to offices or even hospitals. The key to its success is a desire by the company to improve its efficiency and reduce its cost.

Some of the characteristics of a lean process include:

- Very little work in process. Processes execute quickly from beginning to end with minimal disruptions.
- Single piece flow. The elimination of buffer between processes. A task does not begin until the next step in the process needs the product.
- Just-in-time materials delivery. Instead of receiving truckloads of material and warehousing it all until needed, a lean organization might receive new equipment only when it is needed.
- Cross-trained employees who are empowered to make decisions about the work process and ways to improve it.
- The work time among all stations is perfectly balanced. At each "heartbeat," the material advances to the next station.

Paybacks from a lean process include:

- Less rework since there is higher first-time quality. Complexity adds opportunities for defects.

- Reduced inventory expense in storage space and handling and carrying costs. Material arrives as it is needed.

- Reduced cycle time enables a faster response to changes in the marketplace.

- The result is lower overall costs due to reduced inventory costs and high labor efficiency.

[A] The 5S Process

The first step in applying lean processes is to clean up work areas. Messy work areas hide problems. Clutter wastes floor space, takes time to walk around, and decreases employee morale.

Is the user's process a mess? Is the project's work area a wreck? Is equipment lying around, spare parts everywhere, manuals not where they should be, software scattered about, etc.? The Japanese use the five-step approach of sort, straighten, shine, standardize, and sustain to reduce the confusion. The 5S process is organized and run by the team members after some brief training. If 5S is new to the organization, it is best to find a "lean master" consultant to lead the effort.

> A good time to 5S an area is at the beginning of a project. If the team is provided dedicated work areas, take time to get them in order before project tasks consume all of the time.

[1] Sort

To sort is the first step. Purchase a large supply of red and green tags. Walk through the work areas and tag *everything* as "green" (it stays) or "red" (it goes). Immediately send everything tagged "red" to a warehouse or storage area. Keep anything the project will need over the next week and discard the rest. Sort through all of the discarded material for the following:

- Scrap—Follow company procedures for throwing something away. (The accounting department has policies controlling the proper way to scrap a tagged asset.)

- Reissue—Give away something good but not needed by the project. Send it to the warehouse or a higher company echelon to give to someone else.

- Return to vendor—if it is still in the wrapper, maybe a refund is possible.

- Archive—Send old records to deep storage.

The sort step is a ruthless process. Root out the old keyboards, monitors, and PCs and send them away. Open every cabinet, every drawer, and every closet—anywhere materials may hide. Free cabinet space by eliminating old files. Removing clutter often frees floor space for more productive uses. Be sure to send unneeded shelves and cabinets away as well. Otherwise, they will attract more junk.

This can be a traumatic event for some people. Secret caches of spare parts, emergency equipment, etc., will surface. These "security blankets," however, cost projects a considerable amount of money.

After removing clutter, tally the savings. No more time will be lost wandering around looking for something buried under the clutter.

[2] Straighten

The second step is to straighten up the work area. This means that everything has a marked, assigned place. Reference files, shared materials, office supplies, etc.,—anything used in the process has its assigned place. Whenever used, it is returned promptly to that spot.

Label where everything goes. The goal here is to have a visual workspace so it is obvious when something is missing or put out of place.

> Marking where things go applies to shared work areas, such as worktables, cabinets, shelves, closets, etc. It is a bit too much to do to a person's desk—marking where the mouse goes, where the keyboard goes, etc.

[3] Shine

The third "S" is to shine up the area. Now that the clutter is gone and everything is in its designated place, clean the entire area from top to bottom. Cleaning provides an immediate and visible impact on the work area. It includes repairing any structural problems, painting if necessary—whatever it takes to brighten and clean up an area. Shining includes all closets and storage areas. Make everything as clean as the offices.

[4] Standardize

Identify the best 5S practices and spread them around. If one team has found an effective way to label files, pass that on to other team members. Moving people around a project is simpler when all of the files are marked in the same manner. The same goes for reference materials, etc. A visitor should be able to look around a team's work area and know where everything is in a few minutes.

[5] *Sustain*

The last step is to ensure the gains made become a permanent part of the project's business. Sustaining requires making cleaning assignments, following up on facility repairs, and ensuring that the area stays clean and straight.

The key to sustaining gains is to assign responsibilities to the team for ongoing area maintenance. Another useful tool is to have a printed list of outstanding 5S issues that need to be resolved. These are often things that take time to complete, such as replacing the rickety cabinets or obtaining new workbenches.

[B] Waste—Leaches on a Project

Identifying and eliminating waste is a simple concept to sell to team members. Waste is any action or material used that does not add value to the project. People have a tendency to do things "because it was always done that way," or for other equally poor reasons. Take the time to rejustify why a specific action is "required" and if possible, eliminate that step.

A tool for digging out the sources of waste is asking "why" five times. As the questions dig deeper into why something is done a certain way, often the waste can be easily seen. Lean techniques recognize eight different types of waste:

- Overproduction
- Waiting
- Unnecessary transportation
- Overprocessing
- Excess inventory
- Wasted motion
- Defects
- Underutilized technical workers

[1] *Overproduction—Making More of Something Than Is Needed*

Overproduction often occurs when the various process steps are not balanced. Workers continue until everything in their in-basket is processed and passed on to the next step, even if that step cannot process it. This results in work being completed in batches and then passed on. Based on that worker's preference, the batches are scheduled and addressed. Since this is not synchronized with the later steps in the process, paperwork jolts from queue to queue through the system. Processing in batches makes it easier for the worker, but the customer wants the processing to flow through the process as quickly as possible.

> For example, a software development project is working too far ahead of the critical path. Later a customer change to the critical path tasks and requirements alters the project. The tasks completed in advance must be scrapped.

[2] Waiting—Delays in Progress

Waste from waiting is easy to find. Has anyone ever lost time on a project waiting for a "quick" (and clear) answer from a customer or boss? Has a project been delayed because of late materials? Address waiting waste through accurate project planning.

The entire project team has a part to play in driving out waiting waste. They can always provide prompt responses to team or stakeholder requests. If everyone does this, it becomes a part of the team's culture and that aspect of waste can disappear.

Try meeting with executives to obtain quick answers to questions and approvals. Work to reduce the number of approvals required to speed completing documents.

[3] Unnecessary Transportation Is a Waste

Over-ordering material requires someone to receive, move, and store it somewhere. If the project includes servers and space is not ready for them in the computer room, then they must be moved to a safe storage area, and then moved again later to be installed. The first movement is a waste because they should have gone straight in and saved that effort of moving them twice.

> For example, transportation waste is evident in a project where the server is delivered to the home office in Ohio to be configured and then shipped to Europe for installation. A less wasteful approach would be to buy it in Europe, pay someone there to minimally install it, and remotely load and configure the software.

[4] Minimize Waste from Overprocessing

Overprocessing is doing more work than required by the customer. For example, if the customer approves a change based on an estimate, then when the actual amount is determined, they do not need to reapprove the final cost. Another example of minimizing waste is trying to build a parallel set of cost accounts using a project management tool "so it is all in one place" instead of pulling all accounting information out of the accounting system supporting the project.

Much of the overprocessing will be identified by the team members. Often the tasks are based on some worker trying to satisfy his own preferences instead of the customer's desires.

[5]   Excess Inventory Is a Costly Waste

Order materials to arrive when they are needed. The more uncertainty there is for their timely arrival, the sooner they must be brought in. The solution is to require the vendors to deliver the material on the appointed day. Reliable vendors are worth paying a bit more for.

Excess inventory (computers, peripherals, network cards) is expensive to shuffle around and requires floor space to store it. If it is valuable, it must be locked up to prevent theft or safeguarded against damage and corrosion. Sometimes, the project changes direction and the bought-too-soon material is no longer needed. (This may be inevitable.)

> Toner cartridges for printers are likely the most abused IT item. They typically cost $100 each and yet they are sprinkled about the work area—everyone seems to own his own spare cartridge. Add up the money sitting idle! Gather and eliminate these personal caches. They only exist because the normal supply process is not reliable.

[6]   Wasted Motion Is Something We All Have

Some people think that if they are very busy that they are productive. This is not the case. Non-value-added motion is waste and should be eliminated. This might include the walk time to a printer in a distant location. Moving teams from personal printers to shared printers wastes time walking back and forth.

Motion waste can be reduced by carefully planning work areas. People and equipment that tend to interact often should be placed close together.

[7]   Defects Waste Everyone's Time

Defects waste time. Additional time and materials are required to rework the defect, adding cost. The best time to catch a defect is when it occurs. Do not let it proceed longer than necessary. Taking time to correct defects may delay the follow-up steps.

Each person should inspect the work by the previous task to identify problems. Failure to do this is a major reason for small and frequent batches. If the worker is doing something wrong, then he or she might make the same error on each item in the batch.

> Steps to improve results and reduce defects include peer reviews, validation tests, etc. These actions both increase the confidence in the final product and catch defects before the customer sees them.

[8] Waste of Underutilized Workers

Sometimes it is more convenient to use team members already in place to perform minor tasks not related to their actual tasks. For example, server administrators might be asked to fill in routine system documentation. Although they are capable of this, the work could be done by a lower-paid clerk and the more expensive team members could focus on tasks that require their talents and expertise.

This type of waste is primarily caused by poor task management. Tasks may be completed sooner than expected, but often it is caused by inflated time estimates. The project manager should have a set of lower-priority project tasks off the critical path that could be addressed by these technicians. Often when more expensive people are requested, a clerk picking up routine tasks is more effective and cheaper.

[C] Value Stream Mapping

Processes are a sequence of actions. If someone does not have personal experience with a process, it may be difficult to understand the flow of tasks needed to complete it. A value stream map is a high-level illustration showing the flow of work through the various steps.

Each box on the map represents a person or workstation. The job tasks are listed beneath the box. Tag each task as one of three categories:

- Value added (VA) identifies tasks that add value to the work product. It might be to fill in a place on a form, to order material, or to approve a document.

- Non-value-added (NVA) indicates tasks that add no value to the work product. It represents some form of waste. Examples are making unnecessary copies of documents, maintaining a separate set of project accounts (in addition to the official project accounting).

- Non-value-added-business required (NVA-BR) is for tasks that do not add value to the work product, but are required to meet regulatory requirements, such as recording serial numbers or environmental controls readings.

§ 14.03 SIX SIGMA—A QUICK PRIMER

The Six Sigma approach is not new. It contains elements of many other quality programs, such as lean, mistake-proofing, total quality management (TQM), and quality function deployment. Six Sigma incorporates these programs into a statistical framework for identifying the root cause of difficult problems. A company dedicated to Six Sigma methodologies is focused on processes that affect the design and delivery of products and services.

Just what is a "sigma?" In the Greek alphabet, it is the letter s. In quality statistics, sigma is a Greek letter used to indicate the amount of variation in a product or process.

So just what is this beast called "Six Sigma"? The Six Sigma methodology originated at Motorola's manufacturing operations in the 1980s. As word of their achievements spread, other major manufacturers gave it a try. They applied Six Sigma techniques to combat ineffective processes and chronic product defects. As successes mounted, Six Sigma's reputation as an effective breakthrough (not incremental) quality improvement methodology grew.

Six Sigma is too broad a subject to cover in a single chapter. However, it contains many elements familiar to IT project managers. Applying Six Sigma methodologies to project processes will result in more efficient and predictable results. Applying Six Sigma techniques to the design of an IT product or process will result in more stable and effective systems—along with happier customers!

Companies embrace Six Sigma as a way to save money. They invest money and time in Six Sigma projects to reduce waste in their processes and improve product quality. Like all "magic bullets," Six Sigma is not a guaranteed success. Poorly selected projects or leaders and a lack of executive support will eventually doom Six Sigma to the trash heap of the latest management "flavor of the day."

Six Sigma is a collection of statistically driven defect reduction techniques that concentrate on the quality of the customer experience. The customer experience, known in Six Sigma as the voice of the customer (VOC), is a crucial feedback mechanism into product design or service delivery. Companies can listen to the VOC through complaints, product returns, calls for service, and a wide range of customer dissatisfaction communication channels. On the other hand, the VOC is also heard through increased sales and popular acclamation of the product. Everyone has encountered products or services that were such a disappointment that they told everyone about them, or products that they have heard nothing but good things about.

Six Sigma defines the problem that is to be solved (the goal) based on what the customer is saying about the product or service that was delivered or is desired.

The VOC may point out something that no one is even considering. Recently, a major hospital was trying to decide which of several expensive and beautiful building designs to use so they polled their patrons. Overwhelmingly, the customers said they didn't care what the building looked like—they wanted quick service with a minimum of delays.

Products do not make products; people make products through the application of repeatable processes. Six Sigma is a study of these processes. IT departments depend on a wide range of processes for software development, hardware implementation, and end-user support. Processes that at the start of the project were clear and straightforward, over time become tangled with unnecessary steps, unused paperwork, and delays for approvals. When applied to IT operations, Six Sigma gathers together the charts and statistics that decorate a manager's wall and shows how they can be used to improve processes, which reduces the potential for errors, reduces delays, and improves customer service.

[A] Why "Six" Sigma

Unlike many other quality processes, Six Sigma methodology is firmly rooted in statistics. Every conclusion must be statistically proven or it is just a theory. The title "Six Sigma" references this statistical foundation. The term *sigma* refers to standard deviations from an ideal level of operation. The higher the sigma value, the fewer the number of defects found. This is illustrated with a normal curve as in Chart 14-1.

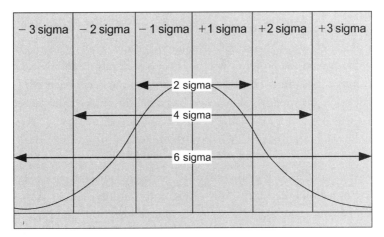

Chart 14-1: Sigma Levels

Six Sigma projects are ideal for tackling tough, seemingly unsolvable problems. The statistical analysis of process factors—both inputs and outputs—makes apparent the many hidden relationships and interactions that provide the final result. All of the activity obscures the causes, but statistics lay them and their interrelationship bare. As Six Sigma practitioners always say, "Show me the data—show me the numbers!"

[B]   The Language of Six Sigma

Σ	DPMO	COPQ	% of Products Defect Free
1	500,000	>40%	50%
2	308,537	20–40%	65%
3	66,807	20–30%	93%
4	6,210	15–20%	99.4%
5	233	10–15%	99.976%
6	3.4	<10%	99.9997%

Chart 14-2: Six Sigma Operation

As Chart 14-2 shows, a two-sigma company performs correctly 65 percent of the time. A four-sigma company, which is approximately where most companies operate, is 99.4 percent defect free. A Six Sigma operation allows only 3.4 defects per million outputs, for a score of 99.99. For an IT operation, a Six Sigma process results in faster executing projects, faster call response times, fewer problem calls, and better overall service delivery.

Consider the following example. Imagine rating the local electrical utility by the ready availability of power at an office's electrical outlet. Think about the complexity of creating electricity and delivering it to a building! Generation stations are located in remote areas. They use high-voltage cross-country lines, relay stations, and smaller electrical lines to send the power down the street and finally to an office. Given all of the opportunities for failure, how often are electrical outages experienced? Chart 14-3 indicates the electric company's Sigma level based on the average daily power outage in a year.

More Six Sigma terms are defined in the following list.

- $Y = f(x)$ is stated as "Y is a function of X." Six Sigma analyzes processes. A process is a set of actions that transforms inputs into outputs. Y is used to signify the output of a process. It can be any *result* of a process from a finished item to the noise of the machine to the amount of scrap created. Y also may be the symptom under examination. An x is an *input* such as a piece of raw material, a cutting tool

Company Sigma Level	Daily Duration of Electrical Outage
1	12 hours
2	7.4 hours
3	1.6 hours
4	8.9 minutes
5	20 seconds
6	0.29 seconds

Chart 14-3: Sigma Level and Daily Power Outage

bit, the operator, etc. There are many Xs that make up a single Y. Six Sigma studies the variation and impact of the Xs on the Ys.

- Voice of the customer (VOC)—Products and services must satisfy some customer need or they have no reason to exist. Six Sigma digs these needs out, quantifies them, breaks them into their component parts, and determines what is interfering with them. Customers do not care what a company's problems may be. They only care about products that fulfill their requirements. Six Sigma techniques emphasize metrics that monitor customer satisfaction.

- Critical to quality (CTQ) breaks down customer requirements into three basic areas:

  —Critical to (product) quality (CTQ)—These characteristics are the ones that customers require to be present in a product to meet their expectations.

  —Critical to delivery (CTD)—This details how, when, and in what form customers want to receive the final product.

  —Critical to cost (CTC)—This identifies the main cost drivers for the process.

- Rolled throughput yield (RTY)—This is the number of units of output received for a given number of units of input.

- "Hidden factory" is a term for the reworking of defects throughout the process. In many companies, the final product is inspected at the end of the manufacturing cycle for acceptance, rework, or rejection as scrap. This much is visible. The "hidden" factory is where workers take time and materials to inspect and rework problems introduced or overlooked by previous process steps. Rarely is this effort or the number of defects found ever recorded. Therefore, no one ever addresses these issues. Information system examples would be to manually audit report totals to ensure that the current data were used and to correct data entry sheets before entry.

In an electrical assembly company, personal computers were custom built to customer specifications. One operation picked the parts and placed them into a tub while a later process assembled them. Whenever a part was missing or was incorrect, the assemblers stopped work and sent someone to fetch the required item from the parts-picking area. This went on for so long that everyone accepted this as part of the normal process. The hidden factory costs included delays in assembly, picking a part a second time, and a person's time to search for and deliver the missing component. So why not fix the problem at the source and save money instead of dancing around the issue?

- Monte Carlo simulation is a "brute force" simulation that uses random values for factors, based on probability distributions. The simulation is run thousands of times to obtain an average value that will indicate the likely result of running that process.

- Design of experiments (DOE) is a tool for identifying the statistical impact of input factors affecting a process's output. It is often used to statistically determine the optimum combination of input factors to achieve the desired process output.

§ 14.04   TRADITIONAL SIX SIGMA

[A]   The Six Sigma Approach

Six Sigma efforts are project-oriented. A Six Sigma problem analysis and resolution typically runs three months—often longer. No one knows all there is to know about a process (especially the Six Sigma analyst), so a team is assembled from the various areas that feed into or use the output of a process. As every project manager will attest, it takes a good project plan to keep a team focused. Six Sigma projects are managed according to a life-cycle that parallels the elements of a well-run IT project.

[B] DMAIC

Six Sigma projects are all different. Some of the initial steps are the same but as the project unfolds, the analysis and actions will gravitate toward wherever the data takes it. In general, a Six Sigma project follows a five-step life-cycle built around DMAIC (pronounced as "Duh-Mae-Ick"), an acronym for the basic phases of a Six Sigma project to define, measure, analyze, improve, and control.

- The *define* phase develops a clear picture of the problem to be solved, lists the project goals, and details customer requirements. Some of the Six Sigma analyst's tasks during the define phase include:

  —Clearly state the issue to be addressed. In project management this is normally achieved through a project charter or scope statement which identifies the issue, the costs, key stakeholders, the sponsor, etc.

  —Identify who the customer is and what they want. Critical to quality (CTQ) aspects of cost, quality, and delivery are crafted from the customer's perspective to more clearly define the problem. In project management, these are the project goals or criteria for success.

  —Illustrate the process as a flowchart that identifies inputs and output of the process that drives it. Visual representations make it easier for everyone to follow the workflow. Include as much of the upstream and downstream processes as possible. In short, identify the Xs and Ys.

  —Identify the workflow within each process in a step-by-step manner. Steps taken within a process are labeled as value added or non-value-added (the customer would not want to pay for this work).

- The *measure* phase sets the baseline of the process's current overall performance and for each major part of the process. A data collection plan is created and data gathered to identify error rates and variation. The baseline is important for later gauging the amount of process improvement that has been made.

  —Gather data on all of the inputs and outputs. How many units of input are required to produce one unit of output? Are there delays, scrap, or waste? Are there product defects created that must be reworked? What is the engineering description of all materials used? How does this compare to the material being used? Inputs also can be time delays in transaction processing.

  —What data are already available? This might be defect reports, scrap materials reports, customer complaints, times when products or parts were sent by express delivery, etc. For process analysis, there may be transaction timestamps on when data arrived at each stage of processing, etc.

—An important step is to define what a defect may be. Sometimes considered to be part of the define step, the defect definition describes when something passes the boundary from a less than perfect item into a defective one.

How is the defect defined? Consider a recently repainted vehicle. If the new paint has a single piece of dirt in the middle of the driver's door, is the entire paint job defective? If there are 20 pieces of dirt scattered across the hood, does this count for 20 defects or just one?

How about defects in a printed report? If two pages are readable but severely wrinkled, is that one defect or two? If a page from the laser printer is smudged and partially illegible, is that a single defect? If two pages are smudged on a 100-page report, is the entire report defective (one error) or are there two errors?

The definition of what a defect is must be completed before error counting and data analysis can begin.

—Determine if the measurement process used is reliable and repeatable. Before collecting anything, be sure that a reliable and accurate method or tool is used to identify defects. Six Sigma practitioners will apply a statistical process called a gauge reliability and repeatability (R&R) study to validate the measurement process used.

—It isn't necessary to stand in one spot all day with a clipboard inspecting every item that passes. Before gathering data on a particular process, calculate the size of a sample required to be statistically valid.

• The *analyze* phase is the fun part, where data are chewed and reviewed to pinpoint the root cause of the problem.

—Based on a review of the process flow model, where are the most likely places to collect data that pertain to the defect?

—The 80/20 rule holds true for defects and can be used to narrow the focus to the significant few process drivers. Sort the data into different sequences and plot them on a Pareto chart. Continue this down three levels where the largest category on the Pareto chart is itself broken into its various characteristics. Statistically check for a correlation between the Pareto results to uncover hidden interrelationships. Does undesirable result "C" most often occur when inputs "A" and "B" are present?

—During the investigation, how much waste or hidden factory work was uncovered? Can these issues be resolved quickly or must a subproject be scheduled to address them?

—Based on the data collected, calculate the sigma level of the current process. This identifies how capable it is of meeting the customer's requirements. It is not unusual to uncover processes that are doomed to failure before they even start.

—How much does this defect cost the company? Use the data collected to calculate the cost of poor quality.

> Most companies "don't know what they don't know." This means they operate on "tribal knowledge" where everything is done a certain way (despite what the engineered process is) because that is what has always worked. A Six Sigma analysis takes nothing for granted—even a company's "articles of faith." Every input is measured and proven to be what it is expected to be and the same with each output. Frequently, Six Sigma projects uncover inaccurate test or measuring equipment, untrained operators, raw materials or components that have been quietly changed by the supplier, or workers who shortcut the published processes.

- The *improve* phase is the alteration to the process or materials that eliminates the problem.

   —Design a set of theoretical changes to the process.

   —Using a simulation technique, such as design of experiments (DOE) or Monte Carlo simulation, statistically test the impact of each change.

   —If initial analysis is promising, install a prototype of the process fix and collect data on its results.

   —Review the solution to incorporate mistake-proofing.

   —With the fix in place, review the process end-to-end for further opportunities to eliminate waste.

   —Calculate the Sigma level of the revised process.

   —Use an FMEA analysis to reduce the risk of the process introducing more errors.

- The *control* phase ensures the fixed process stays fixed!

   —Implement a control plan to ensure the process change remains a permanent one.

—Control plans detect when the process (or operator) is "backsliding" to the way the process was executed prior to the change.

[C]   Use Six Sigma to Drive Out Waste

An important goal in applying Six Sigma to a process is to identify and eliminate waste. The hidden factory that was previously discussed is a common form of waste. Time, materials, floor space, tools, and everything used to repair products that should have been assembled or created correctly the first time are all costs that represent waste in a process.

The first step is to illustrate the flow of work in a simple flowchart. This is usually a block for each major action or workstation in that process. Below each process block, list the steps used in that process. Each step is then labeled from the final customer's perspective if it is value added (VA) or no value added (NVA). In short, would the customer pay you to take that action? A typical VA step might be to connect a cable, validate a credit card transaction for antifraud, or create a help desk trouble ticket.

An NVA step might be to accumulate transactions for a nightly batch computing job—a delay instead of real time processing meeting the customer's desire for speed. It might be to store and inventory a warehouse of personal computers (multiple handling of the same material) or to expedite an overdue materials order (a defect in the shipment of a materials order). Effort spent to perform each of these steps can be defended, yet the additional handling they require is an unnecessary additional cost, or waste. Processes redesigned to eliminate these sources of waste should be cheaper to run and less prone to failure.

Speed of execution is considered to be a key component of a high-performing department. Speed means that when the IT department receives a request it is acted upon immediately. The waste saved is storing the request, rereading it later to sort it, rereading it later to shuffle to another pile, and finally rereading it again to act on it. Would the customer be willing to pay for all of the extra shuffling?

[D]   Cultivating a Six Sigma Attitude

Executives must make clear that Six Sigma is about focusing on the customer's experience and not about eliminating jobs. Almost always, the problem is in the process—not in the people performing it. Improved quality will result in increased sales and improved profits, which will mean more employment for everyone.

The long-term goal of a Six Sigma program is to introduce everyone in a company to Six Sigma concepts, terminology, and techniques. Driving a Six Sigma attitude into a company motivates the entire workforce to examine daily processes for waste and drive it out. No one understands the intricacies of a job like the person who is doing it! A Six Sigma culture empowers people to challenge why some steps in their processes exist instead of continuing to unquestioningly perform the same actions as the previous worker on that job did.

One of the "big" payoffs of a Six Sigma program is the way it transforms people's thinking from passive workers into critically thinking partners. Companies that embrace Six Sigma become data driven and fact oriented. Mediocrity is no longer acceptable to the workers. It takes a lot of training to achieve this goal but it pays off in many ways as everyone questions the value of process steps and focuses on improving the customer experience.

This requires a change in management attitude. Empowering people means they will want to know the *why* of a directive along with the *what*. Managers who do things for reasons that they themselves do not understand will not feel comfortable with this situation and will typically attempt to obstruct the program.

§ 14.05   PROCESS ANALYSIS TOOL CHEST

[A]   Overview

Six Sigma takes the best from a variety of quality approaches and ties them together with statistical analysis to create a fact-based, data-driven solution. Many tools are used to organize data and to understand how it all fits together. A few of the more common Six Sigma tools are provided here because they are very handy in the analysis of IT projects in such areas as risk analysis, requirements gathering, and task decomposition.

If IT processes are not properly documented before introducing Six Sigma, they will be afterward! Even companies with ISO ratings were surprised by the number of undocumented processes uncovered by Six Sigma projects. A company that does not clearly know its own processes can never take adequate action to improve them.

It is difficult to give justice to the power and capabilities of these Six Sigma tools in just a few short paragraphs. Detailed explanations for these tools and a number of others can be found in Six Sigma books at bookstores and at *www.isixsigma.com*.

[B] Failure Modes and Effects Analysis

A failure modes and effects analysis (FMEA) is conceptually very familiar to project managers. It is a tool used to develop a detailed risk analysis and mitigation plan for a process step. It begins by examining all of the things that can go wrong, then it assigns a score to the error based on the likelihood, impact, and how easily it is detected. This list is sorted to bring the most important risks to the top, then a list of mitigation actions is identified along with an action list of who is going to do what.

An FMEA is typically a group effort. A team is assembled to draw up a process flow and then examine each step of the process. This is very useful, but time-consuming, so it is either applied to small processes or to segments of larger processes. For example, a team could be assembled to analyze "receiving help desk calls," a form used to collect end-user software specs, or to debug the company's IT performance evaluation and pay raise program.

FMEAs are usually built using spreadsheets. The cells in Exhibit 14-1 are shrunken to fit the page. In actual use, the cells expand as needed to contain the text. This version of the FMEA has four main sections:

- Problem description—describes and categorizes the problem. Later analysis can group problems with similar characteristics. Each problem can have more than one failure. For example, a process for entering data into a screen can have multiple issues, each with several possible resolutions.

  —Part/Process: name the process step, such as "enter help desk ticket" or "establish user ID."

  —Failure: what caused the problem, such as "a paper jam," "file contention," or "duplicate IP addresses."

  —Failure impact: this describes what occurred, such as "ID did not work," "tape did not load," etc.

  —Failure effects: notes the "damage" that was done, such as a "report was late" and "missed a required deadline."

- Impact—establish a score for how terrible this event would be should it occur.

  —Severity: the degree of damage caused by the error, usually on a scale of 1 to 10, with 10 being the worst.

  —Frequency: how often the error occurs, usually on a scale of 1 to 10, with 10 being the most often.

  —Detection: how obvious the error is when it occurs, generally on a scale of 1 to 10, with 10 being the hardest to detect (not obvious).

—Score: the product of severity times the frequency times the detection. The results are sorted in descending order to bring the most serious issues to the top for action, and push the least likely and least damaging ones to the bottom.

- Resolution—This section identifies potential resolutions to an issue and evaluates the anticipated impact on the severity, frequency, and detection of the problem once the resolution is applied. Use the same scoring scale as before.

  —Action recommended: Explain the proposed solution. In project management, this is a mitigation action.

  —Severity: After the solution is applied, what is the anticipated severity of the mitigated problem?

  —Frequency: After the solution is applied, what is the anticipated frequency of occurrence of the mitigated problem?

  —Detection: After the solution is applied, how obvious will future errors be?

  —Score: The product of severity times the frequency times the detection. The results can be compared to the earlier score to determine a magnitude of improvement.

  —Risk: Proposed solutions are nice, but what is the likelihood they will improve the process without hurting it? A solution that requires major changes, such as reconstructing the help desk office just to see if it really helps, is rather risky. This factor acknowledges the cost and effort required just to test the solution.

  —Risk × Score: Multiply the anticipated improvement score by the risk value to identify which solutions to try, and in what sequence.

- Implementation—This section assigns tasks and responsibilities for implementing these changes. There is no need to detail these fields—they are just typical project assignment tasks.

  —Responsible person

  —Schedule date

  —Action taken

  —Completion date

One of the more powerful uses of an FMEA is as a quick process debugging tool long after the process is in place. The FMEA form can be sorted by the "Failure" or even the "Failure Impact" columns. For example, if the paper in a high-speed laser printer is jamming, then sorting the "Failure" column would bring together all of the potential causes for jamming (as identified by the team during process implementation) along with their mitigation steps.

Exhibit 14-1: Failure Modes and Effects Analysis

Problem Description				Impact				Action Recommended	Resolution						Responsible Person
Part/ Process	Failure Impact	Failure Failure	Effects	SEVERITY	FREQUENCY	DETECTION	SCORE		SEVERITY	FREQUENCY	DETECTION	SCORE	Risk	Risk X Score	
							0					0		0	
							0					0		0	
							0					0		0	
							0					0		0	
							0					0		0	
							0					0		0	
							0					0		0	
							0					0		0	
							0					0		0	
							0					0		0	
							0					0		0	

When a process is evaluated for improvement or replacement, its FMEA highlights areas for process improvement and pitfalls to avoid. FMEAs should be reviewed and updated whenever a significant change is made to a process. They should also be reviewed and updated annually to reflect the process's current usage.

[C] Pareto Charts

A Pareto chart is a tool for breaking down a process or problem into its component parts and quickly identifying the most significant ones. It is based on the 80/20 principle where 80 percent of a result is generally caused by 20 percent of the input. A Pareto chart breaks down a problem into no more than seven factors. The frequency of those factors occurring is plotted on a vertical bar chart. This process is repeated two more times for the top category (or top two categories, if close) of each round for a total of three iterations. The result is said to be a most significant factor in that situation.

Consider this example and refer to Chart 14-4. Imagine a problem accessing an important but complex database. Users must fill in a screen and several fields on that screen are used to link to various tables. After observing the problems encountered by a number of users, the Pareto chart on the left groups the problems into four error types. The largest number of errors seems to be misspelled key words.

The Pareto chart on the right examines the most common error (misspelled key words) and determines that the error is primarily caused by the key word being case sensitive. For some reason, some users type in all capital letters most of the day so the Caps Lock is often on. In this case, all key words searches can be made non-case-sensitive or the entry fields will force all but the first letter of an entry to be lowercase. However the issue is solved, the problem has been "Pareto'd to the top!"

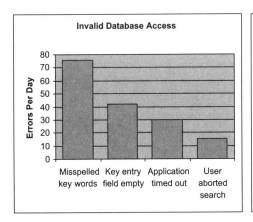
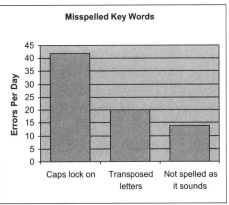

Chart 14-4: Pareto Chart

[D]   Critical to Quality Tree

The critical to quality (CTQ) tree tool provides a visual representation of the voice of the customer (VOC). The third column of Exhibit 14-2 lists factors that drive the product or process. They are grouped according to the three key customer requirements: price, quality, and delivery. The problem under issue might be the size of the programming staff, the speed of a server to be installed, or the timeliness of Web content updates.

To the right of the box with the "Factors" label is where the features requested by the VOC are listed. Above them in row 2 is where each of the desired features is ranked in importance. The number 1 feature is most important, number 2 is next, etc. Some people sort the columns by this value to keep the most critical features to the left.

The CTQ tree is useful since it illustrates the relationship between the customer requirement and the factors in the process. This makes it easier to see where to apply scarce resources or management attention. In this brief example in Exhibit 14-2, if the customer began pressing for a January 1 delivery (or sooner), there are four factors indicated that would have a bearing (plus or minus) for achieving this date.

Exhibit 14-2: Critical to Quality Tree

		Ranked importance to customer	2	4	3	1	6	5
		Factors	Quick loading screens	Database	Relevant features	Ready by Jan. 1st	Interface with old Web system	Maximum Web availability
Process Factors	Critical to Price	Server disk speed	X	X				
		Install latest middleware	X			X		X
	Critical to Delivery	Dedicated DBA support	X					
		New equipment lead time	X					
		Available network support	X	X				
	Critical to Quality	Validate reference data	X	X				
		Customer approves design	X	X				
		Disaster recovery plan in place	X					

A CTQ form might be filled in for every important stakeholder, or for all customer requests. If a single chart is used, add a weighting measure to indicate those factors that are required by the more important customers so that requests from minor players do not drive project durations or cost.

[E] Fishbone Diagram

A frequently used illustration of "cause and effect" is the Ishikawa, or fishbone diagram. Developed in Japan, this diagram breaks down a process into its various inputs (remember $Y = f(x)$). Because the shape is similar to the bones of a fish, it is often referred to by its other name.

Fishbone diagrams are best assembled by the entire problem-solving team. If too many "bones" appear, then break out those sections into their own diagram. In general, this tool only expands three levels since beyond this the picture becomes too crowded to be clear.

A cause-and-effect diagram highlights the various factors that make up a process. It provides some insight into what might be the source of a problem but it does not point to what causes the problem nor does it rank the solutions. It is most useful when first analyzing a process to see what factors are involved.

The diagram breaks down a process into the "6Ms":

- Men—This factor describes the operators of the process.

- Machines—These include any tools used, which could be network tracers, UNIX servers, compilers, workstations, special devices, etc.

- Measurements—These are the metrics that can be obtained from the process and tied into the other five major factors. Always identify any existing metrics that may provide some process performance history.

- Method—This involves both official and unofficial steps that are to be done in the process.

- Materials—These include any materials used in the process, such as toner cartridges, category 5 cable, manuals, etc.

- Mother nature (or environment)—This details the environment that the work takes place in. Is it noisy, dusty, or windy? Is it inside or exposed to the weather? Is it local or in a remote area in a foreign land?

Along the horizontal axis is the fish's "body." The "head" holds a brief title of the problem. At angles to the body are the major factors for a process. Each of these major categories has smaller subcategories that impact on the "body." In turn, these subcategories may have their own contributing factors.

In Chart 14-5, some of the factors for creating an engineering drawing are listed. A full analysis can require many "bones" on the fish.

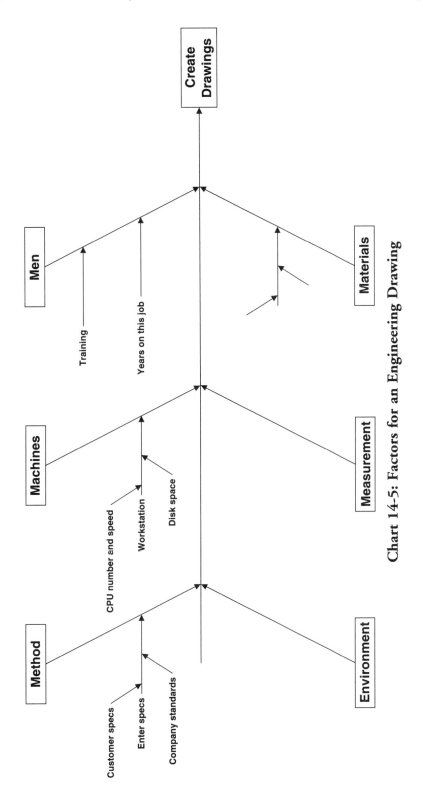

Chart 14-5: Factors for an Engineering Drawing

§ 14.06   DESIGN FOR SIX SIGMA

All of this talk about quality is nice, but how does it apply to IT projects? Quality is like all forms of goodness: no one is against it, yet time to follow proven quality practices is not often found. Quality steps sound so easy to follow in the classroom but seem hard to apply back in the office!

Originally, Six Sigma was a process for identifying the root cause of problems. Along the way, it proved to be valuable for cleaning up processes while also making them highly efficient and mistake-proof. It did not take long before companies began to adapt Six Sigma techniques to product and process design. After all, isn't it cheaper to design something properly in the beginning than to wait and fix it later? Applying Six Sigma to a design adds the dimension of customer expectations, which must be thoroughly understood before a successful design can be completed.

[A]   IDOV Format

Six Sigma (DMAIC) is a problem-solving methodology designed to dig out the root cause. The "design for Six Sigma" (DFSS) methodology is not as clearly defined as the traditional DMAIC approach, but has emerged over time generally following the identify, design, optimize, validate (IDOV) format. Each company adapts these techniques according to their own internal culture.

[1]   Identify Phase

Identify is analogous to the scope statement and project charter of starting a new project. This phase ties various requirements into a clear identification of what is being asked for. An important tenet of DFSS is to listen closely to the VOC before beginning any process or product design. These requirements are broken into the various critical to quality components to identify the specific aspects requested.

   a. The identify phase begins with a clear determination of who the customer is. Is the customer the person purchasing the item or the one who will be using the product? For IT, is the customer the person who will use the software, the manager who must approve it, or the programmers who must support it? Most customer lists are rather long with each customer (or stakeholder) expressing their own particular requirements.

   b. Establish what the customer is looking for.
     • Locate the VOC by determining where they are. Are they in office buildings? On the road? Strolling through stores?

- Determine the channels of communications to hear from the customers, such as interviews, polls, focus groups, etc.

- For a new piece of software, what does each customer seek? Is it most important to be easy to use, easy to maintain, stable and reliable, highly secure, or quick executing? Each requirement has its own priority depending on who the customer is. Low-priority requirements should not be prime design considerations. Prioritize the customers and then prioritize their requirements.

c. Break the customer comments into the CTQ categories as follows:

- Critical to delivery—How do they want to receive it? What is their definition for high satisfaction delivery? It might be a legally-mandated date; it might coincide with a trade show, or the more common "right away."

- Critical to cost—How much would they pay for the ideal product? How valuable is each feature to them? Some "important" features may fade in criticality if their individual costs were known.

- Critical to quality—What features of the product are most important to the customer? How are they measured?

d. Build a business case for creating this project. It should be based on customer requirements along with a list of the costs to create it. Some companies include a detailed competitive analysis.

e. Assemble a project team since no one knows all there is to know about something. Include participants from the upstream and downstream processes.

[2] Design Phase

The *design* phase takes the functional requirements gathered during the *identify* phase and crafts the product. Based on this information, alternative concepts are created and evaluated for a best-fit. Each design is measured against the CTQs identified during the *identify* phase through the application of simulations and design of experiments (DOE), a statistical analysis of factor interaction. Six Sigma statistical tools then predict how capable the design is of meeting the customer requirements and establishing technical parameters.

An important part of the *design* phase is a consideration of how this product will be created. This "manufacturing" plan must include mistake-proofing components and data elements. Mistake-proofing only permits things to fit one way and increases customer satisfaction. A common tool for identifying mistake-proofing opportunities is the failure modes and effects analysis (FMEA).

Mistake-proofing includes such things as ensuring that a cable can only plug in right side up, and that it only fits a single jack on the equipment. Other IT mistake-proofing includes real-time validation of data entry fields, compilers (interpretive languages just run until they hit an error), the way a PC mouse plugs into a PC, and tape management systems that verify the data header before writing to the media. Mistake-proofing sometimes adds cost to a process and may not seem justified. However, by broadening the search for return on investments, it should show savings in service and customer satisfaction.

Examples of IT mistake-proofing we see every day:

- RJ45 plugs can only enter the jack right side up.
- Compilers prevent programs with obvious errors from becoming executable modules.
- Drop-down tables in data entry boxes only permit specific values.
- Bar code scanner guns can read bar codes both right side up and upside down.

The *design* phase goes beyond just the end product. As applicable, a materials procurement plan is developed. Imagine purchasing a new high-speed mainframe-attached printer only to discover that printing supplies were expensive and hard to find! Many major companies purchased ERP software and discovered the technical assistance (consultants) necessary to convert to the new system cost far more than the software.

[3]   Optimize Phase

In the *optimize* phase, advanced statistics and modeling are used to predict how a process will perform. Running simulations, such as the Monte Carlo, provides information for optimizing a process design. The *design* phase uses simulation to test various product designs for proper selection. The *optimize* phase uses simulations to improve the production process. In a sense, this modeling allows the developer to gain the same experience as running a new process without the cost of first building it. Adjustments are easier to make in the model than in an actual process.

An important part of the *optimize* phase is to determine how capable the process is of achieving the desired quality goals. An elegant design is useless if the developers are not capable of creating it. Statistical tools are applied to determine the ability to achieve product tolerances and estimate process design performance. This estimated performance is compared to the customer's critical to quality goals to compare performance to expectations.

Optimization includes identification of the factors that influence the outcome of a process. Using a Pareto chart, the most significant influences are identified and the process is adjusted to minimize their ability to create poor-quality process output. A statistical analysis of influences can reveal unseen interactions between process factors, such as different materials, operators, the time of day, etc.

[4] Validate Phase

During the *validate* phase, the design is tested and compared to the VOC. Share the testing results with manufacturing and sourcing, and future manufacturing. Document design improvements for future reference.

During the *validate* phase, perform an FMEA on the finished process. Compare the results to FMEAs in the earlier phases of the design to gauge quality improvements. This review will highlight what could go wrong at each step of the process and identify actions that can be integrated into the process to mitigate the issues.

When all of the processing and fine-tuning is done, the true measure of success yet remains. The final result must be measured against the customer's critical to quality objectives. In IT project management, this would mean that, for example, the software delivered would be compared item for item against the critical list to see how well it compares against the desired customer "ideal."

§ 14.07 SUMMARY

Effective and efficient project execution is the project manager's responsibility. This chapter described tools that can be used to improve team processes. Keep in mind that lean techniques and Six Sigma are both team efforts where the people who use a process daily are the ones to fix it.

Lean and Six Sigma are complex techniques. There are many things that both approaches can do to improve project and PMO procedures. If these are unfamiliar, then these efforts are best led by an experienced consultant. Lean techniques are a valuable project management tool for improving team productivity. These techniques include the following:

- Value stream mapping illustrates the process for identification of waste.

- The eight wastes show the various things that can sap time and money from a project's prompt conclusion.

- Six Sigma is a great tool for seeking out the root cause of problems and driving at more effective solutions.

Chapter 15

Business Continuity Planning

§ 15.01   INTRODUCTION

Business continuity planning (BCP) is an essential part of an IT project. It mitigates the risk that an unplanned event will significantly disrupt a project's budget or timeline. Once the final product is delivered to the customer, it is the customer's responsibility to cover it under their BCP. Until then, the project manager is expected to safeguard its assets.

Project managers have long implemented individual business continuity actions as a part of their risk assessment. However, those risks normally do not cover the same areas as a BCP. This results in the mitigation of risks pertaining to project resources and scope but not to business continuity.

Including a BCP in the project plan adds some work both up front and at the end. Not a lot of effort is required in the middle of the project. However, without a plan, some unforeseen event may undo all of the project's work. A BCP for a project manager has two stages:

1. During the project, the plan ensures that the damage caused by manmade or natural disasters is minimized and that the company's investment is protected. As the project progresses, there will be more to back-up, etc.

2. After the project is completed, this section of the project plan provides a smooth transition of the finished product to the company's existing BCPs.

> Consultants should add business continuity actions as a value-added service to their project proposals.

§ 15.02   BACKGROUND

Business continuity planning is a lot like car insurance. If it is not in place when needed, then it is too late to get it. Most project managers are optimists by nature. There are so many urgent, exciting, or challenging things to work on that it is hard to find time for something as doom-and-gloom as a BCP.

Over the years, business continuity planning has evolved as the business environment has changed. Thirty years ago, it was primarily concerned with disaster recovery planning (DRP). DRP focused on recovery from catastrophic problems, such as how to rebuild a flattened facility. An IT DRP was only activated if the damage required moving the data center to another site. A DRP contained its own "dirty little secret:" that it was sometimes easier and cheaper to take the insurance check and walk away from the business than to rebuild it. Examples of this might be a department store roof collapse, a factory fire, or even an accusation of selling less-than-wholesome foods.

Law mandates disaster recovery planning for financial institutions. It assumes that financial institutions hold assets belonging to others and closing up is not an option. Hospitals also have tested plans since a major crisis could open them to a slew of lawsuits. However, most industries do little disaster recovery planning and only apply it to their data processing operations.

A major problem with DRP was testing the adequacy of the plans. Testing is expensive and company funds are always under pressure to address the day's immediate issues, rather than being concerned about a pessimistic future that may never happen. Testing, if ever done, usually occurs when the crisis is at hand with no time left to repair flaws in the plan. Still, the DRP concept survived.

Eventually, disaster recovery planners recognized how important a company's customers and suppliers were to a long-term recovery. What good was recovering a facility if, in the process, neglected supplier and customer relationships withered away? This led to the addition of business recovery planning (BRP) to the disaster recovery plan. BRPs address customer concerns; they might also include explaining to customers where to find other suppliers in the interim. Supplier cooperation includes requests to help by taking back delivered goods not immediately required. A BRP keeps suppliers informed as the recovery progresses. BRP made these two critical groups participants in the recovery efforts.

Time marches on, and companies have recognized the huge expense that results in holding materials in inventory and in large queues of work-in-process material. Impressed by the results of Japanese automakers, many companies have adopted lean production practices. Under the previous model, a factory might hold a 30-day supply (safety stock) of a key material to protect against interruptions to the supply chain. The assumption was that carrying extra inventory was necessary to protect the continuous flow of goods down the production lines. Multiply this carrying cost across all materials company-wide and the corporations were paying a lot of money to buy, store, and handle safety stock.

Chart 15-1: Recovery and Continuity Planning

Under lean production methods, companies realized this was not necessary and drastically cut their safety stock. In return, they became dependent on the reliability of their suppliers to deliver quality goods on demand. Many customers now rate their suppliers on the credibility of delivery promises. Late goods may idle their own factory. On the other hand, keeping delivery promises in the face of adversity can be a major competitive weapon!

Taking this on-demand requirement even farther, the Internet has made most companies 24/7 (24 hours a day, 7 days a week) sales centers. Interruptions to a company's operations cause customers to go elsewhere. Every company has charts that show the longer their customers must wait for their goods, the more the cancellation rate increases. Few companies can afford this.

Out of lean production and the around-the-clock world arose a need for business continuity planning. BCP acts as the outer shell of disaster recovery planning. It addresses not only major tragedies such as burned warehouses, but also covers the occasional major disruption such as severe weather, the loss of electrical power, or the loss of a key machine. BCP is more than a set of dusty plans: it is a continuous proactive method of examining business processes to avoid problems and maintain workflow.

We all use business continuity every day. Consider a car. There is the risk of an accident. In this case, transfer the risk of loss to someone else (insurance company). This could be similar to disaster recovery if the insurance money was used to buy another car. If the car was severely damaged and there were difficulties making the journey to work every day on time until repairs were finished, a mitigation plan would inform your employer, family, and any other outside parties of potential delays. If a small, inexpensive "commuter car" was used for driving to work and a larger car for family outings, then the business continuity plan is to drive the larger car to work until the commuter car is repaired.

There is an even more important reason for project managers to develop a business continuity plan—keeping their jobs. A project that loses all of its source code or misses a deadline because the server was stolen, for example, can pile cost onto a project. Not every catastrophe is avoidable, but project managers are expected to analyze and take prudent steps to prevent problems.

[A]   Refer to an Expert

If a company has an in-house business continuity planner, refer to the planner at the beginning of every project milestone to identify risks and mitigation actions. The planner can quickly identify problem areas and his or her voice adds more credibility to BCP-mandated scope changes.

[B]   Business Continuity Planning Basics

Assembling a business continuity plan is a long but valuable process. It helps to uncover weaknesses that must be addressed before an actual problem occurs. BCP planning involves three steps:

1. Identifying what is critical to the organization
2. Identifying what risks (threats) these critical functions face
3. Developing action plans to reduce these risks

§ 15.03   IDENTIFY THE CRITICAL PROCESSES

What are the essential few functions of the business? For some companies, delivering a high level of customer service is critical. For an electrical power supplier, it might be a high level of service availability. For a materials supplier, it may be the on-time shipment of promised materials to customers. In a crisis, there is not enough time to restore everything, so it is important to avoid diverting scarce resources to restoring low-value functions. To focus resources and reduce the recovery time required, companies zero in on the "essential few" functions that keep the cash flowing in the door.

> Pareto's Law indicates that roughly 20 percent of the business's effort (the critical tasks) provides 80 percent of its value.

These critical elements are the foundation of a continuity plan. They address what the company is trying to protect. Any functions that do not directly support these activities may still have a plan, but they are secondary in a recovery. It is an executive management responsibility to identify the critical few functions.

> One author has worked for companies whose critical functions were, "to build, ship, and invoice product on time." Another company's vital few functions were, "to maintain 24 by 7 customer services, the ability to receive orders, and the timely shipment of goods."

In a small company, the executives identify critical business functions based on their experience. Larger or more sophisticated enterprises may conduct a business impact analysis (BIA), which identifies critical business functions based on their cash flow impact and their legal necessity. A business impact analysis involves a series of interviews with company executives to identify:

- The origins of the company's cash flows, and the impact of losing them, over time. This analysis might indicate that after one day's loss of a specific business function, the company would not lose any money at all. However, by the third day, the daily loss would be a large amount of money.

- Potential negative impacts to the company. An example is a contractual performance penalty for failing to perform a customer service. An example might be inability to perform customer support, or to deliver goods on time.

- Actions required demonstrating legal compliance, such as air pollution monitoring systems.

- The IT systems that support each of the critical business functions. This prioritizes them for IT recovery and drives the data center recovery planning. (Most plans assume that in a crisis, office space could be found but the IT systems will be the most complex thing to restore.)

Essentially, the BIA quantifies the impact on the company of a total outage—or a partial outage affecting numerous business functions. The quantified impact is used to make tradeoffs between the risks of the loss versus the cost of mitigating actions. Therefore, the BIA justifies the BCP budget.

During a project's design phase, the project manager should arrange with the company's business continuity planner to conduct a miniature business impact analysis of the project's product to see if it is a critical one. If it is, the mitigation action should be included in the project development plan.

The BIA tracks the losses to the company over time. This is important as some companies cannot tolerate a single day of total outage (such as an internet service provider), while others can tough it out with little more than some lost productivity and wages. The duration of a tolerable outage is the recovery time objective (RTO) and drives the strategy of the data center recovery plan.

BIAs are time consuming and expensive to conduct, but are valuable to the company in many ways. They benefit not only IT analysis, but also the company's strategic planning processes. Based on the revenue loss of a disabled business function, the IT department can rationally set system recovery priorities.

Most business managers lack a big picture perspective of their company. Even executives with long company tenure typically have a narrow view of departments other than the ones through which they advanced. BIA results are useful for allocating future capital and highlighting the costs/revenues of marginal operations.

> Always ensure that software development storage is regularly backed up (never assume this is done automatically). Verify exactly what is backed up and how often, and where the backup tapes are taken. Ensure all work stations have a place to back up their code and project documents, and that workers are trained in good backup practices.

§ 15.04   IDENTIFY RISKS (THREATS)

Project managers manage risk every day. A BCP risk assessment is very similar to other risk assessments. However, the risks examined are different from the ones normally found in a project. For example, the risk of damage by fire is usually regarded as a problem for the IT department's BCP. However, if the fire occurred during the project, the equipment, software, etc., used by the project are not yet included in the IT department's plan and are at risk. The project manager must step into this gap and provide a plan to protect the assets, the loss of which would delay the project.

Every day the company's "critical few" functions face a series of risks. The first step is to identify what these threats are. The second step is to raise defenses against the more likely or damaging risks. To evaluate these risks, build a spreadsheet to sift through the threats and help identify the key ones to address. An example is found in Exhibit 15-1.

A risk, or threat, is the potential that something may happen. Although risks can be positive as well as negative, business continuity planning focuses on the damaging risks, or those things that can go wrong. Risks have many dimensions. The main four dimensions are impact, likelihood warning, and recovery time.

1. First, examine risks based on their impact to the project if a specific event occurred. Impact is typically measured by lost revenue and the time and resources it takes to restore normal function.

   For example, if the facility was located in Minnesota, the impact of a blizzard can be high due to problems of shipping raw materials in and finished goods out. Contrast the snowstorm with a department store fire. Damage from the flames is small. However, there is now an odor of smoke on all of the goods in the store. Recovery time to clean out all the smoke-damaged inventory and refill the building with fresh goods can be quite long.

   A bank has a risk of robbery. The impact is high but the recovery is quick. The police are usually finished within a day and with a fresh stock of money, the bank can reopen.

2. This leads to the second dimension of risk—likelihood. Many horrible things *might* happen, but realistically, what is the chance that they will? If the chance is very, very small, then ignore it. Yes, the sun might quit shining tomorrow, but its likelihood is too small to address. What is the likelihood that a crazed person with a gun will rampage through the offices? What is the likelihood of an electrical outage? What is the likelihood that severe weather will shut down the facility for more than one day?

3. The third dimension of risk is warning. A weather report will warn about incoming severe weather. This allows some time to prepare. However, the theft of a server or a fire in the shipping unit arrives without any prior indication. Therefore, threats that can be anticipated allow more time to react. Threats that emerge suddenly allow no time to mitigate and may be more damaging.

4. The fourth dimension is how long it will take to recover. For example, a critical device in a remote part of the facility may be susceptible to lightning strikes. Any outage of that device is a critical emergency. However, the recovery time is quick by exchanging it with an onsite spare. Another example is a server. If a server is physically destroyed, the recovery time is how long it takes to bring in a spare server and then reload it.

Exhibit 15-1: Risk Assessment Form

Date:		Likelihood	Impact	Restoration Time	Score
Grouping	Risk	0 - 10	0 - 10	1 - 10	
Natural Disasters					
	Earthquakes				0
	Tornadoes				0
	Severe thunderstorms				0
	Hail				0
	Snow / Ice / Blizzard				0
	Extreme temperatures				0
	Floods / Tidal surges				0
	Forest/Brush fires				0
	Landslides				0
	Sinkholes				0
	Sandstorms				0
Man-Made Risks					
	Highway access				0
	Railroad				0
	Pipelines				0
	Airports				0
	Harbors / Industrial areas				0
	Chemical users				0
	Dams				0
	Rivers				0
Civil Issues					
	Riot				0
	Labor stoppage / Picketing				0
Key Suppliers					
	(list your suppliers here)				0
					0
					0

Refer to Exhibit 15-1 for some possible risks to consider. Managers can use this example to get their plans started. The process of developing risks works best as a team exercise so that many points of view are gathered. Managers should change the list to address the local situation. Once a risk list is flushed out, assign scores (1 through 10) for likelihood (10 means almost certain), impact, and restoration time. The score for the warning column is "1" for the most warning and 10 for no warning at all. Multiply the scores together and sort them in descending order so that the highest scores are on top. Address these top risks. At some point, draw a line across the list and ignore anything below it.

A look at the risks shows that some of them would have the same recovery actions, such as a fire that gutted a building or a tornado that wiped it away. They are two different risks, but have essentially the same recovery plan.

§ 15.05   OTHER RISK CONSIDERATIONS

Some risks are local. If a branch bank is robbed, that location will be out of service for the day but the rest of the company's banking branches would still be operational—it is just a bad day for that one branch office, but the company as a whole experiences little disruption. Another localized risk is a tornado—terrible where it hits, but generally the rest of a distributed company is able to conduct business.

> It is essential that a project manager reviews the BCPs of the project's critical vendors. Otherwise, the vendors' disasters may become the project's disasters.

The opposite of a local risk is a wide-area risk, such as the snowstorm in Minnesota example. The snowstorm may close roads across the state, keep employees form coming to work, and prevent the movement of materials on the highways. The factory is intact, but nothing is moving outside the facility's four walls. No fresh materials come in and no finished goods flow out until the highways re-open. Other wide-area risks to consider are floods, hurricanes, and earthquakes. Wide-area risks often affect both customers and suppliers.

Manmade threats come in many forms. There could be a terrorist threat against the company, a truck carrying toxic chemicals could crash outside the facility and force evacuation, or an angry person with a gun could be looking for victims. Manmade threats tend to be localized.

Infrastructure threats include problems with the things essential for the company to continue operating. Electrical power is an essential need of any company. Without it, there are no lights for the offices, desktop workstations fall dark, and the heating and air conditioning systems stop. Another infrastructure threat is to the telecommunications lines outside the building. These lines also carry data traffic, so this risk carries a double whammy.

Possible subsets to the previously mentioned infrastructure risks are associated with the facilities. These include roof collapses, interior electrical failures, etc. Many things can cause water pipes to leak and water damage spreads quickly.

A very common risk facing companies is the security of their assets and employees. Computers make attractive theft targets as do a wide number of things within a company's walls. The severity of losing a computer can be significant if the stolen PC is full of company secrets, confidential legal files, and the only copies of accounting records. A comprehensive internal security program is a key part of any business continuity plan.

> Imagine the impact of losing a developer's notebook PC with over a week's worth of work completed and no data backup.

Few companies do not have at least one disgruntled employee. As an insider, this person knows company processes and what would hurt operations the most if damaged. Employee sabotage may be difficult to stop. Another risk factor is employee theft. Sometimes a thief will try to cover his crime by setting a fire to destroy evidence. Address all of these and similar possibilities through the company's security plan and policies.

§ 15.06 DEVELOP ACTION PLANS TO ADDRESS RISK

After spreading enough "doom and gloom" to depress the most persistent optimist, the manager can begin fighting back against risk. Once the element of surprise has been stripped away from these risks, a manager can take steps to address them. There are three basic strategies to consider:

Avoidance. Are there any actions possible to avoid the risk? If hurricanes interrupt operations, could the company move to Wisconsin? This move *avoids* the threat to the flow of work from hurricanes. However, avoidance actions often introduce new threats to the company.

Mitigation. Unavoidable risks require steps to reduce the likelihood or impact of the threat. Examples of mitigation actions are everywhere. Consider the fire sprinkler system in the offices. A sprinkler does not stop a fire from starting. It requires the heat from a fire to activate it. A fire sprinkler contains and may douse the fire, reducing the damage it causes. To reduce the impact of losing electrical power, some companies install generators.

Transference. After trying to avoid and mitigate a problem, the third option is to transfer the risk to someone else. Transfer losses from a threat to insurance policies. For example, product liability insurance can protect a company in case someone is hurt using one of their products. Reduce insurance rates through the introduction of well-written and tested business continuity plans. Insurance companies will often provide advice for writing a plan, since this also reduces their risk.

With these three strategies in mind, reexamine the list of threats to the company and see which strategy is best suited to meet each threat. The steps required to carry these actions out become the continuity planning action items. Some actions should have already been taken, such as the installation of fire sprinklers. Often mitigation actions must wait for next year's funding.

The third step of planning includes the development of specific plans to address threats to the critical few company activities. Managers should start by comparing the risks to the list of solutions found in the notes of the local expert. Discussing this list in a staff meeting may also bring out some solutions used in the past.

To keep the planning efforts focused, continually refer to the following list of questions.

- What are the critical processes and the critical assets that enable them to work?
- What threatens them?
- What actions reduce the likelihood of a threat becoming reality?
- What will minimize damage if it does occur?
- What does the team do if a problem occurs?
- Where can more information be found on this?

§ 15.07   PLANNING THE NEXT STEP

Before writing the plan, a manager should check to see what information is already available. Writing a plan can be time consuming and yet much of the source material is not that far away. Assemble a basic continuity plan with a few calls and a notebook. *In most crises, three keys are needed—key people, keys to the doors, and key support contract information.* Be sure to label the origin of any information collected, as there may be a need to go back for further clarification.

Ten Steps to a Basic Recovery Plan. When executing these steps, think about the team's work areas (all of them), the servers used, the network closet, etc.

- **Start with the basics—Who do I call?** Obtain a current organization chart for the facility. This will show who works in what areas. Now get an organization chart for the entire company—specifically the key technical areas and executives. In a crisis, their help is useful. For example, if there was a severe crisis with the data network, the IT manager could call on the network experts from other company sites to come in on short notice and help for a few days.

- **With these names in hand, match them to three telephone numbers.** This is very important for people directly supporting the facility and less so for people at peripheral sites. Try to obtain the 24-hour contact information for at least one contact person for each of the other company sites (usually this is their IT manager). For each person on the contact list, obtain their:
  - Office telephone number
  - Home telephone number
  - Cellular telephone number

- **Check with the security staff to see if they keep a key to every door in a secure key locker.** Keys are easy to copy. It is impossible to know who has a key to what doors. If possible, use electronic locks on the critical doors. A report can be generated by the server controlling the electronic locks listing who has access to which doors protected by electronic locks. A part of this step is identifying the doors that individual IT staff members need access to.

- **Build a spreadsheet of service contract information.** The sheet should indicate who to call for which items, the terms of service (24/7, Monday through Friday, etc.), how to call for help, and the contract expiration date. This could be a long list. A copy should reside at the help desk.

- **Build a vendor list of anyone who supplies critical materials or who provides critical services.** This could be the company that prints IT's special forms (such as invoices and checks), the place from which the company buys backup media, etc. Service companies could be hardware repair services, the company that provides offsite storage of backup tapes, or companies that support software tools.

- **Take a walk-around asset inventory.** Walk around the entire facility and note every major piece of equipment and its location on an asset list. Which device is important to critical operations? Compare the asset list to the service contract list. Are all of the critical devices covered? Is the service coverage adequate?

- **Talk to the systems administrators and make a list of software assets.** This includes purchased software as well as homegrown code. Do the purchased packages have service agreements? Are these agreements included on the service contract list? Are the software licenses securely stored offsite?

- **Identify the various business functions that IT supports.** Make a list of them and then fill in the technologies that are necessary to support them. (This information is in the BIA report.) This could be a big list.

- **Perform a security check of the project team area.** Project teams are often stuffed into whatever space is available. Ensure that the work area is secure from theft or sabotage. Also, verify that it is structurally sound.
- **Build an employee skills matrix for the IT department.** This will give some idea of who to call on for emergency backup on a specific technology. It can also be matched against the critical equipment list and software asset list to develop a staff training plan. Identify the skills gaps now and begin training the IT staff.

To complete these ten basic steps, the IT manager will probably spend a couple of days pulling the information together. However, now the staff has a lot of information for the help desk and other key people in the organization. Much more is needed, but this forms the nucleus of a formal business continuity plan.

The essential ingredient for IT recovery is the ready availability of readable backup media. Back up *all* files onto other media as often as possible, and store this media offsite in a secure location. As media rotates back to the data center, verify that it is still readable.

One way to see how ready the staff is (and to uncover any more hidden caches of information) is for the manager to make an unannounced visit to the support people and ask for their critical information. Some will reference the "sticky notes" that encircle their monitor; some will dig deep back into an address book for bypass codes, and some will bring out the "cheat sheets." Others will give a blank stare. Imagine the ball of energy they would become fumbling for this same information in a real emergency! Be sure to copy all of this information into the files, as it will be useful later.

Some people will declare that they already have a plan. Ask for a copy. In most cases it will lack many of the essential details. This shows they have at least already bought into the recovery plan concept. Make sure that the plan is executable by someone familiar with the technology, but who has not worked on that business process.

After organizing what has been collected so far, the manager should begin validating it with people other than those who provided the information. It is especially important if the notes copied might be out of date. All information should be neatly typed (or copied) and placed in a three-ring binder, broken down by subjects with tabs to divide the sections. In an emergency, the tabs allow quick access to needed information without fumbling through many pages. Be sure to mark the binder and all sheets as "company confidential."

[A] Distributing Interim Copies

There is now enough of a plan to make copies and distribute them to key people. This is an important step, as the project has progressed from a one-person show to a team effort. Ask each of these people to help improve the book by filling in the gaps and commenting on what has been collected so far. The minimal number of copies that should be distributed follows.

- One copy of the book at the project manager's office desk. (Use this when problems arise.)
- One copy at the project manager's home to address problem calls when they come in (and in case something happens to the copy at work.).
- One copy to the IT manager.
- One copy at the IT manager's home.
- One copy at the IT help desk.

At this stage it is best to keep the number of copies in circulation to a minimum since there will be many updates as the plan evolves. Store the IT manager's copy and the help desk's copy on a CD and on the network as a read-only file.

[B] Adding to the Plan—More Contact Information

During normal work hours, it is easy to find people when problems arise. Rather than chase them down, obtain a facility telephone directory. The company's telephone technician likely has one. This list provides all of the daytime telephone numbers. However, emergencies have a habit of arising in the middle of the night, on holiday weekends, etc. Using the telephone list and the company organization chart, the key managers to call in the event of an after-hours emergency should be identified. Their home telephone and cell phone numbers should be collected.

These numbers are useful for advising key people of IT problems during off hours. They are forewarned so when they come into work in an emergency, they are prepared for the situation. For example, the materials managers may be told that the warehouse management system has failed and will take many hours to repair. By calling them in the wee hours of the night, they can decide if their staff needs to come in early and work around the problem. The same situation holds for almost every department: accounting, payroll, human resources, engineering, etc.

The manager should respect the personal privacy of these home telephone numbers and never give them out to anyone. These personal numbers will likely be covered by the company's privacy policy, so they should not be left lying around. While on the subject, draft guidelines explaining the circumstances that are severe enough to call someone at home.

[C]   Limit Access to Critical Equipment

An important step in business continuity planning is keeping people away from critical equipment. Some people are curious, like to push buttons, and are intrigued about what will happen next. There is the occasional discontented person who wants to express their outrage by turning off a server or unplugging a network hub. So whenever possible, limit the ability of anyone to disturb the operation of equipment. Keep critical equipment in locked closets, hard wired into the electrical outlet, and away from the wondering masses.

> If the project manager is not a company employee, then entrust company confidential information and door keys with a team member who is also the customer's employee. Be sure the IT manager approves of this arrangement.

After keeping everyone else out, make sure the IT staff can get in! Problems can arise at any hour of the day or night. If technical support staff must work on something, could they get in? If there is a company security force, they should have a duplicate key to every door. If not, then establish an IT key cabinet that holds one copy of every key to every door or cabinet the IT staff needs to access. Be sure each key is labeled because in a small pile, they all look alike.

Some people will attach their own locks to doors and tool lockers. They typically forget to provide a key to the locker. Fortunately, a well-stocked key locker includes a master key named "Mr. Bolt Cutter." Whenever encountering a personal lock on one of the equipment room doors, introduce that lock to Mr. Bolt Cutter. If this is not done, valuable time will be lost in a crisis looking for someone to open a $2 lock that did not belong there.

> The company's security policy should require the security office to stock and provide approved locks for doors and cabinets, or a process for the

security office to obtain two keys to each. The same policy must prohibit the use of personal locks on anything other than company lockers. This, together with an employee orientation, should greatly reduce the use of personal locks on company equipment.

It is easy to copy physical keys without anyone else knowing about it. No one knows for sure how many copies of a particular key may be floating around. The security office should always sign out keys to people for eventual retrieval. Otherwise, these keys may end up in the possession of people who should not have them.

Physical keys can effectively keep out most people, but by far the best approach to limiting access is the use of electronic locks. Instead of turning a key, an electronic "key" checks the database to see if there should be entry through that door. It also maintains a log of who unlocked which door and when. In addition, a record is available of anyone who propped the door open.

Electronic keys allow the IT manager to grant or remove access easily. Over time, some people forget their pass card and ask for a "temporary" one for the day. Then they forget to return it. Some people will do this frequently. When issuing a temporary card, always limit its access to one day. Otherwise, the result is like the duplicate physical keys floating around. It is impossible to be sure who is walking through what door and what they might be carrying out!

Passwords are the logical keys to IT equipment. Just like a master key, a system administrator password is the golden pass to anywhere and anything on a computer system. Guard these passwords closely. The problem is that in a crisis, the support staff may need specific passwords to shut down or restart servers, mainframes, computers, etc. Establish a secure place to store them so they are available in an emergency.

[D] Service Contacts—HELP!

The company probably pays a princely sum every month for someone to be on call to repair its vital equipment. This is a common practice. However, paying someone to come in at any hour to fix something is useless if the support staff does not know how to contact them! Take the time to pull information on all service contracts and put it in the BCP book. This is important information for the help desk to have as well. Ask everyone in the department for a copy of their service contract information. This should include:

- **Vendor's name.**
- **What is covered.** Sometimes this is specific equipment (by serial number), or the agreement is for everything on the premises.

- **Hours of coverage.** The company pays one rate for service to cover normal working hours, and a higher rate for around-the-clock coverage. If the company pays for 24-hour coverage, do not let the service company off the hook if they try to defer until morning. Around-the-clock coverage is about double the cost of standard "daytime" service.

- **Who to call during usual working hours and after hours.** Every agreement must include a 24-hour number. Try to get an after-hours telephone number for the companies only providing 8-to-5 service. It will be expensive to bring them in on a Saturday to help with a repair, but it might be worth it.

- **When the contract expires.** This information should go on a calendar to reevaluate the service level before the contract expires. Reevaluate the importance of the covered equipment, its incidence of repair, and if the current service level is adequate.

- **Any limitations or extra cost provisions.** Sometimes the agreement covers parts and labor; sometimes it only covers the labor cost of "best effort." Know what this is in case an emergency purchase order is required.

- **Contract number.** Some companies will check to see if the caller has paid their bills before sending anyone out. They will look up the contract number in their database to see if the item in question is covered. In some cases, they want the unit serial number as well.

- **Company-appointed contact person.** Usually, a company designates one or two people as the person(s) who can make the call. It helps to know who they are. Often, these are people who know how to make minor adjustments to the equipment and avoid service calls.

- **Guaranteed response time.** How long will it be before they show up? Usually this is something like four or eight hours. If they do not show up on time, start escalating the requests!

There are five basic types of service agreements. Select the one that best suits that piece of equipment's failure rate, the degree of criticality of the equipment, and the availability of alternate devices until that machine is operational.

- **Cold call for service.** This is where the IT manager's fingers do the walking through the phone book and find someone to come out. The result will be a long service call since they know nothing about the site or its equipment. They may also take several days to get around to coming out.

- **Time and materials.** The service vendor will come out for a set rate per hour and work until the machine is operational. They will also charge for the parts. Although the hourly rate is expensive, this may be cheaper than a service contract.

This approach is good for equipment that rarely breaks down and for equipment where there are onsite spares. Under the time and materials arrangement, there is an existing business arrangement so the service company should be somewhat familiar with the company's equipment and its business processes.

- **Standard working hours.** This is usually 8 a.m. until 5 p.m. Under this agreement, the service company will do what they can during these hours. If the job will run past 5 p.m., they will go home and pick up where they left off during the next business day.

- **Full service.** This is 24/7 service, with unlimited calls at any time of day, for any day of the week. The contract includes all costs. Always use this type of service contract for mission-critical equipment.

- **Exchange.** This is a good approach for smaller items like bar-code scanner guns. Keep some spares onsite and send in the broken ones for repair—usually at a set rate. However, it may take weeks to get the device back.

With the service contract information in hand, walk around and look at all of the critical equipment. Is it on the service contract list? Did someone forget to mention something or is there a gap in the service agreements? Does each critical device have the appropriate level of coverage? Business requirements change and often the service contracts do not keep pace with them.

After collecting all of this information into a spreadsheet, provide a copy to everyone who has the BCP book. The help desk will find this all very handy.

To ensure that everyone knows what to do, make up small cards with the service contract information on them. Attach the cards to the major devices such as large printers, servers, etc. If possible, put it somewhere inside the machine where it is easy to find, such as under the dust cover of a printer. Be sure to remove any old service information. If there is a lot of equipment in a room, just post the collective information on the wall.

[E] Vendor Contacts

Like service contracts, the support staff needs to know what vendor to call for a particular service or material. This is not an all-inclusive list. It should only include current vendors or someone the team may need to contact in an emergency. This list will do more than help in a major crisis; it can help with the more mundane emergencies that pop up everyday. Has an off-brand printer ever run out of toner at a critical business time? Knowing who to call for a replacement could get the ball rolling.

A vendor list provides a single point of reference for everyone in the department who needs materials. (Of course, they would still need to work through the usual approval process.) In addition, this list reduces the time required to look for vendors to bid on projects.

For each vendor, give their company name, account manager's name, daytime and after-hours telephone number, fax number, e-mail address, website address, street address, and a description of what they supply. The vendor list should also contain every company on the service contract list.

When drafting the list, remember the "other" vendors such as the electric company, telephone company, water company, waste removal service, and local ambulance. These numbers may be needed in a crisis.

If the project is at a customer site, the customer may handle the asset management. If so, be sure to tag consultant equipment and record their serial numbers. Task the consultant to provide lists of software (and their versions) for the software asset list. The goal is to replace something quickly if it is stolen or damaged beyond repair.

If the project is internal to the company, engage the asset management team early. Sometimes assets brought in for a project are "below the radar screen" until they are placed into production.

[F] Walk-Around Asset Inventory

Grab a pad and pencil and walk around the different company areas. Begin in the IT department. Make a note of every major item found, like a server, network hub, major printer, etc. Do not try to do this from memory. In particular, look for equipment that has popped up in user departments. Indicate which of these items support critical company processes. Walk everywhere. Be curious and open cabinets and look into every closet. Look *everywhere*—especially where equipment does not belong.

The project manager should have an inventory of the materials purchased for the project. However, often the customer will provide other items essential to the project. Even if they were handed over without requiring a receipt, the customer wants them back, so the project manager must identify and safeguard them.

When walking through, note the location of disconnected equipment. Send someone out to pick it up for potential reissue. Likely some pockets of new equipment will be uncovered that someone keeps as a personal emergency spare-parts stash. Arrange to have all of this equipment collected into one spot and lock it up. Repair and reissue the good material and scrap what is broken.

Compare the asset inventory to the list of service contracts. Are all the critical devices covered? Is the level of coverage adequate? Sometimes the machine itself will have a sticker saying who to call for service. When in doubt, ask the operators who they call with questions.

Include supporting equipment that enables other devices to work. This might be an uninterruptible power supply or a critical air conditioning unit. It may also include electronic time clocks or electronic door lock servers. An important goal is to identify "nonstandard" equipment that is essential to a critical operation. (Often this equipment is too old to find replacement part to repair.) The trouble with one-off equipment is that may be impossible to replace in a crisis.

[G] Software Asset List

With the easy part out of the way, move on to backup copies of software and data. A look will probably reveal a vast proliferation of computers: from departmental servers to special client software that interfaces with other companies, to shop floor equipment controllers. Inside each of these is valuable and potentially irreplaceable software and data. The BCP must *ensure that someone makes a periodic backup, or safety, copy of this data*. Clearly label and store offsite.

Software developers are an interesting group. They often resist any assistance they view as interference. Consequently, they install servers in computer rooms or even in their offices without first ensuring that the server's disks are included in a comprehensive data backup program. The project manager must ensure that every server added to a project (or "idle" server assigned to it) is included in the daily backup schedule.

For each critical piece of equipment, make a list of its critical software. It is often easier to replace the hardware than the software. Some software is unique and almost all software has been customized to a particular use.

Ensure that every device has more than one backup copy of its software and that these are stored separately (preferably offsite). For equipment not maintained in the computer room (such as in offices or on the shop floor), store one copy offsite and one copy in the data center's tape library room.

Some devices to include:

- Telephone PBX, automated attendants, and voice-mail system—these are simply special-purpose computers requiring data backup in the same manner as a mainframe computer

- Programmable network devices

- Shop floor control systems, such as PLCs, robots, CNC devices, etc.

- Special-purpose PCs that perform critical but highly-specialized functions such as clearing credit cards

- Servers that control electronic door locks

- Copies of software source code developed locally

- Licenses for purchased software

[H]   Toxic Material Storage

For safety's sake, everyone on the IT staff should know where toxic materials are stored and used within the facility. Technicians should take precautions in case whatever damaged the equipment also damaged the toxic materials containers.

Move or safely isolate equipment found in or adjacent to toxic materials storage areas. If moving this equipment is expensive, include it in the upcoming year's capital budget. This becomes a future planning item to isolate or move the equipment far away from the toxic storage area.

Ensure that the work area is secure from theft or sabotage. Also, verify that the work area is structurally sound.

[I]   Perform a Security Check

Project teams are temporary and often forced into whatever space is available. Often the space is available because there is some aspect about it that no one likes.

Whatever the situation, be sure that the work area is locked when not in use and that the team holds the keys. Some projects change the status quo within an organization, whether it eliminates jobs or interferes with someone's personal empire. In any event, securing the area reduces the likelihood of internal sabotage. Secure servers in the computer room if possible as this will also provide environmental support.

Before moving the team in, inspect the area for structural soundness. Are the ceiling tiles stained? That could be a sign of a weakness in the roof. Do water pipes run overhead? (This does not apply to sprinkler pipes.) Is the electrical power stable? Are adequate cabinets available for locking up documents and software?

[J]   Employee Skills Matrix

If a key support person is on vacation in a far-off place, who is the next person to call to fix the problem? The IT manager can guess or ask around, but in the meantime the problem is simmering and so is the boss. Save time by building an employee skills matrix before problems arise.

Begin with a list of the critical processes supported. Each of these processes uses a set of technologies (hardware and software) to accomplish their mission. Technologies exist within a business reference, so a degree of understanding of how they fit in the customer's operations is useful. The skills matrix breaks down the critical system into its components to identify the support requirements. The components might be a programming language, specific hardware knowledge, or an understanding of the database management system. This list of components translates into a list of skills required to support them.

A spreadsheet makes an easy-to-use tool for building the matrix. The skills matrix lists the technologies along the vertical axis (which can be a very long list) and the staff names along the top (column headings). Rate each person according to their skills at using each of the technologies.

Add a few more rows to this list to identify other useful expertise, such as who is a qualified emergency medical technician (EMT), who is a volunteer firefighter, etc. As an important added benefit, use this list to identify people for training.

§ 15.08   WRITING A PLAN

[A]   Overview

Some people are reluctant to write recovery plans because they do not know where to start. Writing a plan is as simple as stating the basics of any story: who, what, where, when, why, and how. Base the format on what to do first, what to do second, etc. If the plan addresses these basic points, then it should be sufficient. The goal is to develop a set of instructions so that employees can take the right action in a disaster. BCPs are intended as guidelines and advice. The technician on the scene should review the plan and then proceed as the circumstances dictate.

If there is a good risk analysis available, then everyone has an idea of the various things that could go wrong. No one can predict exactly what will happen. However, a set of generalized actions fit most situations. When working through the risk analysis, it is apparent that most plans contain the same details. Recovering a destroyed office is the same whether burned out in a fire or a snow-packed roof collapsed.

A plan is not a complete set of instructions to rebuild something. Typically, a plan consists of specific actions to repair something or contain the spread of damage to operations. Full recovery plans are created while the containment effort is still under way. When writing, always remember the target audience. Emergencies affect people in different ways. Emergencies are chaotic. A good plan reduces this confusion by providing guidance on what to do. Once the team is working on the problem, they will feel more in control and the chaos will diminish.

Cynics will say that a disaster will occur at the worst possible moment. For an accounting system, this might be when closing the year-end books, etc. For a project, this would be right before delivery. Write plans as if the crisis erupted at the worst time in the annual business cycle, usually during the busy season.

Write the plans clearly. Think of the person who is likely to come in after hours to handle the emergency and imagine explaining it to him. Perhaps begin with a short overview paragraph that explains the business purpose of the process and essentially how it accomplishes this purpose. Another way to proceed is to imagine the room during the emergency. What is the clearest way to address the problem?

A picture is worth a thousand words. Include pictures of hard-to-describe locations, or drawings of how the major pieces work together. Digital cameras are common in companies, so it is easy to include some photos in the plan. Pictures can also shorten the narrative, and who has time to read more than a few pages in a crisis?

[B]   What to Write About

Every department should have a plan that addresses natural and infrastructure risks. People should not sit helplessly waiting for things to happen; they should be active participants in creating the results they want. All department processes depend on some basic infrastructure support to be in place for them to be successful. This includes electricity, telecommunications, data communications, and data systems. Therefore, the facility-wide continuity plans should begin with supporting these areas. Each plan should include three major sections:

- **Immediate actions.** The first section is the "first aid" applied by the technician on the spot. This includes things like shutting off the sprinkler valve once the fire is out to minimize the amount of water damage. Another immediate action is to use employees' cell phones for communications during a telephone system outage. Many things are possible if thought out in advance.

- **Containment.** The next section describes containment actions to reduce the spread of the damage until the primary support people arrive. This is not busy-work. These are the same actions as the "experts" would take when they arrived. In the fire sprinkler example, it would be to contain the water on the floor, picking up computers and vital records from the floor to minimize water damage, etc.

- **Establish minimal service levels.** The third major section of the plan contains the actions to return the process to a *minimal* level of service. A company cannot sit idle until a full recovery is completed. This could involve establishing a temporary office, shifting this process to a different company site, implementing manual procedures, etc.

With these three sections in mind, formulate a basic plan format. In this way, all plans at the facility will have a similar "look and feel."

[C]   Contents of a Typical Plan

Base the plan's terminology and the level of explanation on the assumed audience. The plans are for others in the department who either are onsite during the emergency or are the first ones in. Assume they are familiar with the technology, but not with that particular business system.

Begin with how obvious the problem is. A building hit by a tornado is obvious. Magnetic damage to backup tapes is not. Hard-to-detect problems may require detailed step-by-step instructions to discover them.

How much warning will there be before a problem hits? Some natural disasters, such as hurricanes, are usually preceded by extensive warnings. Other disasters, like a lightning strike or blue smoke wafting from the back of a computer, provide little advance warning. Emergencies that have a warning time can trigger containment actions before they begin. Again, a hurricane is an excellent example of an emergency for taking actions to prepare. This can range from covering all of the windows with wood to testing the emergency power generator.

The second consideration in writing a plan is how long the plan's user must hold out before expert help arrives. Will the expert be onsite within an hour, two hours? The plan-user will need enough information to contain the problem and fight it until the expert arrives.

Finally, if a key process is out of commission, is there an alternative that can keep the facility running? Could materials be shipped out of the front of the building until the network is restored to the shipping docks? Can the factory manually perform the processes that the defunct machine used to accomplish? Can the payroll office issue "40 hour" paychecks until the payroll system is restored? So in each plan, remember:

- The target audience
- How obvious the problem is
- How much warning you will have
- How long until expert help arrives
- Are there any manual work-arounds?

[D]   Which Processes Need a Plan?

It is not practical to write a plan to cover every eventuality for every item. A plan is only required for critical processes (although a prudent IT manager has a plan for recovering every process). The facilities department should have a plan to address all natural disasters and manmade disasters (as described in the previous risk analysis section). Other departments, such as human resources, are also involved in these areas.

> Disasters happen. The project manager's disaster plan should focus on how to recover from the problem. Some equipment can wait for replacement and some needs express delivery. If the team must wait, put into the plan actions they can take to remain productive in the interim. Think of where assets could be borrowed on short notice.
>
> Think about what could be done on PCs. For example, configuring a desktop PC as an interim server. Preplan the steps for the server software installation, network connections, data backup loads, etc. This may be the same action as used to set up a new server and may already be documented somewhere. This recovery plan can be reused in numerous projects (so long as it remains current).

All infrastructure risks should also be addressed by a mitigation plan. This includes electrical service, data processing, and telecommunications. Even if the facilities department is handling the loss of electrical power, the IT department needs a plan for managing the UPSs for maximum availability, a power-shedding plan to relieve pressure on the UPS by turning off low-value equipment, etc.

Most companies have a few other critical pieces of equipment or processes outside of the infrastructure area for which they should also produce a plan. It might be an expensive and unique machine in the factory. It might be special equipment to route incoming calls to individual salespersons or even a very old machine that manages the finished goods inventory. Whatever specific critical processes are, they need a plan.

Even in a mechanical world, there are still manual critical processes. They need recovery plans too! Ensure that the manual processes are clearly documented.

[E]   Recovery Plan Testing

Testing is a vital part of recovery planning. Often business managers view testing as a time–consuming, expensive, and nonessential activity. This is completely wrong. An untested plan is a risk. Such a plan may provide a false sense of security if it misses the mark and no one takes the time to validate its contents.

Testing provides many valuable benefits:

- Testing a plan validates that it works. It uncovers any gaps in the document. The author may have known what was meant by a passage but someone reading the document might draw the wrong conclusion.

- Testing ensures that the document is up to date with the latest process it is supporting. Keeping recovery plans in sync with process changes is a major challenge. With so much to do, busy people leave changes to the plan for last. Testing catches any missed documentation and updates the plan accordingly.

- Testing trains the participants in their roles during a crisis. It is one thing to read a plan, but something different to enact it. Involving people in a test helps to debug a plan as others interpret it. It builds confidence in the participants that they could fulfill their responsibilities in a crisis.

Testing a project's BCP takes several forms. During the project, it includes verifying that the backup tapes can be read. Before the project delivery, the entire plan can be tested with the participation of the customer receiving the product.

Document the project's installation validation tests and create a stripped-down version for verifying proper restoration of processes from backups. This is a useful section in the finished product's recovery plan.

Preparing for a test requires considerable planning. People and materials must be gathered. A test scenario is required to provide a backdrop for the exercise. The primary types of tests are:

- Walkthrough—The plan's author walks peers through the plan step by step. The goal is to identify omissions and clarify difficult-to-understand passages.

- Tabletop exercise—The plan is talked through by both the IT support team and the department they are supporting (such as Payroll). A disaster scenario is provided to make the plan more "real." An example might be a fire in the server room, a data security breach, or a multiday electrical blackout.

- Simulation—The IT team and the supporting departments act as if a real disaster has occurred. A good simulation places the teams in separate rooms (to complicate communications) and feeds information in a bit (or complication) at a time. Simulations require considerable preparation and many companies hire a consultant to develop and run the test.

- Wide-area simulation—This is a company-wide exercise. It is a worthwhile effort but is not commonly done due to expense. A simple example is a fire drill.

Few companies can afford to shut down their operations to conduct testing. Often testing is accomplished in "slices," such as for an entire department, or a subset of it. The exception is for "hot site" testing. IT departments must test this at least annually. It is also a good idea to rotate the IT staff through the hot site. In a crisis, the team will be more familiar with the location, its limitations, and rules of operation.

§ 15.09   SOURCES OF ADDITIONAL INFORMATION

The following describe sources to consult for additional help in business continuity planning.

[A]   Publications

There are many books concerning this subject. Most of them are general in nature and a great place to start. As the planning program matures, look for something that is specific to your industry.

Some publications include a regular column about disaster recovery, such as Computerworld™ (*www.computerworld.com*). Two popular and free periodicals dedicated to business continuity are:

- *Disaster Recovery Journal* (*www.drj.com*)
- *Continuity Insights* (*www.continuityinsights.com*)

[B]   Training and Certification

Many organizations offer formal training on the concepts of disaster recovery and business continuity. Some colleges offer degrees and others offer a few classes. These schools can be located by searching the Internet, and through the FEMA site.

The most popular training organizations offering classes, certification, and ongoing professional information are:

- *Disaster Recovery International* (*www.DRII.org*)
- *Business Continuity Institute* (*www.theBCI.org*)

[C]   Web Sites

The most comprehensive web site on disaster recovery is run by the U.S. government's Federal Emergency Management Agency (FEMA) at *www.fema.gov*. This site contains information on training, developing plans, and links to many other useful sites. Take time to explore the contents because the deeper into this site a person goes, the more interesting it becomes. It is the best site for all around (and free) information.

Another useful web site for developing the risk assessment for your location is also run by the U.S. government's National Oceanic & Atmospheric Administration at *www.NOAA.gov*. This site provides information about severe weather for your area, based on historical data.

§ 15.10   SUMMARY

Business continuity planning should be a component of any large project. In smaller projects, the plan should at least ensure that software development storage is backed up regularly (never assume this is done automatically). Verify exactly what is backed up, how often, and where the backup tapes are stored. Include a place to back up workstations.

The project plan should include periodic reviews of the project's BCP at each milestone. In the beginning, this should be quick. However, as the project nears the end, there will be a lot more to protect or quickly to recover from a disaster.

A well-run project should hand over a documented business recovery plan with the finished product. The plan is developed in cooperation with the organization's business continuity planner. Its nature depends on the product delivered and its criticality to the customer's organization.

Chapter 16

Project Information Security

§ 16.01   INTRODUCTION

> "He is best secure from danger that is on his guard even when he seems safe."
>
> —Publius Syrus (50 B.C.)

Information security has always been an important business concern. This is nothing new. Companies have long held secret processes, formulas, financial information, etc. Today's issues are not so much about protecting secrets as they are about protecting the data itself. Companies compile histories of customer purchases as leads for future sales. Customers leave their credit card numbers on account for quick purchases. Companies keep both of these in online storage for reference. Therein lies the problem. What is accessible by authorized people may also be read by criminals.

The problem is exacerbated by the ease with which large quantities of data can be stolen. Instead of loading box after box of paper onto a truck, a data thief can download large databases to a CD or a USB-connected "pin drive" and get away undetected. Rather than sift through piles of papers, data can be quickly extracted and used. Data thefts leave no tell-tale signs since only a copy is taken and the original object still exists.

Further compounding the issue is an ongoing stream of new laws whose details ignore the technical complications for their compliance. Project managers must be aware of the legal compliance risks to their projects. The products that projects create, and the process changes they make, may open a gap in a company's legal compliance program. Changes may even expose data to theft that everyone thought was well protected.

> Although this chapter speaks of protecting data, information security is also concerned with protecting the misuse of equipment, such as network high-jacking, employees loading unlicensed software, theft of software, etc.

Information security controls are a combination of:

- Technical—firewalls, authentication technologies, encryption
- Administrative—processes for granting/revoking access, background checks
- Physical controls—locks on doors and drawers

To ensure that a project does more good than harm, project managers must assess every aspect of a project for risk it imposes on the company. From access controls to data protection to document shredding, the project manager and the project team must know what to protect and the proper way to safeguard it. Not only is it good business, but it might save someone's job!

There is no need to reinvent the wheel. To build the project plan's security annex, start with the company's security policies and add anything unique to the project.

---

§ 16.02 ADDING INFORMATION SECURITY TO A PROJECT

The best time to identify information security issues is during the project definition phase. This allows the inclusion of time and materials for security measures to be included in the project plan and budget from the beginning. Adding these to the plan later may be difficult.

Security is a three-step process:

1. Identify what to protect—Not everything is worth protecting. Focus limited resources on protecting the essentials.

2. Select the most cost-effective defense—Do not spend $10 to protect a $1 asset.

3. Prepare to react to an attack—Plan a standard response before it is needed.

Types of defense:

- Prevent it—Do not permit the attack to occur. A server not connected to a network cannot be attacked remotely.

- Deter it—Reduce the likelihood of an attack by implementing controls. This is the most common defense.

- Deflect it—Use a "honey pot" server that is easy to enter but contains false data.

- Detect it—Monitor networks and servers for unusual activity and react promptly.

- Recover from it—Make data backups to restore damaged databases or servers.

> There are no foolproof defenses. Given enough time and money, anything can be overcome. In 332 B.C., Alexander the Great demanded the surrender of the city of Tyre. Since the walled city was a small island off the coast of Phoenicia, they refused. Over the next six months, Alexander's army (and a large group of involuntary laborers) built a causeway to the island wide and strong enough to support siege towers that battered the walls down.

§ 16.03   INFORMATION SECURITY BASICS

There are three basic concepts to information security. They are vulnerability, threat, and control. These three concepts can be used to describe any situation.

- Vulnerability is like an unlocked door—a weakness that can be exploited.
- Threat is the potential to do harm. In most cases, this is from people. Threats can be internal or external to a company.
- Control is the action (or technology) that prevents a threat from exploiting a vulnerability.

For example, imagine a room full of valuables. The *threat* is that someone outside of the room will enter and steal something from it. The *control* is the locked door. The threat (a thief) cannot get past the door and is stopped. However, if the room has a window, a *vulnerability* that bypasses the strong door, then the threat may gain entry through that other path.

In short, threats are blocked by control of the vulnerabilities. Whenever examining a security issue, begin by identifying the vulnerability, the threat (who might attack this way), and the control (how the attack will be thwarted).

[A]   Security Goals

There are four information security goals:

1. Confidentiality—The protected item must be accessible only by authorized people or applications. Clearly define the people and technologies that have authorized access.

   a. Examples of confidentiality:

      - Protection of information in the system from unauthorized disclosure.
      - In some cases, it may be advisable to protect even the existence of a data file.

- Systems should be accessible only by authorized parties.
- Prevent downloading of confidential data. If download is necessary, ensure only properly authorized users can do so.

b. Confidentiality controls:

- Limit the users who can read from files and access programs that can read files. This can be done with operating system security, internal database security, etc.
- Ensure all data backups and reports are properly safeguarded and shredded when no longer needed.

2. Integrity—Protect from accidental or intentional unauthorized changes. An accidental change that erases critical data is just as damaging as an intentional act.

a. Examples of integrity:

- Protection of systems from intentional or accidental unauthorized changes.
- Assets that can be modified only by authorized parties.

b. Establishing integrity control:

- Encrypt communications through virtual private networks.
- Store regular data backups securely offsite.
- Separate duties between developers and system implementers.
- Rotate duties.

> The "principle of adequate protection" states that an object only requires protection until it loses its value. Also, the price of protecting something should not exceed its value.

3. Availability—Assets are accessible to authorized users when needed.

a. Examples of problems with availability:

- Denial of service.
- Loss of data processing capabilities as a result of natural disasters.
- Fires, floods, storms, earthquakes make facilities unavailable.

b. Establishing availability control:

- Create an alternate data center in a separate location.
- Maintain mirrored databases.
- Segment network into virtual networks.

4. Authenticity—assurance that user is who they say they are.

    a. Example authenticity assurance:

      • User ID/password.

    b. Establishing authenticity control:

      • Require strong passwords, change frequently.

      • Biometric identification.

      • Authentication tokens.

§ 16.04   RISK ASSESSMENT

It is not possible to protect everything forever and there is no such thing as a 100 percent foolproof defense. A determined opponent with unlimited time and resources can crack whatever defenses have been built. The trick is to outlast the attacker until he gives up and goes after a weaker target.

> After project scope is determined, the project manager must perform an information security risk assessment on the data, hardware, and network.

[A]   What to Protect

Begin with a classification of what data needs to be protected. These areas of company confidential data should be detailed in the organization's information security policy. A bit of common sense and experience can identify data elements that need protection. Any data file or database that contains a single element of a protected class must be protected to that level. Examples of data classes to protect include:

• Banks—transaction queues, accounts payable, accounts receivable, and securities records

• Hospitals—medical records, accounts receivable, accounts payable, and logistics

• Manufacturing—processes, marketing, accounts payable, accounts receivable, and logistics

• Retail—client information, marketing plans, accounts payable, accounts receivable, and logistics

> "Distrust and caution are the parents of security."
>
> —Benjamin Franklin

Confidential data can also be identified by legal requirements, contractual requirements, trade secrets, patents, research and development, brand protection, sensitive materials, or other items that, if compromised, altered, or stolen would have a significant impact on the business.

Each type of confidential data should be protected as appropriate to its value. You may identify data as low-, medium-, or high-value data. A company might decide that:

- High-value data must be stored encrypted, with limited access to read/write. Software programs must be reviewed and tested by a separate team. Files should be stored on a VLAN with limited access.

- Medium-value data must be reviewed and tested by a separate team and files should be stored on a VLAN with limited access.

- Low-value files are accessible for read-only with limited update capability.

- Uncontrolled data are files that do not contain any controlled data elements.

Data has a useful lifespan. A password that has expired no longer requires a high level of protection. Similarly, a money order that has been cashed long ago no longer needs extensive protection.

> Likely the most secure site in the United States is the U.S. gold bullion repository at Fort Knox, Kentucky. It is possible that a determined group could breach the walls, but before they could haul off a part of the trillions of dollars of gold, they would need to fight their way through an Army armored division.

[B]   Examine the Project for Security Issues

Once the project scope has been determined, take time to identify the security characteristics of files created, read, or updated by the project.

Exhibit 16-1, Information Security Matrix, provides a method for identifying data that must be secured.

1. List all of the data files and databases that the project will touch.

2. Identify their security classification.

3. Down the left side, list all of the technologies used to touch the data. Typically the data sit on one type of technology, are managed by a database management system (DBMS), and are accessed by software and connected together through a network route.

4. Indicate which technologies touch which files. In most cases, more than one technology can be controlled to protect multiple files.

5. Indicate the value for each data type, based on the organization's standard, such as high, medium, low, or no control.

Exhibit 16-1: Information Security Matrix

Security Type	Data Files / Databases					
	B	B	B	n/c	C	A
	File	File	Inventory	File	Financials	Locks
Hardware						
Apps Server 1	X					
Apps Server 2		X	X			
Disk Farm 1	X	X				
Database Server A			X			
Database Server B	X	X				
Rating System						
Windows Server 2003		X				
Windows Server 2000			X			
Windows XP						X
Sun Solaris	X				X	
Sun Zones				X		
Database Management System						
Oracle	X				X	
Sql Server				X		
Sybase		X				
flat file			X			
dBase						X
Network						
Firewall #1 (DMZ)				X		
Firewall #2				X		
Firewall #3	X				X	X
Router 276	X		X	X		X
Router 73		X			X	
Data Value	High	Medium	Low	Medium	High	Medium

A   Legal compliance
B   Personal privacy
C   Company financials
n/c Noncritical files

Chart 16-1 shows one way to determine which technologies support a data file. Begin with the data object and start working outward. Data are created by some application and maybe through a data collection device or Web page. Unless the file is sequential, it is likely to be controlled by a database management system of some type. All of this is tied together over a series of network components.

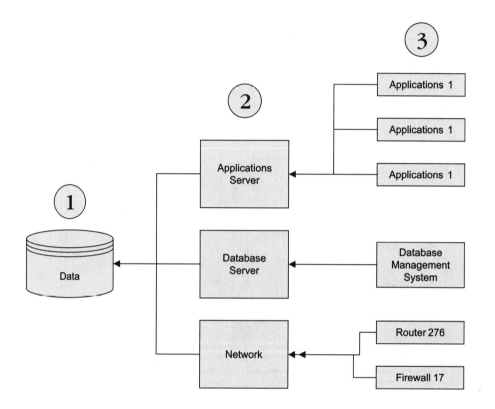

Chart 16-1: Determining the Technological Support of Data

When the things that can touch a data file are identified, this indicates which items require control. If the file is encrypted before storage, then stealing the file is useless unless the program that encodes the data is also taken. And to even get close to the program and file, a series of network controls must be overcome.

§ 16.05   INFORMATION SECURITY PROCESSES

Information security is a combination of technical and nontechnical issues. All processes ultimately begin and end with people, who are often the weakest link.

> Information security protects the company from lawsuits by preventing loading of unlicensed software. This stops individuals from exposing the company to civil penalties due to unauthorized employee behavior.

[A]   Physical Security

The most basic control is to secure information from physical contact with unauthorized people. Companies keep their servers and network equipment carefully locked away to reduce the chance of someone casually turning off something, physically damaging it, or taking the backup media. Any lock can be overcome, but taking precautions dramatically reduces the number of potential miscreants by removing casual opportunities. However, information security includes physical objects as well as electronic ones.

- Printed reports may contain the same critical information as that contained in a database. Examples of this are credit card numbers, check numbers, personal information, customer lists, product specifications, program source code, etc. *All* of these documents must be shredded and not merely thrown away.

- Backup media contains the same data as the databases—and in an easy-to-carry format! All backup tapes, cartridges, disks, etc., must be as carefully guarded as was the data when it was in the computer room. Once backup media is no longer required, it must be shredded and never merely thrown away.

- Test data used by the project may be sensitive. Also, data used in implementation testing will likely be live data. Shred it all!

> So why should seven-year-old backup tapes be shredded instead of thrown away? Social Security numbers do not change. Many people keep the same bank and credit card accounts for many years. People inclined to steal and misuse such information are willing to stumble through a few obsolete data elements to obtain some of the real thing.

Of course, the ultimate information physical security is to never connect the company's network to the outside world. Although subject to other types of attacks, such a network drastically reduces the chance of compromise.

Physical security of portable equipment is often overlooked. Minimize the amount of confidential data and software on PDAs and notebook computers. Encrypt the confidential data. Once these devices leave the secure confines of the office, they are liable to theft. The loss of a notebook or PDA should be reported immediately so that it can be locked out of the network and all passwords changed.

> Caution! Executives love to have windows in their offices. If their computer screens can be seen through the window, then they can be read from a distance.

[B] Technical Security

Technical security means using hardware and software to foil an electronic attack. Physical security issues evolve slowly, but technical security seems to change daily. A project manager should either have an information security technician on the project team or quick access to one.

A basic understanding of a few information security principles can help a project manager to identify some of these security issues during the project definition or planning phases. Technical security falls into one of four technologies.

[1] Applications

Software vulnerabilities come from inadequate coding practices. Projects creating software must ensure that only valid, acceptable values can be entered into fields of a predetermined maximum length. Typical software vulnerabilities include:

- buffer overflow
- invalid input
- command injection
- SQL injection
- information substitute
- insufficient encryption
- logic bombs
- back doors.

Defenses for application security problems include:

- Input validation—only acceptable values can be entered.
- Use peer reviews to detect problems in all software before installation.

- Scan all code for future dates, login IDs, passwords, copy, or FTP commands.
- Data entry fields are never used to build a SQL statement.

Information security must be a component of *every* program written. Too many applications are written as one-time, short-lived projects that seize system roots and last forever; security rarely being considered in the initial design. Consider the security impact on every program no matter how small. A one-time application left on the production system can be accidentally executed again by the staff or a hacker.

[2]   Databases

Databases are an attractive target for a hacker. This is where the data resides. While some attacks may maliciously damage a network or other technical capability, data are where a criminal finds personal information, financial keys, etc. Typical database vulnerabilities include:

- Inferring the existence or values of data
- Database patches that disrupt security
- Old programs that access the data but have not been updated to prevent misuse.

 Defenses for database security problems include:

- Encryption—even if data are intercepted, the data are unusable
- Internal authorization used to segment records into confidential and generally available data elements.

[3]   Operating System

A computer's operating system is a major obstacle to criminally accessing a company's data systems. Operating systems provide a wide range of services and each of them requires the appropriate permission to use it—assuming that the operating system has been properly locked down! Typical operating system vulnerabilities include:

- Default passwords left in products after installation
- Excessive user privileges on accounts, including full administrator rights for developers.

Defenses for operating system security problems include:

- Turn off all services not required. They can always be reinstalled later.
- Forbid or tightly control guest accounts.
- Immediately change all default passwords after installing hardware or software products.
- Account for every user ID on the operating system. Beware of anyone installing a "back door" account with administrator privileges.
- Schedule unannounced server audits to ensure the team is following published security practices.
- Lock down outlets for data on every PC workstation. Examples include:
  - USB ports—anyone can attach a "pen drive" and extract a substantial amount of data. An Apple iPOD can hold up to 60 gigabytes. USB ports may also open a company's liability through loading unlicensed software or by loading unlicensed MP files.
  - CD and DVD writers can make walking out with a lot of data very easy.

Project managers must ensure that as servers are installed for their project, all appropriate security measures are immediately put into place. Do not permit team members to argue against cumbersome and time-consuming steps that hinder system development. Otherwise, such a server may enter service without many of the underlying security provisions in place. Do it right, do it safe, from the beginning.

---

[4] Network

Networks are the glue that binds all of the technologies together. They provide the outer layer of protection for all of the other technologies. As the front line, networks should have well-designed and multilayer protections. Typical network vulnerabilities include:

- Default passwords left in products after installation
- Network devices not patched to latest security level

Defenses for network security problems include:

- Encryption—Even if data are intercepted, the data are unusable.

- Firewalls—Screen out incoming traffic, only pass what is valid.

- Routers—Screen out addresses not within a specific range.

IT administrators love to standardize technologies to reduce maintenance expenses. However, the best network defense mixes multiple vendors and technologies to increase the time required for unauthorized access.

[C]   Access Authorization

The most common approach to securing data systems access is through a user ID/ password combination. A "user ID" identifies to the computer the person (or entity) who is seeking access. A password is paired with a user ID to determine that the person requesting access is really that user. A poorly-chosen password may compromise the entire corporate network.

For maximum protection, require all passwords to:

- Be at least eight characters long (the longer it is, the more secure it is)

- Include at least one uppercase letter and one lowercase letter

- Include at least one number and one special character

- Not be a common word.

One way for users to remember passwords is to have them use certain characters and numbers for vowels. For example, use ! for I and @ for A. This might make "password" into "p@$$w0rd". Adding a special character throws off things a bit. Using Internet notation, "P@ssw0rd;", is pronounced as "password wink."

Another approach used to confound hackers is to link two small *unrelated* words together with a special character like "T!p:t0ck" (tip tock). Do not use related words because hackers also check for that, such as "Ear;tag1."

[D]   People Are the Weakest Link

Companies employ many people. Each of these complex beings has his own hopes and fears, desires, and aspirations. Some of these people also can view, modify, or download confidential company data. The key is to limit the number of people who can do this, and to carefully screen the ones who can.

Policies to protect against employee security threats include:

- All employees and contract workers to sign a confidentiality contract to provide legal recourse to recover damages.

- Carefully screen new team members (unless the company can certify this has been done) to include a background check. If an existing background check is more than 24 months old, rerun the process to catch anything new.

- Limit who has access to sensitive information. Many people often handle reports, data extracts, backup media, etc.

- In all contracts, specify that ownership of software developed under the contract belongs to the company.

- Minimize the number of people who have the authority to grant access to IT resources.

> Separate the functions of development, test, and production. Restrict the number of IT people with access to the production accounts. Do not provide developers direct access to production systems. The temptation to slip in a simple, no-risk software change is too much to resist.

Control internal threats from people by employing the following strategies:

- Management at all levels must be aware of IT security risks and procedures. Security should be a mandatory requirement in every person's job appraisal.

- Training should be periodic and updated.

- Hire an outside organization to audit portions of the data systems to ensure they are following security practices.

§ 16.06 INFORMATION SECURITY PLAN

For some projects, it may be advisable to create a formal information security plan. This document explains how the project will examine a risk, address it, and maintain the project's viability. It provides direction for team members facing a potential information security issue when making design tradeoffs. As always, use the company's existing plan if one exists.

> The amount of security included in a final product has a significant impact on the amount of time required to install it. If security controls are lacking in the finished item, substantial rework may be required.

[A]   Parts of the Plan

The information security plan is an annex to the project plan. In many cases, it can be based on one from a previous project plan. The primary sections are outlined below.

A. Purpose—A statement of the main goals of the policy, and the why the policy is needed. (Include references to legal compliance issues here.)

B. Scope—A statement of the infrastructure and information systems to which the policy applies.

C. Responsibilities.

D. Policy guidance.

E. Related documents—A list of references to additional documents that provide more specific guidelines and procedures.

[B]   Assuring Project-Wide Commitment

Each technical group in the project team must be represented when creating the security plan. Each has its own perspective and experience of what works best. Senior management must approve the plan and enforce its policies.

To ensure that the project team does not run afoul of information security issues, provide each member with a printed copy of the information security policies and procedures. Train all new team members on the features of these documents and require that they acknowledge attendance in the orientation. If the project exceeds six months, conduct a refresher session. Be sure to include information security as an agenda topic during project risk assessments at every milestone or phase completion.

§ 16.07   OFFSITE SUPPORT

Company employees are easy to work with. They know what is required and are already tuned in to the company's information security requirements. Employees are reluctant to risk their ongoing employment by cutting corners and rushing something. There is, however, a gap in the defenses. While local employees are easy to find to talk to, finding offsite contractor's team members is another matter. However, some contract workers are onsite every day and can be briefed about information security just like an employee.

For offsite project team members, different strategies are required. Offsite project team members have remote access to company servers, software, and even data. Ensure that they understand and are accountable for information security. Security bonds, insurance policies, and other legal instruments help to ensure that contractors closely manage their security practices. Do not be shy about insisting on this because it is good business and likely the requirements are the same restrictions they place on their own internal data.

Often, an outside organization has its own information security program. If it is adequate, refer to it in the purchase order to tie it to the agreement. Like any other organization, the policies are effective only to the extent that they are enforced, so review how compliance is audited. If work is done offsite, conduct periodic security audits of the work site.

> Be careful about allowing offshore companies to access sensitive company systems. Their civil liabilities are set by their local laws, not necessarily by the buyer's contract.

Another issue for offsite vendors occurs when trusted vendors access the company's network. Trusted vendors have already been screened to ensure that they follow appropriate information security practices. Still, erect defenses against attacks from this direction. Then if the trusted partner is attacked, that attacker cannot use the open door to enter the local data systems.

§ 16.08 SOURCES OF FURTHER INFORMATION

Information security is a rapidly changing field. New threats appear, common vulnerabilities are announced, patches are tested and reviewed, etc. It pays to keep abreast of new development; use these resources to assist.

- CERT Coordination Center—Carnegie Mellon University Software Research Institute—federally funded research and development center that studies

Internet security vulnerabilities, researches long-term changes in networked systems, and develops information and training to help improve security. *www.cert.org*

- National Institute of Standards and Technology, Computer Security Resource Center—shares information system security tools and practices. *csrc.nist.gov*

- U.S. Department of Energy, Office of Cyber Security—provides tools, information, and news on the latest vulnerabilities. *www.ciac.org/ciac/*

- System Administration Audit Network Security (SANS)—contains a wide range of information on the latest vulnerabilities, general information, and training. *www.sans.org*

"We will bankrupt ourselves in the vain search for absolute security."

—Dwight D. Eisenhower

---

§ 16.09   SUMMARY

Project managers must be aware of the information security risks that may affect their projects, the products they create, and any process changes they make. Any one of these may open a gap in a company's technical shield or otherwise expose data that everyone thought was well protected.

To ensure that a project does more good than harm, project managers must assess the risk that every aspect of a project imposes on the company. From access controls to data protection to document shredding, the project manager and the project team must know what to protect and the proper way to safeguard it. Not only is it good business, but it might save someone's job!

Every project that involves confidential company information should include an explanation of the information security policy during new team member orientation. Everyone must understand the proper way to address security issues. If this step is completed prior to making project time estimates, then information security tasks can be included in the baseline project plan instead of added later as changes.

Chapter 17

Legal Issues

§ 17.01 INTRODUCTION

> "No Connections, Interests, or Intercessions . . . will avail to prevent strict execution of justice."
>
> —George Washington

Project managers can be assigned to a wide variety of projects. If they have always worked in one area of the company, they should be aware of the legal restrictions in that area. But if assigned outside of their normal work area, they could brush up against regulated parts of IT. Project plans must ensure that new systems include the appropriate safeguards to protect data and applications.

The best time to define legal issues is during the project definition phase. Large companies often have a compliance team that can review project proposals to avoid problems. This can ensure that the compliance requirements are included in the project scope and reflected in the budget.

The challenge is in small to medium-sized companies. They typically lack in-house experts to advise the project team. In these cases, it is up to the project manager to dig out the information from other sources. Recent laws have addressed the following areas.

- Ready availability of critical information such as medical records. This has moved some archived data from tape to online disks (running offsite).

- Records availability through data retention. These laws mandate how long specific data elements must be retained. The problem is that data are often mixed up on storage devices, forcing the retention of entire pieces of media (such as an entire backup tape) for as long as the longest period for any data element on that media is required to be kept.

- Data accuracy through software controls. Companies must now identify internal control processes and verify that they provide adequate safeguards for the accuracy of financial reporting. These controls must be in place and monitored regularly to identify tampering.

- Security of data records. Companies must safeguard specific types of data from disclosure. The data may have been protected by companies for some time, but now there is a legal requirement to ensure compliance. Examples of such data are customer data and health records.

> As with all legal questions, IT managers must refer to their company's legal counsel for written guidance on what they must do to comply. Further, IT managers must monitor changes in the legal landscape to ensure their policies, procedures, and strategies do not lead the department into activities outside of the limits of these laws.

§ 17.02 GUIDING THE PROJECT THROUGH THE COMPLIANCE MINEFIELD

Each legal compliance area has its own emphasis and rules. Rules tend to be aimed at solving some problem in a specific industry. In general, they address:

- Data security. Keeping personal and company data secure. This includes printed material, backup media, etc. The project team must be cleared for the material it will work on. This may require segmenting the project so that no one group has enough of the data to compromise the organization or violate any applicable regulations.

- Data integrity, ensured through:
  - verifying that the software's calculations and data manipulations are correct
  - tracking changes to software that makes these verified changes
  - ensuring that calculations are accurate after each change.

> The last point may sound silly, since who would not verify the accuracy of a critical data system after every change, but there is always someone whose "simple fix" does not bear testing (at least according to his limited experience).

- Retain project records of development and design decisions and tradeoffs for these systems. If a problem later occurs, it will make tracing its origin much easier. It will also help to pinpoint if one or more people were adding things that they should not.
- Business continuity has moved, in some cases, from an option to a requirement. At one time, data were stored on tapes to provide for disaster recovery. If needed, it could be searched at a leisurely pace. Today's regulations require a prompt retrieval even after a disaster, forcing online backup storage of critical data. Check to see if this must be added to the project plan for new development.

> "If you have ten thousand regulations you destroy all respect for the law."
>
> —Winston Churchill

§ 17.03   HEALTH INSURANCE PORTABILITY AND ACCOUNTABILITY ACT

Health Insurance Portability and Accountability Act (HIPAA) requires securing and maintaining personal health information (PHI) for specific retention periods (depending on the type of information). While organizations possess this data, they must safeguard the data from unauthorized access. Although the information may be on a wide range of media (x-ray photographs, paper records, electronic records), the primary challenge to the project manager is electronic availability, security, and retention.

Consideration for implementing HIPAA is similar to any other data security issue. Common practices include:

- Password protection and authorization controls
- Hierarchies of security based on need-to-know. A doctor might need different information than a nurse
- Backup and retention of data and ensuring 100 percent data reliability
- Forms and releases must be scanned, saved, and made available
- Health records must be retained for at least six years
- Automatic audit trail
- A business continuity plan is necessary to ensure records are readily available—even after a disaster

The safeguarding of data is moving toward an increased use of fixed disks. DVDs and CDs create a security and control problem for both the media stored and the ease of copying it. Such portable technologies bypass physical and electronic security measures. This fact will drive up online storage requirements over time.

HIPAA's reach is long. Some professionals believe it extends to electronic mail and instant messaging communications that discuss patient conditions or that include other medical data. These types of messages must use encrypted communications to avoid interception. They must also match the retention levels for similar types of information.

A good place to start researching a compliance program is the National Institute of Standards and Technology's (NIST) HIPAA Resource Guide. These standards provide a general requirements framework that should be a part of any compliance program.

§ 17.04   SARBANES-OXLEY ACT

Because of major corporate accounting fraud, legal requirements have been enacted to protect sensitive corporate data. This is the Sarbanes-Oxley Act (SOX), and it contains many sections. The part generally applicable to IT, however, is Section 404.

> An ironic twist is that SOX Section 404, the one that causes IT management the most problems, has the same identifier as the HTTP 404 error.

Section 404 required the Securities and Exchange Commission (SEC) to publish rules governing internal controls to ensure that a publicly traded company's financial data are accurate. Since all companies rely on information technology to create the data, the IT department falls squarely in the middle of this law. IT processes must be certified annually as secure, comprehensive, and repeatable.

IT departments must prove there are appropriate internal controls to manage any changes to software that plays a significant part in financial controls or reports. The impact for IT is that if a project touches on, adds to, or updates these controlled areas, extra time must be allowed to address compliance issues. Certification of information provided may be required. Also, controls must be documented, tested, and added to the company's existing program. Special attention should be paid to:

- Financial record retention systems and the policies that manage them since they affect information collection, validation, analysis, and storage.
- Data mining, scrubbing applications, and analysis systems because they jeopardize data integrity.
- Data and systems security, because unauthorized access could severely and negatively impact the quality of reported information.
- Updating the appropriate IT policies and procedures because they are part of a compliance review.

The local IT policies and procedures may indicate if the project falls into one of the compliance areas.

SOX constantly refers to "controls." A control is a checks-and-balance process ensuring that new systems or changes to existing systems function properly. This is present in most companies as their change control process. However, in most companies there is a way to bypass the process or it is just one of an automatic approval. Correctly done, the change is properly tested, verified by others, and verified again after implementation.

"The best way to get a bad law repealed is to enforce it strictly."

—Abraham Lincoln

Common control concepts encountered when implementing a SOX program include the following.

- Document each control and how it is supposed to work.

- Separate the responsibilities between the person requesting a change and the one approving it.

- All approvals must be written and recorded. Keep these records in a safe place. In most cases, there will be multiple people authorizing changes (IT manager, IT quality technician, requestor, manager of department affected, etc.). Some of the most common approval control points are change prioritization, test result approval, and rollout.

- Audit and verify that controls are still in place and effective. The details are important. Event logs, audit trails, and reporting are critical to meeting this goal.

- Include a formal test in the project plan if the project impacts on or adds a control. Keep records of all such checks along with what was checked, how it was verified, who did it, when, etc. Use a formal test plan and record the results.

SOX compliance does not end at the four walls of the company's offices. It includes any outsourced functions as well. Be sure that any outsourced support (or contract labor) that touches any of the company's controls or controlled objects is also compliant with the company's SOX program.

Privately owned companies do not fall under the Sarbanes-Oxley Act. However, many companies adopt these requirements as good business practices.

---

§ 17.05 SECURITY AND EXCHANGE COMMISSION RULES

SEC rules have long mandated the collection and retention of financial records and records pertaining to securities transactions. More recently, requirements were updated to include electronic mail and instant messaging. The SEC found that these types of messages were used to communicate to customers and among securities employees, and yet the records of these communications were not made or retained.

Exchange Act Rules 17a-3 and 17a-4 have implications for IT managers and for IT securities team members. Companies now require comprehensive, auditable, and legally credible policies, practices, and systems to manage e-mail. Typically, these records must be retained for six years.

§ 17.06 COMMITTEE OF SPONSORING ORGANIZATIONS

In 1992, the Committee of Sponsoring Organizations (COSO) established a framework for the proper authorization, recording, and reporting of transactions. The Securities and Exchange Commission officially recognizes the COSO framework as adequate for establishing internal controls over financial reporting.

In the COSO framework, an internal control is a process—a way to approach an issue. It is about what people do, not what manuals say they ought to do. Internal controls only provide some assurance that something will occur; they are not an absolute guarantee. Each internal control addresses a specific objective.

COSO identifies internal controls as processes designed to provide reasonable assurances regarding objectives in three areas:

- Effectiveness and efficiency of operations

- Reliability of financial reporting

- Compliance with applicable laws and regulations

> "There is one kind of robber whom the law does not strike at, and who steals what is most precious to men: time."
>
> —Napoleon Bonaparte

The COSO framework measures five internal controls for each of the three areas:

- Control environment—processes for managing and developing people in the organization and delegation of authority systems

- Risk assessment—identification and analysis of risks to achieving assigned objectives

- Control activities—policies and procedures for execution of management directives

- Information and communication—effective communication for running and controlling the business

- Monitoring—ongoing activities or separate evaluations

[A] Control Objectives for Information and Related Technology

A mandate known as Control Objectives for Information and Related Technology, or COBIT^{TM}, was created by the Information Systems Audit and Control Association (ISACA) and the IT Governance Institute (ITGI). (COBIT is a trademark of the Information Systems Audit and Control Association and the IT Governance Institute.) It describes a set of control objects for maximizing the benefits derived from the use of IT. It also describes appropriate IT governance and control. It can keep IT in compliance with the requirements of SOX.

COBIT uses COSO definitions as the basis of its control objects, but extends the notion of control throughout the enterprise. It also makes the COSO principles and objectives applicable to the IT function. The COBIT control objectives provide a working document for IT management and staff, the control and audit functions, and business process owners. The conceptual framework includes:

- Information criteria
- IT resources
- IT processes

The COBIT framework focuses IT processes on the company's business. It strives to ensure IT resources are used responsibly and appropriately. Project managers working in a COBIT environment must ensure that their project's product is consistent with the COBIT IT governance model.

While the full COBIT framework exceeds SOX Section 404 requirements, companies should consider customizing the applicable portions of COBIT for their own compliance requirements.

COBIT has 34 high-level objects that cover 318 control objectives in four domains:

- Planning and organization
- Acquisition and implementation
- Delivery and support
- Monitoring

The IT Governance Institute advances international thinking and standards in directing and controlling an enterprise's information technology. It can be found at: *www.itgi.org*.

COBIT control objectives:

- Planning and organization
  - Define a strategic plan
  - Define the information architecture
  - Determine technological direction
  - Define IT organization and relationships
  - Manage the IT investment
  - Communicate management aims and direction
  - Manage human resources
  - Ensure compliance with external requirements
  - Assess risks
  - Manage projects
  - Manage quality
- Acquisition and implementation
  - Identify automated solutions
  - Acquire and maintain application software
  - Acquire and maintain technology infrastructure
  - Develop and maintain procedures
  - Install and accredit systems
  - Manage change
- Delivery and support
  - Define and manage service levels
  - Manage third-party services
  - Manage performance and capacity
  - Ensure continuous service
  - Ensure systems security
  - Identify and allocate costs
  - Educate and train users
  - Assist and advise customers
  - Manage configuration
  - Manage problems and incidents

- ○ Manage data
- ○ Manage facilities
- ○ Manage operations
- • Monitoring
  - ○ Monitor the process
  - ○ Assess internal control adequacy
  - ○ Obtain independent assurance
  - ○ Provide for independent audit

A criticism of COBIT is that it describes what needs to be done but never states how to do it. COBIT helps define processes for identifying and managing IT risk. Other existing standards must take up where COBIT leaves off. While every control objective is applicable to every organization, few companies are able to implement the entire COBIT process.

§ 17.07   GRAMM-LEACH-BLILEY ACT

The Gramm-Leach-Bliley Act covers any business significantly engaged in financial activities (and it is a rare one that is not). The Act addresses the confidentiality of customer data. Responsibility for protecting the data from disclosure remains with the company even when the data are passed to a third party for use. An implication here for a project manager is if the project involves shipping data offsite. Ensure that all third parties are required by contract to secure the data at all times.

The Gramm-Leach-Bliley Act has two areas of emphasis:

- • The financial privacy rule governs the collection of a customer's personal and financial information. It also applies to companies who receive this information.

- • The safeguards rule requires the design, implementation, and maintenance of safeguards to protect the data.

The Act encourages the encryption of data in storage and in transit. It also recommends destroying data that are not needed, since this ultimately protects the data from disclosure.

A criticism of the Gramm-Leach-Bliley Act is that it is more descriptive than prescriptive. The Act leaves the definition of "protecting the security and confidentiality of information" up to each company.

> More information is available from the Federal Trade Commission at: *http://www.ftc.gov/privacy/privacyinitiatives/glbact.html.*

§ 17.08   FAIR AND ACCURATE CREDIT TRANSACTIONS ACT OF 2003

The Fair and Accurate Credit Transactions Act of 2003 (FACTA) governs records disposal. Consumer information includes any record (paper or electronic) about a person's credit worthiness, reputation, characteristics, etc. The Act applies to companies that possess or maintain consumer reports for business purposes, regardless of industry.

FACTA reduces the risk of consumer fraud created by improper disposal of any consumer report record. FACTA requires that anyone who possesses or maintains covered consumer information take reasonable measures to protect against unauthorized access or use in connection with its disposal.

[A]   ISO 17799

ISO 17799 is the International Standard Organization's standard for information security. It is an adaptation of the earlier British standard BS-7799. In the future, ISO will change the numeric designator to ISO-27002, as the ISO-27000 series has been set aside for information security.

ISO 17799 provides best practice recommendations on information security management for initiating, implementing, or maintaining information security management systems. The 2005 version of the standard contains the following 11 main sections:

1. Security policy
2. Organization of information security
3. Asset management
4. Human resources security
5. Physical and environmental security
6. Communications and operations management
7. Access control
8. Information systems acquisition, development, and maintenance
9. Information security incident management
10. Business continuity planning
11. Compliance

§ 17.09   CANADIAN BUDGET MEASURES ACT

Drafted in response to major corporate accounting scandals in the United States, the Canadian government enacted a law similar to the Sarbanes-Oxley Act. The Budget Measures Act, known as Bill 198, increases the level of executive responsibility and accountability in Canadian companies. The law describes certification requirements, disclosure controls, and internal control requirements.

The law requires an annual certification by executives that their filings are true and do not omit facts. Like the SOX legislation, this means that the IT processes that contribute significantly to these reports must be tightly controlled to avoid accidental or purposeful manipulation. Internal controls must be established, tested, and used. Controls encompass the collection of information and its processing and summation.

These controls will significantly impact the design of data management systems. Records retention, security, and overall management will force project managers in Canada to examine their entire project product for gaps.

A legally defensible records management system is an important part of the Budget Measures Act compliance program. Consistency in process across all IT systems is essential. This includes procedures, data retention schedules, policies, data disposal methods, etc. An important tool in consistency is clear documentation explaining what to do, how to do it, and when deviations are permitted.

> "Reduce the number of lawyers. They are like beavers—they get in the middle of the stream and dam it up."
>
> —Donald Rumsfeld

§ 17.10   CANADIAN PERSONAL INFORMATION PROTECTION AND ELECTRONIC DOCUMENTS ACT

> Project managers implementing data systems across the northern border must be aware of Canada's strict laws on personal privacy. It may be advisable to engage a Canadian compliance expert in this area to ensure data systems remain within the law.

Canada has enacted the Personal Information Protection and Electronic Documents Act (PIPEDA). Among other things, this legislation governs the collection, use, and disclosure of information in commercial activities. Personal information is factual or subjective information in any form about an identifiable individual.

PIPEDA addresses the following ten principles for protecting, gathering, retaining, and destroying information about people.

1. Accountability—An organization is responsible for protecting both personal information in its possession or any that it transfers to a third party. Accountability for PIPEDA rests with designated individuals in a commercial enterprise.

2. Identifying purposes—An organization must identify the reasons for which personal information is collected either prior to or at the time of collection.

3. Consent—An organization is responsible for collecting, using, or disclosing personal information only with the individual's consent and knowledge. This requires an organization to document and retain all consent given and withdrawn.

4. Limiting collection prohibits organizations from collecting personal information indiscriminately or through deception. Each data element must have an identified purpose.

5. Limiting use, disclosure, and retention means organizations must use or disclose personal information only for the purposes for which it was collected. The company must retain personal information only as long as necessary to fulfill the identified and consented-to purpose.

6. Accuracy to ensure that personal information is correct, complete, and up to date. The validity of the data is the commercial enterprise's responsibility. Inferred is a process for identifying and correcting errors and cross-validating data.

7. Personal information must be secured against loss, theft, or unauthorized access. Safe destruction of the data is required when it is no longer needed. Always document data destruction.

8. Organizations must publish their information management policies to employees and customers. Make it easy to find and understand.

9. Individuals can request access to their personal information, determine its appropriate use, and be advised of the names of third parties to which it will be disclosed.

10. Legal guidelines for challenging a company's compliance to this Act. Individuals dissatisfied with a company's collection or use of their data have a legal process to correct it.

§ 17.11   SUMMARY

Project managers can be tasked to work in any area of a company. They must be aware of the various regulations that apply in different areas. Otherwise, when the project is ready to deliver its final product (and the project budget balance is about zero), they may face a long and expensive certification process that should have been incorporated in the product development.

If there is a company training module for compliance with some legal aspect, such as HIPAA or SOX, become aware of it before beginning an assignment. It should include local information and examples.

When a project is running late and scope is being closely scrutinized, there is a temptation to sidestep time-consuming compliance and documentation tasks. Even if no harm is done to the customer's data systems, it leaves open the possibility of legal sanctions at some point in the future. It may also leave the project manager open to pressure to avoid disclosure of an expedient shortcut.

Chapter 18

PRINCE2 The UK Standard

§ 18.01   INTRODUCTION

> "To improve is to change; to be perfect is to change often."
>
> —Winston Churchill

The project management method most familiar to project managers is the Project Management Institute (PMI) Project Management Body of Knowledge (PMBOK). However, other organizations have also tackled standardizing best practices into a formal model. One of these is PRINCE2, developed by the United Kingdom's Office of Government Commerce (OGC) (*http://www.ogc.gov.uk/prince2*).

PRINCE2 was created to improve project results. To maintain a high standard of implementation, OGC collaborates with a number of organizations to support PRINCE2. For example, the APM Group Ltd. (*http://www.prince2.org.uk*) is the official training accreditation organization for PRINCE2.

The manuals for PRINCE2 are available from The Stationery Office (TSO), the official publisher of PRINCE2.

> PRINCE, the older version of the process, is focused on IT projects. Some companies did not change to PRINCE2 since it is another variation of a method rather than an upgrade.

Some people feel that since PRINCE2 was created by a government entity that it is available to everyone for free. However, PRINCE2 is protected by copyright and, therefore, it is not in the public domain. People are free to use the materials, but the right to copy those materials must be secured from the copyright holder.

§ 18.02   WHAT IS PRINCE2?

PRINCE (Projects IN Controlled Environments) is a process-based project management method developed by the government of the United Kingdom and used internationally. It focuses on supporting information technology projects. PRINCE was based on the best practices from a variety of industries and was characterized by its templates and decision points.

In 1996, PRINCE2 was released as a generic (non-IT-focused) project management process. It is commonly used in the United Kingdom and many other countries for a wide range of endeavors. The latest update was published in 2005. Features of PRINCE2 are:

- A focus on the product and its business justification. The project plan is centered on the product creation as described by the customer.

- A clear project team structure describing authority, delegation, and communication. The roles and responsibilities of each team member are described before the project begins.

- Divides the project into manageable "stages" (similar to "milestones").

- Uses status reports to minimize routine meetings while focusing on exception handling.

- Ensures resource commitment from executives prior to proceeding to the next stage.

- Provides a common language across all stakeholders.

§ 18.03 PRINCE2 IS PRODUCT FOCUSED

PRINCE2 uses product-based planning rather than activity-based planning for creating and managing projects. It centers planning activities on the product deliverables with less emphasis on individual tasks. It measures progress against objectively measurable products rather than subjectively defined and measured activities.

A PRINCE2 project is driven by the project's business case. During the project, the case is reviewed to ensure the business objectives are still relevant to the products being produced.

[A] Product-Focused Planning

PRINCE2 provides a wide range of tools but it is up to the implementing authority to select the ones most appropriate for a given project. This flexibility allows tailoring to the project's size. However, it may compromise the integrity of the best practices used to create PRINCE2. Therefore, if a company adapts PRINCE2 as a standard, it could enable them to continue business as before but claim to be PRINCE2 compliant.

PRINCE2's product-based framework is applicable to any type of project. This is a three-step process.

1. Create a product breakdown structure that decomposes the project's final product into its basic components. This simplifies estimates, planning, and project

execution. PRINCE2 views all deliverable items as a "product" in one of two classes:

    a. Management products—lists, logs, and reports created to facilitate project execution

    b. Specialist products—components of the final product created by the project

2. Document complete product descriptions as soon as their requirement is identified. The description should contain the specifications and how each is measured for quality.

3. A product flow diagram illustrates the sequence of product creation during the project. This identifies dependencies and where products can be worked in parallel.

[B] Configuration Management

As can be imagined, a method that is product-centric would tightly control product configuration. PRINCE2 configuration management controls all project deliverables. The project's products are the primary assets created by it. Configuration management tracks each of the project's products from its initial description in the project definition to its final acceptance by the customer. Deviations to the baseline description must be approved. Deviations might be a recommended improvement or a forecast of a failure to complete something.

All changes are treated as "project issues." Anyone can raise an issue about any project-related topic. This is typically a request for change to a requirement or product. It may also be the result of a product failing to achieve a quality measurement.

All issues are recorded in the issues log. The project board decides who is responsible for approving issues for addition to the log. No issue is acted upon without approval.

> "We occasionally stumble over the truth, but most of us pick ourselves up and hurry off as if nothing had happened."
>
> —Winston Churchill

[C] Business Case

The business case proposes the problem to solve and explains the reasons why it is important to the company to perform the project. It demonstrates how the project's goals are aligned with the company's objectives. The owner of the business case is termed the project's "executive."

If a satisfactory business case does not exist, a project should not start. Review the business case at the end of each stage. If the business case changes significantly, either revise it or end the project.

The business case contains:

- Reasons for the project

- Options for different solutions

- Benefits expected from successfully completing the project

- Risks for the project, both of completing it and of not performing it

- A rough estimate of cost along with a brief explanation of what the estimate is based on

- Timeframes where the project fits into other efforts or is mandated for completion of other efforts

- An appraisal of the benefits to be derived from the project

[D]   Project Board

Each PRINCE2 project has a project board to oversee the project. The project manager reports regularly to the project board on progress and potential problems. The project board reviews results at each stage and decides if the project is to proceed. A project board consists of:

- Executive—The individual responsible for ensuring the project remains consistent with the business case, and that it meets its objectives

- Senior supplier—A representative of the group providing the technical resources to the project or to the product's ongoing maintenance. Examples are designers, developers, purchasing agents, and accounting personnel. The senior supplier has the authority to commit resources to the project.

- Senior user—A representative of the people who will be using the product or service created by the project. The senior user represents the interests of those who will be using the product and ensuring its functionality, ease of use, and quality.

The board reviews planning documents to ensure that the appropriate quality standards and company processes are used. It reviews the project documents to ensure that the project fits within the business strategy it supports. The project board also ensures that the appropriate people are involved with the project and that critical stakeholders are not excluded.

During project execution, the project manager regularly issues status reports to the board. However, meetings are not conducted unless the project is trending outside of acceptable limits. The board, based on information provided by the project manager, examines these exceptions. The project board approves all changes to the project definition, timeline, and budget.

When the project is ready to close, the project board examines and verifies that all of the project's products meet their goals and stated quality standards, and ensures that the project manager communicates the project closure to all stakeholders.

[E] Manage by Exception

PRINCE2 strikes a balance between keeping busy senior executives involved in a project and providing the project manager with latitude in managing the project's daily activities. It specifically tries to avoid regular time-consuming project status meetings.

The project board provides a set of tolerances for project execution based on the project plan. So long as the project resource utilization and timeline remain within these tolerances, the periodic status reports suffice for progress reporting. However, if a project exceeds or is about to exceed the stated tolerances, an exception report must be provided to the project board. Tolerances may be set for the project as a whole or for specific stages based on business risk.

An exception report explains what aspect of the project is trending out of tolerance, and gives the root cause of the problem. The report is accompanied with an action plan to address this specific situation and an analysis of any other parts of the project that may be affected. For example, if a resource has been underestimated for an activity early in the project, the estimates will be revisited every other time that resource is scheduled within the plan for future activities. An exception report includes:

- Cause of the problem
- Impact of the problem
- For each available option for future action, describe the impact to the:
  - Business case—Does this issue change the justification for the project?
  - Risk—Will this option reduce or increase future project risks?
  - Tolerances—Will this require an increase or tightening of project tolerances?

Create an exception plan to resolve most out-of-tolerance cases. This plan reexamines the remaining activities within that stage, including the out-of-tolerance issues, along with their mitigating activities. After the project board approves the exception plan, it replaces the remaining plans for that stage. It covers the period from the present to the end of the stage.

§ 18.04   PRINCE2'S EIGHT-STEP PROCESS

PRINCE2 breaks down a project into eight processes.

1. Start-up (SU): Select a project manager and define the project. Identify the processes for executing the project.

2. Initiate a project (IP): The project manager prepares the project initiation document for approval by the "project board."

3. Directing a project (DP): The "project board" monitors the overall success of the project and directs the project manager.

4. Planning (PL): The heart of the project. Select products to create and the activities required to create them. Estimate the time/cost required, analyze the risk, and create the schedule.

5. Controlling a stage (CS): The project is broken down into manageable stages. The conclusion of each stage is a decision point for the project board to halt the project or authorize resources to continue. The number of stages depends on the project's size and risk. Complete each stage before the next one begins (no overlap).

6. Manage product delivery (MP): The project manager validates the products to the schedule and project goals.

7. Manage stage boundaries (SB): Review the results of the current stage and update all paperwork. The plan for the next stage is developed. The project board approves the results and approves continuing to the next stage.

8. Closing the project (CP): All documents are completed and filed for project board review. The project manager conducts a post-project review to compare the product to the project initiation document.

> "The farther backward you can look the farther forward you are likely to see."
>
> —Winston Churchill

[A] Starting Up a Project

Efficient projects are the result of careful preparation. Start-up is a pre-project process that validates a project's viability and worthiness. It begins with a project mandate, which outlines the high-level reasons for the project and how to execute it. The project mandate describes:

- The business function that is requesting and authorizing the project
- Background to the project, which is usually an explanation of the business environment and customer interest
- Project objectives to generally describe what the project is to achieve
- Project scope to draw some boundaries around what is and, specifically, is not included within it
- Specific constraints within which the project must operate, such as budget, timeline, or quality
- Interfaces to other departments, products, or projects. For example, does this project rely on the product created in a previous project to be successful?
- Quality expectations for the final product. These will drive the product development and cost and are based on the business case.
- Project tolerances to guide the project manager
- Appointment of key project personnel, such as the executive and the project manager
- Identification of other interested parties

The startup phase identifies senior decision-makers for a project board to oversee the project. The project board selects the project manager. The project brief outlines the reasons for the project. The project's approach is decided, and the initiation stage plans are approved.

The following is a list of the steps involved in starting up a project.

- SU1. Appointing a project executive and a project manager
  - Project executive—The single person who owns the project and who ensures that objectives are met and results are delivered
  - Project manager—Has the authority and responsibility to manage the project day by day
- SU2. Designing a project management team

- ○ Produce a job description for each team member
- ○ Identify skills required and detail staff responsibilities
- ○ Senior supplier—Represents those supplying the products or solutions for the project
- ○ Senior user—Represents those who will ultimately benefit or use the outcome of the project
- ○ Project assurance—to work alongside the project in a "trust and verify" role
- SU3. Appointing a project management team
  - ○ Review job descriptions with team members to ensure everyone knows their responsibilities
  - ○ File the signed job descriptions and acceptances
- SU4. Preparing a project brief based on the project mandate to include:
  - ○ Project definition
  - ○ Outline of the business case
  - ○ Project tolerances—The margin of error open to the project manager to manage at his or her discretion. When this is exceeded, an "exception" is said to have occurred
  - ○ Customer's quality expectations
  - ○ Acceptance criteria
  - ○ Risk assessment of the likelihood of the project's success given the information contained in the project mandate
- SU5. Defining project approach—Decide if the project is to be produced in-house or the solution purchased from elsewhere (make or buy decision).
- SU6. Planning initiation stage—Create a plan for initiating a project for approval by the project board.

The key products created by the start-up stage include:

- Project mandate
- Project brief
- Job descriptions
- Risk log
- Initiation stage plan

[B]   Initiating a Project

This process lays the foundation for managing the project effort. Collect information describing the business case and prepare it in a document format.

The project manager gathers information on how the project will be conducted for review by the project board. This is a critical action toward the project board accepting ownership for the project.

The resulting product is the Project Initiation Document (PID), which must be approved by the project board. The project manager plans the next stage for approval by the project board. A PID builds on information included in the project mandate.

Initiating a project has the following elements:

- IP1. Planning quality—Detail quality-monitoring responsibilities, criteria, and configuration management plan.

- IP2. Planning a project—Create a project plan based on the project approach, project brief, and quality plan. The plan must:
  - identify all of the project's products
  - include countermeasures to risks and assumptions
  - estimate resources required (time, money, and skills)

- IP3. Refining the business case and risks—Refine the justification for the project. Evaluate business risks and review with the project board.

- IP4. Setting up project controls
  - Create a communications plan so that all interested parties are notified of the project's progress
  - Establish project change control procedures

- IP5. Setting up project files—Create project files for use throughout the project. Examples are the issues log, quality log, and lessons learned file.

- IP6. Assembling a project initiation document
  - Project's background—updated from the project mandate to include clarifications
  - Project definition—updated from the project mandate to include clarifications
  - Organization—as created during the start-up phase
  - Communications plan—describes how the team members will communicate, minimally how often and in what format

○ Quality plan—a description of how to conduct the quality assurance and control programs. It is based on how each product is to be measured and includes information from company and industry standards. Assign specific responsibilities to ensure the products adhere to the business case, etc.

○ Tolerances—the amount of leeway the project manager has in executing the project without further reference to the project board

○ Controls—description of the change control process to ensure that product configuration is closely controlled

○ Business case—updated from the project mandate to include clarifications

○ Project plan—Attach a copy of the project plan

○ Risk log—Creation of a risk management log containing all risks known to the project to date.

The key products created by the start-up stage include:

• Project initiation document

• Quality plan explaining the key products to create and how they will be measured

• Identify stage boundaries

• Resources required (time and money)

[C] Directing a Project

The "project board" consists of members of senior management. The project board has overall responsibility for directing the project (DP). The board authorizes the commitment of resources to each stage of the project, reviews risks to ensure that they are properly monitored, and makes decisions requested by the project manager.

The project manager provides periodic status reports to the project board. The project board primarily focuses on exceptions and avoids routine status meetings. Board members sit in on stage completion and initiation reviews.

Following is a list of elements involved in DP.

• DP1. Authorizing initiation—Approve the project brief and business case project initiation document.

• DP2. Authorizing a project—Approve the project initiation document that authorizes the project to proceed.

- DP3. Authorizing a stage or exception plan—Authorize the commitment of additional resources based on results to date.
  - A stage plan is a project schedule for one stage of the project.
  - An exception plan is a replacement stage plan based on actions to mitigate an adverse situation.
- DP4. Giving ad hoc direction—Monitor progress and react to exceptional situations. Provide ongoing advice to the project manager.
- DP5. Confirming project closure once the project is completed or terminated. It ensures an organized hand-off of any product to the customer.

"Let our advance worrying become advance thinking and planning."

—Winston Churchill

[D] Planning

The planning process has the steps that are traditionally associated with project management. It identifies the products to produce, the activities required to produce the products, and the resources needed. Create a project schedule and an analysis of the risks. These documents should be maintained throughout the project's "life."

The anchor for the project is a clear description of what is to be produced, including a description of all quality verification points. Translate this "what" into a plan detailing how it the products are to be created and what resources are required. The result will be an estimate of time and money required, along with a list of risks to be considered.

PRINCE2 uses work packages to represent project activities. A work package contains:

- Description of work to be done
- Description of products to create
- Techniques to use—Standard company or industry practices to follow
- Interfaces to satisfy—Create linkages into other project components
- Interfaces to maintain—Ensure that changes do not undo the work of previous work packages
- Estimate of resources required—time, cost, skills, etc. required to complete the work package. This is a joint agreement between the project manager and the person working on the package

- Constraints—Any limitation placed on this task, such as a firm timeline, critical to quality specification, etc.

- Independent quality verification arrangement—When and how the quality of the work packages' products will be checked

- Reporting—How information about the status of work will be conveyed to the project manager

- Requirements for the finished product before the work package is complete

Planning elements include:

- PL1. Designing a plan—The planning approach is used to create a project plan. The plan lists the actions, time estimates, and costs to create the project's products. Estimates may be top-down, bottom-up, or based on industry standards.

- PL2. Defining and analyzing products—Focus planning on the project's products. Describe all of the intermediate products produced during the project along with their quality measurements and sequence.

- PL3. Identifying activities and dependencies—Identify interdependencies between tasks to ensure they are properly sequenced. Identify tasks assigned to external organizations.

- PL4. Estimating—Include the details of the time and resources for each activity: skills required, level of expertise, and assumptions made in identifying this resource.

- PL5. Scheduling—This encompasses the steps of sequencing activities into a network that identifies dependencies and a logical sequence of work. This initial schedule assumes that all resources will be available when needed. After the draft is completed, it is re-evaluated to ensure that resources are not overcommitted for a given time period.

- PL6. Analyzing risks—Evaluate every activity and resource in the project plan for risks of assumptions proven incorrect, or that an activity will overrun its estimates. Add mitigation actions into the plan to reduce the possibility or avoid adverse situations.

- PL7. Completing a plan—Total the resulting estimates of time and cost to create an initial project budget. The plan and all of its supporting analyses and assumptions are presented to the project board. Based on this information, the project board establishes tolerance margins for the project. This is the project's baseline.

[E]   Controlling a Stage

PRINCE2 uses "stages" to break the project into manageable pieces. A stage is a portion of the project that concludes in a decision point. It provides a place for the project board to pause and review how well the project's performance to date compares to its business case. The project board approves the planning for the next stage as capable of meeting its objectives.

The number of stages in a project depends on the project's complexity and risk. Some of the stages deal primarily with administrative details, such as the startup. Other stages are technical and are where the project's actual product is created. Stage control covers the day-to-day monitoring and control activities of the project.

Controlling a stage is event driven and based on project performance. It details the responsibilities of the project manager, such as assigning tasks, ensuring quality, managing changes, etc. The project manager ensures that product development stays within acceptable quality limits, schedule limits, and resource utilization. Following is a list of steps included in controlling a stage.

- CS1. Authorizing a work package—This is the point where the project manager assigns work packages to specific team members.

- CS2. Assessing progress—The project manager reviews the checkpoint reports and quality log to update the stage plan.

- CS3. Capturing project issues—The project manager captures issues into the issues log and issues change control notices as required to resolve the issues.

- CS4. Examining project issues—The project manager examines the issues log and updates the risk log as appropriate.

- CS5. Reviewing stage status—The project manager compares project progress to the plan and its acceptable tolerances. If performance is outside of the tolerances, then the issues are escalated.

- CS6. Reporting highlights—Create a highlight (status) report for the project board, based on the communications plan.

- CS7. Taking corrective action—Determine the root cause of deviations and update the stage plan.

- CS8. Escalating project issues—Create an exception report for the project board describing the impact on the business case.

- CS9. Receiving completed work package—Ensure that the work package is the same as the product description and is confirmed as the package configuration baseline.

The key products created by the controlling stage include:

- Work package
- Highlight report
- Exception report
- Checkpoint report

[F]   Managing Product Delivery

PRINCE2 focuses on product creation. It ensures that the team's work is authorized and accepted by checking work packages for completeness and quality. PRINCE2 considers anything created by the project—including documents—to be a product. A product is not finished until it has been accepted by the customer. The project manager ensures that suppliers produce the correct products at the right time.

Depending on the size of the project, there may be team leaders appointed to assist the project manager. A team leader is a technical person skilled in a single discipline, such as networking or disaster recovery. That person receives the work package, verifies that it is complete, and ensures its execution is within tolerances. A list of managing product delivery elements follows.

- MP1. Accepting a work package—The team leader reviews the work package and lays out the tasks involved for the team to deliver the product within tolerances.

- MP2. Executing a work package—The team leader (or project manager) monitors execution of the work package, ensuring that the appropriate quality checks are performed and status reports are made at the appropriate time. If an offsite supplier performs the work, the team leader ensures that it meets all required quality measurements.

- MP3. Delivering a work package—The team leader submits the finished product to configuration management for delivery.

[G]   Managing Stage Boundaries

The project manager updates the business case, the project plan, and the risks and issues logs to reflect the completed stage and the upcoming stage. The project manager also verifies that the project's progress supports the business case and that performance remains within tolerances. At the end of each stage, the project manager conducts a "lessons learned" session to capture team impressions and experiences.

The project board approves the completion of each stage prior to beginning the next stage. Approval is based on the satisfactory completion of all products in the current stage. The project board bases its decision on the project manager's assessment of the likelihood for the continued success of the project. Managing stage boundaries includes the following elements.

- SB1. Planning a stage—The project manager reviews the next stage plan in the project plan.

- SB2. Updating a project plan—The project manager updates the stage plan.

- SB3. Updating the project business case—The project manager reviews and updates costs, timing, and benefits in the business case. As needed, the manager presents changes to the business case to the project board.

- SB4. Updating the risk log—The project manager reviews risks for the upcoming stage and updates the risk log to reflect changes.

- SB5. Reporting stage end—As the stage nears its end, the project manager creates a report for the project board detailing variances between the planned schedule and actual requirements. The report includes a copy of the issues log.

- SB6. Producing an exception plan—This is created when a stage's performance exceeds tolerances. The exception plan details how the remaining tasks of the stage will be completed; it is approved by the project board.

[H]   Closing a Project

After a project has delivered all of its products or services, it is ready for a controlled closure. This involves a post-project review in which lessons learned are recorded and formal acceptance is made of the project's products by the project board. A project is to be closed even if cancelled prior to completion. Most of this effort is to prepare information for the project board to obtain approval to close the project.

Closing a project can be tedious because of the many details, large and small, that must be addressed. The project initiation document (PID) must be checked and every product delivered to the customer's satisfaction. The customer and technical support team must take over ongoing maintenance of the product where the project left off. Finally, the project manager must notify all stakeholders that the project is closed.

The majority of this administrative work is to gain approval from the project board to close the project. These steps may be performed in parallel. Product closure is also a good time to look back and congratulate the project team on its accomplishments.

Closing a project involves the following elements:

- CP1. Decommissioning a project—The project manager hands over the finished products. The goal is to obtain formal agreement by the customer and the supplier that the project has met its goals. Inform all project stakeholders that the project has concluded.
- CP2. Identifying follow-on actions—The project manager documents any required follow-up actions and coordinates a post-project review meeting.
- CP3. Project evaluation review—Look back over the entire project for areas of excellence and where things went wrong. Compare the initial quality plan against the final product delivered. Review the initial risk assessment and the actual events.

The key products created by the closing stage include:

- End project report
- Lessons learned report

§ 18.05 MANAGEMENT OF RISK

Projects are unique undertakings into the unknown. A risk may have a negative or positive effect on the success of the project. A risk may come from a too-low estimate of time or expense. It may come from diminished executive support or from failure of a supplier. The project manager monitors risks to keep them within acceptable bounds using three principles.

- Risk tolerance
- Risk responsibility
- Risk ownership

Managing risk is an essential part of project management. All projects have the risk of failure, budget overrun, timeline overrun, poor product quality, etc. The identification and minimization of risk is at the heart of project planning. PRINCE2 addresses this in two parts:

- Risk analysis—Identify risks and record them in the risk log.
- Risk management—Monitor and control the likelihood, impact, or degree of warning of adverse situations.
  - Estimation—Assess the potential of occurrence and possible impact.

- ○ Evaluation—Determine which risks to accept and which ones require mitigation actions.

- ○ Ownership—Assign someone to monitor the risk.

The project board makes the decisions on the project manager's recommended reactions to risk. The project board notifies the project manager of external risks to the project. Risk tracking begins with the project initiation document and continues throughout the life of the project.

§ 18.06   QUALITY IN A PROJECT ENVIRONMENT

PRINCE2 defines quality as all quantifiable product dimensions requested by the customer. Steps for monitoring product quality are detailed in the project mandate, project brief, and project initiation document. Throughout the life of the project, the quality of products is verified against the project's quality plan.

PRINCE2 uses a project quality plan that explains all of the processes and specifications in a single document. The quality plan has four main elements:

- Quality management system—Outlines how products are checked.

- Quality assurance function—Verifies that the processes and tools used to make the products are suitable for creating a correct output.

- Quality control—Verifies that the processes delivered the intended results.

- Customer's quality expectations—A customer's quality expectations are defined before the project begins.

PRINCE2's project board provides additional quality management. The three different perspectives, represented by user, supplier, and executive, ensure that the various perspectives of product quality are all included in the final product.

Product assurance is responsible for providing an independent view of how the project is progressing. In PRINCE2, there are three views of assurance: business, user, and specialist. Each view reflects the interests of the three project board members. Assurance is responsible for checking that the project remains viable in terms of costs and benefits (business assurance), checking that the users' requirements are being met (user assurance), and that the project is delivering a suitable solution (specialist or technical assurance). On some projects, the assurance is done by a separate team known as the project assurance team, but the assurance job can also be done by the individual members of the project board.

§ 18.07 STRENGTHS AND WEAKNESSES OF PRINCE2

PRINCE2 has a number of strengths:

- It produces standardized projects that share a common approach, vocabulary, and documents. Consequently, employees familiar with the method can join a properly applied PRINCE2 project with minimal preparation.

- It is a method that embodies best practices in project management.

- It enshrines management by exception as a guiding rule, which allows the project manager to work with minimal interference. Executives are not involved until things go badly off plan, or in PRINCE terms, out of tolerance.

- It provides a controlled start, middle, and end for projects.

- Each type of document required by PRINCE2 is supplied as a template, which produces standardized documentation.

- It can be tailored to the needs of a specific organization and/or project.

PRINCE2 has the following weaknesses:

- PRINCE had considerable specific organizational training (OT) best practices included in it. PRINCE2's drive to become generic removed these, such as the practice of post-deployment of a software application. The product's life cycle requirements are not included. Once the application is delivered, the project is considered closed and a new project is required to continue life cycle support. Other programs, such as Capability Maturity Model Integration (CMMI), have subdisciplines specific to the type of project that adds in the best practices for what is unique.

- PRINCE2's considerable paperwork distracts project managers from focusing on the project itself.

- PRINCE2 is long on implementation and short on requirements analysis. Projects built on false premises will fail.

- PRINCE2 may impose significant overhead on small and medium-sized efforts.

- Reference and training books essential for the training courses are quite expensive.

- Companies may claim to use PRINCE2, but ignore any parts of it that are inconvenient. This destroys the benefit from using carefully interrelated techniques. It would help if companies promoting themselves as "PRINCE2" compliant were certified by an outside organization, similar to ISO 9000.

§ 18.08   CERTIFICATION IN PRINCE2

Like PMI's PMP certification, practitioners of PRINCE2 are certified in their knowledge and ability to apply the techniques to a project. The Office of Government Commerce's partner, the APM Group, controls training for the exams. APM Group accredits companies to provide training and administer exams. There are two levels of PRINCE2 certification:

- Foundation examination—A one-hour exam of 75 multiple-choice questions about the PRINCE2 method. Thirty-eight correct answers are required to pass. The foundation training and exam are suitable for anyone who will participate in a PRINCE2 project. The foundation level details the fundamentals of project management and acquaints students with the PRINCE2 process and terminology. To pass the exam, participants must understand the purpose and roles of the eight process components and their subprocesses and techniques. Knowledge of the major management products is required.

- Practitioner examination—Open to anyone who has passed the foundation exam, the practitioner test is a three-hour case-based examination. This examination tests the candidate's ability to apply PRINCE2 techniques to running a project. The candidate is expected to execute and tune an existing PRINCE2 project. The examination explores all of the processes and their components and how to apply them to a given situation. It requires an understanding of what goes into PRINCE2 products.

The typical training school approach to PRINCE2 certification is to provide an intensive week-long training session. During this session, both the foundation and practitioner's exams are offered.

An alternative is to purchase the books or an online course to study PRINCE2. The exams are offered at several places in the United Kingdom and, on occasion, outside of it. However, these exams are not cheap—it may make better sense (and like a good project manager, reduce some of the risk) to attend the one-week course.

§ 18.09   HOW DOES PRINCE2 COMPARE TO PMI'S PMBOK?

Both PRINCE2 and PMI's PMBOK are valuable tools for organizing and managing projects to a successful completion. The differences described here are purely for contrasting the two and not a condemnation of either approach. Skilled project managers are expert "borrowers" and use the best aspects of any technique to improve their ability to complete a project satisfactorily.

At this point, PRINCE2 and PMI's PMBOK are the two major players in project management processes. There are likely others around but both of these are internationally recognized.

In general, PRINCE2 is more of a "cookbook" wherein it lays out many of the details that PMBOK implies or expects project managers to already know. PRINCE2 provides a tool kit of standard templates which tends to force a more methodical approach to tasks, where PMI's PMBOK leaves these decisions to the project manager's discretion.

Another interesting difference is in the breadth of the two processes. PRINCE2 focuses on implementation while PMBOK begins with talking to the customer so as to turn vague ideas into a proposal.

This comparison is not exhaustive and is intended only to contrast the two techniques. In both cases, the local organization must tailor the process to meet their specific requirements and filter out unnecessary action.

[A]   PMBOK Advantages

- PMBOK describes a more responsible project manager with interfaces to a sponsor, while PRINCE2's project manager handles day-to-day issues under the strategic direction of a project board.

- PMBOK shows its governmental roots by its detailed chapter on project procurement.

- PMBOK encourages use of earned value to monitor progress and detect problems.

- PMBOK details issues around people, such as team acquisition planning, training, team building, and recognition.

[B]   PRINCE2 Advantages

- PRINCE2's eight processes are more detailed than PMBOK's five phases.

- PRINCE2's forms make it easier to provide consistency between projects within an organization. The local organization must establish guidelines for small, medium, and large projects to determine which level of documentation is required for a given effort.

- PRINCE2 has a formal and detailed set of customer expectation requirements including quality measurements.

- Project execution is more detailed in terms of planning, assigning work, and validating results. (PMBOK stays at a higher level.)

- PRINCE2 provides a more detailed change management process.

- PRINCE2's project and stage tolerances are more detailed than PMBOK's contingency approach.
- PRINCE2 provides a more formal project organization than PMBOK.

[C]   Evaluation

- PRINCE2's stage is essentially the same as a PMBOK phase.
- The product breakdown schedule is essentially the same as a work breakdown structure There are differences, but both break down the whole project into manageable pieces.
- PRINCE2's PID is similar to PMBOK's project charter but contains more detail. However, many companies use a more comprehensive charter which incorporates the same areas as PRINCE—not surprising since PRINCE was based on best practices.

There are some very good reference sites for PRINCE2, with new ones emerging every day. Professionals need to demonstrate their expertise through certification, and then continue to build their understanding by learning about different ways to address project issues.

Some of the better-known web sites are:

- The official PRINCE2 Website: *http://www.ogc.gov.uk/prince2/*
- The governing body for PRINCE2 worldwide is APM Group, Ltd.: *http://www.prince2.org.uk*
- A set of PRINCE2 templates are available for download from *http://www.ogc.gov.uk/prince2/downloads/view.htm*
- The Project Management Institute has a wealth of information on all aspects of project management at *www.pmi.org*

"You can always count on Americans to do the right thing—after they've tried everything else."

—Winston Churchill

---

§ 18.10 SUMMARY

PRINCE2 provides a valuable and easy-to-understand approach to project management. The processes follow a logical flow and build on the results of the previous ones. Smaller projects could manage nicely using fewer of the PRINCE2 products.

PRINCE2's project board is an interesting alternative to PMBOK's project sponsor. By including the key supplier of resources and the user of the final product in a committee with the project executive, the critical perspectives are always available when reaching project decision points. PMBOK includes these under the communications plan and in managing stakeholders, but PRINCE2 keeps them firmly in the decision-making process.

PRINCE2's step-by-step approach ensures that the project manager gathers the essential information at the right time during the project and avoids trying to recreate it later. For occasional or new project managers, PRINCE2's forms and detailed approach will provide a high-quality project.

However, the very things that make PRINCE2 so useful are also its downfall. Lock-step actions, decision points, and numerous documents add an administrative burden to the project manager. For this methodology to be effective, the entire organization must understand and adhere to the PRINCE2 approach. Otherwise, a well-intentioned project manager will be swamped in documents that mean nothing to anyone else.

> "One ought never to turn one's back on a threatened danger and try to run away from it. If you do that, you will double the danger. But if you meet it promptly and without flinching, you will reduce the danger by half. Never run away from anything. Never!"
>
> —Winston Churchill

Chapter 19

Capability Maturity Model™

§ 19.01　INTRODUCTION

"Dare to the level of your capability then go beyond to a higher level."

—Alexander Haig

Software development has always been a problem. The IT trade press is littered with stories of multimillion dollar projects so riddled with defects that the entire effort was scrapped. Even if a problem project continues, it runs far longer than planned and costs much more than expected. Given this poor record of project performance, executives everywhere are looking for ways to improve the predictability of project outcomes.

One approach is to create models of how effective companies conduct their projects to a successful conclusion. This framework of best practices is then compared to how an individual company actually works. Several of these models are OPM3™ by PMI, P3M3 by the United Kingdom's Office of Government Commerce, and CMM by the Software Engineering Institute at Carnegie-Mellon University. Each of these models:

- Identifies standard practices that should be followed
- Has different levels to indicate organizational "maturity"

- Provides a process for comparing an organization to the "ideal"

- Provides training on their model

- Has their own following of consultants ready to do all this for you.

> CMMI is not an all-or-nothing arrangement. Many companies are content to achieve CMMI level 3 and then approach their quality issues using difference techniques.

§ 19.02   BACKGROUND

The United States Air Force funded the original study for a capability maturity model (CMM) at Carnegie-Mellon's Software Engineering Institute. The purpose was to create an objective way to evaluate software subcontractors' ability to produce quality software on time and on budget.

The CMM is a framework of practices for improving software development. It centers on engineering software, managing its development, and providing ongoing maintenance. CMM uses questionnaires and analysis to rate an organization's software development capabilities into one of five maturity levels. Each level contains a set of practices an effective organization uses to improve software development capabilities.

Multiple CMMs were developed over time to handle various IT areas, such as software acquisition, systems engineering, and integrated product and process development. Originally released in 1990, CMM has been updated and adapted for use in other fields. This presents a challenge for companies utilizing multiple models, so CMM Integration, or CMMI, was created to provide a unified solution. CMMI combines these different CMMs into a unified approach that eliminates the difficulties of using several different models simultaneously.

[A]   Benefits of CMMI

A company's CMMI level of maturity can be gauged through a process called SCAMPI (Standard CMMI Appraisal Method for Process Improvement^{TM}). In order to actually set about improving, organizations should either develop their own methods or take a cue from existing management theories on implementing improvements. As with all organizational changes, CMMI will fail unless the company's management team actively supports it.

A successful CMMI implementation rewards an organization with more predictable software development projects. All projects are a journey into the unknown, but if everyone uses the same standard processes, the company can better predict the quality, time required, and cost of a project. Also, when everyone is using the same processes (essentially) the same way, the processes can be continuously adjusted for better performance.

> The requirements for some of CMMI's key process areas are also found in other quality improvement techniques, such as ISO, TQM, and Six Sigma. If a company is already using some of these programs, the transition to CMMI will be easier and faster.

Organizations can use CMMI as a guideline for improvement in best software development practices. This can lead to more accurate estimations for project schedules and budgets and a substantially more stable development environment. The improved environment will help yield superior quality software (relative to the current quality of the organization's software) in a predictable time on a stable budget.

§ 19.03   FIVE LEVELS OF CMMI

CMMI has five levels of increasing process maturity, as shown in Chart 19-1:

- Level 1—Initial: Chaos, as everyone does their own thing.
- Level 2—Repeatable: Standard practices appear to track cost, schedule, and functionality. Similar projects are getting similar results.
- Level 3—Defined: Company processes are documented and used throughout the software development program.
- Level 4—Managed: Time to measure how well the processes work so they can be tuned as needed. Software development processes become measurable and verifiable.
- Level 5—Optimizing: Continuous process improvement from quantitative feedback and piloting innovative ideas.

  Each level is broken down into key process areas (KPAs) which address:

- Support, process management;
- Project management; and
- Engineering.

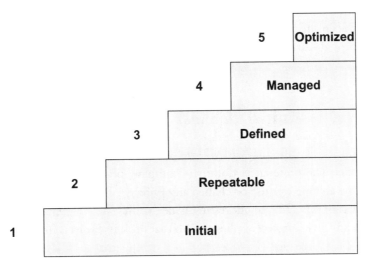

Chart 19-1: Five Levels of CMMI

A company's rating is determined by its adherence to that level's KPAs. Each level is obtained sequentially. The rating is based on the lowest level for which the company does not meet all of the KPAs. The reasoning is that part of achieving each of levels 2, 3, and 4 is to provide a solid base for advancement to the next level. To some extent, most companies use KPAs from all levels.

Companies have encountered problems implementing CMM. The biggest problem occurs in companies already using a waterfall technique for requirements creation, planning, and procedures. These organizations try to convert the waterfall technique into CMM, which results in either a watered-down waterfall approach or a weak CMM.

Criticisms of CMMI

- There is no emphasis on architecting processes such as deployments, which are important for project success.
- CMMI emphasizes traditional quality control methods that are used after the defects have been created and is not focused on prevention.
- CMMI reviews reveal defects, but do not reveal structural problems in the software.
- CMMI's heavy documentation requirements are contrary to driving simplicity into processes.

> • CMMI credits an organization for performing an activity, but it does not ensure it was done correctly. Doing the right thing the wrong way provides a false security.

[A] Level 1—Initial (Chaos)

In an organization classified as "CMMI level 1," everyone pretty much does what he or she sees fit. Personal preferences dominate company practices and results are unpredictable (since anyone can use or change any process). Projects are run in an ad hoc basis, blundering forward and addressing issues as they are encountered. The process followed for any given project applies only to that project. Projects frequently run over budget and over schedule.

Consider level 1 as a starting point. Before something can improve, it must have a baseline from which to improve. A CMMI assessment at this point identifies the gaps between what the processes are and what they should be. Remember, all organizations, at any given time, function in various parts of every level of CMM.

A level 1 organization lacks a stable environment for software development. It depends on poor practices and does not use recognized project management techniques. Even the best software engineers and programmers cannot compensate for lack of support and mismanagement. Plans change frequently. As problems arise, plans are abandoned for ad hoc actions.

Key Process Areas to Achieve a Level 1 Designation

Until they are formally rated, all organizations are rated as level 1. Level 1 does not have any key process areas (how can someone measure chaos?) as the organization lacks systematic methods.

> "If the staff lacks policy guidance against which to test decisions, their decisions will be random."
>
> —Donald Rumsfeld

[B] Level 2—Managed

Level 2 organizations use a consistent set of practices that are repeatable for any software project. Its processes document basic project data such as budget, schedule, and software progress. The organization now has the discipline necessary to repeat past successes. The primary level 2 focus is on project level activities.

Level 2 organization policies are established and practiced. New projects are planned and managed based on experience. For each project:

- Software requirements are formally solicited and controlled throughout the project's duration.
- Project managers track costs, schedule, and product configuration.
- Subcontractors are carefully managed and treated as "partners in success."
- Formal product and project quality programs are established.

Key Process Areas to Achieve a Level 2 Designation

Level 2 KPAs help an organization develop repeatable successes. These competencies form a solid base for developing level 3 practices.

[1]   Support

[a]   Configuration Management

Configuration management (CM) ensures that each feature of the final product maps to a feature in the design specifications. Each of the specifications includes an explanation of what is needed and why. (Once the baseline product definition is set, all changes must be carefully controlled to verify that the customer truly wants the change and that the schedule and project budget have been updated to reflect the change.)

Configuration management ensures that approved processes and tools (such as forms) are used as designed. A fast, easy-to-use process is provided that manages suggestions for improvement. This ensures that standard processes remain standard and a mechanism is available to promptly incorporate continuous improvement in all tools. However, unauthorized changes are never permitted.

Consider the collection of standard software development tools used daily by the developers. A standard tool set makes people mobile between teams, and eases future support staffing.

[b]   Measurement and Analysis

This KPA describes collecting data to develop sound management policies. Developing a strong measurement and analysis (MA) program involves setting relevant metrics for activities for which a measurement can be consistently taken. After analysis, this information is used to create a defined, managed process. This information will help in making future estimates on budget and schedule, as well as helping determine whether one method of software development is generally superior or inferior to another for developing quality software.

Implementing systematic measurement provides an organization with feedback on process performance. A review of this data can detect problems and trends before they become critical. It also provides for budget and schedule decisions, as well as identifying which practices are more and less effective than others.

[c]   Process and Product Quality Assurance

For process and product quality assurance (PPQA), management and the technical staff develop objective methods of understanding the current state of the project. This involves making plans to perform software quality assurance activities, such as a peer review of code and testing. All involved parties need to be aware of these plans. Verify that software development processes are following company standards and procedures. An issue that cannot be solved within the group or organization is brought to the attention of upper management.

These activities ensure that quality code is developed in a consistent manner so that later on, little or no crisis-mitigation is needed to keep the project on track. The benefits of PPQA in short are that all software development activities have a meaningful result and that the project does not stray far from its intended scope.

[d]   Supplier Agreement Management

Supplier agreement management (SAM) develops a formal agreement for acquisitions necessary for operations. Part of SAM is to determine how products are acquired and how they are incorporated into the project. It also includes supplier selection. For each of these parts, a formal process is developed and documented.

A sound SAM policy decreases the likelihood of the organization suddenly falling short of needed materials. Also, forming good relationships with suppliers may result in preferential treatment during a shortage, or perhaps result in better prices.

[2]   Project Management

[a]   Project Monitoring and Control

Project monitoring and control (PMC) is monitoring and understanding the project's progress. This entails regular monitoring of both the project's plan and its execution. In the event that the project has gone awry, a plan to fix the situation is created, executed, and revised until the problem has been resolved. Project progress monitoring may be an enterprise-wide effort.

The benefits of PMC are that it complements PPQA in guiding process progress. PMC is a warning system that something has or is about to happen.

[b] Project Planning

Project planning (PP) establishes and maintains plans to map out activities for the project. Estimates for completion of various tasks, along with actual time and resources utilized for completion, are documented. These are used to help make plans for monitoring progress. Also, those involved with the project agree to their roles for the period of development.

Project planning is a crucial practice for reliably completing any project in a set amount of time. It helps determine where the project is at any given time, and to determine where it is going.

[3] Engineering

[a] Requirements Management

Requirements management (RM) seeks to methodically divide the duties of developing various parts of the software to various team members. All products, plans, and activities align with software system requirements. This prevents multiple people from tackling the same task while leaving others unfinished. More importantly, it helps to ensure that tasks that need to be accomplished are worked on and no work is done on unnecessary tasks.

[C] Level 3—Defined

At level 3, companies see a dramatically improved performance over level 2. It creates, publishes, and trains employees in the use of standard project management practices for use across the organization.

A level 3 organization has a standard set of integrated documented processes. All software projects use these processes during planning and execution. They are updated as necessary to reflect better practices.

Organization-wide training is used to ensure that all employees have a proper understanding of the standards. All activities are still stable and repeatable and relevant data are collected.

Key Process Areas to Achieve a Level 3 Designation

The goal at level 3 is to have all processes laid out and well established in the form of accessible documentation.

[1] Support

[a] Decision Analysis and Resolution

Decision analysis and resolution (DAR) is the practice of analyzing potential decisions using an objective, formal evaluation process. This process identifies the optimal solution given the situation. One of the more important aspects of DAR is to develop a solid list of alternative solutions so that each is evaluated for strengths and weaknesses. Obviously, some decisions are more critical than others or will have more solutions than others—for items like "how often should the lawn be mowed" or "should the leaky roof be repaired," large amounts of deliberation and discussion may not be required.

However, issues such as "what programming language should be used for this project" merit detailed discussion. As always, a defined process with a consistent evaluation methodology helps. This is one place it is especially important to continually revise and improve the process so that the evaluation tools are not skewed toward one or two schools of thought.

A decision analysis and resolution policy is an objective, systematic method of handling a problem and developing a conclusion that incorporates sound decisions.

[2] Process Management

[a] Organizational Process Definition

For maintaining an organizational process definition (OPD), develop and keep up-to-date a standard set of processes by which activities are performed. The way the standard affects projects should be documented and regularly reviewed. Both the standard and the comments regarding its implementation should be public within the organization. These processes are the way by which a company conducts its daily affairs and provides direction on the best way to achieve a certain goal. There should be enough information stored so that if a critical manager or technical staffer leaves the company, the processes still make sense.

The main benefit of an OPD is that the knowledge developed over time will not be lost when critical employees depart the company.

[b] Organizational Process Focus

Organizational process focus (OPF) entails monitoring and improving the organization's software development process. Activities are directed toward developing and improving the process; specifically, identifying the strengths and weaknesses of the process and how it can be further improved.

By having employees focus on processes, the organization should be able to improve their existing procedures for handling projects. These changes should reflect better ideas that have come around over time.

[c]   Organizational Training

It is important to keep both the developers and managers up to date. Organizational training (OT) deals with planning instruction activities for skills and knowledge needed by employees. Without proper training, employees may struggle an inordinate amount of time learning something that could more easily be taught in an efficient manner.

Training is not a one-time deal; it should become a permanent part of the organization's procedure for helping employees grow in their positions and helping them become capable of carrying out future projects successfully. Accordingly, training on an organization-wide basis needs to have a defined process set in place for company use.

Organizational training should help everyone to carry out his or her responsibilities in an effective manner. It can prevent unnecessary trial and error in the learning process.

[3]   *Project Management*

[a]   Integrated Project Management

Integrated project management (IPM) is the practice of working with project stakeholders to gather input on important issues. A stakeholder here can be the end customer, the technical staff developing the product, or anyone else affected by the project or the resulting product. IPM addresses stakeholder concerns in a timely fashion during product development. Stakeholders should be consulted not only at the beginning of a project and during a crisis, because this style of contact makes a messenger from the organization a harbinger of bad news. Also, routine consultation with stakeholders could avert problems. The company should develop a formal method of conducting IPM and then document it.

The benefits of IPM are that if the client says "apples" and somehow the organization hears "fruit," then oranges will not be produced for more than a very short time before this is corrected and apples are once again made. If that analogy doesn't make sense, think that IPM keeps everyone on the same page or helps everyone know what needs to be happening and when.

[b]   Risk Management

The practice of risk management (RSKM) identifies potential problems before they happen. Obviously, it is not possible to predict every problem that could arise. This is one of the places that information about past problems is most useful, as it will help with identifying and analyzing risks. Once a list of risks has been developed, a plan should be made on how to rectify the situation should it arise. RSKM is one of the processes that benefits the most from having not only a well-defined process available, but also a large amount of data available.

Risk management prevents or quickly mitigates threats, such as a mainframe or server being zapped by a power surge or an important developer having to leave for a family emergency when a project is due very soon. While risk management cannot prevent every mishap, it can help protect the company from the fallout from some disasters.

[4] Engineering

[a] Requirements Development

The idea behind requirements development (RD) is to formally create and analyze customer, product, and product subcomponent requirements. These requirements will be used as the basis for product design. RD involves formulating requirements based on customer needs, and then elaborating on these to further develop guidelines necessary for software success. A formal process for requirements development should be defined and documented.

If the client says "I want fruit," but in his mind he sees a bunch of grapes, it is important to find this out before developing a lot of bananas. Practicing RD will help a little with "reading the mind" of a client or other stakeholder.

[b] Product Integration

Product integration (PI) is the process by which all of the product components are assembled. The product as a whole is tested to ensure that the components were properly integrated and that it interfaces properly with all relevant internal and external components. When this has been done, the product is then delivered. As with the other KPAs, it is important that lessons learned are recorded and molded into a repeatable process that the organization can use.

Just because all of the parts of a program have been finished does not mean they function together. One of the main benefits of PI is to make sure that all the parts work together so that a product with many good components does not fail in production.

[c] Technical Solution

The technical solution (TS) KPA deals with developing a way to satisfy the set of requirements for the project. On a more detailed level, this process works out the solution in terms of various product components and is mapped out in a product life cycle as necessary. As this solution is worked out, notes should be taken regarding the effectiveness of the process. These notes can help form an efficient institution-wide defined process.

Once all of the requirements are developed (note that they are not always "set" at first), a technical solution is a well-thought-out way of handling the problem.

[d] Validation

Validation (VAL) places the product in its intended environment, such as at the company where it will be used or in the homes of a few beta testers, and determines whether it has the desired functionality. VAL activities can be applied to more than just software—they can be used for training, maintenance, etc., to make sure the job was done right. Once validation has been carried out, a defined process should be published for the company's use.

Validation uncovers unforeseen problems—perhaps this software was developed on the newest version of the Mac OS or Windows, but is really intended for a version several years older, or even for another platform such as Linux. VAL can help find such compatibility issues.

[e] Verification

Verification (VER) serves to ensure that the product fulfills the specifications. CMMI specifies that plans should be made for verification, which includes peer review and software testing. Ultimately, the process developed by the organization should be documented to help make future verifications more efficient, useful, and predictable.

The benefit of VER is that the organization can be officially cleared as having completed the requirements set forth in the specifications so that the product is officially ready to be delivered.

> "If a policy is wrongheaded, feckless and corrupt, I take it personally and consider it a moral obligation to sound off and not shut up until it's fixed."
>
> —David Hackworth

[D] Level 4—Quantitatively Managed

A CMM level 4 indicates that a company has methods of making detailed measurements, and documenting software progress and company processes. Both the software and the development processes are understood in a quantitative manner and are controlled.

Level 4 organizations use a quantified feedback system to monitor both the development process of the software as well as the software itself. All measurements made are taken in a consistent manner and are documented. These measurements form the basis for evaluating the progress of the project.

These organizations are generally on time and on budget. If the budget or schedule is exceeded, then action is taken to rectify the situation. Control is achieved by reducing the variation in performance to within an acceptable range. Significant variations can be identified amidst all the random variation and noise. This makes the operations of level 4 organizations very predictable. The software produced is generally of high quality.

Key Process Areas to Achieve a Level 4 Designation

Level 4 has only two KPAs. Many of the critical organization functions are already in place, so the remaining behaviors seek to help the company become more efficient.

[1]   Process Management

[a]   Organizational Process Performance

Organizational process performance (OPP) provides a quantitative understanding of the organization's set of processes. It measures virtually everything about an organization's activities and provides a feedback mechanism to change the system as necessary. For example, when programmers on the team do not document their code as they create it in order to save time, is this time-saving worth the amount of time another programmer needs to take to understand what is going on at another point in time? Almost always, this documentation is worth doing, though it is possible to be at a point when too much is written. OPP helps deal with scenarios such as this. This is especially useful for quality control and project management, as it provides objective numerical feedback that can be used to help improve the system.

The main benefit of OPP is to identify inefficient practices and change them so the company is more productive.

[2]   Project Management

[a]   Quantitative Project Management

The purpose of quantitative project management (QPM) is to handle software development using processes that are based on measurable features and activities. These processes are used to verify the project's performance specifications. In order to perform the process, requirements must be laid out regarding the performance and specifics of the software and its environment. Each feature must have a way to be measured, such as the size of the set of files for the software (less than so many n-bytes) or the amount of time it takes to execute a certain command (for things such as databases, this is perhaps less than a few seconds). In addition to software specifications, the progress of the development team should have measurement standards. All of this data should be recorded so it can be analyzed statistically for problems and be monitored in other ways as necessary. Ultimately, a sound process should be documented for the company's future needs.

QPM allows a manager to say "Our project is successful because we have met or exceeded expectations of time and budget, and have met all of the technical requirements." It also helps an organization see where it falls short and where it excels.

Six Sigma uses similar processes to CMMI levels 4 and 5.

[E] Level 5—Optimizing

Level 5 organizations use quantitative feedback to improve company processes. This permits an agile response to changes in the environment or in the process performance. They also seek out and test new, innovative ideas and technologies.

At level 5, continuous process improvement is the focus of all parts of the organization. A systematic method exists to help identify weak or problem areas and to methodically strengthen these areas. Data determine the effectiveness of the various procedures utilized by an organization to determine whether a measure is effective. Ultimately, the goal is to prevent defects from happening. Defects that do occur are analyzed to determine the cause, which is then systematically dealt with. Any lessons learned are shared with other projects within the organization.

Organizations operating at level 5 improve both through innovation as well as the evolution of the internal process. Organizations continuously improve their overall capabilities through this process.

Key Process Areas to Achieve a Level 5 Designation

As with level 4, level 5 has only two KPAs in which to become competent. A company is considered "optimizing" once it has reached the final maturity level.

[1]   Support

[a]   Causal Analysis and Resolution

Causal analysis and resolution (CAR) helps to determine why defects occur and prevents them from happening in the future. This is easier when a detailed data production process is recorded so that the company can see patterns. However a company chooses to implement this, it should be documented so it can be disseminated and understood by all employees. If managers and technical staff alike understand why it is being performed, there will be more support for the process.

Practicing CAR can help greatly reduce wasted time and effort. CAR is supposed to help identify problems that the company may not notice in its process. It is comparable to a carwash—first, lathering a car in mud and oil, only to then have to wash it. If mud is found in the car's windshield wipers, CAR is used to determine what the cause is. The process is then adjusted, saving a substantial amount of future time, money, and probably stress.

[2]   Process Management

[a]   Organizational Innovation and Deployment

Organizational innovation and deployment (OID) is a system through which company processes and technologies are improved through measurable changes that can be implemented one step at a time. These improvements can be demonstrated to have supported the objectives of the organization in a specific way. An example of this could be implementing a new programming interface and compiler—first, one team switches to the selected interface, and they begin coding and testing either more or less efficiently (likely measured in lines of code or time spent testing). To govern this process, a documented system should be made that prescribes how to select and deploy improvements.

The benefits of OID are that a company improves using new technology, but if something goes awry during or after the implementation, it can be easily reversed to restore the former procedure.

§ 19.04   RATING A COMPANY'S CMMI LEVEL

A company's CMMI level of maturity can be gauged through a process called SCAMPI (Standard CMMI Appraisal Method for Process Improvement^{TM}). In order to actually set about improving, organizations should either develop their own methods or take a cue from existing management theories on implementing improvements.

Many organizations can perform this assessment. In addition, SEI offers training so an in-house assessor can learn the SCAMPI method. However, often it is the fresh eye of an outsider who can spot the obvious and who can bring in best practices from other sites.

§ 19.05   USING CMMI IN YOUR ORGANIZATION

Implementing CMMI does not have to be a great burden on a company. The benefits of its use should make it worth implementing. Implementing CMMI can be relatively painless if a few key processes are developed at a time. Trying to implement it all at once will probably lead to frustration and a sense that nothing is being accomplished, which will lead to the entire process being dropped. Instead, try to implement one or two key processes from the next level at a time, and when the organization is comfortable with those processes, add a few more.

CMMI does *not* have any instructions for how to implement each of these processes; instead, it simply spells out what an optimally performing organization is capable of. To find methodologies for actually implementing the processes, try checking out some other programs for project management, such as Total Quality Management (which is also known by its acronym TQM) or Quality Function Deployment (QFD).

§ 19.06   SUMMARY

CMMI provides a framework for a company's software development to transform it into a more predictably successful effort. However, the transition to CMMI requires a long-term company commitment to change. This change may be a significant culture shock for many workers.

However, after the investment in training and documentation is complete, the company may see significant benefits. Software development results will more closely match the official specifications. Timelines will be closer to the predicted duration. Costs will remain within tolerance. In short, the entire process becomes controlled and predictable.

Organizations adopting CMMI should anticipate a multiyear effort. It takes time to adjust attitudes, train teams, and document everything. However, as the benefits roll in, resistance will crumble.

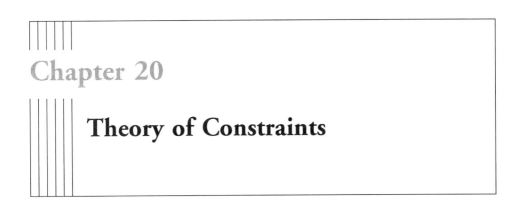

Chapter 20

Theory of Constraints

§ 20.01   INTRODUCTION

An essential part of project management is the efficient use of time. The project team estimates the amount of time required for each activity or task in the project plan.

These estimates are then used to track the performance of project execution and to schedule the application of resources. The scheduling of time is therefore a big part of a project manager's effort.

> "Take all swift advantage of the hours."
>
> —Shakespeare, *Richard III*, Act iv, Scene 1

The problem is that results using the "traditional project management techniques" are spotty. Most projects fail to meet their schedules. Some projects seem to run on schedule, while others are constantly rescheduling and updating plans with ever-slipping dates.

Many people have tried to figure out how to fix this problem. Dr. Eliyahu Goldratt applies a unique approach to an old dilemma. He extended his existing work on the "theory of constraints" to encompass this project management issue. (*See* E. Goldratt & J. Cox, *The Goal: A Process of Ongoing Improvement*, 3d rev. ed., North River Press, 2004). He called this technique "managing the critical chain." This proven approach to project management provides many benefits:

- Projects complete more quickly.
- Project completion is more predictable.
- The team feels satisfaction with reduced uncertainty.

A project's critical chain is a combination of resources and task sequencing. Managing a project through its critical chain is easiest to understand through an overview of managing processes through the theory of constraints.

§ 20.02   THE BASICS OF CRITICAL CHAIN MANAGEMENT

Dr. Goldratt views organizational activities as chains of processes. Each process chain has some point or constraint that limits how much that entire chain can produce. Process improvement efforts that address any point other than the constraint can only have a limited impact. The theory of constraints identifies and manages limitations on maximum throughput.

[A] Prepare the Organization

The first step in managing by constraints is to identify the organization's primary goals. This anchors all future decisions. Typical goals are to be the low-cost provider of a product or service, to provide the best on-time delivery, or to create and deliver the best quality service. Whatever the goal is, it is usually centered on the organization's profitability. Write down these goals in priority order.

Next, determine how to measure the goal. This will be used to gauge the amount of improvement achieved by managing the constraint. Easy-to-obtain measurements should be used whenever practical. If the goal is focused on profitability, then the measurement is likely to be monetary.

The theory of constraints focuses on whatever is constraining or limiting the company's goal. Usually, this means that the process steps leading up to the constraint can move faster than the constraining process bottleneck. The tasks further along the process likewise can run faster. In a factory, the constraint might be located at the point in the process where material piles up awaiting assembly.

[B] Follow the Five Steps

Managing the constraint is a five-step process:

1. **Identify the constraint.** Most constraints are in the last half of the process. If the constraint was near the beginning of the process, it would be too obvious and would be easily resolved. The constraint sets the rate at which the process can operate. In Goldratt's terms, it is the "drumbeat" of the process.

2. **Exploit the constraint.** Take measures to clean up the process step that is limiting throughput. Ensure the constraint is worked to its limit without clutter or distractions.

3. **Subordinate other process steps to the constraint.** The process steps feeding it should run at the same pace as the constraint. The key is for the constraint to never run out of work.

4. **"Elevate" the constraint by expanding its capacity.** This may involve spending money for more machines, or adding a second shift, etc.

5. **Repeat.** Now that the constraint has been resolved—guess what? Something else has become the constraint in the process. Never rest! Immediately start all over again with step one.

Eliminating constraints is a never-ending process. As soon as one is squashed, the next limitation to the process appears.

[C]   Constraints Are Often Resolved Quickly

Constraints can be anything. The careful analysis of processes using a five-step analysis is the best way to locate them. However, in most companies, the constraint is the organization's management. There are two problems that repeatedly appear and which are inexpensive to repair for immediate throughput improvement:

A. **Policies that constrain throughput are often unneeded or obsolete.** Sometimes a policy was implemented to accommodate a situation or an executive's personal preferences. Both justifications may be long obsolete. Require policies to be periodically revalidated or eliminated. Challenge all assumptions!

B. **Managers respond to how they are measured.** Ensure that managers are not rewarded for optimizing their department to the detriment of others. For example, a project management office may be able to estimate new projects far faster than they can be implemented. If the metric is how quickly they turn around a proposal with estimates, then they may pull resources away from project work to help them meet this metric. Their process is optimized to the detriment of the organization.

Many times, the constraint is found to be the boundary between processes. This is the point where one process (usually a department) hands over the work in process to the next process (usually another department). Each department is measured and rewarded for optimizing their own processes and no one is managing or held accountable for the smooth hand-over or interaction at the boundary.

[D]   Constraints and Project Management

Dr. Goldratt postulated that his technique is applicable to the process of project management. Project durations are determined by the time required to complete the tasks along the critical path. If any of these tasks runs over, then the project itself will run longer than expected. The key is to determine what is constraining the project's timely completion. Often, it is management policies and metrics.

§ 20.03   THE PROBLEM WITH TIME ESTIMATES

Time estimation and management is an essential part of project management. Project durations are based on the accurate estimation of time required to complete individual tasks. Correct estimates simplify a project manager's job—poor ones keep a project constantly in chaos. The total project duration is when the organization anticipates the project's completion.

"It is true I must run great risk; no gallant action was ever accomplished without danger."

—John Paul Jones

[A]   How Estimates Are Made

Project time estimates are a combination of human nature and bitter experience. The central issue is uncertainty. On a good day with everything going right, a task may be completed in an hour. On a bad day, when everything goes wrong, the task may take all day.

During project plan development, the project manager asks the team to estimate the time required for the tasks assigned to each of them. Each worker calculates an estimate based on experience. This estimate is usually optimistic and based on events going well. It is an average, which means that half of the time the task requires less time and half of the time the task requires more time.

Then uncertainty sets in. Before saying anything, the worker adds time as a safety factor to account for what may go wrong. All sorts of catastrophes can disrupt the simplest task. The worker adds additional time to ensure that he or she can meet the task's promised date in spite of his or her worst fears. This additional time may double the time estimate.

Chart 20-1 illustrates the application of a normal curve to time estimates. Using this logic, half of the time falls above and below the average. To ensure that a project can be completed with a 90 or 99 percent certainty, more time is required. (This curve is skewed to the left because a task cannot require zero time, but may, in fact, require substantially longer.)

To protect their safety buffer, the worker is adamant that based on his experience, this is how much time must be allowed to complete the task. The project manager then adds an additional safety factor on top of the worker's estimate. In the project manager's mind, this ensures the task is completed with 90 to 99 percent certainty. In reality there are now two unnecessary buffers added to the task duration.

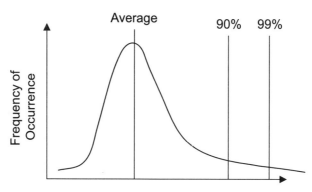

Chart 20-1: Time Estimation Curve

[B]   Estimates Are Overboard

So now the team is working from a bloated project plan when all of the time estimates contain extra time to ensure they are completed on schedule. At this point, human nature sets in again. If someone has 40 hours to complete a task that they believe should only require 16 hours, then why start on it immediately? A 24-hour buffer was added onto the task to ensure on-time completion. From the worker's perspective, other things can be addressed for now and still leave plenty of time to complete the 16-hour task before it is due.

So time passes and as the last 16 hours of the time allotted approach, the worker begins on the task. Several hours into the effort, a problem arises. Apparently the worker will require additional material that must be purchased, and the help of someone who is only available for two days out of the week. The 16-hour task has just hit the "50 percent over estimate" zone. However, since the worker has squandered the contingency time provided for the task, a crisis has arisen.

Why does this occur? In many cases, it is the "student syndrome," as when the college student does not study for an exam until the night before. Similarly, many people will not work on a task until it is almost due. In their minds, this is the time it should be worked on, and the contingency time is theirs to waste.

Why do workers start a task late or if they finish early, why do they absorb the contingency time instead of handing it back to the project manager? There are many reasons people will give for keeping the buffer time in a project task.

- If the task is completed early, the requirements might later change, causing rework for that step. By starting later, the latest information is used to begin the task. (This is a poor excuse since the project manager controls specification changes, which should be accompanied by additional time to complete them.)

- Time estimates are intrinsically pessimistic. The person making the estimates thinks of all of the bad things that might delay the task. In fact these will rarely occur.

- Workers expect executives to make arbitrary project timeline cuts, such as "reduce the project duration by 10 percent." The added cushion to counter these cuts will still keep their tasks in the 90 percent range.

- There is a punishment for being late, but no reward for being early.

- Future estimates will be automatically discounted. Finishing on time protects these estimates.

- Since early finishes cannot be guaranteed all of the time, the team wants to avoid setting a false expectation. The extra time can be used to improve product quality.

- When the next step is not ready to start, workers feel no necessity to rush.

- If the task is finished early, the person working on the next task may add the early finish to their task's embedded margin of safety, and not start work on his or her part of the process right away.

All of this contributes to the basic problem. A delay in one step of the project is passed on to subsequent tasks. Any time savings from an early finish is just absorbed by the other tasks. This can result in schedule "thrashing," as the critical path changes due to overrun tasks.

[C] Encouraging Early Completion Improves Resource Utilization

The primary limitation on projects is resources (which translates into cost). If tasks can finish early, then scarce resources can be applied to more places within the same amount of time. This is not an attempt to wring more blood out of the workers; it takes the excess time and applies it to the greatest benefit to the organization.

Increased resource availability, especially for the constraining resources, permits the organization to complete more projects within a given time. This faster completion reduces the number of disruptive "crisis projects" that muscle existing projects aside.

[D] Multitasking Team Members Is Wasteful

Assigning technical resources to work on simultaneous projects is a waste of time. This results in the people working on one project for a while and then jumping over to work on another one for a while, etc. This approach is wasteful for several reasons:

- Time is lost picking up and putting down work in progress. Reorientation, wrapping up loose ends, etc., all take time that is only required because work is shifting between tasks.

- Projects take longer to complete and for the company to realize benefits from them. For example, consider a resource assigned to support three different projects, each requiring 10 weeks. If they are worked on one at a time, then the first project finishes in 10 weeks, the second finishes at the 20th week, and the third wraps up on the 30th week. However, if the resource rotates among the three projects, spending one week with each over and over again, then all three projects require 30 weeks to complete!

- The longer a project takes, the more likely it is to be disrupted by a "hot" project that pushes everything else aside for the moment. Completing one project at a time allows the hot project to slip in as the next effort instead of halting other projects.

- If one of the multiple projects runs long, then the delivery date of the others will also slip.

[E]   Executive Adjustments

Executives are aware that people add cushions to time estimates to address uncertainty. They typically cut the entire project timeline by some factor that they feel will reduce this cushion. This broad brush approach unfortunately hits the people who fairly estimated as well as the ones who excessively padded their estimates. This unscientific approach of reducing the project timeline (and labor budget) is repeated at each level of management that reviews the project proposal.

The project manager must know where to draw the line on these cuts. Executives that cut the timeline are the same ones who will howl when the project runs over the estimate, since completing a task takes a certain amount of time, and adequate time must be set aside for those tasks that encounter problems.

If a project has a tendency to be always behind schedule, the entire project team will begin to heavily pad their estimates for future protection. The estimates will no longer reflect reality since no matter how hard the project manager tries to weed out the fluff, the workers will not want to go through another project being flogged to do more, and do it faster, for executives who created the situation in the first place.

[F]   Managers Get What They Reward

A critical issue in project management is that workers are seldom rewarded for completing a task early. However, they are rebuked if a task is completed late. Given this situation, if a task could be completed early, the workers will not tell the project manager. The time will be filled with some other task or frittered away. After all, if the project manager agreed to "pay" 40 hours for something, why deliver it early? The reward will be that subsequent tasks may be cut back to remove any cushion. Since the result of finishing early is viewed as a "punishment," it rarely occurs. Instead, workers slow down to be sure they consume all of the time allotted for the tasks.

Consider the effect this has on the project timeline. If tasks are never reported as being completed early, then the cushion added to each task results in excess time *required* for each task. The result is that tasks are only completed on time or late. Since tasks never hand back their excess time, and only take more time for problems, how can a project ever hope to be completed on time?

§ 20.04   PROJECT MANAGEMENT THE CONSTRAINTS WAY

Including a safety cushion of time in a project is not a bad thing. Rather, it is an appropriate risk mitigation step needed to protect the project's completion date. The key here is to place this cushion where the project manager can control it rather than with the people working on the tasks.

This will require a major attitude shift by everyone in the company, so be patient. Beware that people may still pad their time estimates for their own contingencies. It takes time to change ingrained behaviors.

[A]   Plan from the End

Critical chain project management starts with the project's planned completion date and schedules backward from there. The "due by" date is usually included in the project charter. Backward planning begins with the final task, such as customer acceptance, and then works backward one task at a time.

Critical path management uses forward planning. Each task is scheduled to begin as soon as possible. In backward planning, each task is scheduled to begin as late as possible (late start date). The advantages of using backward planning include:

- It minimizes project work in process by pushing all work to begin as late as possible.

- Costs are not incurred early.
- It affords better focus at the critical project start.
- Work begins when it is needed.

Another action is to set criteria for task estimation. Each estimate should have a 50 percent possibility of task completion. Assume that:

- All material and information will be available when needed
- No more than typical interruptions will occur
- No "surprises" will disrupt workflow

By starting a project as late as possible, the project's critical path is already at the critical stage, since any time slip will cause the project to be late. The dates and durations for all tasks are tightly planned. There is no time left for distractions.

To protect the project completion date, buffers are added (as tasks) at strategic points in the project. To do this, the organization must alleviate any fear the workers may have with respect to removing the embedded safety time. Managers should explain that the time is not thrown away. It is accumulated into buffers.

[B] Build a Buffer

Begin by identifying the project's critical chain. This is a combination of the critical path tasks plus the availability of critical resources. (If the project plan has leveled the resources, then it will indicate the critical chain.) Critical chains may jump from task chain to chain due to resource constraints.

Predicting where extra time will be needed in a project is impossible. Imagine a 20 percent buffer added to each task times a project with over 100 tasks. The time wasted would be significant. By collecting this time into controlled project buffers, only those tasks that encounter problems will draw on it.

The guiding principle is that the buffers exist to protect the project's completion date. Buffers are much shorter than all of the contingency time they absorb. This allows the project to be completed more quickly. However, these buffers are not free. There are still those tasks that are on the long side of the 50/50 estimates.

A "project buffer" is added to the schedule as a task at the end of the plan. It is associated with the critical chain. The project buffer is equal to 50 percent of the total project time. Its purpose is to protect the completion date.

Each chain of tasks feeding into the critical chain has a "feeding buffer" attached to it. The feeding buffer shelters the critical chain from delays. They are typically equal to 50 percent of the time in the chain they support.

All tasks are scheduled to begin at their late start times. They must not be measured against a baseline and reported as a problem, since this will push everyone back to the original padding.

> Milestones and managing buffers do not mix. A milestone acts as a hard stop for the project—a gate where performance and ongoing viability are examined. Such an approach prevents passing on any time gains to the next stage.

§ 20.05   EXECUTING A PROJECT USING TOC

Managing a project using constraints is different from the traditional approach. Instead of monitoring individual task durations and fussing over due dates, manage entire chains. Task durations are considered a goal and not something to judge work performance. A due date is provided for the entire task chain. Completion dates for the individual tasks are not reported.

Removing due dates from tasks addresses the problem of work expanding to fill the time allotted. Toss that calendar! The time allotted is now just enough to do the task.

Executing a project using constraints is similar to a relay race. As soon as a runner finishes his part of the race, he passes the baton to the next runner, who immediately runs off. If the first runner is slow, then the second runner starts later, etc. The second runner does not stand around waiting for the next part of the race to begin—it begins when the first runner is completed. When all of the runners in the relay have completed their tasks, then they are finished. In this way, early completions are absorbed into the overall result.

Following is a list of the steps necessary for executing a critical chain project.

1. Stop multi-tasking people. Every task started is worked through to completion. If a task hits an unmovable obstacle, then work another task through from start to end before returning to the interrupted task.

2. When a team member completes a task, he or she notifies the project manager and also the person assigned to work on the next task. This keeps the ownership of urgency within the team. Short task durations increase the team's urgency (and focus) to complete them.

3. Start a task as soon as possible and work it through to completion.

[A] The Buffers Say It All

The key to managing a project using the theory of constraints is to watch the buffers. If tasks are properly estimated, then 50 percent of the time they will dip into the buffers for additional time. Managing the buffers means that a buffer should not be empty before the end of that chain of tasks.

Similar to earned value, if half of the estimated task time for that chain has been unused, then the buffer should be half or more full to protect the rest of that chain. People working on the project do not report the amount of a task that has been completed, only the amount of time projected to complete it. This is used to estimate how much of that chain's buffer will be needed to support that task. Conversely, it may show how much time may need to be added to the buffer.

Buffer consumption should be monitored. When faced with a decision, pick the task with the minimal impact on the buffers to be completed first. Some variation is normal and does not require any action. The focus is on managing the flow of the work, and not the individual tasks.

Manage buffers by in three divisions, as shown in Chart 20-2. Cut the buffers into thirds. The first third is for typical variation. Expect this to ebb and flow. The middle section means that the project manager must pay close attention to what is using the extra time. If the buffer is down to the "Take Action" section, the project chain is in danger of running out of time.

100% full	66%	33%	Dry
Typical Variation No Action Required (green)	Monitor and Make Contingency Plans (yellow)	Take Action! (red)	

Chart 20-2: Buffer Management

The amount of buffer remaining is compared to the amount of estimated time remaining in the chain. If half of the chain's time is consumed and half of the buffer is used, then everything is fine. If one-third of the project chain is completed and two-thirds of the chain's buffer is gone, then there is a problem.

If it looks as though the buffer will run out early, then time can be absorbed from the project buffer on the critical chain. Project manager intervention is required if the critical chain buffer is running out faster than it should.

Buffers eliminate the need to re-plan projects every reporting period. They absorb the variation and only if the "monitor" section is entered does the project manager need to consider revisions.

[B]   Resource Management the Constraints Way

The critical chain is dependent on the availability of resources needed to complete the tasks. Any resource on the critical chain must be available to the workers as soon as it is available. Since a hallmark of the constraints approach is not reporting on task progress, another technique is used.

A resource required for the critical chain is considered to be a critical resource. Each critical resource provides an amount of warning time needed to wrap up or set aside the task at hand. This way, the next task on the critical chain can begin when needed. The person working on the previous task alerts the project manager and the resource when they are within the warning time from completing their task. This sets up the critical resource to be ready when needed.

§ 20.06   SOFTWARE TOOLS

Special software tools are available to use in critical chain project management. However, they may not be necessary. Microsoft Project may be all that is needed. The important step is to ensure that the resource management function is used. Microsoft Project has a resource leveling function, but be prepared for how the project plan will change! Specially-designed software tools will go beyond this in several areas:

- Resource leveling and indication as the critical chain
- Calculates and add buffers to each chain of tasks
- As the project executes, can dynamically adjust buffers to determine if their use is due to typical variation or is in need of attention

---

"Although our intellect always longs for clarity and certainty, our nature often finds uncertainty fascinating."

—Karl von Clausewitz

---

§ 20.07   SUMMARY

Dr. Eliyahu Goldratt's approach to project management recognizes a significant element of human nature. A careless project manager will end up with the opposite of what was intended.

Using constraints to manage projects has one primary advantage over other approaches. It is simple to implement. Traditional techniques require extensive calculations, simulations, and statistical analyses. Constraints focus on monitoring the buffers.

Critical chain project management can bring a number of benefits. Completion dates are more reliable since the buffers are few and closely managed. Projects finish sooner since resources have fewer conflicts. Since workers are not judged on meeting an arbitrary "due date," they feel comfortable addressing problems even if it puts them in the "50 percent over estimate" range. This reduces later rework. All of these directly reduce costs.

Workers will strive to complete tasks as soon as possible. This frees resources for other assignments. It also helps to identify the resources constraining the organization from taking on more projects.

Remember that implementing the theory of constraints for projects in an organization requires system-wide change in corporate attitude toward project management. Shift from a managing-everywhere process to managing throughput and resources. New metrics must be developed and explained to project sponsors, team members, and all other project stakeholders.

Chapter 21

Managing a Troubled Project

§ 21.01   INTRODUCTION

> "Success is going from failure to failure without a loss of enthusiasm."
>
> —Winston Churchill

When a customer complains or when a project's out-of-bounds performance triggers a response from the project management office (PMO), the first question is, "Is this project really in trouble?" It is a rare project that is always on time, on budget, and able to deliver a top-notch product to the customer. Reality is much harsher than that. Delays, budget overruns, or scope issues commonly ebb and flow during a project's lifetime. After all, a project's time and cost are estimates and never advertised as a sure thing. In some cases, a successful project may have been so acrimonious during its progress that everyone has nightmares about it.

Just what is a "troubled" project? Projects routinely encounter problems. It might be a micromanaging customer, the lack of a critical resource, or that the work at hand simply takes longer than expected. Some PMOs identify problem projects through variance triggers, such as 20 percent over budget or 20 percent over schedule. (Often the schedule and budget problems will parallel one another.)

Whatever measure is used, a troubled project is any project where the customer is not satisfied with the progress made. Vague as that sounds, no matter what problems the project faces, if the customer is satisfied, then it is still on track—even if it is late or over budget.

§ 21.02   DON'T PANIC—IS THERE REALLY A PROBLEM?

Before proceeding, it is important to ensure that a project is truly troubled and not just experiencing a temporary problem. Projects never run exactly on time or on budget. At times, the budget appears to be far under (often due to timing of invoices) and other times far over (if the accounting department is pulling expenses into the current accounting period). It is disruptive to an ongoing project to begin poking around looking for a problem when one is not there. It also disrupts team morale. Therefore, before proceeding further, ensure that the project is truly out of control and not just out of bounds due to a passing event.

Why is a project failing? Is it just late or over budget? Is the budget overage tolerance too low? It may be that the project will not be completed by the client's deadline. If completion will come after that date, the client may not want it; similarly, the client may refuse to invest more than a set amount in a project, and the budget is already over that number. Maybe critical team members are leaving the company. Perhaps someone in upper management does not look upon the project favorably and will abort it at the drop of a hat.

Small projects (160 hours or less) rarely fall into the troubled project category. Even if they far exceed their budget, the overall financial impact to the organization is regrettable, but not significant.

From a management perspective, there are measures that can be applied to ongoing projects to identify which ones are trending into trouble. For example:

- A project that is trending toward 20 percent or more over its budget or over its product delivery date. (This number is selected locally depending on customer sensitivity to budget overruns.) This figure assumes that the project was adequately funded to start with. Also, it assumes that a clearly identified one-time crisis (such as a fire or theft) is not included in the variance calculation.

- The client is micromanaging some of the project's tasks due to dissatisfaction with the team's performance. This always delays task completion as everyone waits around for their next order to move.

- Open contention between the client and the team members, or just among the team members. The issues may be technical or personal.

- The client has lost interest in the project or the business requirements have shifted away from the project's goals.

- Looming conflict with a critical resource that will negatively impact schedule or cost.

- The project was started with a vague or inadequate scope and is only now drifting forward. Often this is an example of a customer demanding a project start before requirements are approved or with the announced expectation of designing the product as the project proceeds.

Some project managers revel in the "firefighting" mode where challenges arise daily and decisive action is needed. Although this may seem exciting, it appears to outsiders that the project management process is chaotic and limping from crisis to crisis. A pitfall of the firefighting mode is that trends toward larger problems may not be obvious to the project manager in the midst of the flames. Everyone can see the warning signs except for the project manager, who only sees part of the "fire." By the time a serious problem is obvious, the project is close to implosion and the overworked project manager responds with even more frenzied actions.

In Edward Yourdon's book *Death March: The Complete Software Developer's Guide to Surviving "Mission Impossible" Projects* (Prentice Hall, 1999), he describes four major types of projects. Yourdon gauges projects on the likelihood of success and the happiness of the project team. Although most projects may be rated as somewhere in the center of the chart, project team members can recall times when they worked on projects in one of the quadrants or another.

Yourdon defines a "death march" project as "one for which an unbiased, objective risk assessment (which includes an assessment of the technical risks, personal risks, legal risks, political risks, etc.) determines that the likelihood of failure is less than 50 percent."

Happiness	Kamikaze	Mission Impossible
	Suicide	Ugly
	low high	*Chance of Success*

The horizontal axis indicates the likelihood of the project succeeding from low (on the left) to high. The vertical axis indicates the team member's satisfaction from working on the project.

- Mission Impossible—High happiness and high chance of success. The team is fanatically loyal to each other, thrives on the challenge, and enjoys "living on the edge." The team dreams of fame, glory, and riches if it succeeds.

- Ugly—Low happiness and high chance of success. Projects where the project manager sacrifices the team members to bring the project to a successful completion. The key characteristic is that the project manager is determined to succeed and profit from the project. He or she is willing to sacrifice the team members' health and happiness if necessary to achieve the goal.

- Suicide—Low happiness and low chance of success. In a suicide project, everyone is miserable. The project is doomed to failure but the team keeps working on it to maintain their employment. The team knows from the outset that the project has no chance of success.

- Kamikaze—High happiness and low chance of success. These projects are doomed to fail gloriously! Team members may be attracted to a kamikaze project by the chance to work with an advanced technology. Often this is a "save the company" project that is unlikely to succeed, but the team feels it must try.

The two main themes of the above projects are team morale and chances for success. Any of these projects have the chance to succeed, though the mission impossible and the ugly projects have the best chance. The members of kamikaze and mission impossible projects are in high spirits, as opposed to those in the suicide and ugly projects. The best method to save a project depends very much on the current situation of the project itself and on the team.

§ 21.03   CALL IN THE PROJECT DOCTOR!

Once a project has been determined to be in trouble, the next step is to appoint someone to figure out what the problem is. This assumes that the current project manager could not or did not identify the problem and act on it before it became a crisis. Have the investigator identify a solution or take charge of the project.

> Internal company politics being what they are, an executive may jump on a
> problem with a project as a way to undermine a competitor for promotion.

The usual approach to sorting out a problem project is to bring in someone external to the project to lead it. If the problem involves technical issues, then usually a different project manager internal to the company can be assigned. If the problems are a result of interpersonal conflicts, then someone external to the company should be assigned to lead the project.

Using an outsider to analyze the situation is an attempt to bring in an independent authority with a fresh perspective to sort out the issues—particularly the internal politics. However, an external resource still has political strings to the person who hired him and who can continue or end his employment.

Anyone assigned to investigate a troubled project should ensure that the scope of the situation is clearly understood before accepting the task. Once in place, it will be more difficult for that person to obtain additional latitude for action. The authority that might be needed to rectify a problem project entails the following.

- Firmly remove disruptive team members from the project. In the case of employees, they can be transferred elsewhere. Contractors' engagements can be terminated. This does wonders for gaining cooperation from reluctant team members.

- Hire or acquire internally additional team members with the skills needed over the short term (perhaps 90 days).

- Stop work on the project until a recommendation can be formulated as to how to proceed, or a decision is made to terminate the project. The customer must allow adequate time to determine the root cause(s) of the problem. If they cannot or will not wait for the analysis, then they should order the changes they want and not hide behind a false project review.

- Finally, if the project is to continue, reset the project baseline so the variances of the scope, budget, and timeline are zero. Only future project variances in cost, timeline, and product features are measured.

Some essential information must be identified before beginning this assignment. Now is the time to ask the difficult questions and pin down the sponsor on the options available. Examples of questions are as follows.

- Is there a solid due date, such as may be needed to meet a legal compliance issue?

- Why should this project be recovered instead of cancelled?

- Given the current state of the effort, the budget, and likely completion date, is this project worth the pain of salvaging?

- Does the sponsor have the authority to consider cancelling the project?

- Which is the most important dimension: time, quality, or cost? Is one of them immovably fixed?

> Shaping the battlefield, in military terms, means reducing the enemy's capabilities to fight prior to an attack. In business terms, this means identifying the business objections and political issues and eliminating them.

[A] Assess the Situation

Investigating a troubled project is a project unto itself. It involves a series of logical and related actions building up to a set of recommendations. Managing the data collection and analysis as a project allows the customer to monitor progress toward a recommendation.

The project begins with a statement of work—a clear statement of why someone believes the project is not performing to his satisfaction. This forms the project's statement of work and is the basis for all later actions. The statement must include essential guidance, such as when a recommendation must be delivered, a budget to cover expenses, and any other specifications that limit or guide the project.

The customer must approve the statement of work prior to proceeding. Customer buy-in is essential since the customer may not approve of the final recommendation and should be aware of how it was determined. The customer may be the user requesting the project or the PMO manager who has identified the problem. The key is to identify the real customer. Often the customer contact is an intermediary for the real customer, an executive deeper into the organization who the project manager may not have direct access to.

With an approved statement of work in hand, a plan of action can be assembled. This plan could be involved if the project is large or complex. The project plan should encompass an examination of the project's documents, interviews with stakeholders, a review of the project budget performance, and an analysis of the project's execution from inception to date.

The primary deliverable of this "project-to-heal-a-project" is a proposal for action. Typically this consists of a list of actions to move the project's performance to within the customer's range of expectations—or a recommendation for cancellation. Whatever the recommendation, it must be presented to the customer along with supporting data. A thorough data collection makes a bitter pill easier to swallow. Recommendations should include:

- Which actions to take and the timeline and costs needed to "heal" the project
- Several courses of action and their associated risks
- Details on how the current project will proceed during the transition

Changing a project includes establishing a fresh schedule and budget baseline. This sets a revised (and more realistic) set of expectations against which the revised project's performance can be gauged, from this point forward. Although the overall performance would be gauged against the entire effort from start to finish, a new project manager cannot manage to expectations a budget or timeline that is already substantially behind where it should be.

[B] Root Out the Facts

Assessing a troubled project requires time for the project manager to gain some perspective on the root cause of the problem. This can be difficult if the project is underway and under pressure to press ahead. There are three basic options:

- Pass day-to-day management to a temporary project manager (freeing the current project manager to perform the assessment).
- Retain the existing project manager to address the day-to-day issues.
- Bring in an outside expert to analyze the project.

Most project managers are decisive and action-oriented. Their tendency is to wade into a new assignment and press the team forward while trying to identify problem areas. Although this might work for a small project, immersing oneself in the project details does not leave much time for identifying the root cause of the problems. Ensure that the incoming project manager is focused first on identifying and resolving the basic project problems.

If a project is deemed to be in trouble, the logical question is, "What kind of trouble?". Members of the project team will likely offer their opinions (solicited or not). However, before acting on these ideas, time must be set aside to gather the facts. The root cause of problems is not always obvious. Otherwise, someone probably would have already acted to fix it. Even obvious, serious problems often have other aspects complicating what might initially appear to be a straightforward issue. When performing the assessment, no assumption is safe from scrutiny. Every important fact about the project must be validated.

A new project manager only gets one shot at resolving the problem. He or she must take time to confirm the proposed solution before acting. If the solution is simple, then confirming this reduces the risk of a management error. If the project's problems are complex, then confirming the solution may save the project manager's credibility by not chasing the wrong or an impossible issue.

In reality, few troubled projects have a single problem. The assessment must identify the top few problems for action. Their individual impact is compounded at the point where these issues interact.

> "I'd rather be a failure at something I love than a success at something I hate."
>
> —George Burns

[C] Project Data—Check the Books

A well-run project is (hopefully) a well-documented one. This information should be on file in the PMO and also available from the current project manager. Separately request copies of the project plan, issues log, and status reports from the previous project manager, the PMO manager, the customer, and the team members. Verify that all of the versions provided to the various stakeholders are in sync. It is difficult for everyone to be of the same mind when using different information.

Examining the documents will provide some history on the project problems and how well they have been resolved in the past. The documents will also provide some idea of who needs to be interviewed and some of the key questions to ask. If the documentation is complete, it should paint a picture of a project that (hopefully) started on course and then detail how it gradually drifted off the path.

- Check the project charter.
  - Is the project scope clear and complete?
  - Did the customer sign the charter?
  - Are the assumptions clearly stated?
  - Are the risks listed?
  - Have any scope changes been made?
  - Were the scope changes approved by the customer along with changes to the timeline and budget?

- Is there a thorough stakeholder analysis detailing the participation and interests of each?

- Is there a communication plan detailing what information must be provided to the various stakeholders, its frequency, and preferred delivery method?

- Is the risk assessment complete, up to date, and followed in project planning? Does it reflect each of the assumptions and mitigation plans in case one or more of them are false?

- Is the issues log current? Does it indicate the problem's identification, assignment to someone, and its resolution? Does it seem to be written after the fact? Make a note to cross-check this record with people assigned to an issue during the stakeholder interview.

- Check the project plan. Does it reflect the charter? Is it well-constructed? Are the project charter assumptions about the timeline reflected in the plan?

  - Compare the schedule to the baseline. Plot the project's progress over time to observe the trend of actual time used versus the schedule over time. (Status reports may provide this information.) Could a schedule problem be due to poor estimating?

  - Were the necessary resources available when needed?

  - Were all changes to the schedule documented or was it adjusted to stay within tolerance as the project progressed?

  - Did a single, identifiable event skew the schedule performance? If the impact of this single event were excluded, would the project be performing to schedule?

- Check the project budget. Does it reflect the charter and the timeline? Has it been amended to include approved changes in scope? Are the project charter assumptions about the budget reflected in the numbers? Is it up to date?

  - Plot the budget performance over time. When did it begin to vary from the estimates? Were the original estimates valid?

  - Examine reports on budget variances to detect problems not reported in the project schedule.

  - Were all scope changes reflected in changes in the budget?

  - Did a single, identifiable event skew the budget performance? If the impact of this single event were excluded, would the project be performing to budget?

  - Compare work product so far to the project definition, testing plan, and quality plan.

- Review status reports provided to the PMO and the customer. Is the information in both of them the same? Are they on time? Are there timely requests for resources and funds to support the project? Are there specific "excuses" for something missing in the project? Are there any recurring problems?

> "Develop success from failures. Discouragement and failure are two of the surest stepping stones to success."
>
> —Dale Carnegie

[D] Interview the Key Players

An important tool for gathering data is to separately interview the key stakeholders. Each will provide a different perspective on the issues. Taken as a whole, the interviews will paint a mosaic of the major and minor issues combining to strangle the project.

Based on the document inspection, assemble a list of people to talk to. Interviews take time to arrange and conduct, and it also takes time to validate the resulting conclusions. The interview list should be sequenced by the people with the broadest view (PMO) to the narrowest view (team members). An alternative is to sequence the list from the people closest to the stated problems to the ones most distant. In this way, if the interviews paint a consistent picture of the issues, the project manager can move on to the analysis phase.

Interviewing all of the major stakeholders provides several benefits. First, it provides a wide range of perspectives about the various issues and their interactions. Second, it may identify the minor factors that combined to turn an issue into a crisis. Third, when it is time to implement changes, the stakeholders will be more cooperative since they were consulted during the analysis. When practical, tie recommendations for change to the suggesting stakeholder.

Everyone sees the world through the filter of his or her own experiences, so expect each stakeholder to offer an opinion about the project that reflects his or her views. Some may repeat rumors as if they were verified facts. Statements should not be acted upon until confirmed as true. Critical details should be cross-checked with other sources. Ideally, facts are cross-checked with people that are not in regular contact with each other to reduce the likelihood of an opinion being accepted as a fact.

Another useful tool is a questionnaire. A questionnaire will ensure that the various stakeholders are asked the same basic questions, using the same words. Each question should be open-ended to solicit information. As the conversation progresses, these questions can be pursued to dig deeper into events.

- Project management office—The manager of the PMO should provide historical data on the project's performance in terms of timeline and budget. The PMO can also provide insight into the customer and team members. In addition, the PMO manager can report on the project's use of scarce or external resources.

- Other project managers—Other project managers may have seen or heard about specific areas of the project that are struggling. Ask them about anything they may have seen or heard. They may also provide insights into the various stakeholders—their strengths and weaknesses.

- Project sponsor or customer—Often customers lack the expertise to judge if a technical obstacle is major or minor. A project either appears to be meeting their expectations or not. When interviewing the customer, dig deep into assertions and vague statements to uncover specific incidents or trends that may have reduced their confidence in the project.

- Team members—Interview team members separately. These will be the toughest discussions as some may try to settle grudges by passing on selected information or innuendo. Still, the team members see the inner workings of the team and may provide the quickest path to refocusing the project. This also is an excellent time to identify the most (or least) productive team members.

- Accounting—The flow of funds through a project can sometimes pinpoint when problems have arisen. A discussion with the financial person who reviews the project budget performance reports may provide valuable background information.

- Vendors and suppliers—Many projects depend on vendors for timely and accurate deliveries. Some project managers treat vendors as partners while others treat them as thieving adversaries. Examine this area closely if the project depends heavily on vendor relationships.

In most cases, the project manager conducts interviews in one-on-one sessions. Then the project manager consolidates the information and meets again with small groups, such as the project team, to review it. The goal is to validate the conclusions reached and to identify the significant issues that need to be addressed. This will reduce time spent on low-payback problems pressed by vocal people.

> Of course, a project to save a project that fails in its mission is a complete waste of money. Take the time necessary to dig out the root cause of issues and resist the temptation to jump on the first problem that comes to light.

§ 21.04 DIAGNOSING THE PROBLEM(S)

Projects consist of three major functions: scope, timeline, and budget. The project's performance is an indication of how well these three are kept in balance.

- If budgets are cut, then resource reductions will cause the timeline to extend.
- If the timeline is shortened, then an increased budget may be needed to bring in additional workers.
- If the scope is changed, then the budget and timeline may also change to reflect the new requirements.

A few simple tools can help to identify the components of a project. An example is the "fishbone" diagram. It breaks down a project into the "5Ms and an E," as explained in Chapter 14, "Design for Six Sigma" (§ 14.06). The idea is to list the various parts of a project so they can be methodically reviewed.

[A] Communication

The most common (and easiest to repair) cause of a troubled project is poor communication. When interested people do not know what is occurring or is scheduled to occur, they often fill in the information gap with their darkest fears. If the customer is nervous to start with, or under pressure from his own manager, then he may be sensitive to any rumor or suggestion that the project's progress is anything but perfect.

People are the essential resource for a project. Their primary interaction is through communication, both verbal and nonverbal. Unlike somewhat predictable machines, people often can be unpredictable. The key to a successful project is the free flow of candid communication among the team members, and between the project manager and the external stakeholders. This includes both positive and negative communications, as feedback for corrective actions requires both.

All communications between the project team and the customer must flow through the project manager. The project manager must be seen by all stakeholders as the primary and authoritative source of information about the project. If the project manager is not readily available for questions, then stakeholders will begin seeking their answers from other sources. Many teams have a member who is more vocal than the others and who loves being the center of attention. Of course, the more "interesting" his comments, the more attention this person receives. Project managers must identify and stifle these unofficial commentaries so that all stakeholders receive a consistent message.

Stakeholders should have access to the project's progress—both good and bad—through regular status reports. In-depth, technical reports take too long to prepare and may still lack for the information that sponsors need to make informed decisions. Therefore, a summary report that touches on schedule, scope, and budget is usually advisable.

[1]   Customers

Communication is based on a combination of the message and the audience. Communication with the customer must be carefully crafted to meet the needs of that audience. Often the customer lacks the technical depth to understand what normal development hurdles are and what a problem within a technical project is. For example, testing is a process for identifying and resolving defects in the product. It is normal to uncover defects. Detailing these to the customer may lead them to believe the project is at risk of failure. The key is how well uncovered defects are tracked and repaired.

Some customers expect the product to be perfect. Anything less must be a problem in the development and in the project. Therefore, most project managers provide general statements on the progress of a project and do not detail any issue that will not significantly impact the budget or timeline. However, if the project is behind schedule, and the customer demands detailed reports, then the technical chaos may be more than the customer can comprehend.

> Successful communication with the customer is based on trust. The project manager must establish and then nurture this trust relationship. If it is ever shattered, then the project manager must endlessly justify every action. One way to gain and maintain trust is to provide results to the customer at every project milestone. Another way is to identify the essential elements of information most important to the customer and provide them on a timely basis.

Bad news should never be a surprise to the customer. Disasters can occur suddenly but more often they build slowly. By informing the customer of pending problems (risks about to become reality or of a brewing conflict somewhere in the team), they will be more ready to support a major change to correct the situation.

There are three common pitfalls that create customer communications problems. Project managers must be assertive enough to manage their customers' communications styles and not be fearful about explaining to the customer how their actions are negatively affecting the project.

- Customers who avoid important issues surrounding the scope and tell the project manager to "Just handle it!" will often find themselves in the middle of serious problems. Such a comment implies that the project manager would choose the same course of action as the customer would select. In the absence of further guidance, the project manager may proceed to follow courses of action that the customer would have known were inefficient or incorrect.

- Customers who "shoot the messenger" soon train their project managers to never raise any negative issues. Unfortunately, problems are never addressed at a high level until they are about to overwhelm the project. For these customers, project managers should never present a problem without the mitigating actions to address it.

- Micromanaging customers immediately fly into action at the least implication of a problem. They act as if personally charged with solving the issue themselves. Similar to the "shoot the messenger" customer, project managers learn not to raise issues since the customer cannot handle the news without flailing in all directions—often making more work for everyone and none of it related to solving the issue.

[2]   Project Team Members

Everyone likes to be on the winning team. Team members all have their own opinions on how the project should be run. A skilled project manager will incorporate team ideas into the timeline whenever practical as these ideas may be very good and the team members will be more committed to the project's success. However, if the team lacks information on what is next, on how their contribution fits into the overall success, or even suspect their employment will end with the current task, then they will be defensive and slow to act.

Encourage team members to bring up the bad news with the good, but only to the project manager. Technicians love a challenge. Some feel they work best under pressure. Sometimes when a serious problem arises, they seize upon it as a personal challenge to their expertise. Often this type of person becomes too embarrassed to admit defeat. The project manager must monitor team members' performance to ensure that these personal challenges do not bog down the project. The key is to create a management climate where team members can confess to problems without fear of punishment or ridicule.

Project managers must consider cultural friction within the team. In some cultures, problems are not raised since it negatively reflects on the team. The conflicts simmer and sap the team's effectiveness. In others, if a person is struggling with a task, it might shame him to admit he needs help. The project manager must build individual bridges to the team members whose backgrounds do not easily mesh with the group. The goal is to detect and resolve problems while they are still small and manageable.

People tend to congregate with others of similar background or with like ideas. It is a good practice to occasionally break up small cliques within teams by reassigning members to the other groups. If necessary, bring in the human resources manager to speak informally with the team members to identify and resolve interpersonal conflicts.

[3]   Other Stakeholders

Other stakeholders have their own interests in the project. If the project manager keeps these interests in mind and ensures these stakeholders receive the information they require in a timely fashion, then these people are less likely to cause problems. These other stakeholders include the accounting manager, facilities management, vendors, and a wide range of other people depending upon the project scope.

[B]   Evaluating the Situation

There are many things that can cause a healthy project to fall apart. In most cases, the demise is caused by a combination of events. When investigating a troubled project, look at these areas but do not be limited to them. Each project and every company is unique. Yet if the basics of project management are not addressed, the rest of the project may fall to pieces.

[1]   Lack of Leadership

A project cannot be managed—it must be led. A leader is proactive. Leaders provide a clear vision of what the project is to accomplish (scope) and a good idea of how to get there (timeline and budget). They are cheerleaders when times are good and martinets when times are bad. The project leader learns about the team members and understands how to get the most out of them over the long haul.

The caveat about leadership is that people are never 100 percent anything. Some will resist a leader as a way to rebel against all authority. Some are so wrapped up with outside activities that the project is just a necessary evil. The good worker today may be the dud worker tomorrow. Whatever the team member's motivation, the project leader must take the time to figure it out and use it to obtain productivity. It is also a useful exercise for gauging how long that person will require to complete a task.

Teams do not automatically coalesce into a unit. This merger must be nurtured. If intrateam friction is hindering the project, the project manager can recommend several basic actions:

- Conduct a team meeting focused on team work. Let it be known that cooperation is valued and rewarded and infighting will not be tolerated. Such statements must be enforced or the project manager's credibility may be diminished.

- Take the opportunity to pass out some rewards for work accomplishments, such as a certificate for a free paid vacation day to be used after the project is completed (or even within the next two weeks).

- Bring in food for a lunch on the company. Praise in public and admonish in private. Focus the team on the project objectives and on how important their contributions will be. The goal is to create a positive climate where the team is rewarded for their *collective* accomplishments.

- If necessary, identify the team members who are the worst offenders, and assign them to work together on the same tasks. Make their ongoing employment contingent on their success. If possible, also reward their success with something as positive as practical.

- Although negative leadership actions should not be used liberally, without them the project manager's authority is hollow. As a last resort—or if time is short—identify the chief offenders or instigators of problems and remove them from the team. This may be difficult if they are key participants, but their contributions must be balanced against the cost to the team's productivity.

Leadership is a large and complex subject just as people are complex subjects. The thing to remember is that a project manager cannot leave team formation to chance. Forging a team out of a mob of people is a key project manager task.

[2] Appointing the Wrong Project Manager

Managing a project requires a mixture of skills, some of which are general to project management and some are technical, pertaining to the product or service being provided. Sometimes a project manager's lack in one area can be compensated through the addition of a team member strong in that area who can mentor the project manager through the issues.

A common pitfall is to lump all project managers into one class that is universally applicable across all projects. This approach may provide someone who can lead a project but cannot make technical decisions. In a very large project, this shortcoming might be compensated by assigning a technical architect to make the technical decisions. Listed below are some common errors.

- Pairing a weak-willed project manager with a strong-willed customer

- Assigning a project manager with no knowledge of the technical issues involved with the project

- Assigning too many critical or difficult projects to the same project manager

- Assigning someone accustomed to working on small projects to lead a major effort

- Promoting a strong technician into a people management role with training and mentoring responsibilities

- Assigning a project manager with a strong technical skill to also participate in that project as a team member. A project manager should avoid working as a team member because it will consume too much of his or her time, leaving inadequate time and focus for managing the project.

[3]   The Project Team

The project team is the key to a successful project. It holds the power for making the project a success or a failure through team members' actions or inaction. How are the members of the team doing as individuals? This question really has two components, their quality and quantity of work, and their lives and well-being. Are they and their families healthy? Are they exhausted from something? Are they happy with the company and the project at hand?

Verify that the team members assigned to each task possess the correct skills and expertise levels to successfully complete them within the schedule. This requires assessing the skill sets of the existing members. If they lack sufficient expertise, it may be necessary to replace some of the lesser-skilled team members with more highly skilled outsiders. If outside support is not available, then recommend adjusting the timeline to reflect this new assumption.

[4]   Resource Management

The careful and proper application of resources is essential for a project to be on time and within budget. Resources are usually viewed in terms of people, machinery, or money. All workers are not alike in terms of their expertise, productivity, ability to quickly grasp new situations, etc. The project manager must know the team members well enough to assign them to tasks that maximize their strong points and minimize their weak ones. This is not always possible, but it is the goal. However, sometimes resources get assigned for other than business reasons. Favoritism, convenience, or availability may combine to assign the wrong resource to a critical task, with predictable results.

If the application of resources is too far out of balance, then the project will suffer in a number of ways. Timelines will slip, budgets will overrun, and the requisite quality of the end product will suffer.

Resource problems can arise from a number of directions—a key team member may leave the company, equipment allocated for a task is no longer available, or a disaster occurs that prevents one part of a project from meeting its commitments.

The biggest challenge in resource management is reallocating resources when the timeline slips. Project timelines are used to pinpoint when a certain task is expected to begin. Based on this assumption, expensive or scarce resources are engaged to join the project at that time. If the timeline slips significantly, the expensive resource may sit idle but money must be expended. At the same time, a slip in the timeline may mean that when a scarce resource is needed, the team will be off to their next obligation, leaving the project to scramble to find a replacement on short notice.

A valuable tool for resource management is a thorough risk assessment that examines the requirement for critical resources along the timeline. The assessment must include mitigation actions at various milestones to ensure that resources are still available or to arrange for new ones as the project approaches the period at which they are needed. Otherwise, the project will blunder forward through excesses and famines of resources.

[5] Scope/Project Definition

The scope of the project is the foundation for all that follows. A project built on a vague scope analysis will experience early and serious problems with its performance. The scope should be a clear description of what is needed, when it is needed, and how the project should proceed. The project manager bases the timeline, budget, risk assessment, etc., on this description. If the scope is wrong, the team is working on the wrong things.

Often what an executive calls "specifications" are far too vague for a technician to act on. (In an information vacuum, the developer may make critical design decisions to keep on schedule, without telling anyone.) Always critique project specifications with the developers prior to the customer approving them. It may be necessary to create mock-ups to demonstrate to customers and project sponsors what the current specification would build.

A classic example of a company knowing what the customer needs is the brief introduction of "New Coke" in 1985. What executives thought would revive and expand their brand ended as a major flop. New products should be broken into their target segments and carefully tested. In IT projects, the customer may be the coworkers who will use new Web data entry screens, new time clocks, new user authentication technology, etc.

Changes to the scope of the project must be formally approved. Scope changes will alter the timeline and the budget. Updates to both must be included in the document approved by the customer. Never permit informal scope changes as their full impact on the project may be difficult to determine on the spur of the moment. Projects with scope problems are often the result of the project manager's failure to tightly control formal and informal scope changes, or "scope creep."

Problems with the scope may be caused by any of the following.

- Was the initial project definition clear and concise? Did it identify all of the key functional and quality objectives to be met?

- Did the customer provide written approval of the project definition? If the sponsoring department is supplying all of the answers without involving the customers, the customers may not support the project.

- Were planning assumptions documented and reflected in the risk assessment plan?

- Was a scope control plan in place? Do the stakeholders understand and use it?

- Lack of clear ownership and sponsorship of the project.

- Not consulting all of the major stakeholders in the project during its definition.

- One stakeholder (not the sponsor) dominates the project.

- Project product requirements are not prioritized. Some features are essential but the remaining items may have varying degrees of importance.

- Attempting a project that is too large or too complex instead of breaking it into smaller pieces.

- No common understanding of the acceptance criteria for the major deliverables.

There are three basic types of requirements. A troubled project's definition may have overlooked one or more of the following.

- Business requirements (high-level customer objectives that describe the product's uses and impact on the marketplace).

- User requirements (describe things the new product can do). Imagine how the product will be used by the various market segments it supports. Capture each of these requirements through USE cases.

- Specific functional requirements (created by the technical analysis of the USE cases).

[6] Risk Management

Risk management is an essential element of project management. Through it the project manager looks into the future and takes action that will reduce the likelihood or impact of a negative action. For example, if a scarce or expensive resource is due to start in two months and the project is likely to slip several weeks, the project manager works with that resource to adjust the schedule or locates another resource. A project without a formal risk management plan is blundering forward, expecting everything to work out; it will run smack into situations that could have been anticipated, mitigated, and avoided. Risk-related problems may include:

- Project risk list is incomplete and does not encompass all of the pending project tasks.
- Project risk list is not updated regularly to reflect the current situation.
- Risk mitigation actions are not included in the project plan.

[7] Schedule

A project's schedule is developed by breaking down the scope into its component tasks, identifying the resources required, and estimating the amount of time and resources required. If any of these steps are not correctly completed, the project will encounter problems with those tasks.

Once the schedule is rolled up, the project manager can tell the customer when the project can be completed and provide a budget consistent with that date. Often the customer will want to cut the timeline and budget so the project will be "aggressive." In the end, the project takes as long as it takes and costs what it costs. "Aggressive" projects generally spend extra funds up-front to try and reduce the timeline but generally end up taking the original amount of time since not every task can be collapsed. Following is a list of possible signs of a troubled project with schedule problems:

- The project timeline is too aggressive to achieve with the resources provided. (There are times when executives force unreasonable timelines on a project to fit their personal agenda. Such schedules are doomed from the beginning.)
- The critical path is not identified or managed.
- The project has not been broken down into manageable milestones.
- Project tasks have not been broken down sufficiently to permit reasonable estimation.
- The time estimation for tasks was too optimistic.

[8] *Budget*

The project budget estimate must be based on the approved project schedule. The budget must reflect changes in scope or schedule that occur during the project. Failure to do this will result in a project troubled by an overrun budget.

Assuming a project was properly funded at its inception, some indications of a troubled project budget may be:

- Project manager has not requested a budget adjustment to acknowledge that resources cost significantly more than estimated.

- Significant scope changes are not reflected in the budget.

- Delays in the project timeline have resulted in increased costs.

- The budget was cut without a corresponding reduction in the project scope.

[9] *General Project Management*

There are many things that a project manager must do to make a project a success. In general, the manager presses for scope stability, minimal overhead, and maximum adherence to the timeline and budget. Any instability in these areas will result in problems within the project. Such problems are addressed routinely, yet if they slip out of control, the project may not be able to recover from them.

Managing the project plan is a proactive effort of identifying and resolving roadblocks before they impact the project. Typical project management issues include:

- Internal project processes require an excessive amount of team time to complete; such processes can include status reporting, using the time reporting tools, non-productive mandatory meetings, etc.

- An indecisive sponsor or project manager who causes the team to sit and wait for an answer before proceeding. This can delay tasks and slow down all of the work.

- Customer is not responsive to questions or change requests.

[10] *Vendor*

Some projects depend heavily on outside companies for their success. This might include subcontractors, equipment suppliers, cable installation teams, and a long line of others. The project manager must prequalify these companies' quality of work and reliability. The project manager coordinates the acquisition of outside resources through the PMO, which will have more experience with a range of vendors who have successfully supported other projects. However, if the project manager is directly managing vendors, then he should treat the vendor as a team member who requires project manager support to learn about the organization and to ensure that the vendor stays engaged in the project.

The key to avoiding vendor problems is to bring them along as team members, publicly praising them for good performance but also publicly admonishing them for poor performance. If a vendor places a project at risk of failure, then as early as possible the company's executives need to become involved with ensuring purchase agreement compliance. In most cases, public image and the potential for future sales are as important as the current engagement. Typical vendor issues that can create a troubled project are as follows:

- Salespeople representing vendors sometimes underbid a proposal. They know that once the effort is underway, the buyer has little choice but to provide extra funds to complete the project. Although time could be spent proving who was at fault, litigation is an expensive process and, at worst, the vendor may not be called back again. The salesperson closes the immediate sale but then accepts the challenge of persuading the PMO to hire the vendor again.

- Overpromising performance is another problem when a vendor commits to provide experts or highly-efficient machinery at a set time and place and then does not deliver. The project is delayed as the budget pays first-class rates for third-class service.

- Vendors who promise one thing and work to change it into something substantially less for the same price. These vendors are all smiles before the sale and all tears when it is time to deliver.

- Poorly written or vague statements of work that did not permit the vendor to properly bid for the work.

- Asking the vendors to work in "a little extra work" that is not expected to impact the project scope or budget.

- Disaffected stakeholders can undermine and destroy a project that they feel is a threat to their interests. During the definition phase, the project manager must review all of the potential stakeholders who are involved with the execution of the project or whose work (or life) environment will be changed by its completion. If time is short, focus on the stakeholders with significant influence.

"Victory has a thousand fathers, but defeat is an orphan."

—John F. Kennedy

[C] Making a Recommendation

After collecting and analyzing the data, it is time to craft a recommendation for the project's future. The recommendation should clearly state what to do, how to do it, and the logic behind the decision.

Avoid laying blame in a recommendation as it will slow down the recovery process. If there are lessons to be learned from the problems, conduct a team discussion to capture the issues and identify corrective actions. Blaming someone for the failure should be done only if that person is to be promptly removed from the team. This usually leads to a long-running and bitter argument. It is better to quietly remove someone as part of a "team realignment."

There are two basic recommendations that can be made: to end the project or to continue it.

[1] Ending the Project

Sometimes a project is designed to achieve its goal within a set time window. If that window is missed, the value of the end result is greatly diminished. For example, the goal of writing new income tax software might be to have it operational in time for the upcoming tax year. If the project is delayed three months, the product would miss the prime selling season and be of little value. That project should be cancelled.

Other reasons to cancel might be that the original budget was drastically underfunded, critical resources are no longer available, or that the market requirement for the product has ended. There are a wide range of reasons to cancel a project. The key is for the customer to have the courage (and internal political clout) to cut the company's losses and end the project before committing additional funds.

Companies are reluctant to cancel projects since it means abandoning benefits from the monies that have already been spent on it. In this case, a cost-benefit analysis of the funds required to bring the remainder of the project back on track (plus the funds already paid out) should be compared to the expected value of the end result.

[2] Continuing the Project

Sometimes, an investigation uncovers that a troubled project was not that far off of its path. In those cases, the recommendation may be for tasks that move the project back onto its scope, schedule, or budget. This is the answer that the customer expects. The trick is to understand how to make these changes without losing the project's momentum. All changes are disruptive, however, and should be carefully planned.

> Some projects are needed to achieve legal compliance and cannot be cancelled. It is important that the project manager insist that the customer properly fund the project and accept a realistic timeline.

[a]   Re-Approve the Project

The basis of the recommendation to re-approve the project should be similar to the process for gaining approval of the original project. The proposal is presented as if for a new project but begins with the current state as a starting point. The proposal generally states what must be done, how long it will take, and what it will cost. Based on this project design, the customer can judge the costs versus the business merits of proceeding. If the project is to continue, then a list of the actions and costs to realign it must be provided along with their expected business impact.

As a risk reduction measure, provide the background data used to craft the recommendations. This will demonstrate the logic leading to the decision. Review this information with the customer. If the data or logic are flawed and this is discovered, then the customer can avoid a flawed solution.

Most projects are unmovable in at least one of the scope, budget, or timeline aspects. When crafting a solution, begin by assuming that there are no limitations in terms of budget or timeline to achieve the current project scope. This provides a basis of, "If this is what you want, then this is what it costs." From here, the discussion can shift between reducing the scope, or changing the timeline or the budget.

> Successfully turning a project around does not mean that it will achieve its original goals. Often it will exceed its budget and timeline. However, it does protect the company's investment to date with something to show at the end of the project.

[b]   Review the Recommendations with the Customer

Making a recommendation is the best time for identifying the resources and time required to make a project a success. It is essential that the recommendation clearly communicate the problems found and how to resolve them. It should include modifications to the scope or budget necessary to bring the project back to fulfilling the customer's primary objective.

There are basically four options in any recommendation. If time permits, include all four options. Achieve the:

1. Original project delivery date. This may require trimming the scope and/or increasing the budget.

2. Original budget total. This may require trimming the scope and/or increasing the timeline.

3. Original budget and timeline by trimming the scope.

4. Project scope. Include a new project timeline and revised budget.

Present the approved course of action to the project team in a meeting. This provides an opportunity to answer questions and explain the recommendation. Be sure to publish the approved recommendation to set new expectations for all stakeholders.

> "A battle lost is a battle one thinks one has lost."
>
> —Joseph de Maistre

[D]   A Quiet Exit for a Troubled Project

It takes an act of management courage to cancel an active project. Canceling a project means that a company has accepted as lost the time and money already sunk in the project. For a manager to order this often reflects directly on whether he or she was a participant in the project or not. Project managers appreciate this and do not lightly recommend this course of action.

Yet if a project has little chance of achieving its stated goals, it is better to cancel it earlier rather than to throw more money at it only to cancel it later. Recommending a project cancellation will require that the project manager provide the data explaining not only why it should be cancelled, but also what went wrong. Often this turns into a finger-pointing blame game. For career reasons, some project managers avoid project cancellation until forced into it by the customer. They then point at the customer as someone who cancelled an ongoing project for some mistaken reason.

Due to the potential political fallout within a company, many failing projects stumble forward until either the sponsor or the project manager

---

leaves the company. The departed person is then identified as the villain and the project is cancelled.

Cancelling a losing project can be advantageous to the company. It releases scarce resources to work on ventures that are more profitable. Of course, it also saves the company from throwing good money after bad.

[1] Settle for Half a Pie

The first decision to be made is whether the project can be cancelled. If the project's final product is to achieve something needed for legal compliance or is closely tied to the company's identity, it may press forward no matter what.

However, once the decision to cancel has been made, a project cancellation need not be a total loss. Depending on the end product or service, there may be ways to salvage and use a partially-completed product. For example:

- In a software project, add debugged code modules to the reusable code library.
- In a project to refresh the company's servers, this might be to end the refresh project after a specific server is completed.
- In a construction project, this might be the completion of a smaller building and make use of what was completed.

A well-structured project delivers specific components at every milestone. This provides ready components that the company can begin using without waiting for the entire project to be completed. Cancellation of that project is easier since there are already demonstrated benefits from its "lifetime." Prior to announcing the cancellation, make accommodations to:

- Reassign the team
- Release contractors
- Gather and reassign resources

After receiving formal approval to cancel a project, prepare a formal statement announcing the decision. The statement should explain why the project is being ended. It should also detail the reasons why it is in the company's best interest to end the project. The statement must not assign blame to anyone or anything to avoid arguments. It should also address the interests of all key stakeholders.

[2]   A Plan to Close the Plan

Once the cancellation has been approved, the project moves into a normal project closeout. The PMO may have a standard template detailing the locally required actions for closing out a project. There are a few modifications to be made to account for the sudden nature of the cancellation. Even though the project may have been obviously doomed, the sudden aspects involve employees, contractors, and vendors who were required to continue as usual until notified to the contrary.

1. Review vendor contracts with the purchasing department (sometimes called supply management). Cancellation clauses may require the advice of the legal department to understand cancellation penalties, notification process, the amount of required notice, etc.

2. Review with human resources the issues involved with reassigning employees released from the project on short notice. If it can be arranged, a few paid days off for the team may ease the shock.

> "Defeat is a school in which truth always grows strong."
>
> —Henry Ward Beecher

[E]   Lessons Learned

Learn from the past. Every project encounters problems. After all, a project is only a projection and not a sure thing. Since the company has already paid the financial penalty for the troubled project, gather the knowledge about its cause and potential prevention. Share it with all of the project managers.

Conduct a lessons-learned session with each of the major stakeholder groups, such as the project team, external stakeholders, and the customer. These sessions should draw out opinions from the participants for discussion. The result of these meetings should be published within the PMO along with a list of warning signs.

§ 21.05   SUMMARY

All projects experience problems. However, sometimes the problems pile up until just one too many overwhelms the project. When the timely completion of a project is in doubt, it is considered in danger of failure. Something must be done to protect the company's investment.

Before condemning a project as a loss, have it examined by a disinterested party, usually from outside of the company. If the company's practices are at fault, then other projects may be at risk. If a one-time event doomed the effort or timeline, the company must absorb the loss and move forward.

§ 22.01   THE VIRTUAL WORKER

A virtual worker is someone who is in the office, well, virtually. They work on their assignments, meet objectives, and participate in meetings. Virtual workers can meet with customers, create software, and even troubleshoot technical problems. They can do all of this without ever physically being in the office.

Previously, these workers were called "Telecommuters," since they used telephones to connect to their company office. Instead of driving to their office, they established work areas in their homes. Telecommuting was a tool that companies used to retain talent that had conflicting family responsibilities. Today, it is not unusual for an office worker to occasionally work remotely from home during bad weather or perhaps one day per week to eliminate the commute. All of this has been made possible by modern data and telephonic communications.

Company work culture plays a significant role in determining the success or failure of a virtual workforce. If the company respects its employees as skilled workers motivated to succeed and complete their assigned tasks promptly, then virtual workers may be a good idea. If the company believes workers are lazy, untrustworthy, and that they must be watched at all times, then virtual workers are not suitable.

Long ago, "virtual" was something that a computer did. For example, virtual memory was the place where a computer's Random Access

Memory (RAM) was artificially expanded to a portion of a fixed disk. If more RAM was needed, some of the code in the RAM was "rolled out" onto a special area of the disk and managed by the Central Processing Unit (CPU) as if it were also part of the computer's RAM. Virtual teams are similar to this in concept. People working from home—nearby or far way—act is if they were in the office, laboring alongside everyone else to accomplish the company's goals.

[A] What's in it for the Company?

Traditionally, a company hires people and assigns them work. As the labor progresses, supervisors walk about the office checking to see who shows up for work, who is working efficiently and who is not, and so on. Managers can monitor the progress made on projects and gauge how close they are to completion. A virtual workplace changes all of this. Virtual project managers must regularly check with each worker to gather this progress information.

Companies that use a large virtual workforce may realize other savings. As location becomes of secondary importance to the labor pool, secondary offices can be closed and their servers merged into the primary data center. There is no longer a need for so many offices, each with its own server. The workers all connect to the central office via high speed Internet.

Some of the benefits of supporting off-site employees include the following:

[1] Avoids the High Cost of Office Space

All companies watch their costs. The prime motive for data processing was the way it decreased costs by automating massive manual processing. In its day data processing was considered radical, while today, it is the norm. So what about the high cost of office space? Just the cost of floor space alone can run to $50 per square foot. Add in office furniture/cubicle walls for several thousand dollars, plus parking, utility costs, and more—and it is easy to see that providing employees with an adequate place to work is expensive. Imagine cutting this cost to almost nothing!

So why not change the rules? Just as computers have already eliminated many manual jobs, why not use them dramatically to reduce the number of work areas required by a company, and to reduce the high expense of office space? With the chance to gain such a cost advantage over competitors, why would any organization hesitate?

[2] Scalable Work Force

A virtual workforce is a way to balance labor supply and demand. Skilled workers are often in short supply, and many of them prefer to reside where they wish rather than where the centers of employment are located. For example, consider the situation in Colorado where there is an excess of expert JAVA programmers versus the one in Boston, where such programmers are in critically short supply. In the past, the only way to use these JAVA programmers would be to move them to where the work was located. However, if they did not want to relocate, the talent imbalance would remain. Using a virtual work arrangement, however, the Colorado workers may be employed by a Boston firm and still enjoy the western mountains. In this way, virtual workers can open many new business opportunities to companies at minimal cost to them.

Virtual workers also allow a company to scale its labor pool. Instead of limiting the amount of work by the number of local workers, a temporary work surge can be shared with a virtual workforce from across the entire enterprise. As work increases, it can be shared among the many locations. As it is reduced, virtual workers can be employed on other tasks.

> One aspect of virtual teams is to use them to dramatically shorten a project's duration. Using teams around the globe permits rapid development of software. A team in one time zone writes the code and the team in another location can test it later that same day, feeding results back to the coding team the next morning.

[B] What's in it for the Worker?

Workers have a lot to like about working in the virtual world. It simplifies their lives and saves them money.

Some of the benefits follow:

[1] No Daily Commute

Imagine all of the hours spent every workday commuting to and from the office. How many hours per week, per month, per year does this waste? Imagine recapturing all of that time for other uses! Instead of leaving the house at 7:00 AM to arrive at work before 8:00 AM; a virtual worker can already be at his virtual work place by 8:00 AM and a precious hour of life is recaptured! The same benefit arises again at the end of the workday.

Not driving to work also means savings in fuel. Imagine how much is saved by not filling a thirsty car just to drive to work. This is like an immediate pay raise, since daily expenses would drop precipitously. Does an employee incur an expense to park near the office? Not any more. Wear and tear on vehicles is also saved, making them last longer and stretching the time between required services.

> Is it snowing outside? Is a major storm raging? No problem—it is warm and dry inside! Start in to work on time, safe at home.

[2]   At Home to Handle Simple Issues

Working from home improves employee attendance. Often, domestic issues and responsibilities combine to pull workers away from their work areas. If people normally worked out of their homes, these could be resolved without missing work and disrupting the efforts of all who depend on them. For example:

- Let a repairman in—sounds simple but it requires a round trip from the office, or just as frequently, skipping a day of work entirely, since repairmen often will not indicate when they will arrive.
- Work while under the weather—mild illness can make it too uncomfortable to be in an office with others, but well enough to work from home.
- Staying home to tend sick children or staying with children who are home bound by a school "snow day."

[3]   Save on Business Attire

Typically, those who are more fashion-minded tend to spend more on clothes for work, and some jobs require the purchase and maintenance of expensive clothing. This is no longer an issue when working from home.

[C]   What's in it for Society?

It is not common for IT to be involved with social issues. Yet, virtual workers can engender many benefits for a company and for society in general. Companies constantly complain about a lack of skilled and willing workers. Some of these workers can be found, but for some reason must spend a portion of their day at home.

This might be due to physical mobility difficulties, child care responsibilities, elder care requirements, or any number of other reasons. To tap this skilled work force, companies can establish virtual jobs that can be easily accomplished from remote locations.

There is less wear on vehicles, less land used for parking lots, and fewer traffic jams. It is a wonder everyone does not do it!

A further benefit of working from home and avoiding a daily commute is a reduction in pollution from auto emissions.

[D]   Virtual Pitfalls

With such a rosy outlook, why would anyone want to tramp through rain and snow to work in an office? There are several reasons:

- Lack of direct contact with boss—many find it harder to be promoted without daily personal contact with their managers. Daily contact to let them know that everything is okay.

- Consciously and subconsciously, people use a considerable amount of non-verbal communication. Without visual contact during conversations, communication is incomplete and part of the message is lost.

- It may be more difficult to find quick answers to simple questions. Remote workers trying to contact someone in an office spend more time trying to establish communications—especially if someone will not respond to electronic requests. Who hasn't worked with someone who screened all of his calls and ignored most of his e-mail?

- Virtual workers may feel socially isolated since their co-workers are just disembodied voices.

- There can be too many distractions when working at home. Dogs want out, family members want errands run, and other domestic responsibilities may lure the worker away from his employer's assigned tasks.

- It is more difficult for companies to cultivate a corporate culture and loyalty.

§ 22.02   ESTABLISHING A VIRTUAL OFFICE

Working at home takes more than a telephone line and a corner of the kitchen table. A home office requires essentially the same floor space and furniture as an office cubicle. Office workspaces are configured as they are because that is the optimal layout for a specific type of work. Before volunteering to work from home, be sure enough dedicated space is available.

Be sure there is a dedicated work area with at least as much space as an office cubicle (6' by 8'). There should be plenty of space to spread out papers. If in doubt, find a nice desk in a furniture store and measure it (or buy it for the home office).

> Virtual workers who maintain a home office incur expenses normally borne by the employer in a traditional setting. A prime example is office supplies—pads of paper, paper for a printer, toner, etc. Companies should provide each virtual worker an allowance to cover these expenses—or not be surprised when virtual workers refuse to pay for these things with a corresponding loss of productivity.

[A]   Work Area

Minimally, the desktop space must provide enough room for a keyboard, a monitor (and CPU if it must sit on top), a telephone, and a writing area. Ideally, there will be enough room for several writing areas to accommodate paperwork sprawl, as well as some shelves to hold reference manuals. Since no one is at hand to answer quick questions, reference manuals are important for working through problems.

The work area must be in a quiet part of the house. If no one else is home all day, this is easier. If children come home from school during the work period, they may be disruptive unless a door can keep their noise out. Other interruptions to avoid:

- Noise from outside, such as busy streets, railroad crossings, noisy neighbors, etc.
- "Sounds of the home," such as chiming clocks, cuckoo clocks, squeaky chairs or doors, sounds from televisions in adjacent rooms, etc.
- Demanding pets such as barking dogs, cats who must sit on keyboards, etc.

The work area may include a storage area for printed files. These documents provide background materials and cross reference to business issues. If the worker is someone who is more comfortable with paper, he must also obtain a laser printer (cheaper to use than an inkjet printer). Ideally, virtual workers will store documents electronically, which minimizes the need for file cabinets.

> A quick way to gain weight is to sit all day. In a normal office, there are regular ups and downs out of the chair to attend meetings, discuss things, etc. In a home office, the work effort is to sit by the PC and telephone

(with the occasional trip to the refrigerator). Home workers must schedule exercise into their day in the same way as they schedule their work.

[B] Communications

All team work is based on communication. In the office, this is accomplished through spoken words, gestures, memos, meetings, casual encounters, etc. For the virtual worker, the two main vehicles of communication are data and voice (telephonic). If either of these is out of service, the virtual worker is "speechless."

Many companies provide all of the technical tools used by their virtual workers. This ensures easier tech support and exchange of artifacts. Virtual workers are highly dependent on technology to do their work. Office tools and processes do not always translate well into the virtual work space. Tools for virtual workers must be reliable. They must work together seamlessly. Remote workers do not have a local support team physically present when problems arise.

The primary enabler for virtual workers is the widespread availability of broadband communications and cheap long distance telephone service. Dial-in communication (similar in function and speed of a dumb terminal) could be used for data entry or e-mail but it lacks strong security and is limited by telephone speeds. Dial-up communication could barely keep up with the pace of work. Broadband, however, enables workers to use video conferencing, obtain webinar training, and use groupware to share documents.

Companies employing virtual workers should always provide them with a complete set-up. This includes a workstation loaded with software and a cell phone (with the bill paid by the company), and ensure that they have ready access to high speed Internet.

[1] PC and Software

Some companies provide telecommuting workers with a computer and network connection devices. The advantage of doing this is that the company knows what is on the working desktop, and so can provide prompt tech support for issues. A standard office set-up ensures that documents can be easily exchanged among team members. Telecommuters using their personal computers may introduce problems with virus transmission, and inconsistent software and software versions interfering with document exchange, among other problems.

Many companies, however, dislike spreading their hardware assets all over the country. It is too easy to lose them. These firms require everyone to purchase his own equipment and hope that, if they require that everyone obtain the same software, with the same level of patching, they will do so.

> Home workers PCs also require an Uninterruptible Power Supply (UPS) to filter electrical power and protect it from data losses during a power outage. Since data is stored on the local workstation, some method of backing up the workstation's disk storage is essential.

[2] Network Connection

The telecommuter's PC requires a secure connection to the company's network. The most common approach is a Virtual Private Network (VPN) connection through the Internet. Using this connection safeguards the company's data from interception. In order to implement such a network, special software and some authentication mechanism for the operator are required.

A VPN connection uses "something you know and something you own." It uses a combination of an authentication device, such as a number generating token or fingerprint reader, and a password. Successfully logging on through the VPN authenticates someone as the "real thing" so companies try to make sure only authorized people have access to the connection.

[3] Groupware

Many documents are the result of collaboration among team members. Groupware provides a virtual work place for sharing such team documents, sharing ideas, and submitting ideas or prototypes for team review. For example, a project description document can be drafted by the virtual project manager and then passed around the virtual team, each of whom can add to it or correct some part of it. By posting the document in a shared area, each team member can update it easily, without playing round-robin with the e-mail.

Groupware is also a valuable way to collect all of a project's files into a central repository. When a new person joins the team (or project managers are changed), he can review the files to learn about the project's issues and progress to date.

[4] Telephone

Most homes use a single telephone line. Transforming a simple home phone to a business line may take a bit of effort.

A virtual worker's primary tool is a telephone line. This is the number that will be used by company personnel to contact that person. Since personal calls can come in at any time, it is not advisable to use the family's home number. If family members tie up the line with local calls, some of the workday may be lost. Consider using the family telephone line only for outgoing work calls.

A second telephone line is useful for incoming calls. A cell phone is handy for this since it usually comes with a voicemail feature to catch missed calls. Some companies provide a cell phone and pay for all of the charges.

A connection for low-cost outbound, long distance calls is essential. This can be purchased by the month for the standard telephone line or included on a cell phone account.

The home worker's telephone needs a speakerphone (and/or headset) and a mute button. The speakerphone or headset reduces the fatigue of holding a telephone handset to an ear (many meetings will last an hour or more). The mute button reduces the amount of noise passed over the line when listening to a meeting over a bridge number.

[5] Telephone Bridge Number

Companies will frequently provide a "bridge" number for team meetings. This is a toll- free number (available from telephone companies) through which anyone can join a virtual conversation. If necessary, documents can be distributed via e-mail prior to the meeting, or an online web service can be used and all participants can log onto the site to see the documents under discussion as they are changed.

Since the bridge number is toll-free, workers should consider dialing out on the house line and save the cell phone minutes for other calls.

---

[6] Electronic Mail

Electronic mail (e-mail) can deliver documents and memos to team members. It allows for quick distribution of the same message to many people. Many companies maintain their telephone directories in the same place as their e-mail addresses. E-mail also provides a way to fill in forms, pass on friendly notes, among other things; in fact e-mail is useful for a number of things that an office worker takes for granted but that is vital to a virtual worker.

> Most e-mail systems also include a calendar function for scheduling meetings. This is very important for virtual workers who may be assigned part-time to various assignments. Rather than trying to catch them by telephone in a free moment, time can be set aside on both calendars for a quick chat.

[7] *Instant Messaging*

Instant messaging is the prize tool of a virtual worker. It is the vehicle for informal communication with co-workers, and acts to replace the quick-question-over-the-cubicle-wall. Many people can respond to a quick instant message when they don't have the time to answer a telephone. For instance, a virtual worker sitting in on a long telephone meeting and only listening to the discussion can respond to a quick inquiry that appears on his workstation—without ever leaving the meeting.

[C] Home Office Security

Security is provided for all workers in office buildings. Doors are locked, entrances monitored, and equipment is safeguarded against theft. Not so a home office! Security now becomes the responsibility of the virtual worker! This includes:

- Safeguarding equipment. It's regrettable if a burglar carries off the hardware, but no work can be done until it is replaced. So if no work is done, should a salary be provided? Not only must the virtual worker report theft of his equipment to the police, he must also must report theft of the data to the company!

- Communication connections must be secure at all times. This requires a VPN connection through a wire (not Wi-Fi). A Wi-Fi connection is much easier to intercept than the initial system logon into the company data center.

- Company documents no longer needed on site must be shredded. This reduces the likelihood that the company's documents will be scattered across the lawns when a trash can is accidentally overturned.

- CDs containing company data must be destroyed. (Be sure to purchase a shredder that eats CDs as well as paper.)

- Data backups of the virtual worker's PC must be protected as well as the information in the computer. Stealing a backup provides a criminal with the same information as would stealing the computer and its data.

[D]   Virtual Worker Personality

Working virtually is quite different from sitting in the midst of a sea of cubicles. It can be easy to be distracted when the work is tedious or boring. Virtual workers must be self-disciplined to focus on assignments without constant supervision. Even people who work well by themselves may feel adrift without the traditional office boundaries.

Virtual workers must be skilled communicators. Without visual cues from others on the team, they must pick up conversational nuances and react appropriately. They must also not read dark inferences into hasty or poorly worded written messages.

Virtual teams that cross cultural boundaries pose an additional challenge. Language nuances and different national holidays or workdays can disrupt the project flow. The way team members relate can be drastically different. Even the meaning of basic terms like when a task is "finished" can mean different things to different cultures. In some cultures, it is shameful to admit when someone is unsure of the task or how to complete it, so that person will not ask for help.

Finally, virtual team members must not require a lot of social interaction during their workdays. Telephones, e-mail, instant messaging all provide some sense of community to the isolated worker and a chance to build friendships. Some people, however, may need more than a distant voice to feel accepted within the team, and to take the drudgery of work to a higher level of satisfaction.

§ 22.03   LEADING A VIRTUAL TEAM

Leading a virtual team is a lot like leading any project team. The extra challenge for the virtual team is in the increased reliance on verbal and written communication and the fact of very little personal contact. It requires a sharp focus on what tasks need to be done and when they must be completed. As long as these objectives are achieved, the virtual worker has freedom to schedule his work.

Just as with other office workers, virtual teams often need administrative assistance to complete their assignments. A core group of administrators in the Project Management Office should provide support and advice as requested. This might include assistance with routine clerical tasks, expediting purchase orders through the approval process, following up on non-responsive team members or customers, and fulfilling requests for materials and supplies. Sometimes, virtual team members might just need a friendly voice to chat with.

Everyone has experienced arguing through e-mail. The results satisfy no one. The virtual team leader must carefully choose comments to avoid accidental offense, especially when pressing an issue on a reluctant team member.

[A] Virtual Project Manager

In a traditional setting, a project manager might walk around and visit each team member sometime during the day to see if there are any issues or obstacles interfering with assignments. In a virtual project, the same thing can be accomplished using short instant messages. The difference is that when this is done in person, there is a personal message that we're both okay. The instant message must be cheerful and carefully worded, so that it does not appear to be prodding or micromanaging.

[1] Make Frequent, Short "Visits"

Since team members are out of direct contact with their supervisor and team mates, they may feel out of touch with the organization including peer opinions. A sense of isolation is the primary reason people drop out of virtual teams and return to traditional office positions.

From a project manager's perspective, leading a virtual team takes patience and trust. Patience is needed because it sometimes takes longer to complete virtual tasks than to do the same work in an office where advice and assistance are readily available. Trust is needed that the virtual team member will meet his assignment deadlines.

The telephone is the closest thing to face-to-face communication that the virtual team can manage. The communications feedback loop is closed, with tone of voice and rhythm of the conversation filling in somewhat for lack of body language. When problems arise, the telephone is the quickest way to resolve them.

A valuable team member is someone located on site. This "feet on the street" person can chase down answers, investigate problems, and represent the virtual team at the office. A motivated onsite team member can make the toughest assignment seem (somewhat) easy.

How can someone evaluate the level of work effort that they cannot see, from a person who is just a voice over a telephone? How can someone tell when the worker is struggling and needs some assistance? How can someone provide that assistance without seeing what that person sees?

Virtual team members need more "care and feeding" than those on a typical project team. Without non-verbal communication, these employees may feel uncomfortable about their status in the team, and the project manager's attitude toward them. The project manager must address this higher need for peer approval by ensuring that any conflicts arising between team members are promptly addressed.

[2] Developing Virtual Team

Project team members should be encouraged to frequently chat among themselves. This can be done sometimes just to keep in touch, and sometimes to verify they are available to help with simple issues. There is a potential but significant risk that virtual team members may be floundering and no one knows it. Frequent communication can help to detect that someone is floundering. Frequent communication is also helpful in fostering a team culture and sense of community. As friendships emerge, so will moral support as well as technical assistance.

Just as virtual team members miss out on valuable information from a lack of "hallway conversations," so too does the project manager. The project manager, therefore, must work harder to find out the "team gossip" by dropping in on team members, perhaps via instant messaging or by telephone to "check in" and see how things are going. This process can open an informal communication channel that may serve to make virtual team members more comfortable in speaking candidly about the project and its issues.

[3] Managing Someone You May Never Meet

Virtual projects take longer to complete. More information must be written out since there are fewer chances for actual discussion. Every meeting must be formally documented since, unlike a face-to-face discussion, no one can see if anyone else is writing anything down. Also, without eye contact, the project manager may experience difficulty bringing a meeting to a satisfying conclusion.

Virtual teams often lack the urgency of a collocated onsite group. The project manager, therefore, must work constantly to build and maintain team cohesion and focus on project deadlines. A project manager must keep team members focused on the same schedule and calendar. Virtual team meetings can help the project manger accomplish this, but copying other virtual team members on routine project correspondence fosters a sense of community. Another tool for cultivating virtual team unity is to provide greater detail to the team concerning project issues and progress. The project manager must regularly reach out to each virtual team member to increase his feeling of inclusion.

When someone has a computer problem in the office, he calls the local service desk. However, a virtual team member generally does not have anyone local to consult. The virtual project manager, therefore, must have a plan for supporting virtual team member equipment. If the company owns the equipment, then the project manager should keep a spare PC loaded with software ready for immediate shipment. In a crisis, the computer can be sent out for overnight delivery in exchange for the broken unit. Otherwise the virtual worker sits and waits while the project drags on and on.

If virtual team members use their own equipment, ensure they have pre-arranged local tech support including hardware repair. Don't wait until a problem occurs to prepare to address it.

[4]   Offshore Workers

Some virtual teams include members from outside of North America. This is an extension of the idea that virtual workers can live anywhere. Whoever engages these workers must clarify the hours they must be available for communication with the office and the rest of the virtual team. Typically, this availability must extend to a normal workday wherever the office is located.

Depending on their origins and cultural background, it may be difficult to understand what the various off-site virtual members are saying. Good language skills and possession of a technical vocabulary are important qualifications for offshore team members. As is true for all team members, the use of graphics helps to share ideas.

[B]   Team Members

The single most important contributor to a successful virtual team assignment is proper orientation. New members to a virtual team must be permitted time to settle-in—just as a new office worker should be permitted some time to orient himself to his new surroundings. Further, virtual team members must be trained for their new assignment. Ideally, this training involves bringing them into the support office to pick up their equipment, learn how to use the tools, and to walk through the team processes. Such an onsite experience also allows them to meet the support staff—putting faces to the voices.

New virtual team workers also need time to adapt to their new work regimen. They need time to adjust the home work space, and to adjust to the limitations in communication and limited team interaction. As they become more comfortable with their tools and how to best apply them, their productivity will rise.

> It is *essential* that new virtual team members already possess many years of experience in their field. New people require a lot of attention (as we all did at one time). Answering their questions is very difficult to do in a virtual work environment.

Project managers should aid in the success of every new virtual team member. They should ease them into their new situation with small, non-urgent assignments. This provides time for them to "shake out" their new tools and adjust to communicating with their virtual team mates. As they appear to master their new environment, they can progress to more complex assignments.

Virtual team members must be self-motivated. A strong focus on goals and task completion keeps them working without the need for nagging. These people are not clock watchers and so prefer to be rated based on the results they produce. Goal-oriented workers tend to prefer the independence and flexibility that virtual work situations provide for their schedule. They prefer that the project manager clearly define their assignments and that they be rewarded according to their performance.

Virtual teams develop their own social rules governing communications. Project managers can force the issue early in the team-forming process by providing simple guidelines for communications as follows:

- Carefully prepare all participants for meetings. Distribute documents for advance review. This will result in fewer follow up discussions. A virtual project manager cannot run over to the copier to make copies for the meeting. These documents must be sent out in advance (because e-mail systems add a time lag to document distribution).

- Always debate points over the telephone and not through e-mail. If more than three e-mails are exchanged to clarify a point, it is easier to call and explain the matter than to write pages explaining things in detail.

- Take time before responding to criticism. If something someone says is critical, wait a while and then call. Don't let misunderstandings fester. Be sensitive to the needs of others. It is easier to work patiently with someone courteously than it is to fight and create enemies.

- Respect the normal working hours of others. Time zones count. However, emergencies take priority.

- Always return messages promptly. Do not build unnecessary delays into the project.

- Never hesitate to ask other team members for help—but spread out the requests since everyone is busy. There is no shame in not knowing how to do something—but there is in not asking for help.

- Be careful when using humor, since the body language aspect of interpretation is not present. Also, humor tends not to translate well across cultures.

Because the virtual team is so dependent on messaging and prompt responses, the project manager must ensure that the team members promptly respond to requests from one another. In a physical office, a person can check to see if someone else is on the telephone, but virtual workers cannot see that far, so they leave their messages and move on.

Virtual teams depend upon prompt communication. Team members slow to respond (for whatever reason) to a question will cause the project progress to lag. Further, if the slow responder is intentionally delaying an answer, the team can develop mistrust and considerable dissention. Disaffected team members can choose to ignore messages or leave them for other times. This increases team stress.

§ 22.04 VIRTUAL PROJECT MANAGEMENT OFFICE

Leading a team of independent minded project managers is a demanding task. It is made easier by establishing a framework for data collection and sharing through a set of standard forms and processes.

Trying to do this virtually is hard, much like a "normal" Project Management Office (PMO).

[A] Standards

With workers scattered all over creation, from a range of technical and cultural backgrounds, the PMO has difficulty in obtaining consistent results. As with any other PMO, there must be a set of project management tools promulgated to all team members.

[1] Standardize Document Naming Conventions

A PMO of any type is a busy place. Given that each project manager can run between 6 and 10 projects (at various stages of completion) at any given time, multiplied across a half dozen project managers in a PMO, this means that there are a lot of documents to track. To ensure that documents are filed in the correct place, a standard naming convention must be used. Typically, this is the project number, followed by the official project name, followed by the title of the document. If the document is revised, then a version number is appended onto the end. For example:

PM-1234 Project Manager's Compensation Study—Meeting Minutes 1 Apr 07v2.0

- Project number: PM-1234
- Project name: Project Manager's Compensation Study
- Document title: Meeting Minutes 1 Apr 07
- Version number 2

[2]   Contact Lists

Project managers should not lose time contacting people. Contact lists must be distributed to all new virtual team members. Up-to-date lists should be centrally available for downloading. The list should include:

- Name
- Role
- Telephone number
- Cell phone number
- E-mail address
- Time zone
- Supervisor's name.

[3]   Resources Requests

Project managers must understand how to request resources for their virtual teams. This can be confusing since most virtual team members work for a variety of project managers on a range of projects. Also, it is impossible to walk around the office to see who is sitting back twiddling his thumbs. If virtual team members charge their time to projects, then idle time is easier to determine. The PMO manager must know what resources are available both at the present time and in the near future in order to avoid starting projects that will have no one available to work on them.

[4]   Meeting Minutes

For all virtual meetings, the high points of the discussion must be recorded and distributed to the participants. The project managers are responsible for this task, and must also ensure that a copy is submitted to the central project document store. Meeting minutes are a valuable source of information to the PMO manager in early detection of problems, and to see if projects are spinning out of control. The minutes also provide a valuable historic record of what did or did not happen and when.

[5]   Standard Status Report and Roll Up

There must be performance metrics. Project managers must ensure that their status reports contain the essential information necessary to quickly compile the data into a summary report.

[B]   Processes

The virtual PMO must have clearly documented and published processes. This reduces confusion when virtual team members are working part-time for multiple project managers. If all of the processes are the same, then consistent documentation for comparison can be expected.

[1]   Store All Documents in a Central Repository

Virtual teams have a higher attrition rate than normal project teams. To ensure a smooth transition as required, copies of all key project documents must be sent to the PMO for storage in a central server. This includes:

- Project descriptions and associated changes
- Status reports
- Meeting minutes
- Customer approvals

[2]   Monitor Team Communications and Seek Ways to Smooth Them Out

Communication overload can be an issue. There should be a standard priority for communication among the virtual team members. The sender of a message is responsible for setting its priority status, and including this information in the first part of the message title line. Example levels:

- Hot! Must have an immediate response
- Urgent—answer within 4 hours
- (no urgency listed) 16 hours

[3]   Create a Common PMO Vocabulary to Minimize Misunderstanding

There should be a common vocabulary in use by the virtual team members. The definitions must be clear and understood the same way by the entire team. Although this is most important for cross-cultural teams, it is also critical for every virtual team. Any two people can disagree about the same term. If this is complicated by different regional or international cultural backgrounds, there can be unavoidable problems.

Another communication issue to note is that messages must be sent within context. A simple way to do this is to forward responses to messages that include the original questions. Another way to do this is to repeat the question along with the response in a single message.

---

[4]   Team Members Must Post Their Normal Working Hours on the Contact List

Virtual team members must be readily available at agreed upon times. In the United States, this means the normal working hours for the local time zone. For international workers, however, this means that team members must be available for at least one-half of the normal U.S. working hours, even if this means that they must work during their night. European locations are usually available early in the morning, North American time.

By posting working hours, it is easier for virtual workers to separate work time from family time. There will be times when someone must cut into his normally non-working hours to attend a meeting, but the PMO manager must ensure these times are few. Otherwise, team members may stop accepting virtual assignments.

[C]   "Pumping Up" the Virtual Team

Take time to celebrate the virtual team's successes at milestones. Everyone can use a pat on the back sometimes. For a virtual project office, this requires some new ideas. One way is to plan a virtual team party. Schedule the event in advance. Send out gift cards for national restaurants and ask the team to pick up something to share at the same time (lunch, however, may be difficult to schedule across many time zones).

The PMO manager can help to reduce virtual team member stress by instituting a continuous improvement program. In such a program, team members describe the major obstacles that get in the way of completing their work. The PMO manager then strives to eliminate these obstacles—even if it means standing up to the ultimate project customer (something many PMO managers may be afraid to do). As one of the tasks is completed, the virtual team can nominate another task for that top problem spot.

The second part of the continuous improvement program consists of a list of things that seem impossible to change. In the long run, though, nothing is impossible. The PMO manager must also whittle away at this second list, although successes here take much longer to realize.

Chapter 23

Project Management the RUP Way

§ 23.01   IS AGILE PROJECT MANAGEMENT THE ANSWER?

Traditional project management approaches have had dismal success records. There are many reasons for this. One obvious reason is the time lag between the process of the collection of requirements and their translation into a product desired by the customer. Between the time that requirements are collected and the final product is delivered, many things may have changed. Locking in project requirements too early in the process can result in building what the customer wanted yesterday. One way to address this timing problem is through the use of an Agile process.

Agile (the name reflects its emphasis on agility) project management cuts much of the built-in delays out of project management. It emphasizes face-to-face communication among the team members and between the project manager and the customer. Often the entire group is located in a single work area facilitating many small and quick exchanges as issues arise. (Of course, this requires a significant amount of trust among the participants.)

As the Agile project management movement took flight, it sparked an idea called "The declaration of interdependence for modern management." This extends the basic concepts of Agile development to the sometimes bureaucratic-bound principles of project management.

"The declaration of interdependence for modern management
    We . . .

- **increase return on investment** by—*making continuous flow of value* our focus.

- **deliver reliable results** by—*engaging customers* in frequent interactions and shared ownership.

- **expect uncertainty** and manage for it through—*iterations, anticipation and adaptation.*

- **unleash creativity and innovation** by—recognizing that *individuals are the ultimate source of value*, and creating an environment where they can make a difference.

- **boost performance** through—*group accountability* for results and *shared responsibility for team effectiveness.*

- **improve effectiveness and reliability** through—*situationally specific strategies*, processes and practices."

"http://en.wikipedia.org/wiki/PM_Declaration_of_Interdependence"

[A]   Agile or Traditional Project Management?

Traditional project management has its roots in the creation of physical objects. Pyramids, skyscrapers, and large ships are complex things; construction of them is well suited to traditional project management. A thorough understanding of the customer's requirements is necessary before any work begins. Otherwise, extensive reworking may be required to accommodate changes, or the required changes are never made. In both cases, the customer will be dissatisfied with the result.

This problem, identifying all of the requirements before work begins, is at the heart of customer dissatisfaction with IT programming. Few customers fully understand what they want or the implications of later changes. As the product begins to take shape, new ideas spring to the customer's mind. Also, the business climate might shift and open new opportunities or the perception of the need to keep up with competitors. Depending on customers to identify what they need in advance, and anticipating only minor changes before completion of the project, is not realistic.

So what to do? How can a project manager estimate a budget and a schedule without solid specifications? If the customer has the freedom to change anything, then the concept of rating projects in terms of on time and under-budget cannot work. One solution to this problem is to use the "Unified Process."

> Unified Process is the public version of a proprietary process known as the Rational Unified Process® or RUP® (both trademarks of IBM®).

A traditional project is wasteful because of the tugs and pulls with the customer about paying for new features, or if the team hides problems from the customer to slip the project in on time (the focus here is on time and cost rather than customer satisfaction). Much time is lost debating and negotiating, and through delays in signing an authorization. RUP recognizes the human nature aspect of requirements gathering. Under RUP, projects are designed around smaller "chunks" called "iterations." The first iteration builds a basic version of the desired product. The customer inspects it, and then adds features to the requirements list for the next iteration.

Iterations allow the customer to make decisions more easily about just-discovered design omissions or unpredicted value additions. The project continues through these iterations until the customer decides that the benefits from the next iteration do not justify its cost (or the customer runs out of money).

> The Unified Process is the OpenSource version of the proprietary product, RUP. In fairness, RUP came first and IBM published the open source version

itself. Since to most people, both versions are so very similar, they are incorrectly referred to by most people as "RUP," the legal IBM trademark.

[B]   Rational Unified Process

Rational Unified Process is a software product available from IBM. It is a combination of "rational," the name of a company acquired by IBM and the "Unified Process" (also from the same company). The RUP software provides many tools to facilitate RUP-based projects.

RUP is a framework of principles that are adjusted by each project according to circumstances. This flexibility can be uncomfortable for companies accustomed to lock-step processes. It is ideal for building software, however, since it is easy to add on modules or even to rework the internal architecture (try that when building a house!).

RUP is based on six principles:

1. *Adapt the process to fit the situation.* Rather than a rigid approach, RUP encourages local modifications. It is scalable from small to large projects.

2. *Balance stakeholder priorities against technical and financial considerations.* Keep the focus on the reason the project exists (customer satisfaction). This requires extensive and ongoing customer involvement in the project.

3. *A high degree of communication between the various project team members.* Ideas are shared, test results examined, and project requirements refined. Small, expert teams co-located in the same work area are preferred. Co-location is very important to quickly share ideas since team members can focus on the message and not on the medium.

4. *Value is demonstrated iteratively by growing the product's functionality with each iteration.* This permits shifting the product focus as the business requirements change. It also avoids the analysis-paralysis of a project never beginning at all because the full set of customer requirements can never be assembled to everyone's satisfaction.

5. *Keep a high level of design abstraction to facilitate the use of reusable code and simple tools.* Although it takes time to build a usable library, in the long run, organizations save money maximizing their reusable code.

6. *Require all team members to closely monitor the quality of the product.* Extensive testing and user involvement help to keep the product quality high. Again, this requires a lot of customer interaction.

It is not required for the team to be collocated. RUP relies on just-in-time planning which results in easier to understand requirements, fewer changes and less waste. With RUP, the teams are smaller, more expert, and spend more time discussing issues.

§ 23.02 FOUR PHASES OF RUP

RUP uses a combination of Waterfall and Spiral models. The RUP framework uses the spiral model in which a series of small projects are used to build a base product. This product is then refined using a series of other projects. Within each of the small projects, the waterfall model is used, which means that the processes follow a specific sequence.

RUP is an iterative model that uses a discover-and-improve approach. Imagine the system shaped as a spiral. With each turn of the spiral, more of the solution is uncovered. Essential concepts of RUP are the following:

- *Inception definition and agreement of all stakeholders as to scope.* The scope of the project is determined by many examples that define required functions. Initial systems architecture is developed. Cost, schedule, and risk are estimated.
- *Elaboration.* Project engineering encompassing the details of the problem and possible solutions are formed. Time, cost, and risk estimates are refined. A prototype is constructed.
- *Construction.* A working system is built.
- *Transition.* The product now has sufficient business value to turn over to the customer.

Each of these phases ends with a re-sync of user expectations and a decision point to continue or kill a project. A decision to stop affects the entire project not just the previous effort (phase).

RUP can have a long payback period because it is based on reusable libraries, but has a heavy documentation requirement for reusable code. The four phases are outlined below.

[A] Inception

The inception phase is similar to starting any other type of project. That is, requirements are gathered, risks are evaluated, a business case is assembled, and technical feasibility is checked. These are all of the usual project start-up actions. At this point, the customer must agree to finance the next iteration of the project, which means that the anticipated value exceeds the anticipated costs. If not, the project ends.

The inception phase begins with the collection of customer requirements. This requirements gathering step results in a vision statement for this iteration. The vision statement describes what the finished product will look like and how it will perform. It also includes measurable performance criteria.

The various project initiation steps are consolidated into a business case for customer review. They include:

- Creation of critical use case models for gathering the types of information expected to relate to the requested changes.

- Formation of anticipated project benefits into a business case that compares the projected costs to the projected benefits. This includes verifying the alignment of the project with the company's current goals (via Portfolio Analysis).

- Meetings with all affected stakeholders to determine their opinions and uses for the envisioned product.

- Identification, assessment, and, when possible, mitigation of risks.

At the conclusion of the inception phase, the project is declared to be technically feasible and the basic architecture for the product is proposed. The customer agrees to the project definition (scope, vision, and measurable success criteria). The schedule and costs are approved. The project schedule includes approved plans for the elaboration phase.

[B] Elaboration

The elaboration phase is similar to the typical project design phase. It creates a tested technical design that will form the basis for the final product.

During this phase, the use case analysis is further developed and applied to primary stakeholders. Architecturally significant use case flows are identified. The goal of this phase is to stabilize all explicit and implicit user and technical requirements prior to the construction phase. By the end of this phase, approximately 80% of the use case analysis should be completed. This enables a more accurate time and cost estimate for the construction phase.

A key deliverable of the elaboration phase is a tested technical architecture. The inception phase only proposed a technical architecture. The elaboration phase further develops the project's technical requirements through the development and implementation of detailed use case analysis. This is used to identify the proposed architecture.

The architecture is tested to ensure it can provide the technical performance required by the specifications. Sometimes this may require building a prototype (which pulls some of the work from the construction phase forward to this phase) to create something that can validate the architectural design. Ensuring that the architecture can support the desired construction is a key risk mitigation action.

> Failure to adequately design and test the architecture is a common cause for failure during the construction phase.

At the conclusion of this phase, the risks for the construction phase have been updated, as are the appropriate mitigation actions. This is accomplished through extensive use case analysis plus architecture testing. The project's business case is updated and enough information is made available for a make or buy decision by the customer. If the project is to proceed, the project plan and budget for the construction phase are then approved.

[C] Construction

The construction phase easily consumes 50% or more of the time of the entire iteration. In the construction case, the specifications derived from use cases in the elaboration phase are finalized and coding begins. As coding proceeds, the use cases are finalized and the remaining software specifications are approved.

As the coding progresses, the results are tested extensively. The product is compared to the desired outcomes described in the use cases. Product testing verifies component performance as well as conformance to requirements. Time is set aside to create the user documentation and technical support manuals. The project plan and budget for the transition phase are approved.

The end result of the construction phase is a tested, deployable, documented solution with adequate quality to fulfill the customer's requirements. All functionality should be in place. This phase is considered complete when the customer formally accepts the product.

[D] Transition

The transition phase passes the completed product over to the customer for use. It ends when the customer accepts the final product and the technical maintenance takes responsibility for ongoing support.

Extensive acceptance testing is now performed. Beta testing serves to shake performance and minor functionality problems out of the product. Technical efforts in this phase concentrate on promptly resolving defects. Data may require migrations prior to testing the new system. In some cases, the new technology must also run parallel to the current system. The product is checked against the promised product quality described in the inception phase.

The future support team is now trained on the technical aspects of the product. They verify that the technical support manual created in the construction phase is acceptable.

Training is provided to end users so that they can understand how to use the product features. At the end of this phase, a customer satisfaction survey is provided to those who participated in the use case development effort in order to fine tune future efforts.

At the end of the transition phase, the project is administratively closed and preparations begin for the next project iteration.

§ 23.03   THE NINE DISCIPLINES OF RUP

RUP classifies tasks as being part of one of six engineering or three supporting disciplines necessary to successfully manage a project. The amount of activity under any one discipline varies depending on the phase.

[A]   Engineering Disciplines

- *Business Modeling.* The engineering team develops an understanding and familiarity of the client organization. The team should understand the current client's needs and how the software developed will meet them. Business rules and dynamics within the client organization are also important pieces to this puzzle. End users, the client, and the development team all must agree on the purpose of the software. Their vision for the system's incorporation in the client business should be documented for future reference.

- *Requirements.* Discerning the true needs of the client and end user is the most critical aspect of designing and implementing any IT system. To gather the desired requirements, use cases are written describing how the end user wants to use the system. Use cases are a critical concept in RUP, and are described below. Once the team and client agree on the detail of the use cases, the implementation order should be prioritized based on the risk to the project. Risk has two components: (1) how difficult it will be, financially or in time, to attempt to successfully implement the use case, and (2) the anticipated impact of failure.

- *Analysis and Design.* Once the requirements for the system have been established, the components of the system must be designed. While designing the system architecture, the following things should be kept in mind:

  - The system must fulfill its use cases. How it is to do this should be explicitly laid out.

  - If the requirements change, the system should not need an entire redesign. Ensure the design is as modular or component-oriented as possible. This also allows for easier unit testing later and makes code reuse simpler.

○ Each component must be integrated into the system. The interface between each component should be plotted so that each component can be added to the project with minimal rework.

This part of the process doesn't necessarily involve any coding.

- *Implementation.* Engineers and team members working on the project implementation will finalize the design, making sure the system has a useful amount of subsystems or modules. The team will then create the designed subsystems, being sure to test each component thoroughly prior to integrating it with the rest of the system.

- *Testing.* This discipline further extends the testing work done previously during system implementation. It involves verifying that all use cases and system requirements have been correctly implemented, as well as making sure each component and object interacts correctly. Defects should be identified and handled prior to the software being released. Testing should examine product reliability, functionality, system performance, and application performance. It is also important to be sure during this phase that the system is as user friendly as possible.

- *Deployment.* When preparing to deploy the current iteration of the project, several items need attention. The system needs to be packaged and distributed to the appropriate individuals. Documentation pertinent to installation, maintenance, and use should be provided to assist future developers and end users utilize and improve the system.

[B]   Supporting Disciplines

- *Configuration and Change Management.* Configuration management uses version control to keep track of software updates and document changes. Configuration also involves tracking which work products are affected by what information so that, when the iteration draws to a close, the work product documentation can be updated as appropriate. For example, the installation manual depends on the installation process; if the process changes, then the manual should be changed.

  Change management encompasses multiple versions of a work product. At the end of an iteration, appropriate documentation is written. But, in the next cycle, the document will need to be updated. This updating is likely to be done by those who were most closely involved with the design, implementation, and testing of the work product. Because of this, multiple individuals or groups may update the same document simultaneously. The change management function ensures that all changes made by these team members are retained when the next document is released, and that nothing is lost by overwriting or because one of the multiple updated versions was neglected.

Another important task is keeping track of the status of each change or configuration being monitored. It is helpful to assign names to each, such as new, recorded, approved (or not approved), delegated (assigned), and resolved.

- *Project Management.* RUP has two levels of project planning: phase planning and iteration planning. The phase plan consists of an overview of the project, generally describing it in broad terms, and ignoring the nitty gritty of the individual steps. Finer detail is developed through the iteration plans, which enumerate the work that will be accomplished for each project cycle. For example, the first iteration cycle may be to get a gui running along with a properly functioning basic algorithm. The second iteration cycle may be to implement other features to the system that are perhaps less important, but desirable nevertheless.

- *Environment.* The focus of the environment discipline is to establish a work environment conducive to making quality progress on an IT project. The three types of environments to consider for each project are: (1) the project environment, (2) the iteration environment, and (3) the continued support of the first two types. The main task in this discipline is defining how the work will proceed, including the configuration of software and equipment or the standardization of the format for documentation. At least as important is ensuring that all developers have the tools they need to continue to work effectively and efficiently. This may include their knowing where software libraries and collections can be found, ensuring any necessary networks are running smoothly, and that all necessary or relevant software is readily available.

§ 23.04   START WITH A USE CASE

Use cases are a technique for gathering and documenting user requirements. Developers consult with end user customers to determine what is needed for the project and how the project will achieve the customer's goals. This documentation guides the engineering of the final product to be sure that it matches the customer's true, and often unspoken, needs.

This technique also serves as a way to gather customer requirements when (as is often the case) even the requestor does not really know what is needed. Use case technique is a way to develop a shared vision between the team and the customer, which guides the project.

Key components of the use case technique are:

- *System use case model.* Records the critical and secondary system details.

- *System vision.* Mission statement and a roadmap for the product; provides context for solution detailed in the use case.

- *System supplementary specification.* Anything that does not fit in the use case.

[A] Use Cases Function

As noted, use cases are tools to help elicit project requirements. The contents of each use case are created by the customers and potential end users, but the documentation is done by a project team member. Generally, the team member guides the customer and end users through the process, asking pertinent questions along the way to ensure they have enough information. This will aid in determining the broad objective for the system.

The team will then use the information gathered to set the requirements for the project. It is important to note that some requirements are essential, and some are optional. For example, a person must be able to check e-mail. He may want to have the font be orange on a grey background. The difference here is that the ability to check e-mail is a critical function; being able to pick a custom color scheme is something optional.

When a use case list seems to be fairly exhaustive, the contents should be converted into requirements, and prioritized by investment (time and money) and impact of failure (low to high). The requirements should be communicated to all stakeholders, and they should reach an agreement on them.

[B] Building Use Cases

Constructing use cases is as simple as getting the customer to envision what the system will do, and then writing down every step of the process. A use case can provide information on what the system should do for the actors, or end users. The term "end user" includes those who will be maintaining and managing the end product, and those who will be updating it. The term may encompass a guest user or an administrator as an occasional but rightful user of the product.

Use cases should contain the following:

- *Name*—a brief description of the case.
- *Actor(s)*—who will interact with the system
- *Objective*—what is hoped to be accomplished
- *System boundary*—who or what interacts with system, such as the network or a local processes running on a computer.

A use case description is a more thorough view of the task to be accomplished. This should include the following:

- *Basic flow of events*—This is how the customer or end user sees a typical interaction with the system, and is considered to be the normal way of obtaining value from the system. It should include the expected path through the system for end users and should explicitly state any assumption behind the basic flow, such as "There will be a gui."

- *Alternative flow of events*—These are other ways to reach the state described in the "basic flow of events," or things that may happen "on the way." This could comprise other ways of attaining value for end users, or could explain how the product might generate exceptions and errors. As a general rule, there are usually several alternative paths that accompany any basic flow. For example, if the use case is to exit the system, a basic flow could be to open the main menu and choose exit. However, the user may also achieve this function by clicking a close button. The end user may also achieve the same result by ending the process. But there are other considerations. What happens if there has been a change to the system? What about if the user has not logged off? By using alternative flow scenarios, it becomes much easier to see the kinds of risks involved in the project.

The additive use structure of RUP enables a project to develop its requirements, manage its scope through flow of events, and develop acceptance tests.

§ 23.05 MANAGING A RUP PROJECT

Successfully managing a RUP project requires a different mindset than managing a traditional project. Companies get what they reward. By deemphasizing the project budget and timeline and refocusing attention on value to the customer, even the most hard core traditional project manager can run a RUP project.

Note that the RUP process sidesteps some of the important project management responsibilities such as team forming, managing the project budget, etc. The process falls back on the more traditional project management techniques for this.

[A] Phase Planning

The RUP project is described in broad terms as a "phase plan" or framework. Within this framework are a series of smaller projects known as iterations. Each of the iterations is itself a small and complete project.

The phase plan, developed at the start of the project, applies to all iterations. However, because of the nature of agile project management, if one or more of the project iterations determine something else is required, then one or more of the iterations may be changed.

The phase plan should include the following:

- A process for identifying, measuring and reporting project metrics. This is often detailed in the part of the plan that describes the requirements for status reports and stakeholder notification.

- A risk management process for identifying, assessing, and assigning responsibility for mitigating risks. The individual iterations will use this guidance to address their risks.

- A problem resolution plan (commonly known as an issues list) to track problems that arise and to assure that someone is assigned to resolve them.

- A product acceptance process to describe the types of tests that the customer requires.

The phase plan, then, considers the overall effort and breaks the project down into smaller projects. If the phase is scheduled to last from four through six months, then each iteration period may be set at two months. The actual length of an iteration is adjusted based on the effort required and complexity of those requirements.

[B] Iteration Plan

An iteration plan plots a course of action for meeting the goals for the current or upcoming iteration.

The key points to an iteration plan are the following:

- *A list of requirements for the entire project.* If the iteration plan is not the first one in the project history, then it should explicitly state how each requirement was updated, why it was changed, and who authorized the change.

- *Priorities for development.* Each requirement, corresponding with one or more use cases, should be prioritized based on risk and impact to the project. Prioritization is very important. Objectives should be set aggressively so the team has a goal to strive for, but they should also be realistic. In the event that the project should begin to fall behind, this prioritization makes it easy to choose which objectives to drop first in any iteration.

- *A roadmap of classes, packages, or other software collections should be documented.* This documentation is used, in part, for tracking the progress in fulfilling use cases as well as supplying information to other developers who may need to interface with existing code.

- *A list of risks.* These are items that must be addressed as well as changes, such as bug fixes, that need to be made.

- *The status of the project.* This document should note how the progress being made matches the schedule and proposed budget, as well as noting any large problems that plague the project.

- *Supplementary documentation.* This is used to guide management decisions. This documentation should include:

  ○ A work breakdown structure, enumerating which personnel are assigned to which tasks and in what order the tasks should be handled.

  ○ An estimate of how long each task will take. This can be based on similar tasks completed in past projects, the skill of the worker or team, and predictions from experienced workers.

  ○ The critical path, or a similar diagram, showing which tasks must be completed and/or underway before another task can either begin or be finished.

  ○ A schedule based on the previous information that will be followed during the iteration.

At any time, there are usually two iteration plans being referenced and/or written: the plan for the current iteration and the plan for the next iteration. In earlier stages of an iteration, more focus will likely be placed on adhering to the plan for the current iteration. The plan for the next iteration, however, should not be neglected during this time. Later on, the iteration plan for the next iteration will become more important.

[C]   Scoping Phase

This is the part of the process when requirements are gathered. These allow the project manager to generate a requirements breakdown structure, often called a RBS. This is the time to assess the customer's comfort level for each defined function. Any perceived problems expressed by the customer should be resolved at this time.

When setting the scope for the current iteration the following actions should be taken:

- *Establish a business model.* The framework of expectations for both the customer and the contractor is to be defined and refined as needed for the project.

- *Gather core requirements using a function and feature list.* This is usually accomplished through the development of use cases.

- *Enumerate all cases that flow from the functions/features list.* Use cases are the primary driver of the RUP process and serve as the basis upon which detailed schedules are developed. They are also used to develop methods for acceptance testing.

- *Craft a high level outline of the phases and iterations.*

[D] Launching Phase

The launching phase, the final phase of an iteration, is the assembly of pertinent documentation and software. It includes organizing the distribution of the product, whether through a store, a local network, or other source. Since each iteration is like launching a new project and includes an entire project life cycle, the project should be able to stand alone at this point.

[E] Closing Phase

Finally, the closing phase is when the customer determines whether or not to proceed with an additional iteration. The product may now be deemed to be up to specifications, or it may be deemed to have made insufficient progress to continue. The customer company may not be able to afford more iterations, or there may be enough money to fund a cycle beyond what the customer had originally envisioned. If the customer decides to continue, the next iteration plan must be approved. If a new iteration plan is approved, then the project continues. Otherwise, the project is over.

A big payoff of using the RUP system is the creation of a library of reusable code and reusable case studies. In order to take advantage of this, however, a careful validation that all documentation has been properly completed prior to closing the project iteration is required. Note that even though the project framework sets the boundaries, for the project, a RUP project ends only when the customer is no longer willing to fund the next iteration.

§ 23.06 SUMMARY

RUP attempts to address a lingering problem in project management, which is: "how can a long duration project avoid the large number of design changes demanded by the customer during development?" This has been a significant issue in IT. News headlines point out that many IT projects costing tens or hundreds of millions of dollars that are scrapped before completion. Many excuses are offered for this, but the primary problem is using the traditional approach of completing the entire task in one bite.

Iterative project management makes much more sense for large projects, or projects with poorly defined goals. It allows work to begin knowing full well that changes made later may result in the discarding of some of the work. There is still value, however, in what is cast away because the execution of that part of the project has helped everyone to better understand what was possible for the project, and what improvements might cost.

The key thing to remember from this chapter is that iterative projects are practical. In fact, they already exist in projects with terms like "Phase I" or "Phase II" in their name. Each phase is an iteration toward a project's ultimate goal.

Chapter 24

Maturity Models

§ 24.01 PROJECT MANAGEMENT MATURITY MODELS

[A] Why Bother with Project Management Improvement?

How well run is your company's Project Management Office? Is it as effective as it could be? Is it as effective as a typical Project Management Office for a company your size? Even more important, is it as effective as your closest business rival or even more effective than that? How can a company gauge its current effectiveness and how much more effective could it be?

What aspect of a process would someone focus on to achieve the greatest improvement for the time spent? To examine and judge a process you must know what should be accomplished, when it should be accomplished, and the optimal way to achieve the maximum effect. Project management is a process because it is actually a repeatable series of actions. While the product created by the project is unique, the same basic steps or methodology can be applied to all work efforts. This means that the repeatable process of managing a project is repeatable and can be improved.

Everybody likes to know how well he is doing compared with other companies, especially those considered the best in the class. Once project management caught on in major corporations as a business discipline, people soon noticed that some companies embraced the concept well, while others only claimed to follow it but still did what they pleased. Maturity models began to spring up as a way to gauge how closely an organization follows "best industry practices."

Project management maturity modeling is loosely based on the concept of continuous improvement. Since a maturity model gauges how closely a company's actions adhere to industry best practices, companies are rated against a standard (known as a maturity model) to see how effectively and efficiently their project management operates vis a vis this standard of measurement. This chapter overviews maturity models from COBIT^{TM}, PMI's OPM3^{TM}, and OGC's P3M3^{TM}. Each has its own emphasis and value.

So when might a company want to gauge the maturity of its project management processes? This may occur right after a merger, before and after investing in an expensive tool set, or when making significant changes in its processes. It might also be used at any time to identify shortcomings and to develop a training program, perhaps after coming under serious executive scrutiny.

> Maturity models are one of the many tools used to gauge process effectiveness under IT Governance.

[B] Project Management Payoff

The sad truth is that project management in most companies is very poorly done. Consider Chart 24-1. In the beginning, project management was located in the lower left corner of the figure. Companies assigned projects to people as they assigned any other business task. Little money was invested in project management, and little benefit came out of it.

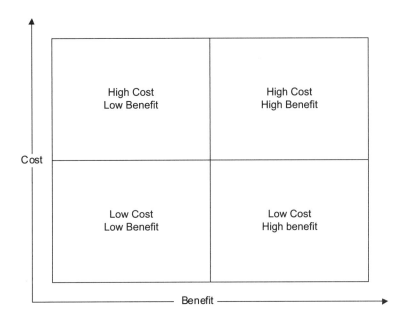

Chart 24-1: Project Management Program Cost versus Return

The second stage of project management is the upper left corner of the figure—high cost and low benefit. Unfortunately, this is where most companies are stuck today. Think not? How many project management offices consistently turn in projects on time and within budget? Most companies would be thrilled with a 30% project completion rate and must make do with much less. They are stuck in the high cost low benefit corner.

In many cases, the goal of the process is to move project management to the high benefit side of the matrix. To do this, project management offices often throw money at their processes to ensure completion—but this means that the result is more expensive than it should be. The high costs come from salaries of highly skilled personnel needed to accomplish the ends of the project, from purchasing necessary tools and training the personnel. The path from low benefit to high benefit may be the result of over allocating resources and the introduction of Project Management quality programs.

The true goal of the project management process must be to reach the high benefit, low cost corner of the figure. Companies must be satisfied with the results achieved so far before they will tinker with the cost aspects of the process. If the money was invested during the high cost/high benefit period, then costs will go down as the project teams progress through the learning curve.

[C]   What Is a Maturity Model?

A maturity model is a gauge of organizational effectiveness. Maturity models provide criteria for identifying the status of an organization with respect to a given objective or desired outcome. Maturity models are often accompanied by a set of descriptions of what an organization's behavior is like at each level of maturity for the specific objective.

Maturity model designs are based on research or discussion of the practices that make an organization most effective. They do not give specific instructions for the "how" of a task—only on the desired outcome. It is necessary to be general in design because of the great differences between companies in size, goals, products created, mandatory quality level, etc.

The freedom of choice in methods that can be used goes hand in hand with the concept of best practices. A best practice is what needs to happen—that is what a method is intended to accomplish, specifically how something is done. A company may use a maturity model for many specific reasons such as: to improve efficiency, to improve customer relations, or as a way to meet certain criteria in order to be eligible to win a contract.

There are as many different maturity models as there are consultants and organizations to market them. Some of these models have a more focused approach than others. Originally, CMMI^{TM} was created for software development, although its use has since been expanded. As researchers evaluate existing practices, new and different models continue to emerge.

Most maturity models use "levels" to indicate just how mature (or conforming to best practices) a company is. Although the lower levels indicate poorer performance, it may not always be cost effective to work toward the upper levels in a maturity model. Some companies are (justifiably) satisfied with a rating somewhere in the middle.

§ 24.02   THE COBIT PROJECT MANAGEMENT FRAMEWORK

[A]   Overview of COBIT

COBIT is an abbreviation for Control Objectives for Information and related Technology. It is a framework for implementing effective IT governance through the use of control objectives. These objectives evaluate or audit processes involving planning and organization as well as logistical issues. COBIT is designed around a set of best practices, which is a consensus from experts regarding what helps a business run as efficiently as possible. These best practices include activities that are carried out by project managers.

COBIT is often used to help a company located in the United States meet the legal requirements of the Sarbanes-Oxley Act, passed in 2002 in response to corporate scandals. Most notably, its framework addresses section 404 of that Act, which requires an "internal control report" be generated. COBIT provides guidelines for a standardized way of generating many of the required internal documents.

COBIT is based, in part, on a framework developed by COSO (the Committee of Sponsoring Organizations). According to the organization's home page, the committee is geared toward "improving financial reporting through business ethics, effective internal controls, and corporate governance." ISACA, the Information Systems Audit and Control Association, developed COBIT as a means of bringing this information and these practices to IT environments.

[B] Strengths of COBIT

COBIT is not an all or nothing arrangement. It can be profitably implemented one piece at a time although the biggest benefit comes from applying the entire model. COBIT's approach to project management is easily adapted to any project, and supplements current business practices instead of replacing them.

Applying COBIT profitably to a company's processes cannot be done overnight since it focuses on auditing and process control. The COBIT framework does not touch on all aspects of project or portfolio management, however. For example, it won't help you build a better team, although it will help the team develop better skills. Also, it isn't the best tool for building a risk management program because it focuses on best practices.

COBIT focuses on best practices as the optimal way to accomplish a certain goal. However, these best practices are not the final word for a company. Businesses change as does the regulatory world in which we live. Each organization must continually seek to improve and add to its manual of best practices that apply to its unique situation and to its industry.

[C] Project Management Maturity with COBIT

COBIT has 34 processes tracks. Of these, the ten from the "Plan and Organize" domain are significant to project and portfolio management. Each process is rated on a scale of one to five. The lowest level that meets all criteria for that level is the overall level accorded to an organization. For example, imagine evaluating a company's ability to obtain good project definitions (a clear understanding of what should be done). Part of what the company does follows the best practices from COBIT level 3 while part of what the company does is evaluated at COBIT level 1. The overall rating for that key area would be level 1 since all practices in the area are not on level 3. The COBIT rankings are:

0. *Non-existent*—No recognizable processes exist. The organization likely isn't aware of a problem or a need to implement controls for this area.

1. *Initial*—The first semblance of structure appears due to the recognition by the company that there is a need to monitor this process. The way it is managed, though, is disorganized and the approaches are made on a case by case basis or developed by each individual. Each time the situation occurs, a different solution may be applied.

2. *Repeatable*—A standard procedure is now followed by different people. No formal training or standardization of the procedures exists. Quality of execution, if measured at all, is based on the individual.

3. *Defined*—Individuals receive formal training or have access to documentation describing an organization-wide standard procedure. The procedures may not be efficient or detailed, but they do exist.

4. *Managed*—Standards are now monitored as they are carried out. Deviations from the procedure are identified so that individuals can be corrected and processes can be improved based on performance. Also, automation of process or other tools may be present.

5. *Optimized*—The processes in question consistently follow best practice guidelines. When possible, automation or pertinent tools are utilized by all individuals involved. Feedback from the monitoring of the processes allows for continual improvement.

[D]   COBIT Plan and Organize Control Objectives

The ten control objectives for the Plan and Organize domain are:

1. *PO1—Define a Strategic IT Plan*
   A strategic IT plan aligns project management efforts with the company's strategic direction. As this plan is developed, key stakeholders learn about IT's strengths and weaknesses. The plan must take into consideration in what manner and with what quality the organization is doing its job, the strategy for becoming/staying pertinent and useful within the company, and which systems are the responsibility of the organization.

2. *PO2—Define the Information Architecture*

Providing a well defined system for information makes it simple to find and report any information that may be useful. This also minimizes the chance that multiple individuals will gather the same information, or prevents individuals from perceiving a need to perform a function multiple times (unless duplication of a single measurement or piece of information is desired!). These steps, in turn, save time in finding information and recording it, and this, in turn, saves the company money.

An important tool in this effort is the creation of a data dictionary that includes the security level of every element. The fewer versions of the "same data" maintained in a system, the more consistent and accurate the reports will be.

3. *PO3—Determine Technological Direction*

The IT department first analyzes the use of existing equipment and software, takes note of emerging trends, and charts a technical direction for the future of both of them. This approach provides end points for the migration of technology over time, allowing for a more cost effective, efficient, and orderly transition from today to tomorrow. Project managers often refer to this published technical direction when designing a project's deliverables.

4. *PO4—Define the IT Processes, Organization and Relationships*

All employees should have a job description describing their responsibilities and permissions. Relationships between tasks performed by employees must be documented and maintained in order to avoid duplication of effort. Further, it is crucial to be aware of the expectations of IT throughout the company and beyond. Are there IT systems that exist outside of the organization's jurisdiction? Why? Any such systems must be brought into compliance with one uniform set of directions for efficient management.

5. *PO5—Manage the IT Investment*

By tracking investments of time and money over a period of time, an IT department is better able to understand where its money is going and why. This tracking also provides historical insight for better budget estimations, which will, in turn, help prevent projects from running severely over budget. The benefits provided by the IT organization are documented to show the relationship between having a good IT system in place and having productive employees. Then, when company budget time rolls around, it is easier to justify the IT budget.

6. *PO6—Communicate Management Aims and Direction*

Company IT policies are based on business requirements, the company's code of ethics, and legal requirements. These policies should be clearly worded and disseminated appropriately to all stakeholders (employees, guests, customers, suppliers, etc.). Most companies post them online so the latest version of the policies is always available. Adherence to these policies by all stakeholders is monitored, and when practical, methods for preventing deviation from policy are implemented. Policies must be periodically updated and reviewed by all stakeholders.

7. *PO7—Manage IT Human Resources*

People are the key to a successful IT organization and the primary tool of a project manager. They are the ones that push the keys, form the code, and interpret the report. A successful organization maximizes the productivity of its people through a wide range of actions.

First and foremost, individuals with talent or at least willingness to learn and follow directions enthusiastically should be recruited. Training pertinent to their responsibilities must be provided to all of these individuals. Those who perform well should be promoted. Before the employees leave, they either must train their successors or at least leave ample documentation. As a safeguard, all employees should be required to document their work on an ongoing basis, in case one of them must suddenly leave for any reason.

8. *PO8—Manage Quality*

The IT organization must establish a quality control and improvement program to continuously improve its services. Quality requirements should be based on customer requirements. They must be quantifiable, achievable, and known to everyone in the organization. Every process in the organization should be open to review, especially Project Management.

9. *PO9—Assess and Manage IT Risks*

Project planning involves both risk assessment and mitigation. Otherwise, the project regularly runs face first into hurdles, fights its way out, and then does it all over again. Project stakeholders depend on the project manager to look ahead, identify risks, and take any possible mitigating action before the risks turn into real problems. By anticipating risks and taking actions in advance (or at least being watchful of the risk), projects are more likely to be on time and on or under budget.

10. *PO10—Manage Projects*

Finally, there must be a project management process to manage the projects. In most companies, this is accomplished through a Project Management Office (PMO). Establishing such an office ensures that the highest priority projects are executed in a standardized fashion. That is, that the various project managers use the same tools the same way.

Projects also must be reviewed at their conclusion. It should be noted if they were on time and on budget, and if not, how far each was off (in either direction). Stakeholders should be consulted to determine how well their expectations were met.

§ 24.03 PMI'S ORGANIZATIONAL PROJECT MANAGEMENT MATURITY MODEL™

[A] Overview

Organizational Project Management Maturity Model (OPM3®) was created by the Project Management Institute (PMI). OPM3 provides a method for an organization to gauge its maturity in the way it manages its projects, programs, and portfolios. The goal of this model is to ensure that the projects in the portfolio are linked to the organization's strategy to provide for their consistent and predictable completion.

In order to develop OPM3, PMI worked with hundreds of project managers from around the world to identify the best project management practices. PMI also reviewed 27 different maturity models to identify the most effective elements of each. Based on this and other research, the OPM3 project team developed best practices, capabilities, outcomes, and key process indicators that comprise the basic parts of OPM3.

OPM3 groups best practices and capabilities into two dimensions. The first is the project management domain. This includes project management, program management and the company's project portfolio. The second domain deals with process improvement. OPM3 divides process improvement into four stages: (1) standardize, (2) measure, (3) control, and (4) improve (somewhat similar to Six Sigma's define, measure, analyze, improve, and control). Across these two domains is a series of capabilities that enable the application of the recommended best practices.

Each best practice is the result of multiple capabilities within an organization. A company that has these capabilities and adheres to the best practice for each should experience specific outcomes. (Of course, it is the outcome that provides the benefit to the company.) The quality of the outcomes is measured by key performance indicators that are quantitatively and qualitatively measured.

A capability is a competency. It is the potential to achieve something, if applied to a requirement of some sort through the actions in a best practice.

The OPM3 process is broken in three primary stages: knowledge, assessment, and improvement. As soon as these are completed, the process begins again to reach even higher organizational project, program, and portfolio maturity.

[B] Knowledge Element

The knowledge element describes the nature of OPM3 and why project, program, and portfolio maturity is important to an organization. Education is an important component of OPM3 online, a web-based application featuring the best practices in organizational project management. It also includes the Knowledge Foundation Handbook that outlines OPM3 principles.

The knowledge element also describes organizational project management, organizational project management maturity, and relevant best practices. Various appendices and the full OPM3 Glossary are also included here. This element is presented in electronic file format (PDF).

[C] Assessment

The assessment element provides organizations with an online OPM3 self-assessment tool. This tool compares the characteristics of a company's current state of organizational project management maturity with those key traits described by OPM3. Through self-assessment in relation to these traits, an organization can quantify its own maturity relative to the capabilities it has achieved. The result is an understanding of an organization's strengths and weaknesses.

An OPM3 assessment uses a series of "yes" or "no" questions for the assessment. There is no time limit for this survey. Some questions may require more thought than others. However, to be of the most benefit, answers to the survey questions must be candid. Once all of the questions are answered, the results are analyzed and reported.

[D] Improvement

Improvement is the process for moving up in the maturity equation. Gauging the maturity level in an organization is a useful exercise, but the big pay back comes from planning a series of efforts for moving the organization to higher maturity levels. The weaknesses identified in the assessment portion are transformed into actions for an organization to address in its improvement plan. The strengths revealed through the assessment highlight areas that must be protected, so that changes made to minimize a weakness do not diminish a strength.

OPM3 is an iterative process. As the weaknesses are identified and resolved, the company starts the process over again to build a new assessment. In most cases, the biggest visible improvement comes from the first iterations, since these changes cost the least and address the most urgent weaknesses.

A unique aspect of OPM3 is that it adds to its own knowledge base with each company that uses it. From the data gathered, patterns are formed illustrating industry-wide weaknesses or strengths. The OPM3 process can also discover new best practices, or reveal some that are optimal for a particular industry on a national level.

§ 24.04 PORTFOLIO, PROGRAM AND PROJECT MANAGEMENT MATURITY MODEL™

[A] Definition

The Portfolio, Program and Project Management Maturity Model (P3M3™) was developed by the United Kingdom's Office of Government Commerce (OGC). It is based on the process maturity framework from the Software Engineering Institute's (SEI) Capability Maturity Model (CMM). Like CMM, P3M3 is a five level maturity framework. Companies that follow the P3M3 process identify and address their limitations and problems, which improve the end result of their projects.

A successful project management effort must encompass the organization's program management results as well. After some research, OGC determined that projects fail because of some aspect of one or more of five general reasons:

1. *"Design and definition failures"* when the project's definition and deliverables were not clearly defined before it began.

2. *"Decision making failures"* when the project's sponsor lacks commitment to see the project through to completion, or when no one is able to make timely decisions.

3. *"Program and Project discipline failures"* because of poor change management and risk control.

4. *"Supplier management failures"* when contractors fail to perform, or the requirements were not clearly articulated to them, or when the project leader failed to manage them properly.

5. *"People failure"* when the local culture, participants, and stakeholders fail to support the project effort.

OGC has also developed a PRINCE2™ Maturity Model called P2MM™. This model does not include program or portfolio management, since neither of these aspects is included in PRINCE2. P2MM™ is analogous to the first three levels of P3M3.

The P3M3 process recognizes that portfolio and project support activities are best accomplished at the organizational level. Without organization level support (one level higher than the individual level project manager), the company cannot expect consistent results. In most companies, this is accomplished by the Project Management Office (PMO).

P3M3 examines certain key process areas of the organization. Based on the competence of these areas, P3M3 assigns a maturity level to indicate where the organization's project management effort is immature and where it is more capable. Programs that are deemed immature are more likely to consistently exceed their budget and schedule. This, in turn, leads frustrated sponsors to impose deadlines. Sponsors are rarely satisfied with the product delivered by the deadline; in order to meet it, the project must trim its scope and skip much of the quality validation process.

A mature organization manages projects by mobilizing a wider part of the company in support. This may be accomplished through the training of team members, definitely by training sponsors, and by building understanding with the many departments the project manager must work with. A mature organization also examines completed projects for lessons learned. They use a defined (and continuously improved) tool set adjusted for each specific project.

[B] How It Works

Each of the 32 key process areas in P3M3 describe the activities that the organization should be achieving. Every key process area is broken into process goals, approach, deployment, review, perception, and performance measures.

Level 1 is the initial process and focuses on two key process areas. Like CMM, this is the time of darkness—the chaotic starting point.

- *Project*: Companies recognize the difference between a process and a project. Companies begin to run projects differently from business processes. Projects are run informally; the project team blundering forward planning the next step only when the present one is completed.

- *Program*: Projects are executed individually with little or no thought about how combining some aspect of them might save time or money. Project teams do not exchange ideas or experiences.

- *Portfolio*: Basically, an executive's list of things to get done this year.

  Level 1 examines two key process areas:

- Project Definition
- Program Management Awareness

Level 2 is when the company begins to use, either accidentally or intentionally, repeatable processes.

- *Project*: Projects are assigned to those managers who have been successful in the past. Out of habit or leaning, these project managers begin to use the same steps that previously brought them success. At some point, these project managers convert their best practices into the basic form of project management procedures for all to use.

- *Program*: Companies begin to group similar projects loosely together, to at least ensure that the output of one is actually useable as input in the next. Published procedures, however loosely written, are imposed on all projects.

- *Portfolio*: Executives become aware of these best practices and press for them to be adapted across all projects in their portfolio.

Level 2 examines 11 key process areas of project, program, and portfolio management.

- Business Case Development
- Program Organization
- Program Definition
- Project Establishment
- Project Planning, Monitoring and Control
- Stakeholder Management and Communications
- Requirements Management
- Risk Management
- Configuration Management
- Program Planning and Control
- Management of Suppliers and External Parties

Level 3 is when the company begins to use, either accidentally or intentionally, repeatable processes. It gathers tools, processes, procedures, and tips together to maximize their use across the company.

1. *Project*: Project management processes and tools are formalized for the organization. All project managers are required to use them, but they still have some discretion on how to apply them.

2. *Program*: Centrally controlled program management is established as separate from project management. Program management defines its own tools for efficient management.

3. *Portfolio*: Centrally controlled portfolio management takes shape along with the tools and processes to support it. Companies examine the value of projects both in-process and pending.

Level 3 examines 12 key process areas:

- Benefits Management
- Transition Management
- Information Management
- Organizational Focus
- Process Definition
- Training, Skills and Competency Development
- Integrated Management and Reporting
- Lifecycle Control
- Inter-group Co-ordination and Networking
- Quality Assurance
- Centre of Excellence (COE) Role Deployment
- Organization Portfolio Establishment

Level 4 is when the project, program, and portfolio efforts are a well-documented and understood managed process. However, for a process to be fully understood, it must be measured in some quantifiable way. Any process that provides consistent results can be measured. These measurement values can provide trigger points alerting management that a project is trending into trouble.

1. *Project*: Specific quantitative measurements are made of the project execution process and the final quality of its projects. These measurements are used to improve current and future project execution, processes, and tools. A quality management function is responsible for reviewing quantitative trends over time.

2. *Program*: Specific quantitative measurements are made of the program management in order to improve reliable performance.

3. *Portfolio*: Portfolios are examined using quantitative data to demonstrate and predict how well the organization manages its portfolio.

Level 4 examines 4 key process areas:

- Management Metrics
- Quality Management
- Organizational Cultural Growth
- Capacity Management

Level 5 is a when project management runs smoothly at all levels. The organization is finely tuning its existing efforts ever in search of better ways of doing things. This is important because organizations change people, change business focus, and hopefully are working with new and challenging customers. Just as IT technologies do not sit still, neither can the management of their projects and programs.

1. *Project*: Project management uses continuous improvement techniques to proactively identify and resolve problems.

2. *Program*: Program management uses continuous improvement techniques to improve performance over time. At times, problems can afflict many of the projects within a program. This approach applies solutions and improvements to all projects in the program.

3. *Portfolio*: Portfolio management uses continuous improvement to improve portfolio performance over time.

Level 5 examines 3 key process areas:

- Proactive Problem Management
- Technology Management
- Continuous Process Improvement

[C] Rating Your Company

To establish an organization's maturity level, a company should begin with level 1 and work upward through all of the key process areas. It is not unusual for a company to be operating at different maturity levels of project, program, and portfolio management at the same time. At this point, a fair assessment is required, so that efforts can be focused on things that are broken instead of on the things that work well.

The second step is to decide which level is best for the company. Is achieving a level 5 rating worth the effort or the cost to the organization? For a hospital, the answer may be "yes." If the company is in the business of digging ditches, then maybe level 5 is too much. In many cases, the level chosen depends on how heavily the company depends on project management for its success.

After a baseline of where the company is and a vision of where the company wants to go, the remaining action is to plan out how to move the organization from here to there. Organizational change is slow and can be difficult, but now the path is easier to see and the vision can be shared by the entire team.

§ 24.05   SUMMARY

So which is the one best model to use? Like all things, that depends on what you want to do with it. Companies are a collection of people and that is where both the problem and opportunity are to be found. The problem is that people cherish stability in their jobs. Even if the current process is universally known to be defective, they are familiar with it and their work days are predictable. They believe the pain of the current situation is less than would be the unknown turmoil caused by a major process change.

The opportunity is that these same people really do want to do a better job and to be on a winning team. By establishing a baseline of today's performance (which these models all do in their own way), and then painting a brighter future to work toward, enough of the people may go along to change, at least, some of the easiest problems with the greatest payback. Success builds confidence to try for more success!

Likely the most significant limitation of the maturity models is that a "best practice" exists within a context of the business environment. Regulatory environment and the degree of risk a company can tolerate vary widely among industries. A "best practice" for building a bridge in New York State may be different than building a similar bridge in New Mexico, Quebec, or other places. Best practices also tend to be grouped by industry. There are some universal truths and those best practices, however, are applicable everywhere. Such basic truths tend to reside in the lower levels of a maturity hierarchy.

When selecting a model, companies tend to select one that aligns with its general project management approach, such as P3M3 and PRINCE2, or OPM3 and PMI's body of knowledge. This simplifies learning about the tools since the terminology and process flows are somewhat similar.

Index

Q

W